5 GROUP BOMBER COMMAND
AN OPERATIONAL RECORD

5 Group Bomber Command
An Operational Record

Chris Ward

Pen & Sword
AVIATION

First published in Great Britain in 2007 by
Pen & Sword Aviation
an imprint of
Pen & Sword Books Ltd
47 Church Street
Barnsley
South Yorkshire
S70 2AS

ISBN 978-1-84415-579-8

A CIP catalogue record for this book is
available from the British Library

Typeset in 10/12pt Times New Roman by
Concept, Huddersfield, West Yorkshire

Printed and bound in England by
Biddles Ltd

Pen & Sword Books Ltd incorporates the Imprints of Pen & Sword Aviation, Pen
& Sword Maritime, Pen & Sword Military, Wharncliffe Local History,
Pen & Sword Select, Pen & Sword Military Classics and Leo Cooper.

For a complete list of Pen & Sword titles please contact
PEN & SWORD BOOKS LIMITED
47 Church Street, Barnsley, South Yorkshire, S70 2AS, England
E-mail: enquiries@pen-and-sword.co.uk
Website: www.pen-and-sword.co.uk

Acknowledgements

Most of the figures used in the statistics section of this work, have been drawn from The Bomber Command War Diaries by Martin Middlebrook and Chris Everitt, and I am indebted to Martin Middlebrook for allowing me to use them.

Generous assistance in the compiling of lists of commanding officers has been provided by Anna McIlwaine at the RAF Museum at Hendon, until her retirement in 1998. Also of considerable help in this regard, and with details of awards, is Clive Richards at the Air Historical Branch of the Air Ministry, to whom I am greatly indebted.

My good friend, author Martyn Ford-Jones, had allowed me to draw extensively from his research material, particularly in respect of losses during 1945. I am also extremely grateful to my friend Steve Smith, an historian of 3 Group in general, and 218 and 623 Squadrons in particular, for conducting research on my behalf whenever he is at the PRO.

A special mention is due to Chris Salter of Midland Counties Publications, without whose generous assistance and encouragement at the outset, I would not have been able to compile a complete list of all operational aircraft on charge with Bomber Command squadrons during the war period, a list, incidentally, which comprises some 28,000 entries.

Contents

General Notes

This profile is a reference work on the activities of the Group and the squadrons serving with it in an operational capacity at some time during the Second World War. Bomber Command operated exclusively from stations in the UK, and used overseas bases purely for shuttle operations, or as advanced staging posts for specific purposes. For this reason, periods spent on detachment, or permanent postings to overseas Commands do not fall within the scope of this work.

This profile is not intended to serve as a comprehensive history of the Group or squadrons, but to provide as much information as possible in a non-anecdotal form. The brief history narrative is basically an account of Bomber Command's war, with the Group's involvement interwoven into it. The publications listed on page 263 are not only recommended reading, but represent the best available sources of information for serious students of the subject. The operational record is based almost entirely on the figures provided in The Bomber Command War Diaries by Martin Middlebrook and Chris Everitt, and I am indebted to Martin Middlebrook for allowing me to use them.

An aircraft is included in chapter two if; (a) it spent time on squadron charge, no matter how briefly, and irrespectively of whether or not it operated and (b) the type was used operationally by the squadron. Information is restricted in most cases to where from and where to, unless it completed its service with the squadron, in which case, some detail of its demise appears. Aircraft which failed to return have the date and target recorded. Where no information follows the serial number of a type still in use when the squadron departed Bomber Command, or at war's end, it can be assumed that the aircraft was still on squadron strength. However, where there is a blank space following the serial number of a type which has been withdrawn from service with Bomber Command, it signifies that I don't know its ultimate fate. An absence of information does not imply that the aircraft flew no operations during its time with the squadron.

CHAPTER ONE

A Narrative History

Organisation

5 Group was formed from 3 Group on the 1 September 1937. Administration remained at Mildenhall until the 2 October, when it was transferred to St Vincents on the outskirts of Grantham. The seven founder squadrons were 44, 50, 61, 110, 113, 144 and 211. No. 44 Squadron was equipped with the Blenheim Mk I, while the remainder operated Hind and Audax biplanes. Nos 44, 50 and 110 squadrons were based at Waddington, 61 and 144 at Hemswell, while 113 and 211 squadrons resided at Grantham. On the 14 March 1938 Scampton was transferred to 5 Group, along with its resident squadrons, 49 and 83. In May 110, 113 and 211 Squadrons were posted to the Middle East. Thornaby was transferred to the Group on the 1 September, bringing 106 and 185 Squadrons within the fold. No. 49 Squadron became the first RAF unit to receive the new Hampden on the 20 September. By the beginning of June 1939 the entire Group was operating the type. For ease of servicing and training it was the sensible policy at this time for each Group to operate one aircraft type. While 5 Group was the lone operator of the Hampden, 1 Group flew the Fairey Battle, 2 Group the Bristol Blenheim, 3 Group the Wellington and 4 Group the Whitley. Air Commodore Callaway was Air-Officer-Commanding 5 Group as war began.

1939. Lessons to learn

At the outbreak of war 5 Group possessed six operational squadrons, 44 and 50 at Waddington, commanded respectively by W/C Bootham and W/C Young, 49 and 83 at Scampton under the commands of W/C Chick and W/C Jordan, and 61 and 144 at Hemswell, led by W/C Brill and W/C Cunningham. W/C Bootham was appointed on the day war broke out, and it was he who had won the Schneider Trophy outright for Britain in the famed Supermarine S6B in 1931. No. 106 Squadron, which would be employed as the Group's training unit for the first year of the war, had just been transferred to Cottesmore in Rutland under the command of S/L Sheen, but both he and the squadron would soon be on the move again. On the first day of hostilities nine Hampdens from 44 Squadron and three and six respectively drawn from 49 and 83 Squadrons, conducted a daylight shipping search over the North Sea. Among the 83 Squadron contingent was a young Guy Gibson, whose exploits later in the war would earn him celebrity status. Having not departed their stations until around 18.00 hours, it was already dark before the Schillig Roads area was reached, and this first operation by the Group was concluded without result, setting the tenor for the rest of the year. AVM Arthur Harris was appointed as the Group's AOC on the 11 September, a post he would retain for more than a year.

There were to be very few operational sorties by the Group's Hampdens during the remainder of 1939, and, indeed, until well into the following year. There was, in fact, a gap of twenty-five days between the Group's first operation and its second, which involved twelve aircraft on the 26th. The Group's third operation, another shipping sweep to the Heligoland Bight area, was mounted on the 29th by twelve Hampdens of 144 Squadron. Two formations of six aircraft led by W/C Cunningham and S/L Lindsay, departed Hemswell to fly independently to the target area timed to arrive at around 10.00 hours. This was the time that previous reconnaissance flights had shown elements of the *Kriegsmarine* to be at sea, on their way home to base after exercising under cover of darkness. One member of W/C Cunningham's formation soon turned back with engine trouble while the remainder pressed on. S/L Lindsay's formation sighted and attacked two enemy destroyers without scoring any hits, but W/C Cunningham ran into a hornet's nest of fighters. One by one the five Hampdens were hacked down into the sea, and sixteen of the twenty crewmen lost their lives, including W/C Cunningham. The disaster afflicting 144 Squadron should have caused alarm bells to ring concerning the ability of self-defending bombers to 'always get through' in daylight. Rather than allowing the evidence to highlight the flaws in this pre-war theory, however, the policy-makers at Bomber Command chose to ignore the obvious and blame the crews for poor formation flying. This stubbornness would cost further lives before common sense and reason prevailed. On the 26 September, 61 Squadron had appointed W/C De Crespigny as its new commanding officer. On the 1 October the popular and well-respected New Zealander, W/C Jordan, was posted in from 83 Squadron to take command of 144 Squadron, and W/C Snaith stepped into his shoes at 83, returning to a post he had held for two years prior to the appointment of W/C Jordan. The next foray by the Group involved just three Hampdens on the 20 November, all of which returned without incident.

49 Squadron welcomed a new leader on the 1 December in the shape of the recently promoted W/C Sheen. He had previously commanded the currently non-operational 106 Squadron for twelve months to October in the rank of Squadron Leader. His place at 106, which had moved to Finningley in October, was now occupied by W/C Montgomerie. The 1st also saw three

Hampdens fly reconnaissance sorties, and a similar number were dispatched on the 4th. The largest operation of the war to date took place on the 14th, and involved forty-four aircraft, including twenty-three Hampdens from 5 Group. A formation of 3 Group Wellingtons sighted enemy warships, but five were shot down into the sea and a sixth crashed on landing after sustaining battle damage. Worse was to follow on the 18th, when twelve of twenty-two Wellingtons were lost to enemy fighters. At last the authorities began to recognise the folly of sending unescorted bombers into enemy territory by daylight. All the preconceived ideas and theories of the past twenty years were swept aside, and a bomber force developed and trained to operate solely by day would have to learn to fly by night. It would not happen at a stroke, but fortunately, 4 Group crews were already able to fly their Whitleys in the dark, and they would undertake the first sorties over the enemy mainland.

On the 21 December twenty-four crews from Waddington and Scampton headed off in search of the pocket battleship *Deutschland*, which had been reported off the Norwegian coast the previous day. At the limit of their range the Hampdens turned for home without having sighted their quarry, and set course for Lossiemouth and Kinloss. Low cloud on the return flight separated the squadrons, but the Scampton element made landfall over the Northumberland coast, and most of them got down without incident. The Waddington contingent, however, having made an alteration in course, and unaware of their precise whereabouts, headed towards the Firth of Forth, an important naval base, where they were intercepted by RAF fighters from Drem. As a result two 44 Squadron Hampdens were shot down into the sea near Berwick by Spitfires of 602 Squadron. Fortunately, P/O Sansome and his crew survived the incident in L4089, and were picked up by a fishing vessel, as was P/O Dingwall with two of his crew from L4090. Sadly, the fourth member of this crew did not survive, having been killed during the engagement. Another shipping sweep by twelve Hampdens took place on Christmas Day, but this was the final operational activity of the year.

1940. Backs to the wall
The 'phoney' war, France's fall, realization

The winter of 1939/40 was particularly severe, and seemed to deepen as the year progressed. This, and what the Americans dubbed the 'Phoney War', restricted operational flying to an absolute minimum, and just one shipping sweep was mounted by Hampdens in January. It was towards the end of February before the icy conditions began to loosen their grip, and no sorties were flown during the month. One shipping sweep was mounted in mid March, otherwise the only activity during the entire period to this point involved a detachment of Hampdens on temporary duty to Coastal

Command for anti-submarine patrols. During this lull W/C Denny took over 61 Squadron on the 12 February. The first occasion on which bombs were aimed at enemy territory came in response to the inadvertent slaying by a stray German bomb of a civilian on the island of Hoy, during an attack on elements of the Royal Navy at Scapa flow on the 17/18 March. Two nights later a retaliatory attack was carried out against the seaplane base at Hörnum on the island of Sylt by thirty Whitleys over a four-hour period, followed by twenty Hampdens over the next two hours. Returning crews were highly enthusiastic about the operation and its successful outcome, and the raid made front-page headlines. For his part in the operation 50 Squadron's F/L Bennett became the first member of Bomber Command to be awarded the DFC. Unfortunately, photographic reconnaissance on the 6 April failed to detect any signs of damage, and similarly optimistic claims in the future would ultimately come back to haunt the Command. On the 8 April W/C Sheen departed 49 Squadron to take up duties with H.Q. 5 Group. W/C 'Downwind' Gillan was posted in from the Air Ministry as his successor on the same day, just as the war began to hot up.

Bombing operations proper began for the Group with the German airborne invasion of Norway on the 9 April, the day on which other German troops marched almost unopposed into Denmark. Because of the extreme range, Bomber Command was unable to support directly the British response at Narvik in the north, and it was required instead to target enemy shipping and the southern airfields at Oslo and Stavanger. Twenty-four Hampdens were sent in search of enemy warships off Bergen on the 9th, and although twelve of the force were recalled, two of the remainder claimed hits on a cruiser. On the 10th W/C Taafe took up the reigns of command at 50 Squadron from W/C Young. Insufficient cloud cover caused the abandonment of another anti-shipping operation by six Hampdens on the 11th, but that night twenty of the type joined a contingent of Whitleys in a similar sweep from Kiel Bay to Oslo, and at least one ship was hit. The 12th brought the largest bombing operation of the war to date, when eighty-three Wellingtons, Hampdens and Blenheims were despatched to attack shipping in the Stavanger area in the face, as it turned out, of fierce flak and fighter opposition. Waddington dispatched twelve Hampdens, seven from 44 Squadron and five from 50 Squadron, under the leadership of S/L Watts, and after crossing the North Sea at low level in conditions of heavy cloud and rain, the weather cleared to allow sight of Kristiansand Bay in the distance. The force climbed to 9,000 feet to carry out the attack in sections of three in line astern, and after bombing, S/L Watts led his section down to sea level to make good their escape. By the time that the second section came across the target area the flak batteries had found their range, and L4099 was hit, damaged and ultimately finished off by fighters. These pounced upon the third section as they dived for the sea. In all six Hampdens failed to return to Waddington, 50 Squadron having lost four of its five aircraft, while three Whitleys were also shot down during the course of the operation. Such losses prompted a further reappraisal of daylight operations, and from this point on, no more would be undertaken by Hampdens and Wellingtons in large numbers.

On the 13/14 April Hampdens carried out the first mine-laying operation of the war, a task to which the type was to prove itself eminently suited. Fifteen aircraft took part on this night, and sowed their vegetables in northern waters between the German ports and Norway. At the end of the month W/C Jordan was posted from 144 Squadron. He would go on to command 3 Group's 214 Squadron between March and August 1941, and eventually reach the rank of Air Marshal. He was replaced at 144 Squadron by W/C Luxmoore, who would barely have time to unpack before his end came. By this time the ill-fated Norwegian campaign was effectively over, and events closer to home were about to grab the attention of the world.

On the 10 May German ground forces began their advance through Luxembourg, while airborne troops dealt with defences in Belgium and Holland in a classic demonstration of *Blitzkrieg*. This was the moment when the gloves came off for good, and all the pretence and shadow boxing of the past eight months evaporated in a few weeks of unimaginable fury. The Battle and Blenheim squadrons of the French-based Advanced Air Striking Force, which had been kicking their heels since a number of bad experiences at the hands of enemy fighters in September, were thrust at once into an unequal fight. They were deployed only after the enemy had established anti-aircraft defences at vital river crossings and road junctions, and this would require them to fly into murderous ground fire and run the gauntlet of marauding BF109s in a vain attempt to impede the enemy's westward drive. The Blenheims of 2 Group were also pitched into the fray from their stations in East Anglia with disastrous results in a clear case of 'locking the stable door after the horse had bolted'. The above mentioned crews displayed the most incredible 'courage by daylight' in the finest traditions of the service to which they belonged, and were hacked from the skies in large numbers for their pains. Some of the Command's finest pre-war airmen would be sacrificed over the ensuing weeks in a battle that had already been lost through political dithering.

The home based heavy squadrons played their part in the battle for France by operating against communications targets behind enemy lines. On the 11/12 May Hampdens and Whitleys attacked road and railway targets at Mönchengladbach in support of the ground forces, the first time that the German mainland had been bombed. W/C Luxmoore's P1326 was hit by flak on approach to its target and severely damaged, but he managed to head back towards the west for an hour, before it became necessary for his crew to take to their parachutes. They landed safely on French soil and returned to the squadron two days later, but W/C Luxmoore was still at the controls when the Hampden crashed in Belgium, and he was killed. He was replaced at 144 Squadron by W/C Watts, who was posted in from 44 Squadron at

Waddington, where he had been a flight commander. No. 5 Group sent six Hampdens mine laying in the Kiel Canal on the 13/14th, while a further six roamed the Dutch/German frontier. A force of a dozen Hampdens was then sent to attack targets at Breda and Roosendaal on the 14/15th. After the controversial bombing of Rotterdam by the *Luftwaffe* on the 15th, which prompted the Dutch surrender, the War Cabinet finally sanctioned operations against Germany proper. This heralded the start of the strategic offensive for which the Command had been prepared. That night ninety-nine assorted aircraft, including thirty-six Hampdens, took off to attack sixteen industrial and railway targets in the Ruhr, while twelve Wellington crews were briefed to bomb communications in Belgium, and this was the first time that a hundred aircraft had been dispatched in one night. Even so, the situation in France demanded the diversion of resources to operations of a more tactical nature, and such attacks on enemy troop movements continued through to the end of the month and into June in a vain attempt to slow the tide. On the 19th W/C G H Sheen (not to be confused with W/C W C Sheen of 106 and 49 Squadrons) took command of 61 Squadron. On the 23/24th fifty Hampdens contributed to a force of 122 aircraft sent to attack communications in the battle area. Two Hampdens failed to return.

The largest operation to date took place on the 3/4 June, when 142 aircraft, forty-eight of them Hampdens, attacked various targets, most of which were in Germany. Earlier in the day, the last remnants of the BEF had been evacuated from the beaches of Dunkerque, bringing the total of those rescued to an incredible 338,000. Later that day, an assessment by a government committee of Germany's oil industry suggested that a concerted effort against it could reduce its output by half a million tons over the summer period. In the light of the massive offensive against the industry by four-engine aircraft in 1944, this was a somewhat optimistic view, and although a sizeable proportion of the Command's effort would be directed against oil refineries and storage sites, the effect on Germany's war effort would be negligible. On the 9th W/C Snaith was posted from 83 Squadron to take up an appointment at Kinloss, and he was replaced by W/C Sisson, an officer with a greater appetite for leading his men into battle. After a brief period in command of 50 Squadron, W/C Taafe stepped down in favour of W/C Crockart on the 12th. The latter's stay would be brief indeed.

That night, the 12/13th, thirty-five Hampdens were dispatched, six on mining duties and the remainder to find worthwhile military and communications targets in France. Not all the crews found suitable targets, and 144 Squadron's P4345 collided with a balloon cable and crashed near Felixstowe on return, killing the crew. The pilot was W/C Watts, and he thus became the third 144 Squadron commanding officer to lose his life on operations so early in the war. He was replaced by W/C Gyll-Murray, who, happily, was destined to complete his tour with the squadron. Hampdens were active over France, Belgium and Holland on the 13/14th, and over Germany on consecutive nights from the 14/15th to the 21/22nd and from the

23/24th into July, while other Hampdens were out mine laying during the same period. With France now out of the battle following its capitulation on the 25 June, invasion fever began to grip Britain. More than one hundred aircraft were dispatched to targets in Germany and to lay mines on the 26/27th, and this included an element from 50 Squadron briefed to attack an airfield at Hanover. W/C Crockart's Hampden failed to return after crashing into the sea, and there were no survivors. W/C Golledge was appointed as the new commanding officer, and he would remain in post considerably longer than his predecessors. Eighty-nine aircraft roamed over Germany and the occupied countries on the 28/29th, and eighty-eight on the last night of the month. During the course of June S/L Stubbs took command of 106 Squadron, and he would oversee the unit's transition from training to operations a few months hence.

There was little change in the nature of operations in July and August, but as the summer progressed the Battle of Britain began to gain momentum overhead. 50 Squadron moved out of Waddington on the 10 July and took up residence at Lindholme. The almost personal association between 5 Group and the Dortmund-Ems Canal, which had begun on the 19/20 June and would extend almost to the end of the war, continued on the 12/13 August. Hampdens of 49 and 83 Squadrons carried out an attack from low level, and it was as a result of 'his complete indifference to personal danger ... regardless of opposition', on this night, that 49 Squadron's F/L Learoyd was awarded Bomber Command's first Victoria Cross of the war. (Donald Garland and Thomas Gray of 12 Squadron were members of the AASF during the action on the 12 May 1940 for which they received the posthumous award of the VC.) Small-scale operations continued as the Battle of Britain reached its climax, and invasion craft in enemy occupied ports became the dominant focus of attention at this time. Many operations were mounted against them beginning on the 7/8th. The Battle of Britain reached its zenith on the 15th, and that night 83 Squadron's Sgt Hannah won the Command's second Victoria Cross, and, at 18 years of age, became its youngest recipient, during an operation against invasion craft at Antwerp. Hannah, a Scotsman, single-handedly fought a raging inferno within the fuselage, and thereby enabled his pilot to bring the aircraft all the way home from Belgium. On the 23/24th, 129 aircraft, including a contingent of Hampdens, were dispatched to Berlin to attack eighteen separate targets. This was a break from the normal pattern of small-scale forays against multiple targets, but it was back to more familiar fare for the remainder of the month.

Although in October the Battle of Britain was still technically in progress, its intensity had diminished, and with it the threat of invasion. Operations would still be directed at craft in Channel ports, but to a lesser degree, and an Air Ministry directive towards the end of the month would reaffirm oil as the priority objective. On the 5th ACM Sir Charles Portal relinquished his post as Commander-in-Chief Bomber Command to become Chief-of-the-Air-Staff. He was replaced by Sir Richard Peirse, whose tenure would be dogged by the inadequacies of the equipment available to him, and the often unrealistic demands placed upon his resources by his superiors. Widely dispersed small-scale raids took place on the 14/15th, among them one to Berlin involving twenty Hampdens. A trip to an oil refinery at Leuna near the eastern city of Merseburg on the 16/17th also provided an opportunity for some crews to drop the incendiary device 'Razzle' into the Harz Forest. Razzle, it was hoped, would set fire to Germany's woodland and crop fields, but it failed to persuade Hitler to sue for peace, and was soon consigned to the 'It was worth a try' file.

The trend of sending small forces to wide-ranging targets continued in November, and this diluting of the effort rendered the operations ineffective and of little more than nuisance value. W/C Valentine became the new commanding officer of 61 Squadron on the 12th. Seventy-two aircraft took off for various targets in Germany on the 13/14th, while on the following night Berlin was one of a number of objectives. The ten failures to return from the night's operations represented the largest night loss of the war to date. On the 22nd AVM Sir Arthur Harris left 5 Group to become second deputy to Sir Charles Portal, Chief-of-the-Air-Staff, but he would return to the Command as its new chief fifteen months to the day later. The Group's new AOC was AVM N H Bottomley, who had been Senior Air Staff Officer at Bomber Command HQ since 1938.

Towards the end of August 1940, S/L 'Hettie' Hyde had been selected as the prospective commanding officer of newly re-forming 207 Squadron, and was posted from his flight commander post at 44 Squadron on attachment to the A&AEE at Boscombe Down. His brief was to familiarize himself with the new Avro Manchester, which the squadron was to introduce into operational service, and he took to the air for the first time in the first production aircraft, L7276, on the 1 September. Among the experienced pilots selected to join him were S/L Kydd and F/Os Burton-Gyles and Siebert, and these would become the nucleus of 207 Squadron, which took physical form at Waddington under the banner of 5 Group on the 1 November. The first Manchester to be taken on charge was L7279, which was collected from Brize Norton and flown to Boscombe Down on the 6th. Two days later it was flown into Waddington, where it was joined by L7278 on the 10th. F/Os French, Eustace and Lewis were posted in at this time, and L7283 and L7284 were taken on charge to double the number of available aircraft. L7280, L7281, L7282, L7285 and L7286 arrived during December, and by the end of the year, eleven Manchesters were on strength. Incessant problems with the type kept them grounded for periods as modifications were carried out, and this would be a constant theme throughout the relatively short service life of the ill-fated type.

While the above events were taking place, life continued for the rest of the war-embroiled 5 Group. W/C Sisson left 83 Squadron on the 3 December, and was replaced by W/C Boyle, who, like the earlier-mentioned W/C Snaith, had commanded the squadron pre-war in the rank of Squadron Leader. The most noteworthy operation in December came in response to recent heavy attacks by the *Luftwaffe* on English cities, in particular, Coventry. A total of 134 aircraft, including twenty-nine Hampdens, took off on Operation Abigail-Rachel on the 16/17th, and headed for Mannheim. The intention was to attack the city centre in a purely area bombing operation, but the leading crews failed to identify the aiming point in clear conditions, and the fires started by their all incendiary loads were not in the centre. The rest of the bombing was scattered, but almost five hundred buildings were damaged, and only three aircraft failed to return. Earlier that day W/C Gus Walker (later, Sir Augustus) took command of 50 Squadron. He was one of the great characters to adorn Bomber Command during the war, and although small in stature he proved to be a giant among men. Three days before Christmas 49 Squadron's W/C Gillan returned to the Air Ministry whence he had come eight months earlier, and W/C Jefferson, a former flight commander with the squadron, stepped into the breach. It had been a backs-to-the-wall year, and one in which a defiant face had been presented to an, as yet, all conquering enemy. The year 1941 was not destined to bring more than a slight increase in effectiveness, and it would be a case of treading water for the foreseeable future. A number of new aircraft were emerging to offer some hope for the future, but the problems arising from pressing them too soon into service would result in a painfully slow development, and the existing types were to bear most of the burden for the next twelve months.

1941. Disappointment and disillusionment
Failure, teething troubles, Butt, under threat

A second successive harsh winter restricted operations at the start of the year, which opened with a campaign against ports in Germany and the occupied countries. Bremen and Wilhelmshaven were the main focus of attention, the former receiving three visits on consecutive nights from the 1/2nd of January, and the latter six of varying sizes between the 8/9th and the 29/30th. On the 15th an Air Ministry directive again reaffirmed that oil was the priority target, on the basis that this industry was approaching a critical period. A list of seventeen oil related objectives was presented to Peirse, the top nine of which represented 80% of Germany's domestic production. Oil targets required decent weather conditions, and when these were not forthcoming, industrial cities were to be attacked. During the course of the month W/C Gyll-Murray was posted from 144 Squadron. In July he would take command of 455 Squadron Royal Australian Air Force, which would be a new addition to 5 Group, and the first RAAF squadron to join Bomber Command. He was replaced by W/C Gardner, who was to enjoy a long spell at the helm.

February began as January had ended, with ports occupying the bulk of the Command's attention, although the accent shifted to those in France and Belgium. Each month was to have a 'big night', when a large force would be dispatched to a single destination. This event in February came on the night of the 10/11th, when 222 aircraft, forty-six of them Hampdens, were dispatched to various industrial targets in the city of Hanover, while Wellingtons and the first three Stirling sorties were sent against oil storage tanks at Rotterdam. On the 16th W/C Stainthorpe assumed command of 83 Squadron, but his period of tenure would be brief. Poor weather continued to hamper operations, and in many cases, only a few crews actually attacked their briefed objectives.

Meanwhile, as the day drew near for 207 Squadron to be declared operational, its ranks were swelled by some new faces, including, on the 15 February, F/O Taylor and P/Os Gardiner and 'Kipper' Herring. On the 18th S/L Stubbs was posted in as the B Flight commander. He had been the commanding officer of 106 Squadron until November, when he was succeeded by W/C Lindlay. 106 Squadron, for its part, moved to Coningsby on the 23rd. Arriving on detachment at 207 Squadron around the same time from 3 Group HQ was S/L Denys Balsdon, a pre-war flight commander with 214 Squadron, whose nickname then had been 'God'. Coincidentally, the other flight commander at 214 at that time was S/L Paul Hill, who had been given the task of forming 7 Squadron in order to introduce the Stirling into squadron service at about the same time as 'Hettie' Hyde was given the 207 Squadron job. Finally, on the night of the 24/25 February six of 207 Squadron's Manchesters were despatched to bomb the harbour at Brest in the company of fifty other assorted aircraft, in the hope of catching the German cruiser *Admiral Hipper*. Selected to launch the squadron's operational career were the crews of the recently promoted W/C Hyde, S/L Kydd, F/O Siebert, F/O Burton-Gyles, F/O Eustace and F/O Lewis in L7300, L7288, L7279, L7284, L7286 and L7294 respectively. All returned safely from an operation which progressed according to plan, although without evidence of damage to the ship, but L7284 suffered a mishap on landing through undercarriage problems. Two nights later F/L French led a contingent of five Manchesters to Cologne as part of a force of 126 aircraft, and again they all returned safely from what was an ineffective operation. Sadly on this night, however, 83 Squadron lost the first of a number of its commanding officers to die while leading from the front. During the return to Scampton W/C Stainthorpe's X3124 struck high ground in Staffordshire, and all on board were killed. The new commanding Officer was W/C Learoyd VC, who took up his post on the 28th. No sooner had 207 Squadron begun operations than B Flight was hived off and posted to form the nucleus of 97 Squadron under W/C Balsdon. Eight aircraft and crews were involved in the move on the 27th, and they were S/L Stubbs, F/Ls Bird and Sherwood, F/Os Eustace and Lewis, and P/Os Ayton, Blakeman and Brown.

A mini campaign against Cologne began towards the end of February, which was prosecuted sporadically into March. On the 9 March a new Air Ministry directive changed the priority of targets from oil to U-Boats, in response to the massive losses being sustained in the Atlantic. Also to receive attention was the U-Boat's partner in crime, the long-range maritime reconnaissance bomber, the Focke-Wulf Kondor. These two menaces were to be pursued where ever they could be found, at sea, in their bases, at their point of manufacture and in the engine and component factories. 97 Squadron moved from Waddington to Coningsby on the 10th. Despite the new directive oil was still on the agenda as opportunity allowed, but the maritime phase began at Hamburg on the 12/13th, when some useful damage was inflicted on the Blohm & Voss U-Boat yards by a force which included forty of 5 Group's Hampdens. Also that night, Wellingtons attacked the Focke-Wulf factory at Bremen, and a number of hits were scored. A return was made to Hamburg on the following night, and the same U-Boat yards were hit again, while an oil refinery was seriously damaged at Gelsenkirchen twenty-four hours later in what was probably the most effective attack on this industry to date. Thereafter during the month Hampdens were involved in operations, among others, to Bremen, Berlin, Wilhelmshaven and Kiel, interspersed with French ports. On the 29th the German cruisers *Scharnhorst* and *Gneisenau* were reported to be off Brest, and by the following day they had taken up residence. This was to be the start of a ten month long saga, which would prove to be a major distraction for the Command, and demand dozens of operations against the port and its guests. It would also result in the loss of numerous aircraft and crews. The campaign against the warships began at the hands of more than a hundred aircraft, including fifteen Hampdens during the course of the 30th, but an absence of cloud cover during their daylight effort forced the Hampdens to abort.

It was a similar story on the 1 April, when a force of eleven Hampdens turned back, and again on the 3rd, although one crew pressed on to bomb with indeterminate results. Many crews were to be lost in the process of attacking these ships, and one of them was that of 106 Squadron's new commanding officer, W/C Polglase. He and his crew all died when AD738 was shot down by flak and crashed in France. They were attacking the cruisers as part of a mixed force on the 4/5th of April, on what was probably his first operation with the squadron since replacing W/C Lindlay at the start of the month. A single bomb fell into the dry dock in which the *Gneisenau* was berthed, and although it failed to explode, the ship was moved to a new position in the harbour, while the danger was dealt with. On the following day a lone Coastal Command Beaufort delivered a suicidal torpedo attack, which seriously damaged the ship, and this would necessitate a six-month repair programme. The Beaufort was shot down immediately after the attack, and its crew was killed, although the pilot was posthumously awarded the Victoria Cross. The new commanding officer of 106 Squadron was W/C Bob Allen, formerly a flight commander at 49 Squadron, who was appointed on the 6th, and he was to lay the foundations for later commanders to mould 106 Squadron into one of the finest units in the Command. Yet another attack was launched against the ships on the 6/7th, and then, in a change of target on the 7/8th, Kiel sustained what for the period was a highly effective assault at the hands of two hundred aircraft, which included a sizeable contingent of Hampdens. On the 8/9th W/C Hyde led the 207 Squadron contingent back to Kiel, in the company of 150 other aircraft on the occasion of 97 Squadron's operational debut with the Manchester. W/C Hyde's L7302 fell victim to flak, and had to be abandoned over Germany, and the entire crew fell into enemy hands. It was a bitter blow for the squadron to lose its popular commanding officer, a man who had inspired by leading from the front. It would be three weeks before his replacement was appointed, and in the meantime, S/L Kydd assumed temporary command.

Persistent technical problems continued to afflict the Manchester, particularly in the engine department, where overheating and component failures were seriously effecting the type's rate of serviceability. As a result the first of a number of grounding orders was issued on the 13 April, while modifications were put in hand, and no further operations were mounted during what remained of the month. In the event the two Manchester squadrons missed little significant activity. Brest and Kiel were the main targets for the remainder of the month, although Berlin was raided on the 17/18th, when 118 assorted aircraft took off. Those reaching the target area failed to achieve any degree of concentration, and lost eight of their number in the process. On the 30th W/C Anderson became the new commanding officer of 207 Squadron, although S/L Kydd continued to lead the squadron in practise, until the new man had converted onto the Manchester.

Operations began again for 207 Squadron on the night of the 2/3 May, when three aircraft captained by S/L Kydd and F/Os Romans and Pinchbeck, joined in on a series of raids against Hamburg. This was the occasion on which S/L Kydd's L7377 became the first Manchester to drop a 4,000 lb 'Cookie'. W/C Anderson's command of 207 Squadron lasted one week, during which time he probably did not even meet his crews. S/L Kydd remained in the hot seat while a successor was found. Hamburg was a frequent destination throughout the war, and this mini campaign of six raids between the end of April and the middle of May was unusually effective for the period. Eighty-three fires were started in the city on the 8/9 May, and ten apartment blocks were demolished by a 4,000 lb 'Cookie'. Even more encouraging results were achieved on the 10/11th, when Hampdens and a Manchester were present, and on the 11/12th, when 5 Group was not involved, it participating instead in a useful raid on Bremen.

AVM Slessor was appointed to replace AVM Bottomley as AOC on the 12th, the former progressing to become Deputy Chief of Air Staff and the first post-war C-in-C of Bomber Command. As the month progressed Cologne replaced Hamburg as the main objective, but there was no night of outstanding success. A second grounding order was issued against Manchesters on the 17th, although some limited non-operational flying would take place. On the 21st W/C Lewis was appointed as the new commander of 207 Squadron, he having formerly acted as the British advisory officer during the formation of the Polish 300 (Masovian) Squadron. While Manchesters were off the order of battle, Cologne and Kiel served as the principal targets for relatively modest forces during the remainder of the month.

The June account opened with a disappointing raid on Düsseldorf on the 2nd/3rd, and there was little further activity for the Hampden squadrons thereafter for a week. During this relative lull, on the 6th, the newly formed 455 Squadron Royal Australian Air Force took shape, on paper at least, under the British Commonwealth Air Training Plan (BCATP) agreement of January 1941. It was based at Swinderby as 5 Group's latest recruit, although largely in the absence of personnel and equipment. The formation process had actually begun at Williamtown, New South Wales in May, when F/O John Lawson had reported to the squadron as its adjutant, temporary commander and sole member. Gradually postings to the unit swelled its ranks, and preparations were made to move to England. In the meantime the German warships at Brest provided the target for over a hundred aircraft on the 10/11th, including thirty-nine Hampdens. The following night brought simultaneous attacks on Duisburg and Düsseldorf, but most of the bombs fell on Cologne. The crews were unaware at the time that they were operating under the scrutiny of civil servant Mr D M Butt, who had been commissioned to analyse the effectiveness or otherwise of Bomber Command operations. Attacks carried out over Germany during June and July were to form the basis of his report, which would be completed in August. On the 12/13 June over three hundred assorted aircraft were airborne to five separate targets in Germany. The 5 Group effort by ninety-one Hampdens was directed at the railway yards at Soest, a few miles north of the soon to be famous Möhne Dam. The attack failed in the face of poor visibility, and only forty-two crews claimed to have bombed the primary target. The rest of the month was devoted largely to simultaneous raids on Cologne and Düsseldorf, these two cities featuring on the 15/16th, 16/17th, 17/18th, 19/20th, 21st/22nd, 23/24th, 24/25th and 26/27th, but not one of these operations resulted in a telling blow. During this period on the 20th W/C Satterly assumed command of 83 Squadron on the posting out of W/C Learoyd to pastures new. He would return to the operational scene in December, to take command of 44 Squadron.

It was not until the 21 June that the Manchester was once more declared fit for operations, and 207 Squadron's S/L Kydd took-off in L7310 to check out a Sergeant pilot for the last time before he took over as a crew captain. Having reached around a hundred and fifty feet the port engine failed, and unable to maintain height, the Manchester flew through trees before crashing in a field beyond the airfield. S/L Kydd died at the scene, the pilot, Sgt Syrett, was severely injured, and the wireless operator, the only other occupant, succumbed to his injuries a month later. That night Manchesters took part in their first operation for almost five weeks, and it was a record number of eighteen which took to the air bound for Boulogne, this figure including a number from 61 Squadron, which was blooding the type for the first time. Seven crews from 207 Squadron took part, and one of them was involved in a chain of events, which had a tragic conclusion. German intruders were known to be active over England, and while heading south over the Midlands L7314 was mistakenly identified as hostile, and a 25 Squadron Beaufighter was directed to intercept. Despite misgivings on the part of the night fighter crew after a visual sighting, they were assured by control that the aircraft was an enemy, and shot it down over Northamptonshire, killing F/O Withers and his crew.

Also aloft that night was F/L Reg Reynolds, one of a number of notables who joined the squadron during the course of the year, and later went on to distinguished careers with other squadrons. Reynolds would command 139 Squadron in 1944, after serving 105 Squadron with distinction. F/L Peter Ward-Hunt began the war with 49 Squadron at Scampton before his posting to 207 Squadron. In 1943, he would became a flight commander under Guy Gibson at 106 Squadron, before eventually moving to Ludford Magna as a staff officer later in the year. S/L 'Penny' Beauchamp was to become the scourge of the Nazi night fighter crews in 1944, as the commanding officer of 157 Squadron, one of 100 Group's 'Serrate' Mosquito units. F/O Wooldridge, formerly with 61 Squadron, moved on to 106 Squadron where he also served as a flight commander under Gibson, before eventually being given command of 105 Squadron during its final months with 2 Group. Having overseen 105's transition to a new role as an Oboe unit with the Pathfinders, he was screened from operations to return to the tri-Service Petroleum Warfare Department, where he had helped to develop FIDO earlier in the war. Wooldridge was also a composer, playwright and author of some standing, and among his many successful works was the book, screenplay and score for the post war classic film *Appointment in London*, which starred Dirk Bogarde as a Lancaster squadron commander, and Dinah Sheridan as a WREN intelligence officer. Wooldridge would survive the war, only to die tragically in a car crash in the late fifties. His widow, Margueretta Scott, is a well known actress, who cameoed as Mrs Pomphrey in the hit TV series All Creatures Great and Small.

Another new squadron joined the 5 Group ranks at Lindholme on the 24 June. No. 408 (Goose) Squadron was born out of Article XV of the BCATP agreement, which had called for twenty-five Canadian squadrons to be formed in the RAF by May 1942. All such squadrons were to be numbered in the 400 to 450 series, to avoid confusion with RAF and other Dominion units. It was the second Canadian bomber unit to form after 405 (Vancouver) Squadron, which had gone to 4 Group two months earlier. The first commanding officer was W/C Nelles Timmerman, a Canadian who had joined the RAF in 1936. He had undertaken at least fifty operations on Hampdens with 49 Squadron by the time of his appointment, during which period he gained the award of the DFC for turning to chase an enemy aircraft while returning from an operation, and shooting it down with his forward machine guns. S/L Clayton was posted in from 83 Squadron as a flight commander, and the other post was taken up by S/L Burnett, who arrived from the OTU at Finningley. All three principal officers of the new squadron were Canadians, but serving in the RAF rather than RCAF. Working up to operational status on Hampdens would not begin in earnest until the squadron moved from Lindholme to Syerston a month hence.

Manchesters became subject to a new month-long grounding order on the 1 July, and it was decided to complete the equipping 61 Squadron with the type while it was inactive. A degree of frustration was also being voiced by the 207 and 97 Squadron crews over the lack of operational opportunities available to them. As a temporary measure 207 Squadron crews were allowed to borrow Hampdens from 44 Squadron to operate on a voluntary basis, and a similar arrangement was put in place for 97 Squadron crews with 106 Squadron aircraft. The Hampden force was used sparingly at the beginning of July, operating against Duisburg on the 2nd/3rd, Bremen on the 3rd/4th, Lorient on the 4/5th and Osnabrück on the 5/6th, all of which were secondary operations to the nights' main activity. On the 6/7th, though, eighty-eight Hampdens led the way in an attack on the German cruisers at Brest, only to find that the highly efficient smoke screens prevented the ships from being sighted. The railway centre of Hamm was the objective for forty-five Hampdens on the 8/9th, with Whitleys of 4 Group in support. On the 9th a new Air Ministry directive identified the inland transportation system and the morale of the civilian population as Germany's most vulnerable points. This meant, that from now on, special emphasis was to be placed on the ring of railway centres around the Ruhr to inhibit the movement in of raw materials and the export of finished goods. These relatively precise targets would require moonlight, while on moonless nights the Rhine cities of Cologne, Düsseldorf and Duisburg should prove easier to locate for area raids. On dark nights, however, when questionable weather conditions prevailed, more distant urban objectives were to be visited.

Aachen received its first major raid of the war on the 9/10th, and extensive damage was inflicted on housing around the city centre. On the following night Wellingtons and Hampdens were thwarted by the weather at Cologne, while on the 11/12th thirty-six Hampdens operated alone against Wilhelmshaven, and deposited most of their bombs in open country. Other targets for Hampdens in mid month were Hanover on the 14/15th, and Hamburg again on the 16/17th. Another change of command at 49 Squadron saw W/C Jefferson posted out to 25 O.T.U. on the 17th, and W/C Stubbs posted in to replace him. Stubbs, it will be recalled, had commanded 106 Squadron in the rank of Squadron Leader between June and November 1940 while it was a training unit, before moving on to 207 and 97 Squadrons as a flight commander. On the same day 61 and 144 Squadrons moved out of Hemswell for what, for the former at least, would be a relatively short stay at North Luffenham in the county of Rutland. The 19th brought a change of address also for 50 Squadron, which departed Lindholme for Swinderby. On the following day 408 Squadron likewise vacated Lindholme to take up residence at Syerston, nestling alongside the A46 Leicester to Newark road in Nottinghamshire. Shortly afterwards crews began to arrive from OTUs, and the first contingent of Canadian ground crews would be on station by early August.

A major daylight operation was planned for the 24 July against the warships at Brest. The original plan involved Wellingtons from 1 and 3 Groups, Halifaxes from 4 Group, Hampdens from 5 Group and Fortresses from 2 Group. At the eleventh hour it was discovered that *Scharnhorst* had relocated to La Pallice, some two hundred miles further south, and it was decided to send the Halifax element there, and leave the rest of the original plan intact. Three 90 Squadron Fortresses carried out a high level bombing run to draw up the enemy fighters, while eighteen Hampdens performed a similar role at a less rarefied altitude under the umbrella of a Spitfire escort. It was hoped, that this would leave a clear path for the assault on the ships by the Wellington brigade, but in the event, they faced much heavier fighter and flak opposition than expected. Six hits were claimed on the *Gneisenau*, although they were unconfirmed, and twelve aircraft failed to return. Ten of these were Wellingtons, and the other two were Hampdens. During the course of the month W/C Gyll-Murray took over command of 455 Squadron from the recently promoted F/L Lawson, but much remained to be done before the squadron became operational, not least of which was to take possession of some aircraft!

Kiel opened the August account for the Hampden squadrons on the 2nd/3rd, but the city authorities reported scant damage. Mannheim and Karlsruhe occupied them on the 5/6th, this time accompanied by other types, and some useful results were obtained. Manchesters returned to the fray on the night of the 7/8th of August, when three from 207 Squadron joined forces with 103 other aircraft to attack the Krupps factory at Essen. It was an ineffective attempt on this hard-to-hit city, concealed as it generally was under a veil of industrial haze. A similarly ineffective attack on Kiel took place twenty-four hours later. An hour into the 12th 408 Squadron launched its first sortie, New Zealander Sgt Bradley heading for the docks at Rotterdam with four 500 lb bombs. Three other 408 Squadron Hampdens followed in company with twenty-seven others, and all four Geese returned safely to Syerston. Krefeld also featured on this night, but only one of the twenty Hampdens and nine Whitleys found the railway yards. A small number of Hampdens joined a Wellington force at Hanover on the following night. While Hanover and Magdeburg were assigned to other types on the 14/15th, eighty Hampdens went to Brunswick to bomb railway installations with indeterminate results. Railway targets continued to be the main focus for the Hampden crews for the remainder of the month, at Düsseldorf on the 16/17th, Bremen on the 17/18th, Cologne on the 18/19th, Kiel on the 19/20th and Mannheim on the 22nd/23rd.

It was on the 18 August that Mr Butt completed his report, and its disclosures were to send shock waves reverberating around the halls of Westminster and the Air Ministry. Having studied around 4,000 photographs taken during a hundred night operations over Germany in June and July, the author concluded, that only a tiny fraction of bombs were falling within five miles of their intended targets. This swept aside at a stroke any notion, that the Command was having a material effect on the enemy's capacity to wage war, and demonstrated its earlier claims to be extravagant and largely propaganda. It would also provide ammunition for the many opponents of an independent bomber force, who were lobbying for Bomber Command to be dissolved, and for its aircraft to be redistributed to other causes, namely the U-Boat war and the Middle East. It was unfortunate, that such damning criticism would forever attach itself to the C-in-C, Sir Richard Peirse, and unjustly blight his reputation.

The Mk Ia Manchesters were now beginning to roll out of the factories, and following discussions on the 1 September, 97 Squadron stood-down from operations to allow new crews to be trained for the establishment of a B Flight. It would be late October before operations were again undertaken, and in the meantime, the Association of British Malay, represented by Captain Gammans MP, conferred the Straits Settlements title on the squadron in a ceremony at Coningsby on the 21st. Crews were briefed for two targets on the 2nd/3rd of September, Frankfurt and Berlin, involving respectively eleven and thirty-two Hampdens and four Manchesters at the latter. Neither operation produced a worthwhile result, and the night cost five Hampdens, two of them from mining operations around the Frisians and Denmark. 44 Squadron suffered a particularly bad time, losing four aircraft and three complete crews. 61 Squadron's Manchester L7388 also failed to return, and it was later established that it had been brought down by flak over the Capital. At the controls was W/C Valentine, who was killed along with his crew and their passenger, the station commander of North Luffenham, G/C Barrett. W/C Weir was appointed as the new squadron commander on the 5th. On the following day W/C Satterly concluded his tour with 83 Squadron, and was posted to a staff job to be replaced by the veteran W/C 'Mary' Tudor, who would enjoy a longer spell at the helm than his predecessors. Almost two hundred aircraft, including forty-three Hampdens and four Manchesters, were dispatched to Berlin on the 7/8th, while a further eighteen Hampdens joined an attack on a U-boat yard at Kiel. Damage was inflicted at both targets, but the loss of eighteen aircraft from 303 sorties was the Command's highest casualty rate in a single night to date.

A daylight raid on the German capital ship, *Admiral Scheer*, at Oslo on the 8th brought about the end of a former 5 Group stalwart. The previously mentioned P/O Dave Romans had served with distinction with 44 and 207 Squadrons, and had survived a number of ditchings during 1940, ultimately earning a DFC. His fine record of service had led first to his selection as a founder member of 207 Squadron and then for 2 Group's elite high-level bombing squadron. This day found him in command of a 90 Squadron B17C, known in the RAF as the Fortress I, which was shot down by fighters in the target area with the consequent loss of all on board. That night Hampdens joined forces with other types to raid Kassel without loss. Operations followed to Rostock on the 11/12th, Frankfurt on the 12/13th, Brest on the 13/14th and Hamburg on the 15/16th for a total loss to 5 Group of four Hampdens. One of these, AE249, was shot down by a night fighter over Germany during the Hamburg raid, and was not only the first 455 Squadron aircraft to be lost on operations, but also the first to be lost by any RAAF bomber squadron. The 15th had been a momentous day in the history and fortunes of Bomber Command, with the arrival at Waddington of the first prototype Lancaster BT308 for crew familiarization in preparation for 44 Squadron to introduce the type into squadron service. But that was for the future, and in the meantime, operations continued with the trusty but obsolete Hampden. It was at this time, on the 12th, that 44 Squadron assumed the Rhodesia title, in recognition of that country's contribution to the war effort. The month ended with two more raids on Hamburg on the 29/30th and again twenty-four hours later, both prosecuted by predominantly Hampden and Wellington forces, and each resulting in very modest damage.

Bad weather had been hampering the bombers' efforts for some time, and frustrating Peirse's attempts to score a convincing victory, which might do something to polish the besmirched reputation of the Command. The unfavourable conditions continued into October, however, and it was the second week before the first sizeable operations were mounted. W/C Fothergill was appointed to command 207 Squadron on the 10th on the posting out of W/C Lewis. That night the destinations for seventy-eight and sixty-nine aircraft were respectively the Krupp complex at Essen and the city of Cologne, but only a handful of crews reached the former, while the slight damage at the latter suggested likewise. In one of the night's minor operations twenty-three Hampdens were sent to Dunkerque. On the following night Nuremberg was the objective for 150 aircraft, not including Hampdens, which participated instead in simultaneous raids on Bremen and Hüls. The total number of sorties for the night was a new record of 373, but in conditions of complete cloud cover, this massive effort was not rewarded with success. Not one of the targets sustained meaningful damage, and a total of thirteen aircraft and crews failed to return. Nuremberg again escaped with only the slightest damage on the 14/15th in the absence of a Hampden contingent, and it is likely that a cloud-covered Duisburg fared equally well on the 16/17th. Hampdens were present in two roles on this night, twenty-six as bombers and eight to suppress searchlights. Earlier on the 16th

61 Squadron began its move from North Luffenham to Woolfox Lodge. The main target on the 23/24th was Kiel, where a U-Boat yard and a naval base suffered some damage at the hands of a hundred-strong force, which included almost forty Hampdens. Only a fraction of the aircraft bound for Frankfurt on the 24/25th actually reached the target area, and this was typical for the period. The month ended with two further raids on Hamburg, that of the 26/27th producing slightly better results than of late. W/C Walker concluded his tour at the helm of 50 Squadron on the 26th. He would later become station commander at Syerston, and we will catch up with him again at the appropriate time. He was replaced at 50 Squadron by another character, W/C Oxley, a bulldog of a man who whipped up Hun-hatred at briefings to galvanise his troops.

There were only minor operations at the start of November until the 7/8th, when Sir Richard Peirse arranged a night of heavy activity, which would see the commitment of the highest number of sorties to date. The main fare on this night of doubtful weather conditions was Berlin, to which over two hundred aircraft were originally assigned. However, the 5 Group AOC voiced his concerns, and was allowed to withdraw his seventy-five Hampdens and Manchesters, and send them instead to Cologne. A third force of fifty-three Wellingtons and two Stirlings were to target Mannheim, while sundry minor operations involved a further ninety-three aircraft. A total of 169 aircraft eventually set off for the Capital, of which less than half actually reached the general area to drop their bombs. These produced scant damage for the loss of twenty-one of their number, and although the 5 Group force returned intact from Cologne, it had left its objective similarly untouched. The Mannheim force likewise missed its target altogether, losing in the process seven Wellingtons, and the minor operations turned into a disaster costing a further nine aircraft. This brought the total casualty figure for the night to thirty-seven aircraft, more than twice the previous highest, and there was nothing to show for it.

In the light of the recently published Butt Report, this was the final straw for the Air Ministry, and a new directive was issued on the 13th, ordering Peirse to restrict further operations, while the future of Bomber Command was considered. In the meantime, Peirse had been summoned to a meeting with Churchill to make his explanations, and would shortly leave his post as C-in-C. Before the new directive came into force some modest success was gained at Hamburg on the 9/10th, when seventy-one of over a hundred crews claimed to have bombed as briefed, and a number of large fires were started. Hamburg was also the destination on the last night of the month, but a third of the force of 180 aircraft failed to reach the target area, and damage was not commensurate with the effort expended and the loss of thirteen more crews. In between, operations had been small scale, and directed mostly at French and German ports, until Düsseldorf on the 27/28th, when almost half of the eighty-six aircraft committed were provided by 5 Group. Meanwhile, 207 Squadron moved to a new station at Bottesford in Leicestershire on the 17th, and after the comfortable surroundings and facilities enjoyed at the pre-war station of Waddington, it was to be something of a culture shock. The air and ground crews were greeted by a sea of mud at this still-to-be completed airfield, and the accommodation was widely dispersed and exceedingly damp. Taxiing would also prove to be a hazardous undertaking, and although the runways were concrete, a wheel on the grass would require a Herculean effort to free it. 50 Squadron also changed address, moving from Swinderby on the 26th for the first of two spells at Skellingthorpe, a new station just a stone's throw from Lincoln's western suburbs. During the course of the month W/C Gardner was posted from 144 Squadron, and he was replaced by W/C Christie, who would remain in post only until early in the new year.

The main focus of attention in December was Brest, to which fourteen separate raids of varying sizes were dispatched, some of which included a Hampden element. The 9th brought a change of address for 408 Squadron, which now took up residence at Balderton on the outskirts of Newark, although some aircraft would be detached to North Luffenham between late January and mid March. On the 13th 44 Squadron lost the first of a number of commanding officers to die on operations, when W/C Misselbrook and his crew went missing without trace during the afternoon while mining off Brest in AE196. W/C Gyll-Murray departed 455 Squadron on the 15th having handed the baton to W/C Lindeman. A daylight raid on the German warships at Brest under the codename Operation Veracity was launched on the 18th. This employed eighteen Halifaxes, an equal number of Stirlings and eleven Manchesters of 97 Squadron led by W/C Balsdon flying with F/S Pendrill's crew in L7490. One Manchester took off as a flying reserve, and as all seemed well by the time the Lizard was reached, F/S Fletcher brought L7463 back home. The Manchester element was the last to pass over the target, by which time the fighter escort had withdrawn, and they were left at the mercy of the enemy flak and fighters. L7490 was hit by flak in the target area, and had already crossed the boundary fence at Coningsby on return when it stalled and nose-dived into the centre of the airfield. The wreckage was consumed by a fire-ball, and all eight men on board were killed. It was a sad end to a faltering eight months of operational activity for 97 Squadron, and W/C Balsdon's influence would be missed, but at least the end was in sight for its association with the ill-fated Manchester, and no further operations would be carried out before the turn of the year. W/C Kynoch was posted in on the 23rd to assume command, and he would preside over the squadron's conversion onto Lancasters, and see it through its first operations with the type. Kynoch had been a contemporary of Guy Gibson at 83 Squadron, which he joined late in 1937 when already in his mid twenties, and he was considered to be good natured and something of an athlete.

The new commanding officer at 44 Squadron was W/C Learoyd, who had relinquished his command of 83 Squadron back in June. He took up his appointment at 44 Squadron on the 19th, at a time when the squadron's association with the Hampden was drawing to a close. A new era was about to begin for 44 Squadron, 5 Group, and, indeed, the Command as a whole, which must have promised much. 5 Group welcomed a new arrival on the 19th in the form of 420 (Snowy Owl) Squadron, which came into existence at Waddington under the command of W/C Bradshaw as the fourth RCAF unit in Bomber Command. Although many of the Group's squadrons had converted to the ill-fated Avro Manchester by this time, and 44 Squadron was about to begin the process of working up to operational status as the first Lancaster unit in the Command, 420 Squadron was to begin its operational career on the trusty, if obsolete Hampden. None of the attacks on German targets during the month, at Aachen on the 7/8th, Cologne on the 11/12th and 23rd/24th, Wilhelmshaven on the 16/17th and Düsseldorf on the 27/28th produced more than modest damage. On a more positive note, though, a return to Wilhelmshaven on the 28/29th did result in some success. The Hampdens did not take part on this night, eighty-one of them taking off instead for a chemical factory at Hüls.

A few days earlier, on Christmas Eve, the first three production Lancasters arrived at 44 Squadron, L7530, L7537 and L7538, and these were followed by four more on the 28th. A number of Manchesters were also taken on charge by the conversion flight, but the Squadron would not use them operationally. Also posted in were some experienced Manchester pilots, for whom conversion to Lancasters would be accomplished more quickly. Among them was W/C Burton-Gyles, who had been a mainstay at 207 Squadron during the year, and who would eventually command 23 Squadron in the Middle East in 1943. Before the end of the month, W/C Learoyd departed the squadron on detachment to Bomber Command HQ, and temporary command passed to Squadron Leader J D Nettleton, who would oversee crew conversion until his return. Initial training on Lancasters was biased towards mining, with an attack on the *Tirpitz* in mind, although the crews were not aware of this. In the event, bad weather caused the plans to be abandoned, and this allowed an opportunity for a number of 44 Squadron crews to assist 97 Squadron in its conversion onto Lancasters. No. 97 Squadron had a sprinkling of Rhodesians among its number, and an exchange took place between the squadrons, to make 44 as Rhodesian as possible. It created a spirit of friendly rivalry between the two units, which would continue into the future through joint operations.

It had not been a good year for the Command, and it was now known through the Butt Report that much of its effort had been wasted, and its claims of success exaggerated. The new aircraft types had thus far failed to deliver, and were constantly beset with technical problems. These had required periods of grounding, while essential modifications were carried out, and their serviceability rate was, as a result, disappointing in the extreme. While this situation would improve, the Lancaster was to show itself to be a thoroughbred from the start, and the coming year would provide an opportunity for 5 Group to demonstrate the type's prowess.

1942. New leader, new tactics, new weapon
Harris, the bomber stream, the Lancaster and the 1,000 raids

The year began for the Command with a continuation of the obsession with Brest and its guests *Scharnhorst*, *Gneisenau*, and from time to time, *Prinz Eugen*. No fewer than eleven operations were carried out against this objective during January, none of which resulted in success. No. 5 Group's first casualty of the year was a 106 Squadron Hampden, which failed to return from a mining sortie to the Frisians on the 3rd/4th of January. On the 8th the unfairly discredited ACM Sir Richard Peirse relinquished his post as C-in-C, and departed for the Far-East, where he would fulfil a similar function. As a temporary measure 3 Group's AVM Baldwin would occupy the hot seat until the appointment of a permanent successor. German targets during the month included Wilhelmshaven on the 10/11th, Hamburg on the 14/15th, which cost two 50 Squadron Hampdens, Hamburg again on the 15/16th, for the loss of two 207 Squadron Manchesters, and Bremen on the 17/18th. Not one of the operations produced worthwhile results. 44 Squadron, of course, would miss almost the entire first quarter of the year as it worked up to operational status. Introducing a new aircraft type to operations was vastly different from simply converting to a type. Although the Lancaster was basically an enlarged Manchester, its engines were different, and there were more of them. The handling characteristics with war loads could only be ascertained under simulated operational conditions in the hands of a front-line unit, as could fuel consumption, servicing and arming. The time would be well spent, however, and tens of thousands of airmen would benefit in the coming years. No. 420 Squadron went to war for the first time on the night of the 21st/22nd when contributing five of twelve Hampdens for an attack by a total of thirty-eight aircraft on Emden. Three Hampdens and one Whitley failed to return, among them AT130, the aircraft captained by 420 Squadron's B Flight commander, S/L Wood. It was brought down by flak over Holland, but the entire crew survived to fall into enemy hands. Two other Hampdens failed to return from a simultaneous operation to Bremen. A bad night for 106 Squadron on the 28/29th saw four Hampdens fail to return from Münster. Sgt Brown ditched off the east coast, and when rescue came after sixteen bitterly cold hours adrift in the dinghy only he remained alive. On the last night of the month three 61 Squadron Manchesters were lost raiding Brest along with two Hampdens from 144 Squadron. During the course of the month W/C Christie was posted from 144 Squadron to be replaced by W/C Simond, whose tenure would be brief indeed.

In the meantime, February began slowly and Brest again featured on the night of the 6/7th, when less than half of a sixty-strong force of predominantly Wellingtons reached the target area. The inevitable first loss of a Lancaster came via a training accident later on that day, the 7th, when F/S Nicholson misjudged his landing, and rendered L7542 beyond economical repair, happily without injury to the crew. Also on that day the Group lost three more Hampdens, two again from 144 Squadron, while they were mining off the Frisians. 455 Squadron moved from Swinderby to Wigsley on the 8th, where it would spend the little time remaining to it as a Bomber Command outfit. The situation at Brest resolved itself just hours after yet another inconclusive attack by Wellingtons on the evening of the 11th. The *Scharnhorst*, *Gneisenau* and *Prinz Eugen* slipped out of port with their escorting entourage under the most atrocious weather conditions, and headed into the English Channel in an audacious bid for freedom. The British government had anticipated such a breakout, and Operation Fuller had been prepared for precisely this eventuality. However, an unbelievable breakdown in communications prevented its implementation until it was too late. It was already 10.30 hours on the 12th before the enemy fleet was spotted, and with 5 Group alone standing by at four hours readiness, it was 13.30 hours before the first Bomber Command aircraft got away. Throughout the course of the day a record 242 daylight sorties were launched, but the low cloud and squally conditions made it extremely difficult for crews to locate their quarry, and few sightings were made. A number of attacks were attempted, and although some ships were straddled, no hits were scored. The German fleet made good its escape through the Straits of Dover and into open sea, where *Scharnhorst* and *Gneisenau* both hit mines recently laid by 5 Group crews. This minor inconvenience slowed their progress to a degree, but all arrived in home ports on the following morning. Fifteen Bomber Command crews were lost on this day, eleven of them from 5 Group, and these came on top of all those who had failed to return from attacking the warships over the past ten months. 144 Squadron's AT175 was lost without trace, and with it went W/C Simond and the four other occupants. 49 Squadron was hardest hit, registering the loss of four Hampdens. The whole affair was a huge embarrassment to the government and the nation, but at least this annoying itch had been scratched for the last time, and the Command could now concentrate on targets to which it was better suited.

The end was now in sight for the Hampden as a front-line bomber aircraft, and most of 5 Group's squadrons had already either re-equipped, or were in the process of doing so. Nos 44 and 97 Squadrons had taken Lancasters on charge, and would carry out their first operations in March, 207, 61 and 83 Squadrons had Manchesters, and 106 Squadron was in the process of converting to that type during the month. This left only 144, 49 and 50 Squadrons of the old guard, 408 and 420 Squadrons of the Royal Canadian Air Force and 455 Squadron Royal Australian Air Force with Hampdens. The Canadian squadrons were to move to 4 Group later in the year, 49 and 50 Squadrons would operate briefly with the Manchester before converting to Lancasters, and 455 Squadron was earmarked for a transfer to Coastal Command as a torpedo bomber unit. It seems likely that 144 Squadron's future had by this time also been determined, and its remaining time with

Bomber Command was short. It also seems probable in view of this, that command of the squadron now passed to one of the flight commanders, S/L Bennett, who, it will be recalled, had been the first Bomber Command recipient of the DFC back in March 1940 while serving with 50 Squadron.

On the 10th, the armed merchant ship *Alcantara* departed America's eastern seaboard to cross the Atlantic. She carried the person of ACM Sir Arthur Harris, who was shortly to take on the arduous post of Bomber Command's commander-in-chief. On the 14th, while he was still at sea, a new Air Ministry directive was issued, which reaffirmed the assault on the morale of the enemy's civilian population, particularly its workers, as the primary objective. This cleared the way for the blatant area bombing of Germany's towns and cities, without the pretence of aiming at specific industrial or military objectives. Indiscriminate bombing had, of course, been a fact of life since 1940, although the general public and all but a few politicians were unaware that this had been the case. The Command had proved conclusively over more than eighteen months, that precision targets were quite beyond the scope of even the most highly trained crews. The technology did not exist, and would not until the advent of 'smart bombs', to hit individual buildings from high level over a cloud-covered, blacked-out hostile country. Even the Americans, who claimed to be able to drop a bomb into a pickle barrel from twenty thousand feet, would eventually resort to area bombing, although it would be couched in different terms. It was the only way forward for Bomber Command, and while the new commander-in-chief would be a fierce advocate of the policy, he was not, as many in Britain and Germany continue to believe, its architect.

A similar accident to that of the 7th accounted for the second loss of a Lancaster, L7538, on the 20th, this time at the hands of Sgt Rowan Parry, but again the crew walked away. Two days later Harris took up the reins at Bomber Command HQ at High Wycombe, and assessed the enormity of the task facing him. He took on the job with firm ideas already in place on how to win the war by bombing alone, a theory, which had never been put into practice before. He recognised the need to overwhelm the enemy's defences and emergency services by concentrating the maximum number of aircraft over the target in time and space. This would bring the introduction of the bomber stream, and spell the end of the former practice, whereby crews largely determined for themselves the details of their sorties. The old system could cause a raid to be spread over many hours, and expose individual crews to the full might of the anti-aircraft guns. Harris also knew, that urban areas are destroyed most efficiently by fire, not by blast, and it would not be long before the loads carried in his aircraft reflected this thinking. For the remainder of the month he persisted with the small-scale raids on German ports, and it was during such an operation on the night of the 26/27th, that the war threw up one of its ironies. While attacking the floating dock at Kiel, a high explosive bomb from one of the forty-nine participating aircraft struck the bows of the *Gneisenau*, now supposedly in safe haven after enduring ten months of almost constant bombardment at Brest. The damage was so severe, that her sea-going career was ended for good, and her main armament was eventually removed for use in coastal defence.

March began for 97 Squadron with a move to Woodhall Spa on the 2nd. The first signs of a new hand on the tiller came on the night of the 3rd/4th of March. A force of 235 aircraft, a new record for a single target, was sent against the Renault lorry factory at Billancourt in Paris. 5 Group's contribution amounted to forty-eight Hampdens and twenty-six Manchesters. The tactics employed were a foretaste of things to come, involving a three-wave attack led by experienced crews, and with extensive use of flares to provide illumination. In the face of what was expected to be a weak flak defence, crews were to bomb from low to medium level to ensure accuracy, and thereby, hopefully, avoid civilian casualties in adjacent residential districts. In a highly successful outcome, almost all of the crews claimed to have bombed as briefed, and 40% of the factory buildings were destroyed, causing a four-week loss of production. This outstanding result was achieved for the loss of just one aircraft, and the celebrations were tempered only by the heavy casualties among French civilians. It was somewhat ironic, that Harris, as a champion of area bombing and critic of precision attacks, should gain his first victory by way of the latter. The Lancaster also went to war for the first time on this night, when four crews, those of S/L Nettleton, F/L Sandford, W/O Lamb and W/O Crum, carried out mining sorties off the north German coast, before returning safely. By this time, W/C Lynch-Blosse had joined the squadron to convert to Lancasters, and he would shortly assume command, although W/C Learoyd was still technically in command, and S/L Nettleton acting commanding officer.

Essen was to feature prominently in Harris's future plans, and on the night of the 8/9th he embarked on an eight raid series spread over the ensuing five weeks. The first three were on consecutive nights, involving respectively 211, 187 and 126 aircraft, with the leading element equipped with the new Gee navigation device. It appears that few crews managed to find or hit the city, as damage was reported by the local authorities to be negligible. 83 Squadron posted missing two Manchesters from the first operation. On the night of the last-mentioned, 44 Squadron sent two Lancasters for the type's first bombing operation, and both returned safely. One was also sent to Cologne on the 13/14th, for what was the first successful Gee-led operation, in which some useful industrial damage was achieved. W/C Allen departed 106 Squadron at the end of his tour as commanding officer, and left behind him a spirit of efficiency and confidence, which future commanders would develop. His replacement was Acting W/C Guy Gibson, whose finest hour lay more than twelve months hence, but who would use his time at 106 Squadron to enhance not only his own reputation, but also that of the squadron. Having completed a tour of operations with 83 Squadron during the first year of war, Gibson had managed to obtain a posting to 29 Squadron as a Beaufighter night fighter pilot, rather than be screened from operations altogether. He had also extracted from Sir Arthur T Harris, his AOC at 5 Group, a promise of a return to bombers in the future. Having redeemed that promise, Gibson immediately set about improving standards of efficiency in all areas of the squadron, and managed to gain from the troubled Manchester an operational serviceability, which other squadrons could not achieve. Gibson's manner would not endear him to his men, and he admitted to an inability to relate to 'other ranks', or to those whose job did not expose them to the dangers of operations. To a select few aircrew officers, however, he was an inspirational leader, and he collected around him pilots with potential, who, under his tutelage, would achieve reputations in their own right. Among those who would grace the Squadron as flight commanders during Gibson's reign were the already mentioned John 'Dim' Wooldridge and Peter Ward-Hunt and also John Searby. Among the as yet unknown pilots were future Dambusters John Hopgood, David Shannon and Lewis Burpee.

Almost two weeks of minor operations followed for the Command, during which, on the 24/25th, two 44 Squadron crews went mining off Lorient. Only one returned, the other, R5493, captained by F/S Warren-Smith, having disappeared into the sea with the loss of all eight men on board, and this was the first operational loss of a Lancaster. Major bombing operations resumed on the 25/26th, with the fourth of the series against Essen. This went the way of the first three, despite the commitment of 254 aircraft, a new record for a single target. Both 61 and 83 Squadrons lost two Manchesters, three to enemy action and one to a barrage balloon cable at the Kent coast. There was no improvement in effectiveness on the following night, when a little over a hundred crews tried again and lost 10% of their number. W/C Timmerman stepped down from his command of 408 Squadron on the 26th, and was posted back to Canada to become the Director of Training at No. 34 OTU. He left behind him a highly efficient squadron, which he bequeathed to S/L Clayton who was promoted from flight commander. On the following night he had the sad task of posting missing three of his crews from a mining sortie. The first real success for the area bombing policy came at the Baltic port of Lübeck on the 28/29th. Aware of the difficulty of navigating without reference points on the ground, Harris selected this target for its easily identifiable coastal location, its weak defences and the half-timbered construction of many of the buildings in its old centre. Employing similar tactics to those used at the Renault factory at the start of the month, the operation proceeded according to plan, and this fire-raising attack by almost two hundred aircraft destroyed around 30% of the city's built-up area. On the 31st W/C Kynoch was posted away from 97 Squadron, before completing his conversion onto Lancasters, and he was replaced by W/C Collier, another former 83 Squadron contemporary of Gibson.

April began with minor operations until the 5/6th, when a new record force of 263 aircraft took off for Cologne. The outcome was disappointing, and this carried over into the following night's attack on Essen, which again failed to impress. Yet another record force of 272 aircraft was unleashed on

Hamburg on the 8/9th, this time with a Lancaster presence, but the weather produced icing conditions and electrical storms, and only a few bomb loads found the mark. The penultimate raid of the series on Essen passed unspectacularly as far as the Germans were concerned on the 10/11th, but the Hampden element suffered at the hands of the defences and six failed to return, two each from 49, 144 and 455 Squadrons. Later on the 11th the start of low-level training at Waddington gave rise to much speculation. The final raid on Essen took place on the 12/13th, and was another failure, at which point Harris accepted defeat for the time being at least. The eight operations against this giant industrial city had involved over fifteen hundred sorties, and had cost sixty-four aircraft and crews in return for no significant damage. The problem was largely the industrial haze, which hung perpetually over the region, cloaking it from the eyes of bomber crews even on clear nights. Until the advent of some device to 'see' through this blanket, the problem would remain. As events were to prove, the solution was already under development, but it would be a further year before it was fully operational. W/C Pitt Clayton's brief reign as commanding officer of 408 Squadron concluded on the 14th, but no replacement would be appointed until mid May, and it was S/L Price who probably filled the breach in the meantime. Also on the 14th W/C Crighton-Biggie became the new commanding officer of 83 Squadron, and two days later the first Lancasters arrived, making the squadron the fourth to receive the new type.

Meanwhile on the same day 44 and 97 Squadrons carried out a practice flight, which equalled the round trip distance to southern Germany, culminating in a simulated attack on the Scottish town of Inverness. This was to prepare the crews for an audacious daylight attack on the M.A.N. diesel engine factory at Augsburg on the 17 April. The operation called for six Lancasters each from 44 and 97 Squadrons to fly at low level to the target, arriving at dusk, so that the return flight could be undertaken in darkness. In the meantime, attempts to hit Dortmund on the 14/15th and 15/16th went the way of the recent series against Essen, with only a proportion of the crews claiming to have reached the target, and hardly any of these actually landed their bombs anywhere near it. Another bad night for the Hampden brigade saw four of them lost to enemy action and two more crash on return to England.

Briefings for Augsburg took place on the morning of the 17th, the crews incredulous at the prospect of such a deep penetration foray into enemy territory by daylight. Take-off was timed for shortly after 3 pm, 44 Squadron from Waddington led by S/L Nettleton, and 97 Squadron from Woodhall Spa led by S/L Sherwood, each element proceeding independently to the target, and, although only a few miles apart, out of sight of each other. Flying across France in two vics line astern and half a mile or so apart 44 Squadron was spotted by German fighters, which were about to land at their base at Beaumont-le-Roger, having earlier been scrambled to meet a diversionary raid by Bostons at the coast. In a furious engagement lasting half an hour, four of the Lancasters were downed. The first to attract the fighters' attention was W/O Beckett's L7565, which had an unserviceable rear turret and was in the rear formation. On fire from stem to stern, the Lancaster sank into the ground, and exploded in a clump of trees with no survivors. L7548 was the next to go, its port wing in flames, W/O Crum ordered the bomb load to be jettisoned, and in a masterly display of airmanship, he brought the stricken Lancaster down on its belly in a meadow. The crew members emerged unscathed from the wreckage, and were eventually taken into captivity. Shortly afterwards, R5506 ploughed into the ground with all four engines ablaze, killing F/L Sandford and his crew. Now that the rear vic had been wiped out, the fighters advanced on the remaining three Lancasters, focusing first on L7536 which, in its death throes, reared upwards before stalling and diving in, taking with it to their deaths Sgt Rhodes and his crew. Both Nettleton and F/O Garwell, in R5508 and R5510 respectively, came under repeated attack, and their aircraft sustained damage before the fighters were forced to withdraw through lack of fuel and ammunition.

The two Lancasters continued on to the target, and at 19.56, bombed from chimney-top height in the face of a spirited and accurate flak defence. Garwell's Lancaster was hit by light flak, and caught fire, necessitating a forced-landing beyond the target, from which Garwell and three of his crew survived as PoWs. They watched from the ground as the 97 Squadron contingent ran the gauntlet of fire, and saw S/L Sherwood's Lancaster crash in flames after clearing the city. They would not know, that Sherwood alone had survived in miraculous circumstances. Their thoughts would have been with the four surviving 97 Squadron crews, as they followed Nettleton's westward course into the gathering darkness, to begin the long journey home. W/O Mycock's aircraft had been hit on the run up to the target and was a ball of flame even before it crashed with the loss of all on board. At half past midnight, unsure of their position and with fuel running low, the Nettleton crew sent out a distress call, which, thankfully, was answered. They were over the North Sea, from where they were directed to Squires Gate at Blackpool. A safe landing was made at 00.59, almost ten hours after take-off, while back at Waddington, those awaiting the return of the men they had waved off that afternoon were in sombre mood, as not one, it seemed, had survived. 97 Squadron had fared better on the outward flight and arrived at the target with the formation still intact. Some damage was inflicted on the M.A.N. factory, but not in proportion to the losses incurred, and it was later discovered, that a substantial number of the bombs had failed to explode. In recognition of his epic flight, Nettleton was awarded the Victoria Cross, and he became something of a celebrity over the ensuing months, speaking in a radio broadcast about the operation. He was also followed by film cameras as he paid a morale-boosting visit to a Lancaster factory, and this was later shown on newsreel at cinemas around the country. While the remnant headed homeward from the Augsburg raid, a modestly effective operation was being mounted against Hamburg.

Two squadrons now left 5 Group and Bomber Command to pursue a new career with webbed feet. 455 Squadron joined Coastal Command on the 20th, and 144 Squadron followed suite on the 21st. An attempt to address the problems recently experienced over the Ruhr was mounted on the night of the 22nd/23rd. A Gee-equipped force of Wellingtons and Stirlings flew to Cologne, intending to use the electronic device as a blind bombing aid. Only around a quarter of the bomb loads found the mark, thus demonstrating that Gee was unlikely to be effective for anything other than navigation. Even this was to have limitations once the enemy discovered the device and shortened its range by jamming. On the 23rd/24th, the first raid took place in a series of four on consecutive nights against the Baltic port of Rostock. Such had been the contrast between the failures over the Ruhr and the spectacular success at Lübeck, that Harris possibly decided to return to Germany's northern coast to boost morale. The presence nearby of a Heinkel aircraft factory might also have influenced his decision, and a small contingent of aircraft was sent specifically against this. In the event the factory escaped damage altogether, and most of the bombs intended for Rostock's old centre fell up to six miles away. On the following night the town was heavily bombed by around a hundred aircraft, while a 5 Group contingent again failed to hit the Heinkel works. W/C Guy Gibson of 106 Squadron led the Manchester assault on the factory on the 25/26th, and this time achieved some success, while the town itself suffered further severe damage. The final raid was directed exclusively at the town, and photographic reconnaissance revealed, that over 1,700 buildings had been destroyed in the series, and 60% of the built-up area lay in ruins. AVM Coryton became 5 Group's new AOC on the 25th. His predecessor would become C-in-C Coastal Command in 1943. At the end of the month, a further joint operation was mounted by 44 and 97 Squadrons, this time against the *Tirpitz* at Trondheim, for which, sections of both squadrons were detached to Lossiemouth in Scotland. The operation on the 27th/28th was carried out in concert with Halifaxes from 4 Group, but was unsuccessful, and 10 Squadron's commanding officer and future AOC of the Pathfinders, W/C Don Bennett, was shot down. A repeat effort on the following day fared no better, by which time Bennett was in the process of evading capture and returning to the UK.

49 Squadron operated Manchesters for the first time on the night of the 2nd/3rd of May, when five crews were sent to the Rennes area to drop leaflets. As far as bombing was concerned, the month began with an outstandingly successful raid for the period on Hamburg on the 3rd/4th, to which 5 Group's only contribution was five Hampdens. The Group was more heavily involved, however, in a three raid series on consecutive nights against the southern city of Stuttgart from the 4/5th. No losses were incurred from the Group's commitment of twenty-nine Hampden sorties and twenty-eight by Lancasters, but all three raids failed through a combination of haze,

difficulties with identification and decoy fires, and this particular city would continue for some time to be an elusive target. 61 Squadron was on the move once again on the 5th, this time settling at Syerston. Heroic though the Augsburg raid undoubtedly had been, it was a disaster in terms of losses for the limited level of damage inflicted, and another disaster awaited 44 Squadron on the 8/9th, the day on which W/C Lynch-Blosse officially assumed command.

The docks at Warnemünde on the Baltic coast were selected for an elaborate three-wave attack, involving two medium level forces and one at low level. 5 Group put up twenty-one Lancasters, nineteen Hampdens and nine Manchesters. Six of the seven Lancasters dispatched by 44 Squadron were assigned to the low-level force, and four of them failed to return. W/C Lynch-Blosse, flying his first operation as commanding officer, died with the other seven men on board R5555, when it was shot down in the general area of the target. Close by, F/O MacLagan and six of his eight-man crew lost their lives in the wreckage of R5568. The other two eight-man crews, those of W/O Lamb in L7533 and W/O Jones in R5557, were lost without trace, presumably in the sea. Three Hampdens and a Manchester completed the Group's list of missing aircraft. On the 10th W/C Smales became 44 Squadron's seventh commanding officer since the outbreak of war. 49 Squadron parted company with W/C Stubbs on his departure to H.Q.92 Group on the 14th, and W/C Slee arrived from Coningsby to assume command. The middle part of the month was taken up with minor operations, predominantly of the gardening variety. On the 18th W/C Twigg was appointed as the new commanding officer of 408 Squadron, and while his two predecessors had been Canadians in the RAF, he was the first RCAF officer to attain the position. Early in the month, the squadron had taken a number of Manchesters on charge, and S/L Price set up a Conversion Flight for the training of crews. It was not until the 19/20th that the Command ventured forth in numbers again. The target was Mannheim, a city on the eastern bank of the Rhine in southern Germany, for which almost two hundred aircraft were detailed. There were just thirteen Lancasters involved, but even these could not save the operation from failure.

When Harris took up his appointment as C-in-C he had asked for 4,000 bombers with which to win the war. Whilst there was never the slightest chance of getting them, he needed to ensure, that those earmarked for him were not spirited away to what he considered less deserving causes. In fact, Harris believed that his was the only worthwhile cause for bomber aircraft, and vociferously denounced the siphoning-off of resources, even for SOE duties within his own Command. However, the jury was still out following the damning Butt Report, and critics in high places, principally the Admiralty, continued to call for the dissolution of Bomber Command. The same song was being sung, namely, the reallocation of Bomber Command's aircraft to the fight against the U-Boat menace in the Atlantic, and to help combat the reversals in the Middle-East. To ensure the future of the

Command, Harris needed a major success and perhaps some symbolism to silence the critics. Out of this was born the Thousand Plan, Operation Millennium, the commitment of a thousand aircraft in one night against one of Germany's premier cities, for which Hamburg was pencilled in. Harris did not have 1,000 front-line aircraft, of course, and to reach the magic figure, he would need the support of other Commands, principally Coastal. This was forthcoming in a letter on the 22nd, only for support to be withdrawn after objections from the Admiralty a few days later. Undaunted, and demonstrating the singleness of purpose for which he became famous, he, or more probably his deputy, the affable AM Sir Robert Saundby, scraped together every airframe capable of something resembling controlled flight, and called in the screened crews from their instructional duties. Come the night, the figure of 1,000 aircraft would not only be reached, it would be comfortably surpassed.

There were no major operations during the run-up to Harris's masterstroke, and the arrival of training aircraft on bomber stations from Durham to East Anglia only served to increase the speculation. As was generally the case in these situations of a total information blackout, the only people who knew what was going on were the NAAFI staff and the civilians in the surrounding towns and villages. As the days ticked by inexorably towards the end of May only the weather remained in question, and this was in bullish mood, absolutely refusing to enter into the spirit of the occasion. Harris was aware of the genuine danger, that the massive force might well draw attention to itself and compromise security, and the point was fast approaching for the operation either to take place or be abandoned for the time being. During this period of frustration and high tension W/C Fothergill departed 207 Squadron on the 28th to be replaced by W/C Jeffs, who was posted in from his flight commander role at 50 Squadron, but had yet to be passed out on Lancasters. Finally, at 'morning prayers' at High Wycombe on the 30th, Harris's chief meteorological adviser, Magnus Spence, gave a qualified nod in the direction of the Rhineland, where a break in the cloud might be expected after midnight, with a chance of moonlight. Hamburg in north-western Germany, on the other hand, would be concealed under buckets of nasty cloud, and would thus be spared the dubious honour of hosting the first 1,000 bomber raid in history. The fickle finger of fate swung instead in the direction of Germany's third largest city, Cologne, which, despite frequent visits from Bomber Command in the past, had never succumbed to an effective attack.

The departure of the 1,047 assorted aircraft began before 23.00 hours and continued until after midnight, with the genuine heavies in the third and final wave. A number of the older training hacks took to the air almost reluctantly, lifted more by the enthusiasm of their crews than by the power of their engines. Among these were some unable to climb to a respectable height, which would fall easy prey to the defences, or simply drop from the sky through fatigue and mechanical breakdown. 5 Group managed a respectable seventy-three Lancasters, forty-six Manchesters and thirty-four Hampdens, of which four Manchesters and a 61 Squadron Lancaster failed to return. The operation was by any standards an outstanding success. Over 3,300 buildings were destroyed in return for a new record loss to the Command of forty-one aircraft, but in the moonlight conditions favourable to both attackers and defenders, it was an understandable casualty figure, and in view of the scale of success, an acceptable one. At the pre-op briefings, it had been predicted, that just two aircraft would collide over the target, despite the unprecedented concentration of at least ten aircraft per minute during the intended ninety-minute duration of the raid. It is reported, that at least one 'wag' asked whether the statisticians knew which two aircraft would be involved! Whether or not they did, their prediction was accurate. Among the missing Manchesters was L7301, a clapped-out 106 Squadron aircraft borrowed by the 50 Squadron crew of P/O Leslie Manser. Hit by flak over Cologne, it was eventually abandoned by all but the pilot over Belgium. Five crew members managed to evade capture, and on their return to England provided testimony of Manser's heroism in sacrificing his life to allow them to live. As a result Manser was awarded a posthumous Victoria Cross. One of the crew, P/O Horsley, would become an instructor in Canada before taking a pilot's course and ultimately joining 617 Squadron in that capacity late in 1944.

The Thousand Force carried out its second operation on the 1st/2nd of June, with Essen as the target, but it was a major disappointment. Industrial haze made identification extremely difficult, and bombs were sprayed liberally around the Ruhr, with few finding their intended target. On this occasion 5 Group sent seventy-four Lancasters, seventy-one Hampdens and thirty-three Manchesters, losing four Lancasters and one each of the other types. A series of four smaller follow-up raids was launched over the next two weeks, but they fared no better, and cost the Group eight aircraft from a total of one hundred sorties. Punctuating the disappointing follow-up raids on Essen were effective attacks on Bremen on the 3rd/4th and Emden on the 6/7th, but these were isolated bright spots in an otherwise uninspiring month. Also in June, 44 Squadron sent a detachment of four aircraft and five crews to Nutts Corner in Ireland to carry out convoy patrols for Coastal Command, the first being conducted by R5603 on the 12th. On the 13th this Lancaster was again on duty, clocking up an eleven-hour sortie without incident. On the following day, R5858 was ditched with engine trouble, and the crew of P/O Nicholson had to be picked up by the convoy it was shepherding. On the 15th the crew of R5489 spotted a U-Boat on the surface and attacked it with depth charges, without causing any apparent damage, but this was redressed next day, when F/L Barlow and his crew sank a U-Boat in L7568. Patrols continued until the end of the month, although without further incident, and the detachment returned to Waddington. In the meantime three further attacks on Emden between the 19/20th and 22nd/23rd had failed to capitalize on the earlier success. W/C Coad took over 61 Squadron on the 19th from W/C Weir, who would eventually be promoted to Group Captain and become station commander at Fulbeck. 50 Squadron moved out of Skellingthorpe temporarily on the 20th and returned to Swinderby.

The final employment of the Thousand Force occurred on the 25/26th of June, when 960 aircraft took off for Bremen, among them ninety-six Lancasters, fifty Hampdens and a handful of Manchesters operating with the Command for the final time. This time, higher authority in the person of Churchill himself, ordered Coastal Command to take part, and a hundred of its aircraft carried out what is classed as a separate operation. This meant, that the total number of aircraft converging on Bremen on this night exceeded the figure dispatched to Cologne. While not repeating the success of that night, results at Bremen far surpassed the debacle at Essen, although at a new record loss of forty-eight aircraft. Three follow-up raids spanning the turn of the month added further damage to the city, the operation of the 27/28th of June involving only twenty-four Lancasters, while those on the 29/30th of June and 2nd/3rd of July boasted sixty-four and fifty-three respectively.

49 Squadron would spend the entire month of July off the order of battle while it worked up to operational status on the Lancaster. On the 11 July 5 Group attempted a daring daylight raid on a U-Boat construction yard at Danzig, now Gdansk in Poland, but then a German city. It was undertaken by forty-four Lancasters, whose 750-mile outward flight was timed to bring the aircraft to the target at dusk. In the event it was almost totally dark by the time of their arrival, and the operation failed to achieve its aims. A series of five operations against Duisburg began on the 13/14th of July, and continued on the 21st/22nd, 23rd/24th, 25/26th and 6/7th of August. Each attack produced some modest destruction in residential districts, but nothing outstanding, and certainly nothing in proportion to the size of the forces employed. It was a different story at Hamburg on the 26/27th, however, when extensive damage was inflicted upon housing, and eight hundred fires needed attention from the emergency services. A return to Hamburg two nights later was thwarted by the weather, and only a quarter of the 250 strong force reached the target area to bomb, these leaving a further fifty fires burning. On the last night of the month 100 Lancasters operated for the first time in a force of 630 aircraft, including some from the training units, whose crews were briefed to attack Düsseldorf. It was moderately successful, but cost twenty-nine aircraft, including two Lancasters. 49 Squadron operated with Lancasters for the first time on this night, and all returned safely. Meanwhile, a 61 Squadron detachment had moved in at St Eval on the 16th, and would remain there until the 22nd of August carrying out patrols on behalf of Coastal Command.

During a low-key start to August's operations, 420 Squadron departed 5 Group on the 6th to take up residence at Skipton-on-Swale under 4 Group. In time all the existing RCAF squadrons would find their way to 4 Group in preparation for the creation of the all-Canadian 6 Group in the New Year.

That night the final raid took place of the disappointing series against Duisburg. It was another unsatisfactory effort, which dumped most of the bombs in open country to the west of the city. Modest compensation was gained when a moderately successful attack was carried out against Osnabrück on the 9/10th, and over 200 houses were destroyed by a force containing forty Lancasters. An operation to Mainz on the 11/12th resulted in quite serious damage in the centre of the town, and this was increased after another successful attack on the following night.

A new era in Bomber Command operations began on the 15th with the formation of the Pathfinder Force. Harris had been opposed in principle to the formation of an elitist target finding force, and this was a view shared by all but one of his Group commanders. Once overruled by higher authority, however, and to his eternal credit, he gave the new organisation his unstinting support, and his choice of the then G/C Don Bennett as its leader was at the same time imaginative and controversial, but most of all, inspired. 5 Group surrendered 83 Squadron to Bennett as a founder unit, and it moved from Scampton to Wyton on the 15th. However, in view of 83 Squadron's future return to the 5 Group fold, we will continue to chart its progress. 5 Group was compensated for the loss by the posting in from 3 Group of 9 Squadron, a unit of equal status, commanded by W/C Southwell. He had been the 'Boss' since June after relinquishing a similar post with 57 Squadron in March. Fate, or the 'Powers that be', would lead 57 Squadron also to 5 Group just a month hence, and both these former 3 Group units would have a part to play in the career of the yet-to-be-formed 617 Squadron of Dambuster fame. The 9 Squadron crews arrived at their new home of Waddington on the 7th, which they would share with 44 Squadron, and took delivery of their first Lancasters on the following day. Having operated twin-engine Wellingtons since the outbreak of war, they would need a period of concentrated conversion training before being let loose on the enemy.

A less publicized addition to the Pathfinder ranks was 109 Squadron, a Mosquito unit under the command of W/C Hal Bufton. For the remainder of the year, he and his crews were to work magnificently and untiringly to develop the Oboe blind bombing device. This was designed to guide a single aircraft to a target along a radar beam transmitted from a station in England. A second station sent another beam, and they intersected over the target with an accuracy of a few hundred yards. The system had a limited range because of the curvature of the earth, but it could cover the Ruhr. Once in service on main force operations in the coming year, Oboe would signal the end for the likes of Essen and Duisburg, and render impotent their protective blanket of industrial haze. Whatever the Pathfinder Force was to achieve in the future, its operational career started inauspiciously with an operation to Flensburg on the 18/19th. Situated on the narrow neck of land where Germany and Denmark meet, this shipyard town should have been relatively easy to identify. In the event, the only bombs reported were those falling on Danish towns. The second PFF led raid fared little better when Frankfurt was the target on the 24/25th, cloud cover preventing identification, and most of the bombs fell into open country. 83 Squadron suffered the loss of two Lancasters, its first casualties as a Pathfinder unit. Kassel was attacked by three hundred aircraft on the 27/28th in conditions, which enabled the Pathfinders at last to illuminate the target adequately. The main force exploited the opportunity, and considerable damage resulted, although at the high cost of a 10% loss rate. While this operation was in progress, W/C Gibson led nine 106 Squadron Lancasters on a special operation to Gdynia on the Baltic coast, a round trip of 1,900 miles. The target was the German aircraft carrier Graf Zeppelin, which was thought to be about ready to put to sea for the first time. Seven Lancasters reached the target area with their special capital ship bombs, but haze prevented them from locating the vessel, and the harbour was attacked instead. The Pathfinders managed to mark Nuremberg on the 28/29th, and returning crews claimed an effective attack, although this was not confirmed by local authorities. 49 Squadron suffered its first loss of Lancasters when two failed to return. A simultaneous raid on Saarbrücken by over a hundred aircraft included seventeen Hampdens, all provided by 408 Squadron. It turned into the squadron's worst night to date, and four empty dispersals at Balderton next morning told a sorry tale of its fortunes. AE197, which was carrying the squadron commander and the bombing, signals and gunnery leaders, fell victim to a night fighter over Belgium. W/C Twigg and one other were killed, while the bombing and signals leaders, F/L Fisher and F/O Van den Bok, evaded capture.

The 1 September brought a new commanding officer to 408 Squadron in the imposing form of W/C 'Tiny' Ferris, who, like his predecessor, was a RCAF officer. The Pathfinders posted a 'black' on the first night of September, when marking the small town of Saarlouis in error for its more industrialized neighbour Saarbrücken. Much to the chagrin of its inhabitants, the main force then proceeded to produce a good display of bombing, and left much destruction within the town. This might have been an ill-omen for the remainder of the month's operations, but in fact, from this point the Command embarked on an unprecedented series of effective operations over the next two and a half weeks. The improvement began at Karlsruhe on the following night, where extensive damage was inflicted on residential areas. On the 3rd/4th, Bremen suffered the destruction of over 450 buildings as the Pathfinders employed their new three-phase tactic of illumination, visual marking and backing-up, a system, which would form the basis of all future operations.

57 Squadron was posted in from 3 Group on the 4th and took up residence at Scampton alongside 49 Squadron. Its first Lancasters arrived on the following day, and training began to bring the crews up to operational status. There would be no commanding officer to guide them until the arrival of W/C Hopcroft on the 23rd. As part of the Advanced Air Striking Force 57 Squadron had been in the thick of it since the very start of the war, moving to France in September 1939 with its Blenheims. It returned to the UK to join

2 Group as the Dunkerque evacuations were under way in May 1940, before joining 3 Group in November of that year.

An attack on Duisburg on the 6/7th produced only moderate damage, but it was still the city's heaviest raid to date, and the only outright failure of the period occurred at Frankfurt on the 8/9th, when most of the bombing fell on nearby Rüsselsheim or in open country. Over 900 houses were destroyed in Düsseldorf on the 10/11th, when elements from the training units took part, but the defenders fought back to claim thirty-three of the bombers. This was the night of 9 Squadron's operational baptism on Lancasters. W/C Southwell piloted one of the three Lancasters to take part, and each returned safely. 408 Squadron left 5 Group on the 13th to join the other Canadian units which were now gathering in 4 Group. A return to Bremen by over 400 aircraft on the night of the 13/14th resulted in the destruction of more than 800 houses and damage to industrial premises, a result by far eclipsing that achieved by the Thousand Force against this city only three months earlier. Wilhelmshaven experienced its worst night of the war to date on the 14/15th, as did even Essen on the 16/17th, although the bombing was still scattered, and much of it fell onto other Ruhr towns. Essen had the final word on this night, however, when the night fighter and flak defences brought down a massive thirty-nine bombers, including two from 9 Squadron, its first casualties under the banner of 5 Group. It was a bad night for 106 Squadron also, with three crews failing to return including that of flight commander S/L Howell.

If any period could be said to represent Bomber Command's turning of the corner towards becoming an effective, potentially war-winning weapon, then these two weeks in September might qualify. It can also be no coincidence, that this improved level of effectiveness came at a time, when the Pathfinder crews were emerging from their less than convincing start, and were coming to terms with the intricacies of their exacting and demanding role. It would not be an overnight transformation, but rather a slow and measured evolution, and failures would continue to outnumber successes for some time to come. The unmistakable signs were there, though, that all the elements of technical and tactical advance were coming together, and with other technological wizardry in the pipeline, it augured well for the Command, and ill for the enemy. A large-scale mining effort was mounted along the enemy coastline from France to the Baltic on the 18/19th. Over 100 aircraft were involved, and five of them failed to return, among them two 5 Group Lancasters. On the following night 3 Group Stirlings joined forces with a contingent of sixty-eight Lancasters from 5 Group to carry out a reasonably effective raid on Munich. 207 Squadron swapped Bottesford for Langar on the 20th, and withdrew its detachment from nearby Syerston. No. 5 Group sent a force of eighty Lancasters to the Baltic town of Wismar on the 23rd/24th, with the Dornier aircraft factory as the main objective. A successful operation was reported, but four Lancasters failed to return.

5 Group returned to Wismar with over seventy Lancasters on the 1st/2nd of October, and produced only scattered bombing for the loss, this time, of two of their number. Earlier in the day 106 Squadron moved into Syerston after more than eighteen months at Coningsby. Krefeld escaped serious damage at the hands of a mixed force of over 150 aircraft on the 2nd/3rd, and it was not a too dissimilar story at Aachen on the 5/6th. Osnabrück fell victim to an accurate attack on the 6/7th, in return for the moderate loss of six aircraft, two of them Lancasters. A 5 Group raid on Wismar on the 12/13th provided 57 Squadron with the opportunity to go to war in Lancasters for the first time, the squadron contributing eight of the fifty-nine aircraft involved. Bad weather was encountered, but returning crews claimed to have hit the target. A moderately effective raid was launched against Kiel on the 13/14th, with the Lancaster now firmly the second most numerous type behind the Wellington. Almost three hundred aircraft set out for Cologne on the evening of the 15th, but these managed to find the target with only one of more than seventy cookies, and the disappointment was compounded by the loss of eighteen aircraft. 106 Squadron experienced another sobering night with the failure to return of three aircraft, including one containing the crew of flight commander S/L Hill DFC. 57 Squadron also registered its first missing Lancaster and crew since joining 5 Group.

On the 17th 5 Group launched its audacious daylight raid, Operation Robinson, against the Schneider armaments works at Le Creusot and the nearby transformer station at Montchanin. The company belonged to the very same French Schneider family that had donated the famous Schneider Trophy, now, as mentioned earlier, permanently in British hands. Eighty-eight crews were briefed for the assault on the factory complex, led by W/C Slee of 49 Squadron, while W/C Gibson of 106 Squadron headed the attack by six Lancasters against the other target. The operation was only moderately successful after much of the bombing fell short, but only one Lancaster was lost. W4774 of 61 Squadron contained the crew of flight commander S/L Corr, and was part of the Montchanin element. It seems the pilot attacked from such a low altitude that he crashed into buildings, killing all but one on board. It was also on this day that 50 Squadron began the task of moving back to Skellingthorpe, where it would remain while hostilities persisted. Three days later W/C Oxley concluded his tour in command of 50 Squadron, and was replaced by W/C Russell, an officer who had joined the RAF during the 1920s. This put him in his forties, and therefore considerably older than the majority of operational commanders. A campaign against Italy's major cities began at Genoa on the 22nd/23rd in support of Operation Torch, the Allied landings in North Africa, which would ultimately lead to the final defeat of the Afrika Korps. This first operation by 5 Group was initially led by 44 Squadron's commanding officer, W/C Smales, but he was forced to drop back into the bomber stream after his starboard-outer engine lost power. The raid was concluded successfully without loss, and was followed up twenty-four hours later by a force of over 100 aircraft representing the other Groups. Unfortunately, cloud cover caused most of the bombs to be dropped on Savona, some 30 miles away. 5 Group took on Milan on the 24th in a daring daylight attack, and much damage was inflicted upon city-centre type buildings and some industrial premises. The other Groups followed on that night, but again the attack was less effective than 5 Group's effort. The remainder of the month was given over to minor operations, particularly those of the gardening variety. Milan was the last operation over which W/C Collier presided as 97 Squadron's commander, and he relinquished the post on the 26th to be replaced by W/C Jones.

The offensive against Germany would continue alongside the Italian campaign, but two further raids were sent against Genoa on the 6/7th and 7/8th of November, before the first foray of the month into Germany. The former was a predominantly 5 Group effort with 8 Group support, which resulted in the loss of three 83 Squadron Lancasters, two to enemy action and the third while attempting to land at Mildenhall. Another 83 Squadron Lancaster got down safely at Mildenhall, but crashed shortly after take-off for Wyton later that morning, killing the pilot and two others. A new Squadron was formed at Scampton on the 7th. 467 Squadron RAAF was the third Royal Australian Air Force squadron to form in Bomber Command after 455 and 458 Squadrons, both of which had long since departed to pastures new. Its formation came in response to the Australian government's wishes to group together Australian flying personnel, although initially like all squadrons, it was a polyglot of nationalities, predominantly from Britain, Canada and New Zealand. Ground crews were also mainly RAF, although this would change in time. The squadron was formed under the command of W/C Cosme Gomm, whose expatriate family resided in Brazil. Born there also he was educated in England, and in many ways his life paralleled that of Guy Gibson. Both were born overseas and educated in England, and both were serving officers at the outbreak of war. They each completed a tour of operations, Gomm with 77 Squadron flying Whitleys, and Gibson with 83 Squadron on Hampdens, before joining respectively 604 and 29 night fighter squadrons. Both then returned to Bomber Command to take up commands of their own, Gomm at 467 and Gibson at 106. Twenty-nine years old, tall and quiet, he was every inch the commanding officer, and would lead the squadron in the only way acceptable to the Australians, by example from the front. The two flight commanders, S/Ls Green and Paape, had both served with 207 Squadron at Bottesford, to where 467 Squadron would shortly be posted. Four crews arrived on the day the squadron was formed, and within three weeks twenty complete crews were on strength. Most were straight out of OTUs, although there was a sprinkling of second tour men to provide a leavening of experience. The first Lancaster, W4384, was taken on charge on the 9th, thus making the squadron the fifteenth operational unit to receive the type.

Hamburg was the Command's target on the 9/10th of November, but it escaped serious damage when adverse weather conditions thwarted the force of 200 bombers, and much of the effort was wasted in return for a 7% loss rate. Three of the missing Lancasters came from 57 Squadron. A modest 5 Group and Pathfinder force went back to Genoa on the 13/14th, an operation repeated by elements from the other Groups two nights later. A series of seven operations of varying sizes against Turin began on the 18/19th, when around seventy aircraft started many fires in the central districts, and also hit the Fiat motor works. More than 200 aircraft returned on the 20th/21st, and this was the largest force employed during the current campaign. A successful operation ensued, during which many more fires were started, and only three aircraft failed to return. On the 22nd 467 Squadron made the move from Scampton to Bottesford, the inhospitable plot of farmland on the Leicestershire/Nottinghamshire border that had recently been vacated by 207 Squadron. It lacked all the basic amenities and comforts taken for granted at pre-war stations, like the one the squadron had just left. However, someone said there was a war on, so everybody got down to the business of working up to operational readiness, a process that would occupy the remainder of the year. Oblivious to the trials of 467 Squadron a mixed force of over 200 aircraft headed for Stuttgart that night. It was always a difficult city to identify, and the Pathfinders failed to find its centre, which caused most of the bombs to fall on the outskirts, where only moderate damage resulted. Turin wilted once more under a heavy attack by some 200 aircraft from all Groups on the 28/29th, and W/C Gibson captained one of two 106 Squadron aircraft to deliver the first 8,000 lb blockbusters onto Italian soil.

The Italian campaign continued into December, a month of generally reduced activity, but the first two major outings were against German targets. A little over one hundred aircraft set out for Frankfurt on the 2nd/3rd, and in the face of ground haze deposited most of their bombs in open country. It was a similar story at Mannheim on the 6/7th, when over 200 aircraft encountered complete cloud cover, and bombed on dead-reckoning. Later that day W/C Bain took up his post as Commanding officer of 207 Squadron. Sadly, his period of office was to be brief in the extreme, and came to an end with his first operation on the 8/9th. This was to Turin, when a 5 Group force with Pathfinder support inflicted extensive damage on residential and industrial districts for the loss of just W/C Bain's R5570, from which there were no survivors. S/L Parselle took over temporary command of the squadron, but he would be confirmed in the post, and promotion to Wing Commander would follow on the 7 February. The final salvoes of the Italian campaign were fired against Turin on the 8/9th, 9/10th and 11/12th, with 5 Group aircraft participating in each. The first of the series was highly effective, the second less so, and the third encountered severe icing conditions, which persuaded many crews to turn back before the Alps were reached.

On the 17/18th 5 Group dispatched twenty-seven Lancasters to eight small towns in Germany, in what turned out to be an ill-fated venture costing nine aircraft and crews, one-third of those dispatched. 44 Squadron's element was briefed for Nienburg, north-west of Hanover, and it suffered a disastrous night, losing three aircraft, while 9 Squadron posted missing one from Diepholz and another from Cloppenburg, 50 Squadron two from Soltau and 97 Squadron two from Neustadt. A further tragedy struck the Group on the night of the 20th/21st, when over 200 aircraft set out for Duisburg. Climbing away from Waddington, 44 Squadron's W4259 was in collision with W4182 of 9 Squadron over Lincoln, and both aircraft plunged into the ground on the outskirts of the city with no survivors. A second operation took place on this night, which although passing unnoticed by all but those taking part, was of great significance for future Bomber Command operations. Six Mosquitoes of 109 Squadron went to a power station at Lutterade in Holland, employing Oboe for the first time to guide their bombs. Three aircraft, including that containing W/C Bufton, were able to release their bombs as planned, but equipment failure thwarted the others, and they joined the attack on Duisburg instead. This was to be a calibration test to gauge the device's margin of error, but post raid reconnaissance revealed the area to be pitted by bomb craters from a misdirected raid on Aachen back in October, and it proved impossible to plot the three successful releases. This was only a temporary setback, however, and further calibration tests would be undertaken over the ensuing weeks. On the following night a Pathfinder element led an ineffective 1 and 5 Group raid against Munich, and that proved to be the final major operation of the year by heavy bombers.

At the start of 1942 only 44 Squadron had the Lancaster, and it remained to be proved in battle. Now, as 1943 beckoned, the whole of 5 Group was equipped, and 1 Group was in the process of replacing its Wellingtons with the type. The potential of the Lancaster had been ably demonstrated, and the campaigns of the coming year would see it come of age in spectacular fashion.

1943. Emergence of the unstoppable beast
Campaigns against the Ruhr, Hamburg and Berlin. Oboe and H2s. 617 Squadron enters the fray

The year 1943 would see a number of major campaigns undertaken, which would demonstrate both the burgeoning power and effectiveness of the Command, and its vulnerability to enemy defences. As the year progressed, technical and tactical innovations would bring impressive and spectacular victories, but the potential for disaster was never far away, and many nights of heavy losses awaited the crews. The year opened with the formation of the RCAF 6 Group on the 1 January, and the raising of the Pathfinder Force to Group status as 8 Group a week later. No. 49 Squadron had moved out of Scampton, its long-time home on the 2 January, and taken up residence at Fiskerton. On the operational front, 467 Squadron went to war for the first time on the night of the 2nd/3rd, when five aircraft mined the waters off the Biscay coast. Seven small-scale raids were mounted against Essen and one on Duisburg during the first two weeks of January, as part of the Oboe trials programme. These involved the Mosquitoes of 109 Squadron marking for 1 and 5 Group Lancasters. On the 14th a new Air Ministry directive authorised the area bombing of those French ports containing U-Boat bases and support facilities, and much of the Command's effort over the next three months would be directed against Lorient and St Nazaire, much to the annoyance of ACM Harris. The first of eight raids on Lorient took place that night, but it was only modestly effective. Matters improved on the following night, however, and more than 800 buildings were destroyed.

Two disappointing attacks on Berlin were mounted in mid month, the first of which, on the 16/17th, brought the first use of genuine target indicators. The predominantly Lancaster force of 200 aircraft destroyed the 10,000 seater Deutschlandhalle, the largest covered arena in Europe, but this was the only damage of significance in an otherwise disappointing raid. On the credit side, the operation was concluded for the remarkably low loss of just one Lancaster. In contrast, the totally ineffective operation to Berlin on the following night suffered an 11% casualty rate. 5 Group had ten aircraft fail to return, four of them belonging to 9 Squadron. Three more raids were sent against Lorient with just a token Lancaster presence, but the type made up the bulk of the force at Düsseldorf on the 27/28th, when Oboe Mosquitoes carried out ground marking ahead of the Pathfinder heavy aircraft for the first time. The substantial damage resulting from this attack included industrial premises, public buildings and much housing. The bombing at Hamburg on the 30th/31st was based for the first time on H2s, an electronic scanning device attached to the belly of the aircraft, which produced a crude map on a cathode ray tube. The operator had to interpret the images, and in time, in an improved form, it would become a useful weapon in the Command's armoury, but it was not yet entirely reliable, and much of the effort was wasted. Nevertheless, more than 100 fires had to be dealt with, seventy of them large, and railway traffic was disrupted for two days. At the end of the month W/C Smales was posted from 44 Squadron to be replaced on the 1 February by W/C Nettleton VC, who was returning to the squadron after a period of screening.

February opened with an experimental attack on Cologne on the 2nd/3rd, for which various techniques were used in the continuing quest to find a reliable method of marking aiming points. In the event, both the Oboe and H2s laid markers failed to provide the necessary concentration, and the bombing was scattered. Over 250 aircraft started out for Hamburg on the following night, but icing conditions forced many crews to turn back. Those pressing on produced scattered bombing, and forty-five large fires were started. Lorient was attacked in two waves on the 7/8th with devastating results, and for the loss of only seven aircraft. No. 83 Squadron welcomed

W/C Gillman as its new commanding officer on the 10th, while 61 Squadron followed suite on the 11th with the installation as commanding officer of W/C W M Penman, (not to be confused with D J Penman, a 97 Squadron participant in the epic Augsburg raid of April 1942). On the 11/12th a raid on Wilhelmshaven resulted in a devastating explosion, which laid waste to over a hundred acres in the town and the docks. Lorient hosted its heaviest raid of the war on the 13/14th by over 400 aircraft, and Cologne again escaped with modest damage twenty-four hours later, despite the commitment of more than 200 aircraft. Lorient was bombed for the final time on the 16/17th, and was now nothing more than a deserted ruin. Three further attacks on Wilhelmshaven on the 18/19th, 19/20th and 24/25th were most disappointing, and a predominantly Lancaster assault on Bremen sandwiched in-between on the 21st/22nd was inconclusive because of cloud cover. Nuremberg followed on the 25/26th, but only the northern suburbs sustained damage, along with nearby towns and villages. A generally unsatisfactory month's operations to Germany ended with another failure at Cologne on 26/27th. Having dealt with Lorient, Harris now reluctantly turned his gaze upon St Nazaire on the last night of the month. Over 400 aircraft took part, and destroyed 60% of the town's built-up area.

This was the day that saw the appointment of the Hon. Sir Ralph Cochrane as Air-Officer-Commanding 5 Group. There was something almost inevitable about his appointment to command Harris's old Group. The two men had known each other since late 1922, when Harris was posted to Mesopotamia to take command of 45 Squadron. The two flight commanders awaiting his arrival were F/Ls Robert Saundby, now Harris's deputy at High Wycombe and the Hon. Ralph Cochrane. Once at the helm of Bomber Command Harris relied heavily on Saundby, and trusted him implicitly. Who better than Cochrane then, with whom he had built a similar relationship, to take over and nurture 5 Group. Cochrane was the youngest son of the first Baron Cochrane of Cults. He had spent the first fifteen months of the war as Air Aide-de-Camp to His Majesty King George VI, and the six months immediately prior to his appointment at 5 Group as AOC 3 Group. There is a suggestion that Harris sacked AVM Coryton for refusing to send a small force of Lancasters to Berlin in doubtful weather conditions. He was to move to the Air Ministry.

March began with an attack on Berlin by 300 aircraft on the night of the 1st/2nd, during which, bombs were sprayed over a wide area. Despite the scattering, considerable damage was inflicted on the southern and western districts, and it was the most effective raid on the Capital to date. Many of the bombs meant for Hamburg on the 3rd/4th fell onto Wedel thirteen miles downstream of the Elbe, but those hitting the intended target started over 100 fires. The time had now arrived for Harris to embark on the first major campaign of the year, and, in fact, the first campaign of the bombing war for which the Command was adequately equipped and prepared. Harris had at his disposal a predominantly four-engine force of bombers with highly trained crews, led by a Pathfinder elite, with H2s and Oboe to guide the bombing. The target over the coming months was to be the Ruhr, Germany's industrial arsenal, a massive sprawl of towns and cities, whose boundaries almost overlapped. It represented an almost continuous built-up area, which began at Krefeld and Duisburg, shortly after crossing the frontier with Holland, and ended at Soest, just north of the Möhne Lake. Such a vitally important region was bound to be heavily defended by flak positions and night fighters, and crews would find themselves running the gauntlet from the moment they crossed the Dutch coast on the way in until doing so again on the way out.

It was on the night of the 5/6th of March that Essen was selected to open the Battle of the Ruhr. Although 442 aircraft took off for the target, an unusually high number of early returns and the bombing of alternative targets reduced the number of aircraft actually attacking Essen to 362. These proved sufficient, though, to deliver an outstandingly successful raid and a promising start to the campaign, which left the German authorities pondering over the destruction of more than 3,000 houses, and some useful damage within the Krupp works. A fairly modest fourteen aircraft failed to return. A week passed before the second operation of the campaign, and in the meantime Harris switched his force to southern Germany. A moderately effective raid on Nuremberg on the 8/9th was followed by one of similar success on Munich twenty-four hours later, but most of the bombs intended for Stuttgart on the 11/12th were wasted in open country. This proved to be the final operation as commanding officer of 106 Squadron for W/C Guy Gibson, and, indeed, some of the other 5 Group crews who were shortly to join him at Squadron X. It was Gibson's twenty-ninth operation since taking over the squadron a year earlier, and it was conducted on three good engines at a lower level than was customary.

After twelve months in post Gibson would have been expecting a posting of some sort on his return from the leave he was about to take. He would not have relished the prospect of flying a desk, but he would have tolerated it as long as the promise of a return to operations sometime in the future was a realistic option. About to join his wife Eve in Cornwall, he was surprised to be posted instead to 5 Group HQ on the 15th, and believed, initially at least, that it was to assist in the writing of a book. It was also on this day that Harris met with AVM Sir Ralph Cochrane at Bomber Command HQ at High Wycombe, and told him to form a special squadron under Gibson to carry out an operation against the dams. Meanwhile, over at Scampton, a bomb fell out of the belly of 57 Squadron Lancaster W4834, and in the ensuing explosion and conflagration a further two 57 Squadron Lancasters and three from 50 Squadron were destroyed. For Gibson, the first few days of his new posting were anything but stimulating, in fact, everything to do with it was anathema to a warrior, who needed to be surrounded by the paraphernalia of war, the people, the aircraft, the noises, the smells. On the 18th he was summoned to a meeting with Cochrane at St Vincents, the imposing building set in trees on the edge of Grantham serving at the time as 5 Group HQ. As Cochrane had himself been in post as AOC 5 Group for less than three weeks, he knew of Gibson only through Harris. It seems that the purpose of this initial meeting was to settle just one point; was Gibson prepared to carry out one more unspecified operation? This having been established in the affirmative, Gibson was dismissed, and recalled on the following day, when Group Captain J.N.H.Whitworth, who was known among his peers as 'Charles', joined him and Cochrane. Whitworth was the station commander at Scampton, where, Gibson soon learned he was to form a new squadron specifically, though not exclusively, to carry out an as yet still unspecified special operation.

Prior to these events, a return to Essen by the heavy brigade on the night of the 12/13th signalled round two of the Ruhr offensive, and this time the Krupp complex was in the centre of the bombing area, sustaining 30% more damage than a week earlier, while around 500 houses were reduced to rubble. On the 15th 9 Squadron bade farewell to W/C Southwell, who would be posted to the Middle East in August to assume command of 150 Squadron. His replacement arrived in the form of W/C Smith, who had vacated his last command, 4 Group's 58 Squadron, a Whitley unit now in Coastal Command, back in June 1941. His time with 9 Squadron was destined to be brief, however. On the same day W/C Searby stepped into Gibson's shoes at 106 Squadron. It was on the 21 March that instructions were issued by Bomber Command to form Gibson's new squadron, and included within them were certain principles as a guide to the selection of personnel. The majority of aircrew were to have completed one or two operational tours, and the remainder were to be specially selected. Special attention was to be paid to the efficiency of ground officers, particularly to the armament officer. The ground crews were to be drawn as far as possible from Group resources, and all were to have experience on Lancasters. Aircraft were to be provided from existing squadrons, but would be replaced later by a modified version. The squadron was to be given priority over everything else, and all endeavours were to be made to form it into an efficient unit by the earliest possible date.

Minor operations held sway from Essen until the night of the 22nd/23rd, when the third raid on St Nazaire took place. Returning crews confirmed a concentrated attack by around 250 aircraft. On the 24th Gibson went to Surrey to meet for the first time the designer and engineer Barnes Wallis, who was then working for Vickers, and was responsible for many innovations, including the successful R100 airship and the geodetic design of the Wellington bomber. He showed Gibson film of the revolutionary 'bouncing bomb', but was unable to reveal the intended target. Meanwhile, back at Scampton the first crews began to arrive. Contrary to popular belief and the stated intentions of Bomber Command, not all of the future Dambusters were experienced, and only a relative few were hand-picked by Gibson. 617 Squadron came into the world as the offspring of 57 Squadron, whose

C Flight was simply moved en-masse across the tarmac into the former 49 Squadron hangar and offices. Certainly its recently appointed flight commander, S/L 'Dinghy' Young, had a reputation and would have been known to Gibson, despite undertaking his first tour with 4 Group and his second in the Middle East in 1941/42. On his return he managed to get over to America, where he married his American sweetheart on the 10 August 1942. He was posted back to the United States for special duties in October, before returning to Bomber Command and his 57 Squadron appointment on the 13 March 1943, less than two weeks before his posting to 617. At twenty-seven years of age Young was a tad older than most, and as events were to turn out, he would fail to make his twenty-eighth birthday by just three days. Perhaps his greatest asset was his organizational ability, and this would be put to good use as the burden of responsibility for training fell largely upon his shoulders through Gibson's necessary frequent absences. The other flight commander, S/L Henry Maudslay, was a 5 Group man to the core, with 44 and 50 Squadron blood coursing through his veins, and he was a natural for the job at 617, particularly in view of his recent instructional and test flying. Gibson's hand was undoubtedly at work in the selection of Hopgood and Shannon, both of whom had completed tours under Gibson at 106 and were his closest allies. Hopgood was away from the operational scene, while Shannon had volunteered to join the Pathfinders and had just arrived at Wyton to begin training. Other pilots came from 44, 49, 50, 61, 97 207 and 467 Squadrons, some with crews, some without. On the afternoon of the 27th F/L Bill Astell, also late of the Middle East and 57 Squadron, flew 617 Squadron's first training sortie, to photograph lakes. Training would begin in earnest on the 31st, just six weeks before the operation had to be carried out.

The third raid of the Ruhr campaign was aimed at Duisburg on the 26/27th, but equipment failure among most of the participating Oboe Mosquitoes led to sparse marking, and the operation was a disappointment. The following night brought the first of two attacks on Berlin in the space of three nights. Almost 400 aircraft set off in mid evening, but those reaching the target area mostly bombed short, and, it seems, many of the bombs failed to explode anyway. After St Nazaire was pounded again on the 28/29th, over 300 aircraft set out again for Germany's capital city on the evening of the 29th, only to drop their bombs away from the city centre and mostly into open country. Despite a simultaneous but ineffective attack on Bochum in the Ruhr by Wellingtons, the defenders were able to concentrate their effort against the main raid, and twenty-one aircraft were lost.

April would be the least rewarding month of the Ruhr offensive, largely because much of the effort was directed away from the region, and beyond the range of Oboe. It began promisingly, however, with another successful tilt at Essen on the 3rd/4th by a force including more than 200 Lancasters for the first time. A bad night for 83 Squadron saw three of its aircraft fail to return to Wyton. Thick cloud, strong winds and decoy sites combined to thwart an attack on Kiel by the largest non-1,000 force to date of 577 aircraft on the 4/5th. W/C Slee's highly successful tour as commanding officer of 49 Squadron came to an end after eleven months on the 5th, and W/C Johnson, fresh from conversion training at Swinderby, stepped into his shoes. The second attack of the campaign on Duisburg on the 8/9th produced only moderate damage for the loss of nineteen aircraft, and the following night saw a smaller force of 100 aircraft try again with similar results. This time 9 Squadron suffered the loss of three Lancasters. Frankfurt was another of those city targets, like Duisburg, proving difficult to hit, and it escaped serious damage once more on the 10/11th. 9 Squadron's W/C Smith failed to return from this operation, his fourth sortie since taking command a month earlier, and he was killed along with his crew. W/C Burnett was posted across the tarmac from 44 Squadron on promotion to fill the vacancy, arriving just in time to oversee the squadron's move from Waddington to Bardney, where it would see out the remainder of the war. The disappointing series of operations continued at Stuttgart on the 14/15th, when only the despised creep-back phenomenon saved the night for the Command by falling across an industrial suburb and two others of a residential nature, resulting in the destruction of almost 400 buildings.

On the 16/17th Harris divided his forces by sending the Lancasters and Halifaxes to Pilsen in Czechoslovakia to target the Skoda armaments works, while a predominantly Stirling and Wellington raid took place on Mannheim. The former was a dismal failure, for which the raid planners were partly responsible. Rather than dropping target indicators onto the factory buildings, the Pathfinders were to mark the route about seven miles away as a reference point, so that the main force crews could fly on from there to identify the target visually. Almost inevitably, the main force crews bombed the target indicators, and the Skoda works escaped damage by many miles. The frustration was compounded by the loss of thirty-six aircraft, split equally between the two types. 5 Group posted missing eight Lancasters, including three from 50 Squadron and two each from 49 and 467 Squadrons. 83 Squadron also had two failures to return. The Mannheim contingent produced better results, but also lost eighteen of its number, and this brought the night's losses to a new record high of fifty-four. 97 Squadron was posted out of 5 Group on the 18th to become the latest addition to 8 Group's heavy brigade. When it departed Woodhall Spa for Bourn it left behind three crews who were apparently surplus to requirements. These were to provide the nucleus for 619 Squadron, which was born this day at Woodhall Spa from the remnants of the previous occupant. Sadly, this would be one of only a small number of units never to be awarded a badge or motto to commemorate its existence. W/C I J McGhie was installed as the commanding officer, and ED977, the first of an intended sixteen brand new Lancasters arrived on the 29th. Among other Lancasters taken on charge were some older ones, including seven from 617 Squadron. The most successful non-Ruhr raid of the period was delivered by a three hundred-strong force upon Stettin on the 20th/21st. In contrast to the likes of Duisburg, Stuttgart and Frankfurt, this

Baltic port never seemed to escape the ravages of a Bomber Command assault, and on this night much of its centre was devastated. Duisburg's seemingly charmed life was dented on the 26/27th, when more than 500 aircraft managed to destroy around 300 buildings, a figure that would have been substantially higher, had much of the bombing not fallen short.

Essen was the target on the last night of April for 300 aircraft taking off either side of midnight. The outcome of the operation was declared inconclusive at the time because of complete cloud cover, but later photographic reconnaissance revealed some fresh damage. The month of May would bring a return to winning ways with a number of spectacular successes now that the main focus was back on the Ruhr. A new record non-1,000 force of 596 aircraft set out for Dortmund late on the evening of the 4th, and the massive effort was rewarded by the destruction of 1,200 buildings. The defenders fought back to claim thirty-one bombers, and this was the highest yet at a Ruhr target during the campaign. 83 Squadron lost its commanding officer, W/C Gillman, who was flying as 'second dickey' to Sgt Leigh in R5629, which crashed in the target area without survivors. His replacement was W/C John Searby, who was posted in on the 9th from 106 Squadron, where he had been Gibson's successor on the latter's posting to form 617 Squadron. W/C Edmund Baxter took over in Searby's stead at 106 Squadron. The attack on Dortmund was followed by a period of minor operations until the 12/13th, when Duisburg finally succumbed to an outstandingly accurate and concentrated assault. Almost 1,600 buildings were reduced to rubble, and some 60,000 tons of shipping was either sunk or damaged in Germany's largest inland port. Losses among the bomber force were becoming consistently higher, however, and thirty-four aircraft failed to return on this night. While the main force went to Bochum on the 13/14th, a predominantly 5 Group force returned to Pilsen to attempt to rectify the previous month's failure. The operation was again unsuccessful, as most of the bombing was wasted in open country. Nine aircraft failed to return.

A nine-day break in main force operations allowed the crews to draw breath, and it was during this period, that 617 Squadron booked its place in history. The attack on the Möhne, Eder and Sorpe Dams on the 16/17th would live on as the greatest feat of arms in aviation history, and capture the imagination of the world. Eight of the nineteen participating Lancasters failed to return, and this was felt particularly keenly by Barnes Wallis, who had seen the operation as the final act of an experiment, and had not anticipated the human cost. It would forever change his attitude to the way in which his future theories and designs were proved. The losses were mostly the result of bad luck and the need to fly at ultra low level. Byers was the first to go, shot down by marine flak as he climbed to a few hundred feet over the island of Vlieland to get his bearings. To receive a direct hit by a heavy flak shell fired at the gun barrel's lowest possible elevation was a fluke, but that was war. Barlow flew into an electricity pylon at Rees, and Astell followed suite some twenty-five minutes later near Marbeck. Hopgood was shot down by flak at the Möhne and crashed a few miles north of the dam, the bomb-aimer and navigator escaping by parachute just in time. Burpee was shot down by flak from the fighter airfield at Gilze-Rijen in Holland, and crashed onto the aerodrome, where the bomb exploded causing massive damage to buildings and installations. Maudslay's Lancaster was damaged by his own bomb blast against the parapet of the Eder Dam, and he was eventually brought down by light flak on the outskirts of the town of Emmerich, a few yards from the frontier with Holland. At almost the same moment Ottley was being shot down by flak north of the town of Hamm, and only the rear gunner survived. Finally, Dinghy Young crossed the Dutch coast a little too high on the way home, and was brought down into the sea by flak, crashing just off the beach. It should not have happened. On the profit side, Young's bomb had fatally weakened the Möhne Dam, and Maltby's had finished it off, while Les Knight brought the Eder crashing down. Two gallant attempts on the Sorpe failed to inflict more than superficial damage, but it was impregnable anyway, and should not have been on the target list. Operation Chastise made the headlines, and turned its participants into heroes. Gibson was awarded the VC, and many others were decorated. Fifty-three men died and three spent the remainder of the war as PoWs. It did not bring Germany to its knees, but it did demonstrate that Bomber Command had the wherewithal to strike anywhere in the Reich with precision. Perhaps most importantly, the Dams Raid was a boost to morale in the free world.

The rest period for main force and Pathfinder crews ended on the 23rd/24th, when a new record non-1,000 force of 826 aircraft was dispatched for the second time in the month to the unfortunate city of Dortmund. An outstandingly accurate and concentrated attack ensued, which left around 2,000 buildings totally destroyed, and many war industry factories damaged. The defences fought back, however, and exacted a heavy toll of thirty-eight aircraft, another new record for the campaign. A failure at Düsseldorf on the 25/26th was probably caused by a combination of cloud and decoys. Twenty-seven aircraft failed to return, among them the 207 Squadron Lancaster W5001, which fell victim to a night fighter over Holland. At the controls was the squadron commander, W/C Parselle, and only he and one other of the eight men on board escaped with their lives to become PoWs. He was replaced as commanding officer on the 29th by W/C Jennings, who relinquished his flight commander post at 44 Squadron to take up his appointment. Only moderate success attended a raid on Essen because of cloud and skymarking on the 27/28th, but there was to be no escape for the luckless town of Barmen, for which 700 aircraft set off on the 29/30th. Known jointly with its twin Elberfeld as Wuppertal, it suffered on this night the most devastating raid of the campaign to date, which left around 80% of its built-up area in ruins. Some 4,000 houses were destroyed along with dozens of factories, and close to 2,000 other buildings were seriously damaged. In human terms it was also unprecedented, with approximately 3,400 dead, two and a half times the previous highest death toll, which had occurred on the Dams raid, and that had been the result of mass drowning. Thirty-three aircraft failed to return, thus demonstrating the reputation of 'Happy Valley' to be justly earned.

After spending the entire war to date at Waddington, 44 Squadron moved to a newly opened airfield at Dunholme Lodge a little to the north of Lincoln between the A15 and A46. The move spanned the turn of the month, and a ten-night break from operations for the heavy brigade allowed the crews and maintenance staff to settle in and find their bearings. When the Command next took to the air, on the 11/12th, it was for a raid by almost 800 aircraft on Düsseldorf. It proved to be among the most destructive raids of the war to date, despite an errant Oboe marker attracting a proportion of the bombing. Almost 9,000 separate fires had to be dealt with by the emergency services, and dozens of war industry factories lost vital production. The operation cost another thirty-eight aircraft, and twenty-four more, including three from 50 Squadron, were lost raiding Bochum to good effect on the very next night. An attack on Oberhausen, on the 14/15th proved highly successful although costly, with over 8% of the 190 aircraft involved being lost. This time it was 49 Squadron which had three empty dispersals to contemplate. Two nights later, 200 aircraft of 1, 5 and 8 Groups were involved in an H2s-led raid on Cologne, and despite bad weather and marking difficulties, 400 houses were destroyed and many industrial premises hit. 49 Squadron was among the losses again on this night with two more failures to return.

A special operation was mounted by a force of fifty-six Lancasters from 5 Group on the 20th/21st, with four Pathfinder aircraft in support. The target was the old Zeppelin works at Friedrichshafen, a highly industrialized town nestling on the shore of Lake Constance on Germany's border with Switzerland. The factory was now being used for the manufacture of radar equipment, and was vitally important to Germany's defensive capability against the bomber. The Allied victories in North Africa had made available a number of airfields in Algeria, principally Blida and Maison Blanche, and these were to be used in the future for what became known as 'shuttle' operations. Following certain operations to southern Germany and Italy, aircraft could fly on to Africa to refuel and rearm, and undergo repair if necessary, before carrying out another operation on the way home. This would be the format for Operation Bellicose, which was to involve all the frontline squadrons of 5 Group. Some crews were briefed to bomb on target indicators, while others would attempt the 'time and distance' method currently being developed by the Group. The latter was under consideration as a way of countering the loss of visual target reference through smoke after the first bombs had detonated. G/C Slee, late of 49 Squadron, led the force at medium level across France, but a failing engine forced him to drop back into the stream, and hand over to W/C Gomm of 467 Squadron. The factory represented a pinpoint target, and the necessary moonlight was of equal benefit to the flak gunners. For this reason W/C Gomm added another 5,000 feet to the planned bombing height, and this proved to be prejudicial to the accuracy of both marking and bombing. After carrying out their attack, each crew continued circling the target to split the defences until the raid was over, and then made for Maison Blanche in North Africa, where all landed safely, half a dozen bearing the wounds of battle. Photographic reconnaissance later showed the factory to be severely damaged. That this should be achieved without loss at such a heavily defended target after such a long flight was remarkable.

A hectic round of four major operations in five nights began at Krefeld on the 21st/22nd, when the town suffered a devastating blow, resulting in the destruction of over 5,500 houses, and the deaths of 1,000 people. The attackers paid a heavy price, however, and some of the many thousands of homeless inhabitants might have found some consolation in the fact, that forty-four of their tormentors would not be returning home. This was the highest loss of the campaign to date. Mülheim was pounded on the 22nd/23rd, and registered the destruction of over 1,100 houses and 64% of its built-up area in return for a bag of thirty-five bombers. The heavy brigade remained at home on the following night, while the 5 Group contingent bombed the Italian port of La Spezia on its way home from Maison Blanche. On the 24/25th it became the turn of the Elberfeld half of Wuppertal to experience the fate suffered by its twin Barmen at the end of May. The result of the raid by less than 600 aircraft was, if anything, even more devastating, leaving an estimated 94% of the town's built-up area in ruins, and killing around 1,800 people. Thirty-four Bomber Command crews paid the price for this success. The run of successes came to an end at the notoriously elusive oil town of Gelsenkirchen on the 25/26th, when, in an echo of the past, malfunctions in Oboe equipment led to bombs being sprayed all over the Ruhr. This time there were thirty empty dispersals to contemplate on the participating bomber airfields, four of them belonging to 106 Squadron at Syerston.

After a two-night rest the first raid took place of a series of three against Cologne spanning the turn of the month. Despite the most unpromising circumstances of complete cloud cover, the use of skymarking, and the arrival of only half of the Oboe Mosquito force, the Rhineland Capital received its most destructive attack to date. 6,500 buildings were destroyed, and amidst the devastation lay the bodies of 4,300 people. Bomber Command's casualty figure was twenty-five aircraft. 97 Squadron appointed a new commanding officer on the 1 July. W/C Jones left the squadron on a posting, and he was replaced by G/C Fresson, who relinquished his post as station commander at Oakington to become the station and 97 Squadron commander at Bourn. The initial success against Cologne was followed up by two further highly accurate raids by more than 600 aircraft on the 3rd/4th of July, and by an all-Lancaster heavy element of over 250 on the 8/9th. By the conclusion of this mini series more than 11,000 buildings had been destroyed, 5,500 people had lost their lives, and a further 350,000 had been rendered homeless. The overall cost to the Command of the three operations was sixty-two aircraft and crews missing. Two 106 Squadron Lancasters were among the missing and another crashed in the Fens on return with just two survivors. Another attempt on Gelsenkirchen by almost 400 aircraft took place on the 9/10th, and failed to inflict more than minor damage on the oil and other industrial concerns. Although two further raids would be sent against the region in the final week of the month, this effectively brought the Ruhr campaign to an end. It had been an outstanding success, and vast areas of Germany's industrial heartland now lay in ruins. Harris could look back over the past five months with genuine satisfaction at the performance of his squadrons, and his 'Blue Book' containing the post-raid reconnaissance photographs provided graphic evidence of the damage inflicted upon Germany's most important industrial region. Although losses to the Command had been grievously high, the aircraft factories were more than keeping pace with the rate of attrition, and output was even allowing for a gentle expansion. In terms of manpower, fresh, eager young crews were flooding in from the Empire training schools around the world to fill in the gaps.

Late on the evening of the 12th, almost 300 Lancasters of 1, 5 and 8 Groups took off for Turin, the 44 Squadron element led by W/C Nettleton VC. The operation was highly successful, but Nettleton's aircraft, ED331, was shot down into the sea by a night fighter shortly after crossing the French coast via the Brest Peninsular in daylight on the way home. None of the eight men on board survived. 467 Squadron lost three aircraft, two to enemy action and a third to a crash on return. Nettleton's replacement at 44 Squadron was W/C Williamson, who was appointed on the 15th, and whose own period of tenure would be brief. Meanwhile, 617 Squadron's period of operational inactivity came to an end on this night, when twelve aircraft joined a similar number from the Group to attack targets in Italy. S/L Holden led the squadron for the first time, when he and five others attacked a transformer and switching station at Aquata Scrivia. Meanwhile, S/L Maltby took a force of six aircraft to a similar target at San Polo d'Enza. After moderately successful outcomes the twelve aircraft landed at Blida in North Africa.

With confidence high Harris now prepared for Operation Gomorrah, the planned and systematic destruction of Germany's second city, Hamburg, in a series of heavy raids until the job was done. It was estimated, that this would require around 10,000 tons of bombs. Having been spared by the weather from hosting the first 1,000 bomber raid at the end of May 1942, Hamburg now satisfied Harris's criteria almost perfectly. As Germany's Second City it held the necessary political status, and its importance as a centre of war production, particularly U-Boat and shipbuilding was beyond question. There were, however, considerations of an operational nature which made Hamburg the ideal target, among which were its proximity to a coastline to aid navigation, and to the bomber stations to allow the force to approach and retreat in the few hours of darkness afforded by mid summer.

Of equal importance was the fact that Hamburg lay beyond the range of Oboe, which had proved so decisive at the Ruhr, but in compensation, boasted the wide River Elbe to provide solid H2s returns for the navigators high above.

The offensive began on the 24/25th, and was aided by the first operational use of 'Window', the tinfoil-backed strips of paper, which, when released into the air stream, drifted slowly to earth in great clouds. This swamped the enemy night fighter control, searchlight and gun-laying radar with false returns, making it impossible to single out a genuine target. The device had been available for a year, but its use had been vetoed in case the enemy copied it. Germany, as it happened, already had a similar device called Düppel, which it too had withheld for the same reason. Almost 800 aircraft took off in the late evening, and the dispensing of Window began at a predetermined point over the North Sea. Its effectiveness was immediately made apparent by the few combats taking place before the target was reached. In the target area, the usually efficient co-ordination between searchlights and flak was absent, and a golden opportunity existed to exploit the situation. In the event, the marking did not proceed entirely as planned, and the extensive creep-back caused many bomb loads to be wasted. Nevertheless, a swathe of destruction was cut from the city centre, out across the north-western districts along the line of approach and out into open country, and extensive damage was inflicted for the modest loss of just twelve aircraft. Most of these had fallen victim to night fighters outbound while hopelessly off-course and outside of the protection of Window and the bomber stream. No. 617 Squadron used the activity at Hamburg as a diversion and slipped back to England after bombing the docks at Leghorn on the way.

On the following night Harris took advantage of the chaos inflicted on the enemy defensive system by Window, and raided Essen with highly satisfying results. Almost 3,000 houses were destroyed, and the more industrialized eastern half of the city took a pounding. The Krupp complex suffered its worst night of the war. The second Hamburg operation took place on the 27/28th after a night's rest. The tragedy following the arrival over the city of the 729 aircraft was both unprecedented and unforeseeable, and was the result of a cruel conspiracy of circumstances. Firstly, a period of unusually hot and dry weather had left parts of the city a tinderbox. Secondly, the Pathfinder marking was again slightly wide of the mark, falling two miles to the east of the planned city centre aiming point, but with unusual concentration into the densely populated working class residential districts of Hamm, Hammerbrook and Borgfeld. Thirdly, the main force crews followed up with unaccustomed accuracy, concentration and almost no creep-back to deliver 2,300 tons of bombs into this relatively compact area. This combination allowed individual fires to join together to form one gigantic conflagration, which sucked in oxygen from surrounding areas at hurricane velocity to feed its voracious appetite. Such was the violence of this meteorological event, that trees were uprooted and cast bodily into the heart of the inferno along with debris and people. At the seat of the fire temperatures exceeded 1,000° Celsius, and the flames only subsided once all of the combustible material had been consumed. An estimated 40,000 people lost their lives on this one night alone, on top of the fifteen hundred killed three nights earlier. On the following morning, as a pall of black smoke hung over Hamburg, the first of an eventual 1.2 million people began to file out of the city. Later that day W/C Hopcroft concluded his tour as commanding officer of 57 Squadron, and he was replaced by W/C Haskell, who, as events were to prove, had only three weeks to live.

The third operation against Hamburg followed on the 29/30th after another night's rest, and it was again highly destructive. The Pathfinders approached on a north-south heading but once more two miles to the east of the intended line. The marking fell into an area just south of the districts devastated by the firestorm, and many bombs stirred the embers here before the creep back reached the residential areas of Wandsbek and Barmbek, where fierce fires took hold. Over 700 aircraft delivered their bombs into the city on this night, and the already overwhelmed rescue services on the ground were rendered powerless to reach the afflicted streets. Under cover of this operation nine Lancasters of 617 Squadron dropped leaflets over the Italian cities of Milan, Bologna, Turin and Genoa. A total of 270 aircraft went to Remscheid on the 30th/31st, and destroyed 83% of the town's built up area. and this was the operation that brought down the final curtain on the Ruhr offensive. 44 Squadron lost its second commanding officer in the month, when W/C Williamson, operating with the squadron for the first time, failed to return in JA895, and he and his crew were killed. W/C Bowes became the new commanding officer on the 1 August, and he, at least, would survive his tour. The final round of Operation Gomorrah took place on the 2nd/3rd of August, but it was rendered ineffective by violent electrical storms en-route, and many crews jettisoned their bombs over the sea or on alternative targets in Germany. Those reaching the tortured city were unable to deliver an effective attack in the absence of Pathfinder marking, but the damage had already been done. 5 Group dispatched over 570 sorties during the campaign, and sixteen Lancasters failed to return.

The time had now come for Guy Gibson finally to depart 617 Squadron, having effectively kicked his heels for the past month. His replacement, W/C George Holden, had been at Scampton for a month as commanding officer elect, and was now ready to take over the reins, having learned the ways of the Lancaster and led a squadron element on an operation to Italy. The Gibson era came to an end on the 3rd, when he was officially posted from the squadron to join the Prime Minister's party on a trip to Canada, where he would conduct a lecture tour. Holden had been confirmed as his successor on the 2nd, Gibson's final day on the squadron, when Gibson, his dams crew and Holden enjoyed an eighty-five minute farewell cross-country flight together in ED933.

Why, though, was Holden, a 4 Group man to the core, selected to replace the charismatic Gibson, now the most celebrated squadron commander in the entire service? His selection actually began a trend of appointing 4 Group men to the position: Cheshire, Tait and Fauquier, men who would carry the squadron through to the end of the bombing war in late April 1945. If Harris, and one might reasonably assume some involvement on his part, was prepared to look outside of 5 Group for Gibson's successor, why did he sanction the appointment of Holden from among the wealth of qualified existing squadron commanders available? It has to be said, that there was something of the Gibson character in Holden. His career to this point had been distinguished, and he had been involved in some unusual and spectacular operations. He had also rubbed shoulders with some of the Command's finest young bloods, many of whom were gathered within the squadrons of 4 Group, and were themselves seen as shining lights. Not all had survived to the summer of 1943, and of those who had, whose operational careers had begun in 1940, Holden was unquestionably among the brightest prospects. If Dinghy Young had survived, he a 4 Group contemporary of Holden and Cheshire, or perhaps even Henry Maudslay from the 'class of 41', then they would also undoubtedly have been in the frame, but they were gone, and Cheshire had progressed to the rank of Group Captain, which generally speaking at that time, precluded him from the command of a squadron. This latter restriction was in the process of being revised, however, as Pathfinder squadrons were now being led by Group Captains, with Wing Commanders filling the roll of flight commander.

Holden began basic training, presumably part time as a reservist, in May 1937. On the 1 September 1939, the day German forces began their assault on Poland, he joined 9 FTS at Hullavington, moved on to Benson between January and early May 1940, and thence to 10 O.T.U. at Abingdon, where he learned to fly Whitleys. This was the type operated by 4 Group until the advent of the Halifax, and it would be the spring of 1942 before it was finally withdrawn from operational service with the Command. He passed out as a first pilot, day only, with an average rating on the 18 September 1940, and immediately joined 78 Squadron at Dishforth. Here he began working up to operational status, and undertook his first sortie as second pilot to a F/L Pattison in a raid on Antwerp on the night of the 26/27th of September. His second sortie was flown to Amsterdam with his flight commander, S/L Wildey, who would eventually take command of 10 Squadron, and lose his life in action in October 1942, the same month in which Holden would gain his first command. Finally, on the 11 November, Holden was signed out as a fully qualified Whitley captain by the newly appointed commanding officer, W/C 'Charles' Whitworth. Two nights later he undertook his first operation as crew captain, his eighth sortie in all.

Late in 1940 Churchill pressed for the formation of a paratroop unit, as the forerunner of an airborne force for use in a future invasion of Europe.

Plans were put in hand to carry out a special operation under the codename Colossus, with the purpose of ascertaining the viability of such an undertaking. Volunteers were brought together as X-Troop No. 11 SAS Battalion for an attack on an aqueduct over the River Tragino in Italy to be launched from Malta. Two aircraft were to carry out a diversionary bombing attack on marshalling yards at nearby Foggia, while six others delivered the parachutists into position. 51 and 78 Squadrons were each selected to provide four aircraft and crews under the command of W/C James Tait, who had recently begun a short spell as commanding officer of the former. Among the pilots from 78 Squadron was P/O Holden, who flew with Tait on a container-dropping test as part of the run-up on the 2 February. On completion of their task the surviving commandos were to gather at a point on the coast for evacuation by submarine. The force departed for Malta on the night of the 7/8th of February, and carried out the operation on the 10/11th. In the event, not all of the commandos were dropped within range of their target, and if this were not unfortunate enough, one of the diversionary Whitleys had to be abandoned in the area selected for the ground force's withdrawal, thus alerting the local defenders. Some damage was inflicted upon the aqueduct, but all the soldiers were captured on their way to the rendezvous, to be joined soon afterwards by the Whitley crew.

This operation was Holden's twentieth, and his last with 78 Squadron, which he left with an above average rating to join 35 Squadron at Linton-on-Ouse. 35 Squadron had been re-formed at Boscombe Down in November 1940 to introduce the Halifax into operational service, and was attracting the leading bomber pilots in 4 Group. Holden arrived on the 25 February 1941, and met up again with Tait, who had now reverted to Squadron Leader rank and was a flight commander under the portly personage of the squadron commander, W/C R W P Collings. The Halifax suffered many teething problems, and the demand for modifications ensured only a trickle of new aircraft from the factories. As a result, following its operational baptism in March, the type operated only intermittently and in very small numbers for some time. Holden flew his first Halifax sortie against Duisburg on the 11/12th of June, and over the ensuing five weeks managed ten more. He then participated in the already-mentioned major assault on the German cruisers *Scharnhorst*, *Gneisenau* and *Prinz Eugen* on the 24 July. The *Scharnhorst* having slipped away to La Pallice, some 200 miles further south, was targeted by the Halifax element of fifteen aircraft from 35 and 76 Squadrons. Extensive damage was inflicted on the vessel, but five Halifaxes were brought down in the process, and all the surviving aircraft sustained damage to some degree. Holden was forced to bring his bombs home after flak shot away the electrical release gear. One of his crew was killed, while two others were wounded, one seriously. Holden's flight commander at the time was S/L Jimmy Marks, one of the brightest stars in Bomber Command, and an officer who would gain command of 35 Squadron in 1942, only to then lose his life in action shortly after taking it into the Pathfinder Force as one of the founder units.

Holden concluded his tour on a total of thirty-two operations, and was posted to the Heavy Conversion Flight at Linton-on-Ouse on the 18 August. Here he remained until December, when he was detached to Upavon, before progressing to Marston Moor, Leeming and Pocklington progressively in the role of instructor. At Pocklington, and now in the rank of Squadron Leader, he was put in charge of the Conversion Flight of 405 Squadron, a Canadian unit commanded by W/C Johnny Fauquier. While there, Holden flew on the second 1,000 bomber raid against Essen on the 1st/2nd of June 1942, and the third and final one on Bremen on the 25/26th, his thirty-third and thirty-fourth sorties. In July he was posted to 158 Squadron's Conversion Flight at East Moor, where he remained until the 25 October. In the early hours of the previous day, 102 Squadron's commanding officer, W/C Bruce Bintley, had been killed in a freak accident on the runway at Holme-on-Spalding-Moor on return from Genoa, when another Halifax had crushed his cockpit on landing. Holden was posted in as his replacement on the 25th, and began a successful period of command, during which he operated a further eleven times, bringing his tally to forty-five. He was rested again on the 20 April 1943, and thereafter seemed to be somewhat in limbo until the call came through from 617 Squadron. On the 4 July, two days after his arrival at Scampton, he was taken up by Martin in EE148 for a local familiarization trip, and the two paired up again on the following two days.

Italy was now teetering on the brink of capitulation, and Bomber Command launched a number of raids against its major cities during the first half of August to help nudge it over the edge. The campaign began on the night of the 7/8th with simultaneous attacks on Genoa, Milan and Turin by 1, 5 and 8 Groups respectively. Before the next round, Mannheim received a devastating attack on the 9/10th at the hands of a mixed force of Lancasters and Halifaxes, and much damage was inflicted upon industrial premises as well as housing. The following night was devoted to Nuremberg, where a moderately effective raid was delivered by around 600 aircraft, but this city was still to experience the worst ravages of a Bomber Command assault. W/C Russell was posted from 50 Squadron on the 11th at the conclusion of his tour as commanding officer. After a period of screening from operations he would return to frontline duties in 1944, this time reverting to Squadron Leader rank for the privilege of flying secret operations on behalf of SOE with 138 Squadron at Tempsford. At the beginning of May he would regain his former status as a Wing Commander when appointed commanding officer of the squadron, and die in action within a week. W/C McFarlane became his successor at 50 Squadron. Milan was hit again in the main raid on the 12/13th, while a smaller 3 and 8 Group attack went ahead at Turin. It was Milan again for 140 Lancasters of 1, 5 and 8 Groups on the 14/15th, and for almost 200 Lancasters on the following night. 467 Squadron's W/C Gomm was outbound over France when ED998 was attacked by a night fighter and exploded, killing Gomm and all but one of his crew. It was the twenty-fourth trip of his second tour, and his loss was a bitter blow to the squadron. Temporary command now passed to the A Flight commander, S/L Raphael, but his tenure would be tragically brief. Also missing on this night were three crews from 61 Squadron. The campaign ended at Turin on the 16/17th, when 3 Group Stirlings provided the main force for what was claimed as a successful operation. On return, many Stirling crews found their airfields fog-bound, and were forced to divert to other parts of the country. This would mean, that some were unable to return to their own stations until it was too late to prepare their aircraft for the coming night's vitally important operation.

Since the start of the war, intelligence had been filtering through concerning German research into rocketry, and gradually, attention was drawn to Peenemünde, a location on the island of Usedom on the Baltic coast. Photographic reconnaissance aircraft began to overfly the area as if by accident, and a picture was built up of the activity centred on the establishment there. Churchill's chief scientific adviser, Professor Lindemann, or Lord Cherwell as he became, steadfastly refused to give credence to the feasibility of such weapons, and remained unmoved when a PRU Mosquito snapped a V-2 on a trailer in June 1943. It required the combined urgings of Duncan Sandys and the brilliant scientist, Dr R V Jones, to persuade Churchill to act, and at last, with sufficient evidence to hand, preparations were made to attack the site at the first available opportunity. It was an operation of great importance, and every effort was made to ensure Peenemünde's destruction at the first attempt. It was mounted on the 17/18th by 597 aircraft, the numbers somewhat depleted by the already mentioned late return from Italy the night before of a large part of 3 Group's Stirling force. The operation was to proceed in three waves, each assigned to a specific aiming point, the housing estate, the factory and the experimental site, and the Pathfinder squadrons were charged with the task of shifting the point of aim accordingly. A Master of Ceremonies was appointed to lead the operation, in the manner pioneered by Gibson at the dams, and G/C Searby of 83 Squadron was the man selected. A spoof raid by eight Mosquitoes of 139 Squadron on Berlin, led by its recently appointed commanding officer, the previously mentioned G/C Slee, was intended to keep the night fighters away from the scene while the bombing of Peenemünde was in progress.

The operation began inauspiciously, when the initial target indicators fell more than a mile beyond the housing estate, and onto the forced workers camp at Trassenheide. Inevitably, they attracted a large proportion of the 3 and 4 Group bombs, and many casualties were inflicted upon the friendly foreign nationals trapped inside their wooden barracks. Once rectified, the bombing was effective, and a number of key technical personnel were killed as their houses were demolished. The factory buildings were assigned to 1 Group, but the accuracy of the bombing was compromised by a strong crosswind. Such was the lay of the land, that bombs either found the mark, or fell harmlessly into sand dunes or the sea. Nevertheless, the buildings were hit, and damage was inflicted. The final wave consisted of Lancasters from 5 and 6 Groups, the former at liberty to adopt the time and distance method of bombing if they chose, in case the aiming point at the experimental site was obscured by smoke. It was at this stage, that the night fighters belatedly arrived from Berlin, and a fierce battle developed, both in the skies over the target, and on the route home westwards along the coast towards Denmark. In all forty bombers were brought down, twenty-nine of them from the final wave. 5 Group dispatched 117 Lancasters, and of these seventeen failed to return. 49 and 61 Squadrons each posted missing four crews, 44 and 619 Squadrons three. 57 Squadron's commanding officer, W/C Haskell, was lost without trace, presumably in the Baltic on his way home, and his counterpart at 619 Squadron, W/C McGhie, also died with his crew. 467 Squadron's stand-in commanding officer, S/L Raphael, was shot down into the sea close to the target, and all eight men on board LM342 were killed. Although not entirely successful, the operation delayed development of the V-2 by a number of weeks, and ultimately forced the manufacture of secret weapons underground at a new facility at Nordhausen, while the V-2 testing programme was moved eastwards into Poland, out of range of RAF Bombers.

W/C Fisher became 57 Squadron's new commanding officer on the 19th, while 50 Squadron flight commander, S/L Abercromby, stepped up to the plate on promotion to Wing Commander at 619 Squadron. W/C Balmer was posted in from Syerston to assume command of 467 Squadron on the 20th, and he was the squadron's first Australian commanding officer. Following the successes of the Ruhr and Hamburg, and the reasonably effective attack on Peenemünde, Harris felt confident to embark on the campaign, which he had always believed would win the war. Berlin, as the seat and symbol of Nazi power, held the key, and its destruction might be sufficient to cause an uprising by the civilian population against its Nazi leaders. Less than a week after Peenemünde, on the night of the 23rd/24th he sent 700 aircraft to Berlin to begin the opening phase of what would become a series of nineteen major raids against the Capital over the next six months. Much of the bombing on this night was wasted in open country, and the operation was only a partial success. Any satisfaction was overshadowed by the failure to return of fifty-six aircraft, the heaviest loss to date from a single operation. The next operation was against Nuremberg on the 27/28th, but it was another disappointing raid on the birthplace of Nazism, much of the effort falling short of the target into open country. In contrast, an outstandingly accurate and concentrated raid took place against the twin towns of Mönchengladbach and Rheydt on the 30th/31st. Perhaps the difference was the shallow penetration into Germany, but whatever the reason, around 2,300 buildings were reduced to rubble, and railway installations were severely damaged.

It is remarkable to imagine that Scampton still had a grass track four years into the war. Now, though, the time had arrived for an upgrade, and 57 Squadron moved out on the 28th to take up residence at East Kirkby, where it would remain until war's end. Two days later 617 Squadron began the process of moving to Coningsby. The second Berlin raid, on the last night of the month, was again an expensive failure, costing forty-seven aircraft from a little over 600 dispatched. Proportionally, the Halifaxes and Stirlings sustained by far the heaviest casualties, and a pattern was beginning to emerge. The final operation to the 'Big City' before the autumn break took place on the 3rd/4th of September, and was an all Lancaster affair, perhaps reflecting Harris's concern at the disproportionately high loss rates suffered by the Halifax and Stirling squadrons. Bombs fell into the industrial district of Siemensstadt and adjacent residential districts, where substantial damage resulted for the loss of twenty-two Lancasters.

The heavy losses of the preceding two weeks notwithstanding, the Command was out in strength again on the 5/6th of September to deliver a highly accurate, concentrated and destructive attack on the twin cities of Mannheim and Ludwigshafen. Their location respectively on the east and west banks of the Rhine made them ideal for the exploitation of creep-back. By approaching from the west, and placing the aiming point in the eastern half of Mannheim, the bombing would almost inevitably spread back along the line of approach across Ludwigshafen. This is precisely what occurred on this night, and both cities were devastated. Once more, however, the defences claimed a heavy toll, bringing down thirty-four aircraft. On the following night over 400 aircraft took off for southern Germany again, their crews on this occasion briefed for Munich. The city was found to be completely cloud covered, and no assessment of the performance could be made. It had, in fact, been a scattered attack, falling predominantly into the southern and western districts.

For the next two weeks the main force Lancaster brigade remained largely off the order of battle, while the Halifaxes and Stirlings of 3, 4 and 6 Groups carried out a number of raids against precision targets in France with mixed fortunes. W/C Johnson departed 49 Squadron on posting to Woodhall Spa on the 15th, and W/C Adams assumed command in his place, although he may not have taken up his post until the 1 October. It was also during this period, on the 15/16th, that 617 Squadron undertook its second operation over Germany with disastrous results. Initially launched on the night of the 14/15th, the operation was intended to breach the banks of the Dortmund-Ems Canal at a point near Ladbergen, but the crews were recalled while over the North Sea because of poor weather conditions in the target area. S/L David Maltby and crew were lost when their heavily-laden Lancaster cartwheeled into the sea during the turn, and only the pilot's body was recovered. This was a tragic loss to the squadron of one of its founder members, but worse was to follow when the operation was rescheduled for the following night. The attack failed when thick fog reduced visibility in the target area to almost nothing, and five out of the eight crews were lost. W/C Holden was shot down over Nordhorn on the way to the target, and all eight men on board the Lancaster, including four of Gibson's Dams crew, were killed. Les Knight lost his life in ensuring his crew had time to bale out of their stricken Lancaster after it ploughed through treetops while orbiting the target. Both port engines had to be shut down, making it difficult to fly straight, and this problem was compounded by damage to control surfaces. Knight jettisoned the huge 12,000 lb blockbuster, a weapon being employed for the first time, and coaxed the Lancaster to a height of around 1,400 feet. By the time Den Ham was reached in northern Holland, the aircraft had become almost uncontrollable, and Knight gave the order to bale out. Now alone and unable to leave the controls, Knight made a gallant effort to force land in a field on the edge of the town, but hit treetops and lost all flying speed. The Lancaster nose-dived into the field, and he was killed. Two members of his crew fell into enemy hands, but the remaining five evaded a similar fate through the selfless and courageous assistance of Dutch and other resistance workers.

The two founder crews of F/L Wilson and P/O Divall, who trained for the dams but missed out on the night, were also shot down without survivors, the former close to the intended target, and the latter on the edge of the Mittelland Canal a few miles to the north-east. Finally, flight commander S/L Allesbrook crashed at the conjunction of the Dortmund-Ems and Mittelland Canals after being hit by light flak, and again all were killed. Martin and Shannon eventually carried out an attack on the canal banks, but failed to create a breach. On his return from the operation F/L Martin was given the acting rank of Squadron Leader, and as temporary commanding officer he would begin the process of rebuilding what had now become a 'chop' squadron. Despite the severe mauling only hours earlier, Martin offered to go back to the canal that night to try to finish the job. In the event it was decided to send six aircraft with fresh crews to join six from 619 Squadron to attack the Antheor Viaduct on the Franco-Italian frontier. The ten-hour round trip resulted in some near misses, but that was not good enough at such a target, and the squadron would have to return. While the appointment of a permanent replacement to Holden was considered, Martin began interviewing volunteers, of which, despite the 'suicide squadron' reputation, there seemed to be no shortage.

'Mick' Martin was born in New South Wales in February 1921, and joined the RAF in 1940. He qualified as a pilot in June 1941, and after further training was posted to 455 Squadron RAAF at Swinderby in October. Flying Hampdens, Martin ultimately drew around him an all-Australian crew consisting of Jack Leggo, Tammy Simpson and Toby Foxlee. When 455 Squadron was posted to Coastal Command in April 1942, Martin and crew moved on to 50 Squadron at Skellingthorpe to continue their bomber tour. At the time of their posting 50 Squadron had recently converted to Manchesters, but was about to take delivery of Lancasters. By the end of May,

Martin had passed out on Manchesters, and the squadron put up sixteen of them plus a single Lancaster for the first thousand-bomber raid on Cologne. Martin reported attacking Cologne from 7,400 feet, and described it as a really good trip. He went to Essen for the second thousand-bomber raid two nights later in the same Manchester, and completed the hat trick at Bremen on the 25/26th in what proved to be the operational swansong for the ill-fated type.

After its two week lay-off 5 Group returned to action as part of a 700 strong force bound for Hanover on the night of the 22nd/23rd. This was to be the first of four raids on this city over the coming four weeks, but stronger than forecast winds caused most of the bombing to fall wide of the mark. A return to Mannheim twenty-four hours later brought more misery upon this city, with the destruction of a further 1,000 buildings, most of them of a residential nature. Among the thirty-two missing bombers were three from 57 Squadron and the 49 Squadron Lancaster containing the crew of P/O Cyril Anderson, who had participated in the Dams raid in May. The second Hanover operation took place on the 27/28th, and produced a concentrated pattern of bombing, but it again fell mostly outside of the built-up area. This was a disappointing return for the loss of another thirty-eight aircraft. The month ended at Bochum in the Ruhr on the 29/30th, a target well within the Oboe comfort zone, a fact reflected by the destruction of over 500 houses.

October began in hectic fashion for the Lancaster squadrons. They were included in all six of the major operations mounted during the first eight nights, while the Halifaxes and Stirlings were employed more sparingly. The month's account opened on the night of the 1st/2nd with a raid on Hagen by Lancasters of 1, 5 and 8 Groups. It was a total success, despite the small size of the target and the presence of complete cloud cover, and only two Lancasters failed to return from the 240 dispatched. On the following night the same Groups went to Munich, where a moderately successful raid ensued for the loss of eight Lancasters. The Halifax and Stirling squadrons were drafted in on the night of the 3rd/4th for a tilt at Kassel. This operation was a major success, with severe destruction inflicted on a number of districts for the loss of twenty-four aircraft. One of these contained 61 Squadron's commanding officer, W/C Penman, who died with his crew. Later that day W/C Stidolph was installed as the new commanding officer. The first really effective attack on Frankfurt was delivered by a mixed force of under four hundred aircraft on the 4/5th, and this left a number of districts engulfed in flames. An all-Lancaster assault on Stuttgart on the 7/8th was also moderately effective, and included for the first time radio-jamming ABC Lancasters from 1 Group's 101 Squadron. These were spread throughout the bomber stream, and, apart from a full bomb load, they carried an extra 'special equipment' operator, whose job was to listen-in to enemy night fighter broadcasts, and jam the frequencies with 'Jostle'. To do this he needed only sufficient knowledge of German to recognise the language, and was not required to broadcast himself. A very modest four aircraft were lost on this night, and whether or not this resulted from the presence of the Radio Countermeasures (RCM) Lancasters will never be known. From this point on, however, there would be a 101 Squadron presence on every major operation, whether or not 1 Group was involved generally. Hanover finally succumbed to a devastating assault by a mixed force of under 500 aircraft on the 8/9th. Most parts of the city were afflicted, and almost 4,000 buildings were completely destroyed, with 30,000 others damaged to some extent.

207 Squadron changed address for the final time on the 12th with a move to Spilsby. The final raid of the month-long series against Hanover took place on the 18/19th, after a nine night break from major operations. The all-Lancaster attack failed to capitalize on the success gained in the previous raid, and eighteen Lancasters were lost. This mini campaign had, in fact, cost the Command over one hundred heavy bombers and crews, but the one successful attack had at least left the city devastated. Two nights later the eastern city of Leipzig was selected to host its first major attack of the war. The operation took place in the most appalling weather conditions, and very little damage resulted for the loss of sixteen Lancasters. Kassel received its second raid of the month on the 22nd/23rd, and it became the victim of the second recorded firestorm. Over 4,000 apartment blocks were totally destroyed, and one and a half times that number were damaged, amounting to over 60% of the city's living accommodation. Some of the homeless may have been heartened by the news that forty-three of the bombers would not be returning home, but this was insignificant in the face of more than 6,000 fatal casualties among their fellow inhabitants.

November brought with it the long, dark, cloudy nights that would enable Harris to return to his main theme, the destruction of Germany's capital city. The next four months would bring the bloodiest, hardest fought air battles between Bomber Command and the *Luftwaffe Nachtjagd*, and test the hard-pressed crews to the limit of their endurance. In the meantime, W/C Hilton DSO DFC* arrived at 83 Squadron on the 2nd, having formerly served it as a flight commander. He officially assumed command on the 5th at the departure of G/C Searby, who was posted to command the Pathfinder's Navigation Training Unit. Little did he know, that the fates would require him to return to 83 Squadron within a matter of weeks. The month's account opened at Düsseldorf on the 3rd/4th, and this was a heavy and destructive attack in return for a reasonably modest loss of eighteen aircraft. It was a momentous night for F/L Bill Reid, whose 61 Squadron Lancaster was attacked by a night fighter during the outward flight. His windscreen was smashed, sending shards of Perspex into his face. In the shock of the moment, and with blood pouring down his face, Reid allowed 2,000 feet of height to be lost before gathering himself. Having established that all four engines were in good order, and that it was not a good idea to turn back across the bomber stream, there was no question in his mind that they should press on to the target. Once he was able to take stock he realised he had also sustained shoulder and hand injuries, and noticed that the Lancaster was becoming difficult to handle because of damage to the elevator trimming tabs. The rear turret was also severely knocked about and only a single gun barrel was serviceable with which to defend the aircraft. A second fighter then strafed the fuselage from stem to stern, killing the navigator and fatally wounding the wireless operator. Reid and his flight engineer picked up further wounds, but they managed to find the target by orienting on the stars. By sheer professionalism Reid brought the Lancaster directly over the target and obtained an aiming point photograph. On the way home Reid lapsed in and out of consciousness as loss of blood, extreme cold and fatigue took hold, but with the help of his crew mates a landing was made at the American airfield at Shipdham. The undercarriage collapsed but the surviving crew members were able to walk away, and Reid was ultimately awarded the Victoria Cross. He would later join 617 Squadron, where he would once more narrowly escape with his life.

Earlier in the day Harris had stated in a memo to Churchill, that with the assistance of the UK based American 8th bomber force, he could 'wreck Berlin from end to end'. He estimated that it would cost between them 4/500 aircraft, but it would cost Germany the war. Quite why he believed so fervently that the destruction of Berlin would destroy German resolve to continue the fight is a puzzle. The bombing of British cities had quite the opposite effect, and served only to strengthen the resolve to fight on and overcome. Much earlier in the war there had been a report, which suggested that the German civilian population was less able than the British to withstand heavy bombing. This would prove to be a false assumption. There is no question, that Harris wanted the bomber to win the war, partly perhaps for personal credit, but mostly in order to save Allied lives. Having personally witnessed the carnage of protracted and bloody land campaigns during the Great War, he wished to avoid a repeat this time round. In fairness to Harris, it is only in the light of recent conflicts, that we appreciate fully the need to occupy physically the enemy's territory in order to subdue him completely. The Americans, of course, were committed to victory on land, and there was never a chance of enlisting their support for an all-out bombing campaign against Berlin. Single minded and adamant as ever, Harris would go alone, and for the next two weeks minor operations became the order of the day as he prepared the way for the resumption of the offensive begun back in August. 106 Squadron swapped Syerston for Metheringham on the 11th, and would remain there until war's end. 9 Squadron was to face the Berlin campaign with a new commanding officer, as W/C Porter succeeded W/C Burnett on the 14th.

The Cheshire era at 617 Squadron began officially on the 10 November, although it appears that he did not actually arrive on station until after the squadron got back from North Africa, following another gallant but unsuccessful crack at the Antheor Viaduct on the 11/12th. W/C Cheshire had, like Holden before him, hitherto been a 4 Group man to the core. He had begun his operational career as a Flying Officer flying Whitleys with 102 Squadron in June 1940, where he was a contemporary of the late 'Dinghy' Young. On the 12/13th of November he brought a massively damaged aircraft safely back from Germany, and received an immediate award of the DSO, thus giving an insight into the character that would make him one of the most famous warriors in Bomber Command. With the advent of the Halifax Cheshire was posted to 35 Squadron in January 1941, to join the likes of Tait and Holden, and was awarded the DFC in March. In early May, while the Halifaxes were grounded for essential modifications, he landed a posting to the Atlantic Ferry Organisation and departed for Canada. A surplus of pilots saw him kicking his heels, and he took the opportunity to visit New York. Here he met the retired actress Constance Binney, whom he married in July. He returned alone to the UK soon afterwards to rejoin 35 Squadron, and set about persuading the Foreign Office to allow Constance to join him. This she did in October, and they set up home in a flat in Harrogate. Promotion to Flight Lieutenant had come in June, and at the conclusion of his second tour in February 1942 he was posted as an instructor to 1652 Heavy Conversion Unit at Marston Moor. During this time he was writing his book, Bomber Pilot, which he had finished before he participated in all three of the thousand-bomber raids in May and June. He returned to a front line operational squadron in August 1942 as a Wing Commander, when given command of 76 Squadron, the unit in which his brother Christopher had served as a pilot until being shot down on his way to Berlin a year earlier. Christopher had survived, and was on extended leave in a PoW camp. Cheshire remained at 76 Squadron until April 1943, and at the conclusion of this, his third tour, he was promoted to Group Captain and posted back to Marston Moor, this time as the station commander. Here he had a converted railway carriage transported onto the site, where he lived with Constance.

Although throwing himself into his new job, Cheshire was never really happy at being away from the operational scene, and when offered the post at 617 Squadron, he eagerly accepted it, even though it meant having to revert to the rank of Wing Commander. Despite his own reputation and status within Bomber Command Cheshire's natural modesty left him somewhat in awe of Gibson, and he wondered how those at the squadron, who were survivors of the Gibson era, would receive him. He need not have been concerned. While Holden had been very much in the Gibson mould, Cheshire was entirely different. He was a friendly and approachable person, who took a genuine interest in those under his command. This attitude extended to the lowliest 'erk', whose name Cheshire would remember, along with some details of his family or background. He enjoyed spending time with the ground crews, talking to them, sharing a cigarette, asking questions about technical matters or their personal concerns. This endeared him to his subordinates, and ensured their loyalty and willingness to go the extra mile on his behalf.

467 Squadron escaped the mud at Bottesford after twelve months of living rough, and returned to all the home comforts of a permanent station at Waddington on the 12 November. 630 Squadron was formed on the 15th at East Kirkby. This was another entirely new unit with no past history or tradition, and as was generally the case, it was spawned by an existing operational unit. Its parent was 57 Squadron, whose B Flight, under the command of the American, S/L Malcolm Crocker DFC, transferred en-masse across the tarmac to form the nucleus. This was the second time that 57 Squadron had given birth to an offspring, its firstborn having by now become part of Bomber folklore as the Dambusters. S/L Crocker was promoted to Wing Commander, but as he was approaching the end of his tour, he was to spend only a month in command. With a complement of sixteen Lancasters with four in reserve, and crews already blooded in battle with 57 Squadron, the fledgling unit would be ready for battle within three days of its formation. 61 Squadron also moved from Syerston to Skellingthorpe on the 15th.

The opening round of the main Berlin offensive came on the night of the 18/19th of November, for which an all-Lancaster force of over 400 aircraft was detailed. A diversionary raid on Mannheim by the Stirling and Halifax brigade was designed to split the defences, and the loss of a modest nine Lancasters from the Berlin force suggested that the ploy had succeeded. The attack was scattered across the city with no recognizable point of concentration, although most of the damage occurred in the southern half. Round two was mounted on the 22nd/23rd, when a maximum effort operation took over 700 aircraft back to the Capital. Despite complete cloud cover, which prevented any assessment of the results by the crews, this proved to be the most destructive raid of the war on the city. A total of 2,000 people lost their lives, while a further 175,000 were bombed out of their homes, and many industrial premises were among more than 3,000 buildings destroyed. Following the 10% loss rate among the fifty strong Stirling contingent, Harris withdrew the type from further operations over Germany. An all-Lancaster force returned on the following night, and guided by the glow of fires still burning beneath the clouds, they delivered another crushing blow. Altogether, 2,000 more buildings were wrecked on this night, while the death toll stood at around 1,500 people. Twenty Lancasters failed to return, including three from 44 Squadron, and another of the casualties was W/C Hilton, the commanding officer of 83 Squadron. He and his crew were brought down in the target area in JB284, and there were no survivors. W/C Hilton was a highly experienced bomber pilot, with over sixty sorties to his credit, and his death was a bitter blow to the squadron and to the Command. G/C Searby was asked to return temporarily, until a suitable replacement could be found from among the 5 Group contenders.

The 25th saw the formation at Waddington of 463 Squadron RAAF. It was created by hiving off 467 Squadron's C Flight under S/L Locke, and he became A Flight commander of the new unit, while W/C Kingsford-Smith assumed overall command. The provision of a core of experienced air and ground crews enabled 463 Squadron to become operational immediately, and it made its debut on the very next assault on Berlin, which was undertaken by more than 400 Lancasters on the 26/27th, while a diversionary raid was mounted against Stuttgart. Approaching the city from the south, the Pathfinders overshot the central aiming point, and marked an area well to the north-west. Fortunately, this was still within the built-up area of the city, where much of the bombing found useful targets, and thirty-eight war industry factories were completely destroyed. Among the twenty-eight missing Lancasters were three from 61 Squadron. 50 Squadron also lost one to the defences, one to a crash on return and two more in Landing accidents. 619 Squadron likewise posted one crew missing, while another crew safely abandoned its aircraft when out of fuel. Two other 619 Squadron Lancasters crashed while trying to land, one without survivors, the other without casualties. Such are the fortunes of war.

December opened with a predominantly Lancaster force returning to Berlin on the 2nd/3rd to deliver a scattered attack, which, although creating some useful industrial damage, cost the Command forty aircraft. Having been saved by the weather in October, Leipzig faced another major attack on the 3rd/4th, which this time proceeded more or less according to plan, and resulted in severe damage. Had many aircraft not strayed over heavily defended areas of the Reich on the way home, the losses would have been remarkably light for such a deep penetration raid, but in the event twenty-four were shot down. W/C Hilton's official replacement at 83 Squadron arrived on the 4th in the form of W/C Abercromby, who was posted in from his command at 619 Squadron. His 5 Group attitudes, particularly with regard to the 8 Group practise of weaving as a defensive measure against night fighters, were to ruffle a few feathers, most notably and appropriately those of F/O Chick, whose flying he described as cowardly. Chick refused to abandon a policy which had seen him through more than forty operations, and predicted that Abercromby would survive no more than three weeks if he flew straight and level. Chick completed his tour on forty-eight operations shortly afterwards, and lived to see his prophecy fulfilled. W/C Jeudwine became the new commanding officer of 619 Squadron, but he had to wait until mid month before presiding over his first operation. On the 6th W/C McFarlane concluded his brief tour as commander of 50 Squadron to be replaced by W/C Pullen, whose own period in command would be fleeting. This round of musical chairs continued on the 12th, when W/C Crocker concluded his tour, and was posted from the command of 630 Squadron for a 'rest'. He was rewarded for his efforts with a second DFC, to go with the one he had received while with 57 Squadron. He seems to have remained at East Kirkby in a staff job, however, until returning to operations in the coming spring. He was replaced at 630 Squadron by W/C Rollinson, another officer whose period of tenure would be brought to a premature conclusion. While this was going on, 617 Squadron lent four aircraft and crews to 138

Squadron at Tempsford. 138 and 161 Squadrons had been flying top secret operations on behalf of the Special Operations Executive since early in the war, dropping agents into occupied Europe and supplying resistance organisations with arms and equipment. The attempt to drop arms over France on the 9/10th was cancelled and rescheduled for the following night. The crews of Bull, Weeden and Clayton took part, all flying Dams Lancasters. None of the drops was successful, and Bull and Weeden failed to return. Chuffy Bull and three of his crew were soon captured, but another managed to evade, while the remaining two crew men died in the crash. There were no survivors from Weeden's crew.

After this period of minor operations the next slog to Berlin was undertaken by an all-Lancaster heavy force on the night of the 16/17th. This operation will always be remembered with great sadness, particularly by those involved with 1, 6 and 8 Groups, who were to suffer most from the prevailing conditions. A moderately successful operation cost twenty-five aircraft, most of them falling to night fighters during the outward flight and in the target area. The tired survivors arrived back in friendly airspace around midnight, many of them to find their stations blanketed in low cloud. Few would have had sufficient reserves of fuel to allow them to reach distant clear airfields, and the following two hours witnessed a desperate search for somewhere to land. Some crews elected to abandon their aircraft, and these proved to be the fortunate ones, while others flew into obstacles or directly into the ground as they stumbled around in the murk. A total of twenty-nine Lancasters came to grief either through abandonment or crashing, and around 150 airmen lost their lives in this tragic way, when so close to home and safety. 97 Squadron was among the worst afflicted, losing one Lancaster to enemy action and seven more to crashes at home. Two crews escaped by parachute and arrived safely on the ground, but a total of twenty-eight airmen lost their lives in the other aircraft, on top of the eight killed over Germany. Among those killed on home soil was S/L Deverill DFC, AFC DFM, who had participated in the epic Augsburg raid in April 1942.

617 Squadron was also in action on this night, with Cheshire leading from the front for the first time. It was the tentative start of a new campaign against V-Weapon sites, which would continue until the end of the following summer, when Allied forces overran the Pas-de-Calais region of France. The target for the nine Lancasters on this night was at Flixecourt, for which high-flying Oboe Mosquitoes provided target indicators. Each 617 Squadron aircraft carried a single 12,000 pounder for maximum blast effect. (The bombs employed here were those of the 'blockbuster' type, i.e. light case, high capacity, first used at the Dortmund-Ems Canal in September, and are not to be confused with the Barnes Wallis designed Tallboy medium capacity 'earthquake' bombs of the same weight used by the squadron from June 1944.) 617 Squadron's target lay concealed in a wood at Flixecourt, while another at Tilley-le-Haut was assigned to a force of Stirlings from 3 Group. 8 Group Oboe Mosquitoes were used to deliver the target indicators onto the

aiming points at both targets, but they fell respectively 350 and 450 yards wide. 617 blasted the indicators with their bombs, but as the indicators were a few hundred yards wide of the mark, the target escaped damage.

Frankfurt was the target for more than six hundred aircraft on the 20/21st, when the bomber stream was plotted early by the night fighter controller. He soon brought his forces into contact, and many combats took place during the outward flight, the night fighters scoring steadily throughout. The raid did not achieve concentration, and the creep-back was largely responsible for the destruction of over four hundred houses within the city and outlying communities. Forty-one aircraft failed to return, among them the Lancaster carrying W/C Pullen of 50 Squadron, and he was killed. Eight 617 Squadron aircraft went to Liege on this night to attack an armaments factory, but cloud obscured it and Cheshire sent them home. Geoff Rice, one of the founder members of the squadron, failed to return after his Lancaster was shot down by a night fighter, and Rice alone survived, staying on the run for five months before being captured. Two nights later eleven 617 Squadron crews targeted a flying bomb site in the Abbeville/Amiens area, but returned empty handed when the Oboe markers could not be identified. The penultimate raid of the year on Berlin was carried out on the 23/24th by a Lancaster main force, but scattered and intermittent marking led to a disappointing outcome. A few hundred houses were destroyed in south-eastern suburbs, and sixteen Lancasters failed to make it home. 1943 concluded with another maximum effort operation by over seven hundred aircraft to the 'Big City' on the 29/30th, the first of an unprecedented three Berlin operations in the space of five nights spanning the turn of the year. Cloud-covered as always, the Capital escaped devastation, and settled for the destruction of around four hundred buildings in mostly southern districts. 617 Squadron slipped across the Channel again on the night of the 30/31st to return to the flying bomb site at Flixcourt, the scene of the failure two weeks earlier. The Oboe markers again missed the aiming point by around three hundred yards, which, at an urban target would have represented pinpoint accuracy, and even though the 12,000 pounders fell within 150 yards of the markers, the site survived. The crews returned home frustrated, but the experience set minds working, and a solution would not be long in coming.

Despite heavy losses, it had been a successful year for the Command, the first of the war so far, and the advent of Oboe had been the most significant factor. It effectively signalled the end for the Ruhr, which came within the device's range, and the result of that was the dispersal of industry. However, with so much slack in Germany's manufacturing capacity, it was, perhaps, a greater blow to morale than to the Nazi ability to continue the fight materially. It was a different matter for the Command beyond the range of Oboe, where the outcome of operations was still something of a lottery. Without the ability to 'see' through cloud and haze courtesy of Oboe, the weather became a decisive factor, and H2s was never quite able to bridge the gap, even in the hands of an expert operator. Having recovered from the setback of Window, the *Luftwaffe* had been forced to devise a much more efficient night fighter system based on a running commentary. Out of this emerged a leaner and much deadlier adversary than had existed before Hamburg. The twin enemies, weather and night fighter, stood in wait as the New Year dawned, and challenged the crews of Bomber Command to do their worst.

1944. From disaster to destroyer of worlds

The winter campaign, independence, railways, oil, flying bombs, tactical support, annihilation

Despite the harshness of the winter of 1943/44, there would be no let up in the campaign against Berlin, and a series of heavy defeats for the Command characterized the first three months of the year, threatening the viability of major operations over Germany. It was also a period which would test to the limit the morale of the crews, many of whom found their tours coinciding with the main battle. It is likely that the hard-pressed crews of Bomber Command and the beleaguered citizens of Berlin shared a common hope for the New Year, that the Capital would cease to be the main focus of Harris's attention. Berliners first and Germans second, the natives of the Capital were a hardy breed, who bore their trials resolutely and with humour, precisely as had their counterparts in London during the Blitz of 1940. The persistent bombing served only to strengthen their will to withstand the onslaught, and banners of defiance were paraded through the streets bearing the message, 'you may break our walls but not our hearts'. The war was not yet lost despite the reversals of 1943, and the most popular song of the day, *Nach jedem Dezember kommt immer ein Mai*, (After every December comes always a May) gave promise of a change in fortunes with the onset of spring. In a way, as far as the Berliners were concerned, this would come to pass at the conclusion of Bomber Command's winter campaign, but for Germany as a whole, there was to be no respite.

New Year's Day brought the arrival at 97 Squadron of a new commanding officer to replace G/C Fresson, who had relinquished his station commander role on the 24 November, but had remained at the helm of the Squadron. W/C 'Jimmy' Carter would preside over the next round of operations to Berlin, and see the squadron through until his loss on D-Day. He was an experienced officer, who had formerly commanded 150 Squadron during the second half of 1942. Before New Year's Day was done more than 400 Lancasters were winging their way to the Capital, arriving overhead in the early hours of the 2nd to deliver an ineffective attack for the loss of twenty-eight of their number. As predicted by F/O Chick a few weeks earlier, 83 Squadron posted missing W/C Abercromby and his crew, after ND354 was torn asunder by an explosion, and just one man survived as a POW from the eight on board. He was replaced as commanding officer by W/C Deane, who was posted in from fellow Pathfinders 156 Squadron on the 3rd, having served that unit as a flight commander. In all 5 Group surrendered twelve Lancasters to the defences on this night. The current three raid series against the Capital was concluded by another all-Lancaster heavy force on the following night, when the effort was again not rewarded with success. Only marginally greater damage was achieved, but even so, it was a paltry return for the investment of effort and the cost of twenty-seven more Lancasters and crews, eight of which were from 5 Group. The Pathfinders in particular were suffering grievously, and 83 Squadron posted missing three aircraft, and a fourth Lancaster was lost while on loan to 405 Squadron at Gransden Lodge. 156 Squadron alone registered the loss of nine crews in these first two nights of January, and in mid month it would lose five more in a single night. 8 Group was being bled dry of experienced crews, and could not sustain this level of attrition and remain effective. On the night of the 4/5th Cheshire led a force of eleven 617 Squadron Lancasters back to the Pas-de Calais for a crack at another flying bomb site. Again the Oboe markers were difficult to spot, and although bombs fell around those which were visible, photographic reconnaissance confirmed no new damage to the target.

Mercifully, the Lancaster force was switched to Stettin for the next operation on the 5/6th, and this was a highly destructive raid against residential and industrial buildings, which also sank eight ships in the harbour. The current lull in major operations allowed the weary crews a period of rest and 617 Squadron to move from Coningsby to its final wartime home at Woodhall Spa on the 10th. On the previous day 619 Squadron had moved out of Woodhall Spa to occupy the accommodation at Coningsby just vacated by 617 Squadron. The previously mentioned F/L Bill Reid VC joined the ranks of 617 Squadron on the 13th. When briefings next took place on the 14th there must have been a degree of relief, that the red tape on the wall maps stopped short of Berlin. It stopped, in fact, at Brunswick, a town some fifty miles to the east of Hanover, which itself had proved to be a difficult and expensive nut to crack during the previous autumn. Brunswick had not been visited by the Command in numbers before, and would prove to be equally as difficult a proposition as its neighbour. Almost 500 Lancasters took off for north-central Germany, crossing the enemy coast near Bremen. The night-fighter controller was already plotting the course of the bomber stream, and his night fighters infiltrated it shortly afterwards. The two forces remained in contact all the way to the target and back as far as the Dutch coast, by which time thirty-eight Lancasters had been brought down, four of them bearing the EM code of 207 Squadron. This was the occasion, as mentioned above, on which 156 Squadron lost five more crews, and with most of the bombing falling wide of the mark, there was not even the consolation of a successful attack.

The next Berlin operation, the eleventh since the resumption, was mounted on the 20th/21st by a force of well over 700 aircraft. Complete cloud cover left the crews guessing as to the results of their work, but they had produced quite extensive damage in the hitherto less severely afflicted eastern districts. There were thirty-five missing aircraft, and twenty-two of them were Halifaxes. Among the missing Lancasters were a further three from 83 Squadron. A full month after the vacancy for a commanding officer at 50 Squadron was created, W/C Heward stepped into the breach on the 21st. That night brought the first major raid of the war on Magdeburg, another of Germany's eastern cities. The bomber stream was again picked up early by the night-fighter controller, although he was unable to identify the target until much later. This did not matter to the night-fighter crews, who were again able to maintain contact with their quarry by means of the running commentary system. A combination of stronger than forecast winds, decoy markers and bombing ahead of the Pathfinders by a small number of main force crews combined to produce a disappointing raid, which fell largely outside of the built-up area. To compound this, the defenders claimed a massive fifty-seven bombers, a new record high, and the Halifaxes again bore the brunt by losing thirty-five of their number, or 15.6% of those dispatched. 83 Squadron's casualties continued with the failure to return of two more crews. Also on this night, twenty-two Lancasters of 5 Group carried out a diversionary raid on Berlin with 8 Group Mosquitoes in support, and found themselves unmolested by the defences, although one 630 Squadron Lancaster was lost to flak. 617 Squadron dispatched twelve Lancasters to the Pas-de-Calais in the continuing campaign to wipe out flying bomb sites, and aided by clear visibility for a change, inflicted substantial damage on the target. A return four nights later was less rewarding, however, and reconnaissance could not confirm new damage.

Despite the mauling over the past few operations, ahead lay three Berlin trips in four nights, an unprecedented concentration of back-to-back deep penetration raids, and the cracks in crew morale were now beginning to show. An all-Lancaster heavy force numbering more than 500 aircraft began the series on the 27/28th, and encountered the usual heavy cloud over the target. No assessment could be made at the time, but it was a moderately destructive attack, although dozens of outlying communities were also afflicted by stray bombs, and thirty-three Lancasters were missing. Halifaxes joined in on the following night, when the strain on the crews was manifested by a 9.7% rate of early returns. Breaks in the cloud allowed some ground marking to take place, and western and southern districts were hardest hit, while the spraying of bombs onto outlying communities continued, as did the heavy losses. Forty-six aircraft failed to return on this night, and as generally happened when Halifaxes were present, they suffered the heavier casualties, both in numerical and percentage terms. Among the missing Lancasters was JB666 of 630 Squadron, which had been carrying W/C Rollinson on his fifty-fifth operation, and his third since assuming command of the squadron.

There were no survivors from the crash in Germany. After a night's rest, over 500 aircraft rejoined the rocky road to Berlin, the Lancasters accompanied on this night by only the new Hercules-powered and much improved Mk III Halifaxes. An 8% early return rate reduced the numbers by forty-three aircraft, and those reaching the target hit many parts of the city, with the main weight of bombs falling onto the central and south-western districts. The night fighters caught up with the bomber stream only well into the outward flight, but then remained in contact scoring steadily. Of the thirty-three missing aircraft, all but one were Lancasters. Eleven 5 Group Lancasters failed to return, 207 and 463 Squadrons sustaining the heaviest casualties at three and four respectively.

Harsh weather conditions contributed to keeping the main force on the ground for the first two weeks of February, and during this respite W/C Deas took command at 630 Squadron on the 1st, the same day that 61 Squadron moved from Skellingthorpe to Coningsby. Two days later W/C Bowes relinquished his command of 44 Squadron in favour of W/C Thompson. After a period away from the operational scene W/C Bowes would be appointed to command 214 Squadron of 100 Group, taking up his appointment in March 1945. On the 7th 617 Squadron carried out a secret bombing practice, the result of which would have a major influence on the way 5 Group conducted its operations for the remainder of the war. Cheshire and Martin had conducted an unofficial experiment, which involved diving a Lancaster onto an aiming point before releasing target markers from low level. It was an interesting experience in such a heavy aircraft, and involved a genuine risk of tearing off the wings. The idea was put to Cochrane, a man ever receptive to new ideas, and he authorized a live test at a real target. The Gnome & Rhône aero engine factory was selected at Limoges, for which twelve crews were briefed. They arrived over the target at around midnight, and Cheshire made three low passes across the factory to warn the workers to evacuate. On his fourth pass he delivered incendiaries onto the centre of the factory roof, which were backed up by Martin. A mixture of 12,000 and 1,000 pounders then fell from the ten Lancasters waiting at 8/10,000 feet, and just about every building on the site was destroyed or damaged. The operation was an outstanding success, which was captured on cinefilm.

On the night of the 12/13th Cheshire led as eleven 617 Squadron Lancasters returned yet again to the Antheor Viaduct. This time a heavy searchlight and flak defence greeted the force's arrival, and Martin's aircraft was hit in the nose during the course of marking the target. His bomb-aimer, Bob Hay, a squadron original and the bombing leader, was killed. The flight engineer also received shrapnel wounds to his legs, while the Lancaster lost all hydraulic power. Martin jettisoned the 4,000 lb cookie en route to Sardinia, where he made a safe landing at an American base. Cheshire made repeated attempts to mark the viaduct, but was beaten back by the intense ground fire. He eventually landed some markers on the beach and instructed the waiting crews to adjust their aim accordingly. One bomb fell close, but the operation was another gallant failure. They landed at Ford on the south coast to refuel, and then had to wait out the weather. S/L Bill Suggitt, a Canadian, had joined the squadron as a flight commander from 6 Group in October, and had been a regular on the order of battle ever since. He decided he could make it back to Woodhall Spa despite the weather, and took off with the station intelligence officer on board, and F/S Pulford DFM, who had flown to the Dams as Gibson's flight engineer. Ten minutes later the Lancaster impacted high ground near Chichester and seven of the eight occupants died at the scene. Suggitt lingered on for a few days before he too succumbed.

When the squadrons next went into battle on the 15/16th, it was a record-breaking effort to the 'Big City', and the penultimate raid on Berlin not only of the current campaign, but also by RAF heavy bombers for the remainder of the war. The largest force ever sent to Berlin, and the largest non-1,000 force to date, 891 aircraft, took off in the early evening with a time on target of shortly after 21.00 hours. This was the first time that over 500 Lancasters and over 300 Halifaxes had operated together, and those reaching the target, after the seventy-five early returns had departed the bomber stream, carried a record 2,600 tons of bombs. These delivered a destructive if scattered attack, in which 1,000 houses and hundreds of temporary wooden barracks were destroyed, and many outlying communities again caught stray bombs. On the debit side, forty-three bombers failed to return.

After three nights of rest over 800 aircraft set off for Leipzig on the 19/20th, and headed into the greatest disaster to afflict the Command thus far in the war. The bomber stream was met by a proportion of the enemy night-fighter force at the Dutch coast, and a running battle ensued all the way into eastern Germany. Wrongly forecast winds led to some aircraft reaching the target area too early, and they were forced to orbit, as they waited for the Pathfinders to open proceedings. Around twenty of these fell victim to the local flak batteries, and four others were lost through collisions. The attack, once under way, was inconclusive in the face of cloud cover and skymarking, but what was not in doubt, was the scale of the defeat inflicted upon Bomber Command. When all the returning aircraft had been accounted for, there was an unbelievable shortfall of seventy-eight, a new record by a clear twenty-one aircraft. This was the final straw for the Merlin-powered Mk II and V Halifaxes, which were now withdrawn from operations over Germany like the Stirlings before them, and this would temporarily remove a large part of 4 Group from the front line.

Remarkably, the unprecedented losses did not stop the Command in its tracks, and it 'got back on the horse' on the following night to take a swipe at Stuttgart with almost 600 aircraft. Central districts and those on the northern rim took something of a pounding, and the loss of a modest nine aircraft restored a little confidence to the battered squadrons. A new tactic was introduced for the next two operations in an attempt to find a way of reducing the prohibitive losses of recent weeks. The idea was to split the force into two distinct waves separated by two hours, with the intention of catching the enemy night-fighter force on the ground refuelling and rearming as the second wave passed through. On the 24/25th, an attack on the ball-bearing town of Schweinfurt failed to produce the hoped for destructions because of undershooting. However, the second wave lost 50% fewer aircraft than the first in an overall loss of thirty-three aircraft, and although this was still high, it suggested some merit in the system. On the following night similar tactics were employed against the beautiful and historic city of Augsburg, the object of 44 Squadron's epic but ill-fated daylight operation of April 1942. It became one of those relatively rare occasions, when all facets of the operational plan came together in near perfect harmony. The cultural heart of the city was ripped out and destroyed forever as architectural treasures were consigned to the flames. It was a devastatingly accurate and concentrated assault, which destroyed or damaged by fire thousands of buildings, and bombed out up to 90,000 people.

This was the last operation to be presided over at 207 Squadron by W/C Jennings, and later that day he was posted out to be replaced by W/C Wheeler DFC*. Already in his mid forties W/C Wheeler would not have seemed out of place during the first nine months or so of the war, when many of the squadron commanders were of his age, and had been in post, in many cases, for a number of years. Since that time, however, a new breed had emerged of young, dynamic officers, largely in their twenties, who had been tempered in the heat of battle, and had risen through the ranks with an impressive tally of operations behind them. In fact, W/C Wheeler was a remarkable character, who had been awarded the MC and Bar for service during the First World War, and the DFC and Bar during the current conflict. Towards the end of 1940 while still a Pilot Officer, he joined 85 Squadron, a fighter unit, which was then commanded by S/L Peter Townsend, who post-war, would be romantically linked with Princess Margaret, sister of the future Queen of England. The squadron was based at Gravesend, and was engaged on night patrols. 'Pop' Wheeler astounded his commanding officer by declaring 3,000 hours night flying, and a total of 15,000 hours in his log book altogether, at a time when few pilots could claim fifty hours at night. Most of this experience had been gained as an airline pilot with Imperial Airways. He commanded 157 Squadron, the first Mosquito night fighter unit, during the first half of 1943, before being posted to a desk job, where he languished discontentedly until wangling a posting to 207 Squadron. Sadly, W/C Wheeler's term of office would be brief.

The March account opened with a reasonably effective raid on Stuttgart by over 500 Lancasters and Halifaxes on the 1st/2nd, when thick cloud throughout the operation prevented the night fighters from making contact, and only four aircraft were lost. There was little further activity for most of the main force squadrons until the same target was visited in mid month. On the following night 617 Squadron attacked a BMW aero engine factory and an adjacent machine tool works at Albert in France. Eleven of the Lancasters were carrying 12,000 lb blockbusters, and these were put to good use, ending production at the machine tool works for the remainder of the war, and permanently reducing output at the engine factory to a paltry 10%. During the lull in main force operations, elements of the Command fired the opening salvoes of the pre-invasion campaign against the French railway system. The target on the night of the 6/7th for the Halifax brigade, including the older marques withdrawn after Leipzig, was the marshalling yards at Trappes. These were effectively bombed, as was a similar target at Le Mans on the 7/8th. 617 Squadron's run of successful operations continued on the 10/11th at the Ricamerie needle-bearing factory at St Etienne, where all but one of the buildings on the site were destroyed or extensively damaged. Other railway installations at Le Mans were raided to good effect by over 200 Halifaxes on the 13/14th. Earlier on the 13th W/C Baxter concluded his tour as commanding officer of 106 Squadron and was replaced by W/C Piercy. The main force returned to the fray at Stuttgart on the 15/16th with over 800 aircraft, more than 600 of which were Lancasters. In contrast to the raid of two weeks earlier, this was not a successful operation after much of the bombing fell into open country. Once the night fighter force caught up with the bomber stream on the approaches to the target, the carnage began, and thirty-seven aircraft were brought down. The following night saw 617 Squadron destroy the Michelin rubber works at Clermont Ferrand, and as with the other recent raids on French targets, all the evidence was captured on film by S/L Moyna, now a regular passenger in Cheshire's Lancaster.

The first of two massive raids on Frankfurt took place on the night of the 18/19th for which 846 aircraft were detailed. The operation began with accurate Pathfinder marking, and this was exploited by the main force crews who delivered a decisive blow. Heavy damage was caused from east to west, and more than 6,000 buildings were destroyed or seriously damaged. No. 617 Squadron used the main force raid as cover for another foray into France, this time to target a powder factory at Bergerac. Incendiaries and 12,000 pounders went down with extreme accuracy, and a planned air burst of Bunny Clayton's blockbuster caused the explosives storage area to go up spectacularly, lighting up the sky for ten seconds. A nitro-cellulose explosives plant at Angouleme provided the next success for 617 Squadron two nights later, as this target also suffered near total destruction. Another force of over 800 aircraft took off for Frankfurt in the early evening of the 22nd, and inflicted even greater damage, leaving the city almost in a state of paralysis. Half of the population was deprived of the essential services of water, gas and electricity, for an extended period, and the old Frankfurt, which had developed since the Middle Ages, was obliterated. The combined cost to the Command of the two operations was fifty-five heavy bombers. Among the thirty-three missing from the latter operation was the 207 Squadron Lancaster containing W/C Wheeler, who was killed with three others. The new commanding officer was W/C Grey, who took up his appointment on the 24th. Also missing was the Bardney station commander, G/C Pleasance, who had been flying as second dickie in a 9 Squadron Lancaster. A rare failure for 617 Squadron occurred at Lyons on the 23rd/24th, when an aero-engine factory was the intended target. Cheshire had been ordered not to mark from low level, which should not have been a problem, but the flare force illuminated the wrong area, and in hazy conditions the target escaped temporarily.

The time was now at hand for Harris to launch the campaign's nineteenth and final raid on Berlin. It must have been clear for some time, that this enormous metropolis could not be 'wrecked from end to end' by bombing, at least, not with the resources available to him. There had been no concerted effort since the three raid burst at the end of January, and although this had sorely wounded the city, it had not been a mortal blow, and Berlin remained the seat and symbol of Nazi power. Nowhere were their signs of collapse, but just a grim determination to see things through. Perhaps Harris had been persuaded by his success at Hamburg, but Berlin was a different proposition. It was too modern, with wide thoroughfares and open spaces, it was concrete and less prone to burning, it was too vast, too well defended, too frequently covered by cloud, and ultimately, too far to carry the necessary weight of bombs to do the job. This final assault was by no means a token gesture, however, and more than 800 aircraft lined up for take-off in the early evening of the 24th. During the outward flight the crews became aware of unusually strong winds from the north at cruising altitude. The windfinder system existed for precisely this situation, to update Command on the state of the winds, so that corrections to the briefed speed and direction could be broadcast to the outbound bombers. The problem on this night, was that nothing on this scale had been encountered before, and the dedicated windfinder crews modified their findings, rather than be accused of error. The information received at Groups, though modified, was still not believed, and was modified further before being transmitted back to the aircraft. As a consequence, navigation from this point was based on wildly inaccurate information, and the bomber force became scattered as it was blown south of the intended track. This contributed to bombs falling over a wide area of Berlin, and over 120 outlying communities reported being hit.

The winds drove many aircraft over heavily defended areas on the way home, and two-thirds of the seventy-two missing aircraft were credited to flak batteries, providing them with their most successful night of the war. 630 Squadron suffered 5 Group's heaviest casualties on this night, when posting missing three crews. The Berlin campaign was now over, and never again would Harris send his heavy bombers to the Capital. In future, it would be the task of the Mosquitoes of 8 Group's Light Night Striking Force to harass the residents and rob them of their sleep night after night, right up until Russian troops arrived in the suburbs in April 1945. Throughout the course of the nineteen major raids and the small-scale diversion on Berlin on the night of the Magdeburg disaster in January, 5 Group dispatched a fraction over 3,000 sorties, substantially more than any other Group, and yet sustained the lowest percentage casualty rate of 4.3%. This translated into 128 missing Lancasters, of which sixteen belonged to 44 Squadron and another sixteen to 57 Squadron, while 207 Squadron lost fifteen. These figures reflected the fortunes of the three squadrons during the war as a whole. (See *The Berlin Raids*. Martin Middlebrook). 617 Squadron returned to Lyons on the following night, but confusion over the accuracy of the markers led to scattered bombing, and it was impossible to confirm that the target had been hit.

Although Berlin would not feature again, the winter campaign still had six days to run, and two more major operations for the crews to negotiate. Essen was the first of these, on the 26/27th, and the remarkable run of Oboe inspired successes against this once elusive city since March 1943 continued with another highly destructive attack. Over 1,700 houses were destroyed, and dozens of industrial buildings sustained severe damage. The operation cost only nine aircraft, but what was to follow in four nights time would not only redress the balance, but rock the Command to its foundations. In the meantime, 617 Squadron retraced the now familiar path to Lyons, and this time hit the factory with most of their bombs, destroying sixteen of twenty-two key buildings. The final operation of the winter offensive was to be a standard deep penetration raid on Nuremberg, a target visited many times before, and one, perhaps, which had still not experienced a night of devastation at the hands of Bomber Command. At briefings, crews were given a forecast of protective cloud at cruising altitude, but later, a 1409 Met Flight Mosquito crew reported that this was unlikely to materialize. Despite the warning the operation was given the green light, allowing 795 aircraft to take off in the late evening, and fly into the greatest catastrophe to afflict the Command during the entire war. A conference earlier in the day involving the Group commanders had decided upon a 5 Group inspired route, which would take the bomber stream on a long, straight leg from a point over Belgium to about fifty miles north of the target, from where the final run-in would commence. AVM Bennett, the brilliant Pathfinder AOC, was utterly and violently opposed to the plan, but despite predicting a disaster, he was overruled.

Once airborne it was not long before the crews began to note some unusual and alarming features in the conditions. These included uncharacteristically bright moonlight, combined with crystal clear visibility, which enabled them to observe the other aircraft in the stream, something to which they were rarely accustomed. The forecast cloud did, indeed, fail to appear, but formed instead beneath the bomber stream as a white backdrop, silhouetting the aircraft like flies on a tablecloth. If this were not enough, condensation trails began to form in the cold, clear air, further advertising the bombers' presence. The final insult was the reappearance of the jet stream winds, which had so adversely effected the Berlin raid a week earlier. On this night they blew from the south, breaking the cohesion of the bomber stream, and driving aircraft well to the north of their intended track. Again the wind-finders were unable to cope with the speed of the wind, and modified the findings transmitted back to HQ. Here, as had happened the week before, the figures were disbelieved, and were again modified before being sent back to the aircraft. The result was, that many crews, through either failing to detect the effects of the wind, or refusing to believe the evidence, wandered up to fifty miles north of track, and consequently, turned towards Nuremberg from a false position.

Perhaps of greater significance, was the fact that the disputed route passed close to two night fighter holding beacons, and this, together with the conditions, handed the bomber force on a plate to the waiting enemy. The carnage began over Charlerois in Belgium, and continued all the way to the target, the burning wreckage of RAF bombers on the ground sign-posting the way. Eighty-two aircraft fell during the outward flight and around the target area, and together with the fifty-two early returns, this dramatically reduced the numbers available to attack the city. Other absentees from the target were around 120 crews, most of whom had probably been unaware of their true position when turning towards Nuremberg. At the appointed time, they found themselves over a built-up area, which, on seeing a number of target indicators, they took to be the target. It was, in fact, Schweinfurt, some fifty miles to the north-west, and it was only on return, that the majority discovered their error. In the event, Schweinfurt escaped lightly, as did Nuremberg, but the surviving aircraft did at least face a considerably reduced level of opposition on the way home. The damage had been done, however, and ninety-five aircraft were lost, while others were written off in crashes at home, or with battle damage too severe to repair. 5 Group's contribution was 201 Lancaster sorties, of which twenty-one failed to return, 106 and 630 Squadrons sharing the highest losses of three aircraft each. 50 Squadron also lost three, but one was to a crash on take-off after a tyre burst, and the crew walked away.

The operations now facing the crews were in marked contrast to what had been endured over the winter. The frequent deep penetration forays into Germany on dark, often dirty nights were to be replaced by mostly shorter range hops to France and Belgium in improving weather conditions. An added bonus was that these targets, unlike Berlin, Frankfurt, Nuremberg, Schweinfurt, Augsburg, Leipzig and Stuttgart, would fall within the range of Oboe. The main fly in the ointment as far as the crews were concerned was a diktat from on high, which decreed that most such operations were worthy of counting as just one third of a sortie towards the completion of a tour. Until this flawed and ridiculous policy was rescinded, mutterings of discontent pervaded the bomber stations. The view from the top, that operations against French and Belgian targets would be a 'piece of cake' would not be borne out. They would prove to be equally demanding in their way, and require of the crews a greater commitment to accuracy to avoid as far as possible friendly civilian casualties. Now that the entire Command was available to concentrate on the Transportation Plan it would proceed apace, and despite the prohibitive losses of the winter, the bomber force was in remarkably fine fettle to face its new challenge. Harris was now in the enviable position of being able to achieve that which had eluded his predecessor, namely to attack multiple targets simultaneously with forces large enough to make an impact. He could assign targets to individual Groups, to Groups in tandem, or to the Command as a whole, as dictated by operational requirements, and whilst pre-invasion considerations dominated, Harris was never likely to entirely shelve his favoured policy of city-busting.

Now that Cochrane had successfully tested the low-level visual marking method with 617 Squadron, he took the idea to Harris, who authorized a Mosquito for Cheshire to use in place of a Lancaster. Harris had it in mind, that 617 Squadron could act as a marker squadron for the whole Group, as well as operate independently, and 5 Group's first operation in April was to test the system out. The target was an aircraft factory at Toulouse, for which 144 Lancasters were detailed from the whole Group, including 617 Squadron. The marking was carried out by Cheshire in a Mosquito, and the accurate and concentrated bombing left the factory severely damaged. The operation proved, that ordinary front-line crews could hit a small target without undergoing special training, as long as the markers were accurate. On learning of the successful outcome of the operation Harris began the process of giving 5 Group an independent role. He earmarked the former 5 Group squadrons 83 and 97 for a return to 5 Group on permanent loan from the Pathfinders to act as the Group's heavy illuminator and marker units, along with 627 Squadron for the low-level Mosquito role. This was a bitter blow to the Pathfinder chief AVM Bennett, and it served to deepen the already publicized rift between himself and Cochrane. Both were brilliant men, but they held opposing views on target marking. Bennett believed the low-level approach to be too dangerous, while Cochrane accepted the risks, and considered them justified in the interests of operational efficiency. He was also confident in the ability of the fast and small Mosquito to slither its way through the defences largely unmolested.

The changes would not take place until later in the month of April, and in the meantime the new offensive got under way on the night of the 9/10th. Over 200 aircraft from 3, 4, 6 and 8 Groups attacked the Lille-Delivrance goods station, while elements from all the Groups went for the marshalling yards at Villeneuve-St-Georges, Paris. The former resulted in severe damage to buildings and installations, and over 2,000 items of rolling stock were destroyed. Adjacent residential districts were also hit by stray bombs, however, and 456 French civilians lost their lives. The danger of collateral damage was ever present, and it was a problem without a satisfactory solution. It was a similar story at the night's other target, although the death toll among civilians was substantially lower. On the following night four railway yards were attacked in France and one in Belgium. 5 Group was assigned to Tours, where serious damage was inflicted for the loss of one aircraft. 617 Squadron went to a signals equipment depot at St Cyr on this night, and destroyed it with their 8,000 lb blockbusters. Aachen, an important railway centre, provided a return to Germany for the Command for the first time since the Nuremberg disaster. On the night of the 11/12th it was subjected to its worst raid of the war to date at the hands of over 300 aircraft drawn from 1, 3, 5 and 8 Groups. Minor operations occupied the next few nights, and it was during this period, on the 14th, that the Command became officially subject to the dictates of SHAEF for the invasion period. Much to Harris's annoyance, it would remain thus shackled until the Allied forces were sweeping towards the German frontier at the end of the summer. On the 15th W/C Fisher completed his tour as commanding officer of 57 Squadron, having guided it through the tribulations of the winter campaign, and W/C Humphreys stepped into the breach. On the same day 61 Squadron moved back to Skellingthorpe, where it would spend the remainder of the war.

On the 17th 619 Squadron moved out of Coningsby and into Dunholme Lodge. This was to make room for 83 and 97 Squadrons to make Coningsby their new home. The other ex-Pathfinder recruits, 627 Squadron, had already taken up residence on the 15th just down the road at Woodhall Spa, where they would share the facilities with 617 Squadron. The 8 Group crews, although retaining their Pathfinder status and badge, were dismayed at being posted to 5 Group. They were justly proud of their elite past, and as few if any members of the two heavy squadrons had been with them during their 5 Group days, they felt no loyalty towards their new masters. As far as 5 Group was concerned, it had always believed itself to be the elite of Bomber Command, and probably felt, that the newcomers should view the move not only as a promotion, but also a privilege! All resentment might have been quickly soothed, had the newcomers' arrival been handled more diplomatically, but scarcely had they tumbled out of their transports before they were summoned to the briefing room. Here, they were subjected to a humiliating lecture by the base commander, Air Commodore Bobby Sharpe, a man with no relevant operational experience. Rather than welcoming them as brothers in arms, he harangued them about their bad 8 Group habits, and told them to buckle down to learning 5 Group ways. This was an insult to highly qualified and experienced crews, who were used to handling the most complex of tasks under operational conditions. The episode soured relations between the squadrons and the Group, and although a grudging loyalty would develop in time, it took longer than necessary, and the whole situation could have been avoided. From this moment, 5 Group was known somewhat disparagingly in 8 Group circles as the 'Independent Air Force' and 'The Lincolnshire Poachers'.

627 Squadron had been formed in 8 Group at Oakington on the 12th of November 1943, from C Flight of 139 Squadron. AVM Bennett was planning to beef up his Mosquito strength to enable him to form the Light Night Striking Force in 1944. The highly respected and popular W/C Elliott

was posted in on the 17th from his command of the Pathfinder Navigation Training unit, and he was still at the helm when the move came to 5 Group. He, and the other commanding officers of the new 5 Group recruits, W/C Deane of 83 and W/C Carter of 97 refused to allow their crews to operate that night, the 18/19th, against the railway yards at Juvisy, and the operation went ahead successfully with 8 Group Oboe Mosquitoes providing the initial reference, and 617 Squadron Mosquitoes, now numbering four, the low-level marking. The Group operated with its new structure for the first time on the 20th/21st, a busy night for the Command as a whole. The main target was Cologne, for which 379 Lancasters and Mosquitoes were detailed from 1, 3, 6 and 8 Groups. Meanwhile, two predominantly Halifax operations involving a total of 370 aircraft were mounted against railway yards at Ottignies and Lens. Finally, 5 Group carried out a two-phase assault on railway yards at La Chapelle near Paris. The two waves were separated by an hour, and a number of Pathfinder Oboe Mosquitoes were again on hand to provide an initial reference point. W/C Cheshire and F/L Fawke of 617 Squadron provided the low-level marking for the first wave, while S/L Shannon and F/L Kearns performed the same task for the second wave. Some communications problems between the various elements of the force had to be overcome, but thereafter, the attack proceeded according to plan and was a success.

The real test for the marking system would come at a heavily defended German target, and Brunswick was selected for this purpose on the night of the 22nd/23rd, while almost 600 other aircraft attended to Düsseldorf. Although the 617 Squadron marking was accurate, a thin layer of cloud and communications difficulties between the various elements of the force led to only a modest proportion of the bombing finding the mark. 61 Squadron appointed a new commanding officer on the 22nd in the person of W/C Doubleday, one of many Australians to grace Bomber Command and attain leadership of a squadron. While over 600 aircraft from the other Groups carried out an ineffective attack on Karlsruhe on the 24/25th, 5 Group tested its marking system again at Munich. This time the main force plastered the centre of the city after accurate marking by W/C Cheshire in the face of murderous light flak. Over 1,100 buildings were destroyed, and this operation probably sealed the award to Cheshire of the Victoria Cross at the conclusion of his tour in July. Six other 617 Squadron crews carried out a diversion at Milan on this night, employing four H2s equipped Lancasters on temporary loan, and one of the original prototype dams-modified aircraft. Another busy night of operations on the 26/27th saw almost 500 aircraft pound Essen, while a Halifax main force continued the pre-invasion campaign at Villeneuve-St-Georges railway yards and 5 Group went to Schweinfurt. Having been present at the last three targets to carry out windowing and flak suppression, whilst also watching the 'masters' at work, 627 Squadron was operating in the low-level marking role for the first time. Sadly, it was not a successful debut, and strong winds hampered the heavy illuminator and marker crews' efforts as well. The operation was a costly failure from which twenty-one Lancasters, or 9.3% of the force, failed to return. Hardest hit was 106 Squadron with five missing crews, followed by 49 and 83 Squadrons with three each.

As 106 Squadron's ME669 began the long journey home it was attacked by a night fighter. A fierce fire broke out between the starboard inner engine and the fuselage, which threatened to blow the Lancaster apart. Flight engineer Sgt Norman Jackson took it upon himself to deal with the problem, and gained his captain's permission to climb out onto the wing with a fire extinguisher to tackle the blaze. His crew mates clung on to the rigging lines of his parachute as he edged his way along the fuselage, fighting to maintain a grip in the two hundred mile an hour slip stream. Amazingly, he managed to drop onto the wing, but he lost the extinguisher and found himself in danger of being engulfed by the flames. Badly burned, he lost his tenuous grip and was swept off the training edge of the wing. His crew mates released the rigging lines and watched Jackson being snatched away. There was now no option but to abandon the doomed Lancaster, and four of the crew managed to do so safely. The pilot, F/O Mifflin, and one other were found in the wreckage, while their colleagues became PoWs. Jackson survived his descent at the end of a burning parachute, but broke his ankle in a heavy landing, and was tended to by a woman and her daughter until the authorities came. Jackson spent many months in hospital, but made a complete recovery, and returned home with the others at war's end. It was then that his story was told and he was awarded the Victoria Cross.

May began for 5 Group with successful attacks on two factories at Toulouse and one at Tours on the 1st/2nd. 49 Squadron began the month with a new commanding officer, W/C Crocker, who, it will be recalled, had briefly commanded 630 Squadron before being screened from operations for six months. On the night of the 3rd/4th 1 and 5 Groups undertook what should have been a relatively straight-forward operation against the Panzer training camp and transport depot at Mailly-le-Camp in France. The attack was led by W/C Deane of 83 Squadron, acting as Master of Ceremonies, with W/C Cheshire of 617 Squadron controlling the low level Mosquito force, while 627 Squadron acted in a flak suppression role. The two principals attended separate briefings, which may have contributed to the later confusion, and neither seemed fully aware of the full picture, including the involvement of 1 Group's Special Duties Flight, which had been assigned its own individual aiming point. A delay arose in calling the main force in to bomb, and the communications problem was exacerbated by interference from an American Forces broadcasting station. While the main force Lancasters were milling around in the target area awaiting instructions, the enemy night fighters got amongst them, and aircraft were seen to fall in flames all over the sky. Some crews succumbed to the frustration and anxiety, and this led to a breakdown in R/T discipline, which was manifested in unauthorised and uncomplimentary comments over the radio. Once underway, the bombing was accurate and over 150 assorted buildings were hit, while thirty-seven tanks were among more than 100 vehicles destroyed. On the debit side, forty-two Lancasters were shot down, two-thirds of them from the 1 Group second wave of the attack, but 50 Squadron also lost four. Recriminations abound to this day concerning who was to blame. Many accusations have been unjustly directed at Cheshire, but he carried out his part in the plan on time and as briefed, and advised the raid controller accordingly.

On the 7/8th a 5 Group force of fifty-eight Lancasters attacked an ammunition dump at Salbris. The bombing was accurate, but the relatively high number of seven Lancasters failed to return, four of them from 106 Squadron. Two nights later the Group conducted three successful small-scale operations against factories in France, one of them the Gnome & Rhone aero engine factory at Gennevilliers. The night of the 10/11th involved all the Groups attacking railway targets at five locations. 5 Group went to Lille, where a successful outcome was marred by the loss of twelve Lancasters. 467 Squadron lost three, its highest casualties to date from one operation, and 463 Squadron also lost three, making this Waddington's worst night of the war as home to the Australians. One particularly sad fact was that of the eighty-four crewmen posted missing by the Group, only one survived. On the following night 467 Squadron's commanding officer, the now Group Captain Balmer, failed to return in LL792 from a raid on a military camp at Bourg-Leopold in Belgium. Haze forced the Master Bomber to call a halt for fear of civilian casualties after only half of the force of 190 Lancasters had bombed. Balmer's aircraft blew up after being attacked by a night fighter during the bombing run, and all eight men on board were killed. Later on the 12th W/C Brill became the new commanding officer on posting from 463 Squadron. He had previously served with 460 Squadron RAAF, and as a Pilot Officer had been the first in that squadron to be awarded the DFC for his courage during an operation against the Gnome & Rhone factory at Gennevilliers in Paris on the 29/30th of May 1942. The pace slackened somewhat over the following nights until the 19/20th, when eight separate operations were mounted against railway targets, two of them by 5 Group. At Amiens cloud hampered the Master Bomber's view of the proceedings, and he called the attack off before even half the force had bombed. At Tours, where the target was in the centre of the town, the crews were ordered to take great care to avoid collateral destruction. The target was left severely damaged, and inevitably, some bombs fell outside of the yards.

The first major assault on Duisburg since the Ruhr campaign a year earlier fell on the city on the 21st/22nd. Carried out by 500 aircraft from 1, 3, 5 and 8 Groups it caused severe damage, but resulted in twenty-nine missing Lancasters, thus proving that the Ruhr had lost none of its sting. On the following night, Dortmund was likewise raided for the first time in a year, and also sustained heavy damage. 5 Group was busy elsewhere on this night, attempting to deliver a telling blow against the somewhat elusive town of Brunswick, but unexpected cloud and communications difficulties led to another failure, and almost all of the bombs fell in the surrounding countryside. Of 5 Group's fourteen missing aircraft, three each came from 57 and 207 Squadrons. On the 23rd W/C Jeudwine was posted to 54 Base at Coningsby, where he would join 5 Group's Master Bomber fraternity, and he was replaced as commanding officer at 619 Squadron by W/C Maling. Aachen was pounded by over 400 aircraft on the 24/25th, while 5 Group sent small forces to the Philips factory at Eindoven and the Ford motor works at Antwerp. The former raid was abandoned and the latter failed, but at least no aircraft were lost. With the invasion fast approaching, attention turned to coastal defences, both in an attempt to nullify them, and, more importantly, to reinforce the enemy belief that the main thrust would come in the Pas-de-Calais. For this reason most of the effort against coastal batteries was directed at targets well away from the intended invasion beaches, and only at the last minute would those in Normandy be attacked. On the last night of the month 5 Group sent a small force to bomb the battery at Maisy, between what would be the Omaha and Utah beaches. In the event it was found to be cloud-covered, and only a handful of aircraft bombed. In a simultaneous attack the Group bombed a railway junction at Saumur, and both operations were concluded without loss.

Invasion considerations dominated the first week of June, and 5 Group opened its account with a small-scale return to the railway junction at Saumur on the night of the 1st/2nd. A signals station at Ferme-d'Urville was also attacked on this night by 4 Group Halifaxes, but the operation failed, and it was left to 5 Group to wipe out the site two night's later. W/C Elliott relinquished command of 627 Squadron on the 3rd, and was succeeded by W/C Curry. Four coastal batteries were attacked on the 4/5th, including the one at Maisy, to which 5 Group was again assigned. The target was found to be cloud-covered, but was bombed on Oboe-laid skymarkers with inconclusive results. Over 1,000 Bomber Command aircraft were aloft on D-Day Eve, the 5/6th, to attack ten coastal batteries in support of Operation Overlord. No direct reference was made to the invasion at briefings, but strict instructions were given about maintaining flight levels, and that no bombs were to be jettisoned over the sea. Aircraft were taking off throughout the night, and those returning in dawn's early light were rewarded with a sight of both the giant armada churning its way sedately across the Channel below and American bombers heading for the French coast. There had been little intervention by night fighters, but a JU88 shot down 97 Squadron's W/C Carter in ND739, a Lancaster containing a highly experienced and decorated crew including the squadron gunnery and signals leaders. There were no survivors from among the eight men on board.

617 Squadron also took part in the proceedings on this night in what was in some ways its most demanding yet unspectacular operation. Operation Taxable was one of two Bomber Command spoofs to confuse and mislead the enemy over the location and heading of the invasion force. It required the crews to simulate a fleet of ships approaching at eight knots towards

the French coast at Cap d'Antifer. This was achieved by flying to the most exacting standards of speed, track and timing, and dropping window at precise intervals for two of the four and a half hours they were aloft. The intention was to present a steady return on German radar screens, which, in the darkness could not be verified visually. The force was split into two sections of eight aircraft each. The first section, headed by Cheshire, flew line abreast at 180 mph, with a separation between aircraft of two miles. Window was dispensed at the rate of one bundle every five seconds. After a seven minute leg all aircraft turned to port to adopt a reciprocal course for six minutes, and then resumed the original heading for a further seven minutes and so on. The second section followed eight miles behind mirroring exactly the actions of the first section. Each Lancaster carried two pilots and up to a dozen crew members. Further along the coast 3 Group's 218 Squadron conducted Operation Glimmer in similar manner.

A further 1,000 aircraft were in action on D-Day Night, when nine separate locations were bombed to disrupt enemy communications. The night of the 8/9th offered 617 Squadron an opportunity to reacquaint itself with Barnes Wallis. In order to inhibit the enemy's ability to bring reinforcements to threaten the Normandy beachhead, it was necessary to cut the railway access through the Saumur tunnel between Tours and Angers. Wallis's new 12,000 lb medium capacity Tallboy was now ready for action, a sleek, shark-like giant of a weapon designed to reach supersonic speed in freefall and penetrate deep into the ground to cause an earthquake effect, whose shockwave would literally shake an objective into collapse. Twenty-one of the Squadrons Lancasters were loaded with one each. while a further six, including Martin's Dams aircraft, ED909, were loaded with 1,000 pounders to be employed against a nearby bridge. A number of 83 Squadron aircraft provided the illumination for the hastily put-together operation, and Cheshire was on hand in his Mosquito to mark the target with red spotfires. The operation was successful according to post raid reconnaissance, which showed a massive hole in the roof of the tunnel and road and railway access cut. It was believed that the tunnel remained out of action for a number of months, but documents recovered after the war suggested that the line had been restored to use fairly quickly, but the Germans had purposely left an impression of disuse. A railway junction at Etampes was the objective for 5 Group on the 9/10th, when stray bombs resulted in severe damage to part of the town.

A new oil campaign was opened by 300 Lancasters and Mosquitoes from 1, 3 and 8 Groups on the 12/13th. The target was the Nordstern synthetic oil plant at Gelsenkirchen, and a stunningly accurate attack brought a halt to the production of much needed aviation fuel for several weeks. The importance of this industry to the German war effort was always reflected in the resolute defence on hand to meet the bombers, and this would be brought home to 5 Group in the most painful fashion a few nights hence. On this night, however, 5 Group was in action against railway communications at Poitiers and Caen, just two of six similar targets being attacked simultaneously. The first daylight operations since the departure from Bomber Command of 2 Group a year earlier were mounted against Le Havre on the evening of the 14th. The port was home to the fast motor-torpedo type light naval craft, which posed a threat to Allied shipping serving the invasion beachhead. 617 Squadron opened the attack ahead of a predominantly 1 Group first wave, and 3 Group followed up as darkness fell. The operation was an outstanding success, and the few surviving craft removed themselves along the coast to Boulogne. Later that night elements of 5 Group joined in attacks on enemy troop positions, while other forces continued with the railway campaign. Almost 300 aircraft repeated the slaughter of the E-Boats at Boulogne on the evening of the 15th, when 5 Group again played a small part. Ten 617 Squadron crews dropped Tallboys amidst a degree of confusion caused by cloud and contradictory orders by Cheshire and Munro as to whether to continue or abandon the attack, and the remainder brought their precious Tallboys home. Meanwhile a second contingent from the Group attacked a fuel storage site at Châtellerault with moderate success. Earlier in the day W/C Porter relinquished command of 9 Squadron in favour of W/C Bazin, who would see the squadron through to the end of hostilities. He had served a tour with Fighter Command, during which he was awarded the DFC, and had later volunteered for a posting to bombers. The citation for his DSO in 1945 would make mention of his leadership from the front, and his commitment to the training of his crews.

Another new campaign, or perhaps more accurately, the resumption of an old campaign begun in the previous December against flying bomb launching and storage sites in France, was opened on the 16/17th by elements from 1, 4, 5, 6 and 8 Groups. While this was in progress a second force attacked the Ruhr oil refinery at Sterkrade/Holten, but failed to cause serious damage in the face of difficult conditions. 463 Squadron appointed W/C Donaldson as its new commanding officer on the 18th at the departure of W/C Kingsford-Smith. W/C Donaldson's tenure would only last one week, while W/C Kingsford-Smith would return to the operational scene in April 1945. On the evening of the 19th 617 Squadron attacked a target at Watten, which had originally been intended for the storage of V2s. Attacks during the previous year had caused so much damage, however, that the site, once completed, was now to be used to produce liquid oxygen for the rocket weapon. The operation did not proceed according to plan, and no Tallboys fell within fifty yards of the structure.

5 Group's participation in the oil offensive had to wait until the night of the 21st/22nd. Two operations were planned, one by 133 Lancasters at Wesseling near Cologne, and the other by a similar number at Scholven-Buer in the Ruhr. Each force included a handful of 101 Squadron ABC Lancasters from 1 Group, and a number of 8 Group Oboe Mosquitoes were on hand at Scholven. The intention was to use the low-level visual marking method at both targets, but in the event, low cloud prevented this and in so doing

demonstrated the system's one major flaw. Bombing at Wesseling proceeded by H2s, and by Oboe skymarking at Scholven. Neither attack achieved the desired results, although German reports suggested a useful degree of damage. The Wesseling force was hacked to pieces by night fighters, particularly over Holland, and lost thirty-seven of its number, a massive 28% of those dispatched. Three squadrons, 44, 49 and 619 each lost six aircraft. 57 Squadron also lost six, but one was a ditching off the east coast from which the crew was rescued. 207 Squadron posted missing five crews and 630 Squadron four, plus a fifth Lancaster which was safely abandoned by its crew on return. Among the missing was the 49 Squadron commanding officer, W/C Crocker, who died with his second-tour crew and a BBC correspondent. Later that day S/L Botting was promoted from Flight Commander to take the helm, and he would remain in post for the remainder of the war. 50 and 97 Squadrons had also welcomed new commanding officers on the previous day. W/C Heward moved from the former to the latter as the late and lamented Jimmy Carter's replacement, while W/C Frogley took up the reigns at 50 Squadron. W/C Heward was an exacting and some say humourless man, and a stickler for discipline. There is a suggestion that his appointment was intended to lick 97 Squadron into shape, and banish for good any lingering 8 Group attitudes.

Flying bomb sites dominated the remainder of the month, but 5 Group found itself attacking a railway yard at Limoges on the 23rd/24th. In the late afternoon of the 24th 617 Squadron headed for a V2 storage site at Wizernes, where they delivered a number of direct hits and near misses to leave it in ruins. Seven separate flying bomb sites were attacked that night, including those at Pommerval and Prouville, which were the objectives for elements from 5 Group. 463 Squadron's W/C Donaldson failed to return from the latter, but all seven men escaped with their lives, and W/C Donaldson and three others evaded capture. The squadron also lost two other aircraft, and 9 Squadron also had three empty dispersals as a stark reminder of the fortunes of war. W/C Forbes became 463 Squadron's new commanding officer. He had risen through the ranks with remarkable speed, having been a Flying Officer at 467 Squadron at the time of the Peenemünde raid ten months earlier. 617 Squadron was back in action on the morning of 25th, W/C Cheshire flying his Mustang for the first time. The target was the V-Weapon storage site at Siracourt, which was dealt with in typical fashion. Over 700 aircraft were engaged at six flying bomb sites on the night of the 27/28th, including one at Marquise for which the 5 Group crews were briefed.

The flying bomb store in caves at St Leu d'Esserent, once used to grow mushrooms, became 5 Group's first target in July on the night of the 4/5th. The attack was led by 617 Squadron, whose Tallboys were intended to smash through the 25 feet thick roof, while the 1,000 lb bombs carried by the 230 main force Lancasters devastated the general area and blocked all access to the site. The operation was successful, but night fighters accounted for thirteen aircraft. The 6th was devoted to attacks on V-Weapon sites by more than five hundred aircraft, and 617 Squadron was assigned to a V-3 supergun target at Mimoyecques. The target was difficult to identify because of the craters from previous attacks, and the fact that it consisted of deep shafts cut into the earth covered by a concrete slab presenting a very small visual footprint. Nevertheless, Tallboys rained down onto it, and it was put out of action for good. Although they was unaware at the time, this was the final operation of the war for Cheshire, Shannon, Munro and McCarthy.

The night of the 7/8th brought a return for 5 Group to the flying bomb store at St Leu, where a bloody nose had resulted from the last effort three nights earlier. Worse was to follow this time, however, when the target was attacked by 200 Lancasters and thirteen Mosquitoes. The operation was controlled by the former 9 Squadron commanding officer, W/C Porter, who was now on the staff at 54 Base, Coningsby, home of the 5 Group Master Bomber fraternity. The attack succeeded in cutting all communications to the store, but did so at a cost of twenty-nine Lancasters and two Mosquitoes after the force was again intercepted by night fighters. No. 55 Base posted missing five 207 Squadron crews from Spilsby, three from 57 Squadron at East Kirkby, and one from 630 Squadron. The last mentioned crew was that of the commanding officer W/C Bill Deas, who was killed along with five others in NE688, the wireless operator alone escaping with his life to be taken prisoner. The loss of such an experienced officer, on his sixty-ninth operation, was a bitter blow to the squadron, but the best commanding officers led from the front, exposing themselves to the same risks as the rank and file crews. Many of the finest squadron and flight commanders were lost to Bomber Command in this way, and rarely a week passed without at least one being posted missing in action. Also on the 5 Group casualty list as a result of the St Leu operation were three Lancasters each from 9, 44 and 50 Squadrons. Earlier that evening the first of the major operations in support of the ground forces had been directed at enemy strong points around Caen. The decision to bomb open ground and the northern rim of the town rather than the fortified villages, rendered the operation relatively ineffective.

There was little to occupy the Group over the next few nights, and during this brief lull a new crew arrived in the 5 Group fold to begin a tour of operations. Their experiences would be largely typical of those who survived service with Bomber Command during the second half of 1944, one of the most intense operational periods of the entire war, and we will observe the campaign through them. After completing a heavy conversion course at Swinderby on Stirlings, F/O Davey and his crew were posted back down the A46 to No. 5 Lancaster Finishing School at the former operational station at Syerston. Here they amassed the impressive total of twelve and a half hours on Lancasters between the 4th and 10th of July, before being posted to Dunholme Lodge and 44 Squadron. The other members of the crew were Sgt Jack Rawcliffe, flight engineer, F/L Grant, navigator, who wore pilot's wings, and had already completed a tour in that capacity, F/O Roddie, bomb-aimer, Sgt Oliphant, wireless operator, F/S Arnold, mid-upper gunner and Sgt Morley, rear gunner. We will meet them later, and follow them through their tour.

On the 12th W/C Cheshire was officially posted from 617 Squadron to 5 Group HQ, from where he proceeded to a Senior Commanders course at Cranwell. He had now completed 100 operations in a glittering career spanning four operational tours, and this was to be capped by the award of the Victoria Cross two months later. Cheshire was succeeded on the day of his departure by the highly experienced W/C James Tait, who was apparently known to some as 'Willie'. In keeping with commanders since Gibson, Tait had 4 Group blood coursing through his veins, and had served previously with a number of its leading squadrons. It was no easy matter to find an officer of the appropriate stature to command such an elite body of men, and could step easily into the shoes of someone as unique as Cheshire. Tait was such a man, who had commanded 51 Squadron briefly between December 1940 and January 1941, and led the already-mentioned ill-fated Operation Colossus from Malta, the airborne undertaking by the SAS in February 1941. He was posted to 35 Squadron shortly after its re-formation to introduce the Halifax to operations, and took command of 10 Squadron in April 1942, while its incumbent leader, W/C Don Bennett, now AOC the Pathfinders, was evading capture to return home from Norway. He then moved on to the command of 78 Squadron in July, and remained in post until November. Thereafter he completed a spell at 22 O.T.U. before joining 5 Group as Base Operations Officer at Waddington, where he apparently managed to notch up a number of further operations. Also departing 617 Squadron during the month were the three flight commanders and squadron founder members, Shannon, Munro and McCarthy. It was the end of an era. Munro went to 1690 BDTF on the 13th, McCarthy to 61 Base on the 20th, and Shannon to 27 OTU on the 24th.

W/C Blome-Jones assumed command of 630 Squadron on the 12th, and presided over his first operation that night, when 5 Group delivered an accurate attack on a railway target at Culmont-Chalindrey. At the same time 1 Group attempted to destroy a railway junction at Revigny, but the attack was abandoned partway through because of cloud, and a further attempt two nights later would also fail because of identification problems. This was to have serious consequences for 5 Group a few nights hence. Tait led 617 Squadron into battle for the first time with a return to Wizernes on the 17th. He was in the Mustang, while Gerry Fawke flew a Mosquito with sixteen Lancasters in tow. Tallboys peppered the site, and although no direct hits were scored, this target would require no further attention. In the early hours of the 18th over 900 aircraft took off for a massive effort in support of the British Second Army, as it prepared to launch Operation Goodwood. The targets were five fortified villages to the east of Caen. American aircraft were also involved in the morning's proceedings, but the bulk of the 6,500 tons of bombs was delivered by Bomber Command. The attacks were accurate, and among the most effective of the post-invasion tactical operations. Oil targets at Wesseling and Scholven-Buer occupied much of 1, 6 and 8 Groups that night, while other aircraft from 1, 3, 5 and 8 Groups maintained the pressure on railway communications at Aulnoye and Revigny. The two recent attacks on Revigny by 1 Group having failed, the job was now handed to an element from 5 Group. W/C Jeudwine flew as marker controller in an American P38 Lightning, and he witnessed a shocking night for his former 619 Squadron charges. Whilst the hundred-strong force succeeded in cutting the lines, and consequently communications to the front, the loss of twenty-four Lancasters represented 22% of those despatched. 619 Squadron lost five aircraft to night fighters before the target was reached, and only three of the thirty-five crewmen survived. 49 and 630 Squadrons posted missing four crews each, and 207 Squadron three.

The evening of the 19th was a momentous occasion for the Davey crew, who were about to make their operational debut, and tension was high as they clambered aboard ME694, KM-L, for the trip to a flying bomb site at Creil/Thiverny. They were part of an overall 5 and 8 Group force of 144 aircraft, whose crews were briefed to attack one of three targets, two launching sites and a supply dump, in what was left of the daylight. The Davey crew bombed at 21.32 from 18,000 feet in conditions of partial cloud cover, and returned safely after a round trip of just over four hours. 'L' had sustained flak damage along the whole length of the fuselage, but this was patched up during the course of the following day, and the Lancaster was back on top line in time for an operation that night against railway yards and a junction at Courtrai. The bombing was carried out from medium level, in the case of the Davey crew this meant 11,000 feet, and the attack appeared to be accurate. Night fighters were active, particularly on the way home, and nine of the original three hundred Lancasters failed to return, although all the 44 Squadron participants got back after another relatively short flight of a little over four hours. Invasion considerations had given Germany's cities a rest from the relentless heavy bombing it had come to expect, and none had been attacked for two months. On the evening of the 23rd over six hundred aircraft took off for Kiel, where they appeared suddenly and with complete surprise from behind an RCM screen laid on by 100 Group. The town, the docks area and the shipyards all sustained serious damage in what was the town's worst night of the war, and the success was achieved for the modest loss of just four Lancasters.

A series of three heavy raids in five nights on Stuttgart began on the following night, the 24/25th, and having sat out the Kiel trip, the Davey crew prepared for their first operation over Germany. They took off in ND578, KM-Y, and settled down for the long round trip to southern Germany of more than eight hours. Cloud was encountered over the target, and the crew found themselves coned in searchlights as they ran in to bomb at 19,500 feet shortly before 02.00 hours. They were not hit, and returned home without further incident, while twenty-one other crews were less fortunate. The attack caused heavy damage within the city, but this was surpassed twenty-four hours later, when a force of more than 500 aircraft returned. On this occasion the Davey crew was in LM625, KM-H, which carried them safely to the target, where they released their bombs at 01.57 from 20,000 feet. The return flight was without incident, and the whole trip lasted five minutes under nine hours. This was the most destructive of the three raids on Stuttgart, causing severe damage in central districts, and as events turned out, it was the least expensive. However, among the fairly modest twelve missing aircraft was one from 44 Squadron, ME694, the Lancaster used by the Davey crew for their first two operations. For Jack Rawcliffe, the flight engineer in F/O Davey's crew, this was a particularly sad night. Before joining the crew at Swinderby, he had understudied the engineer in a different crew captained by F/O Walter Buchanan. When Buchanan's crew was posted to 49 Squadron, Jack became a 'spare bod' again, and was reassigned to the Davey gang. Jack learned that Buchanan's Lancaster had also been shot down over France that night, and it was later established that none had survived. 619 Squadron's commanding officer, W/C Maling, also failed to return, but he at least survived with three of his crew as PoWs when ND935 was brought down over France. W/C Millward was appointed as his successor. Earlier in the day, at breakfast time, sixteen 617 Squadron Lancasters took off for a V-Weapon site at Watten. Tait and Fawke took of fifty and forty minutes respectively later, and on arrival Tait decided that marking was unnecessary. A number of direct hits were claimed, and these were confirmed by later photographic reconnaissance.

Only 5 Group was out in strength on the night of the 26/27th, when 178 Lancasters were detailed for an attack on the railway yards at Givors in France. The weather outbound and over the target proved to be atrocious, with electrical storms causing the St Elmo's Fire effect on propellers and fuselages. All aircraft carried navigation lights into the attack to try to avoid collisions, and handling became so difficult, that F/L Davey ordered his crew to put on their parachutes. A moderate amount of flak added to the discomfort, and a close burst left 'E' with a leaking fuel tank and damaged mainplane. The return flight was undertaken with a close eye on the fuel gauge, but a safe landing was eventually carried out at Morton-in-Marsh after a little over nine hours in the air. The last of the three raids on Stuttgart was undertaken by an all-Lancaster heavy force on the 28/29th, while a mixed Halifax/Lancaster force of 300 aircraft took on Hamburg. The Davey crew, as new arrivals on the squadron, did not qualify for their own aircraft, and were consequently in LM645 KM-P, their fifth different Lancaster in six operations. The conditions on this night contrasted starkly with those of twenty-four hours earlier, for where storm and cloud had been, there were now clear skies and bright moonlight, and these very much favoured the night fighters.

As the 490-strong 1, 3, 5 and 8 Group force approached the target across southern France, it was intercepted and a fierce air battle ensued. The Davey crew bombed the centre of a green cluster of target indicators from 17,000 feet at 02.02, and then turned for home. Touchdown at Dunholme Lodge came after eight hours and ten minutes aloft, and was accomplished safely despite a burst tyre, courtesy of a flak splinter. Thirty-nine Lancasters failed to make it back, however, most of them having fallen victim to night fighters over France on the way out, and this represented almost 8% of the force. The Hamburg contingent had been caught by the night fighters on the way home, and the bulk of the twenty-two missing aircraft were Halifaxes from 6 Group. The loss of sixty-one aircraft in a single night harked back to the dark days of the winter offensive, and must have caused some disquiet at Bomber Command HQ.

There was an early start for almost 700 crews on the 30th, after being briefed to attack six enemy positions ahead of American forces in the Villers Bocage-Caumont area. The Davey crew were once more in LM645 for the trip to their target at Cahagnes. The Master Bombers had to contend with cloud in the target area, and it became necessary to send half of the aircraft home with their bombs still aboard. The remainder released theirs on Oboe markers, but accuracy was compromised, and only two of the sites were effectively bombed. The evening of the 31st brought a return to railway targets, with a predominantly 5 Group assault on the yards at Joiny-la-Roche. The six-hour round trip was undertaken by the Davey crew in LM650 KM-M, which carried them safely home from what was described as an accurate attack. The round-the-clock operational cycle resulting from the side-by-side campaigns was taking a heavy toll of aircraft and crews in numerical terms, although, such were the numbers committed to the battle, that the percentage losses remained within acceptable parameters. Even though the Davey crew was advancing through its tour of operations seemingly without undue alarm, July had been one of a number of recent sobering months for 44 Squadron. Ten Lancasters had failed to return during the month, but happily, August would bring an end to this period of worryingly high losses, and it would not be until mid-month that the next one occurred. 617 Squadron concluded its operations for July by leading almost a hundred 5 and 8 Group aircraft to attack a V-Weapon storage site in a railway tunnel at Rilly-la-Montagne. The operation was partially successful, but marred by the loss of F/L Bill Reid VC, whose Lancaster was hit by bombs falling from a higher flying 5 Group aircraft. It took four minutes for Reid's aircraft to crash, eventually breaking up in the air. He and his wireless operator were the only survivors, and they fell into enemy hands.

The first half of August was dominated by the campaign against the flying bomb, and operations against this menace were mounted daily from the 1st to the 6th. The largest effort was by more than 1,100 aircraft against a number of large storage sites on the 3rd, and among the participating 44 Squadron crews was that of F/O Davey in LM625 KM-H. They were able to bomb visually from 16,000 feet at 14.32, collecting flak damage in the process. The mid-upper turret Perspex was smashed, but F/S Arnold escaped with superficial injuries. 617 Squadron's first outing of the month took them to a railway bridge at Etaples, which they attacked with 1,000 pounders. The target disappeared in a cloud of dust and smoke and the crews went home convinced of another resounding success. When they saw the post raid reconnaissance pictures, however, they were astounded to see the bridge still standing and apparently unscathed. The target for the 5 Group contingent in the early afternoon of the 5th was the storage site at St-Leu- d'Esserent, the scene of some recent unhappy memories for the Group. More than 700 aircraft were involved here and at a similar target in the Foret-de-Nieppe, and clear visibility provided good bombing conditions at both targets. 6 Group preceded 5 Group at St-Leu, and the Davey crew in PB192 KM-G reported being unable to see the markers. They bombed at 13.33 from 15,500 feet, and returned home from this, their tenth operation, without incident. Having survived the first half dozen or so sorties, statistics now favoured them surviving the next fifteen operations before they entered the tense period towards the end of their tour. Earlier in the war a tour could be expected to last six months to a year, but in the summer of 1944 it was completed by some in a matter of weeks, and already after less than three weeks the Davey crew was a third of the way through. 617 Squadron, meanwhile, was targeting the U-Boot pens at Brest, where the Germans, it seems, were able to refit their submarines in record time before sending them back into the Allied shipping lanes in the Atlantic. As always, the pens were heavily defended, and the bombing run was a tense affair with shells exploding all around the Tallboy-bearing Lancasters. Canadian Don Cheney's aircraft was hit, and two crew members were seriously wounded. A fierce fire in the starboard wing signalled a terminal problem, and Cheney ordered his crew to bale out. Cheney was last to leave after struggling through the roof hatch above his seat, and he landed in the sea, from where he was plucked to safety by the locals. They looked after him until the Germans were driven from the area, and he soon made it back to England to be joined by three others of his crew. Sadly, the wounded navigator and wireless operator and the rear gunner drowned. On a more positive note, the U-Boot pens received a number of direct hits from Tallboys and were severely damaged.

The target for the Davey crew's eleventh operation on the 6th was the storage site at Bois-de-Cassan. The Master Bomber for the occasion was the former 619 Squadron commanding officer, W/C Jeudwine, who favoured a P-38 Lightning as his mode of transport. Unfortunately, communications problems between him and the main force led to confusion, and half of the 200 strong force retained their bombs. The Davey crew were in LM650 KM-T, which took them to the target and back in five minutes short of four hours. 617 Squadron was U-Boot pen busting again on this day at Lorient, and it was another display of accurate bombing with Tallboys.

More than 1,000 aircraft were dispatched to the Normandy battle area on the night of the 7/8th to bomb five enemy strong points. A 44 Squadron element was assigned to an aiming point at Sequeville, which was attacked from around 7,000 feet in clear skies, but with ground haze. The Davey crew continued to work their way through the Squadron's aircraft until they found one they liked, and were trying out PD222 KM-U on this operation. As events were to prove, this particular Lancaster would survive only one more week, but it brought them safely home on this night after a four hour trip. Tait led 617 Squadron against U-Boot pens at La Pallice on the 9th, and photo-reconnaissance confirmed the collapse of a large section of roof. The went back on the afternoon of the 11th, this time carrying 2,000 lb armour piercing bombs because of a shortage of Tallboys. Another accurate attack ensued, which did little more than demonstrate the futility of throwing conventional bombs at reinforced concrete structures. They each had a Tallboy on board on the following day when the pens at Brest received further attention resulting in two direct hits.

The Davey crew was off the order of battle for ten days after Sequeville, and while they were enjoying the break, Brunswick was selected for a large-scale experiment. The massive demands on the Command during this period were most keenly felt by the Pathfinders, who were called upon to provide aircraft and crews for almost every operation. They were the only source of Oboe-equipped Mosquitoes and Lancasters, as well as heavy marker and illuminator crews, and they provided the Master Bombers and Deputies for all but 5 Group operations. They also carried out their own precision attacks, and as all of their duties put them at the forefront of activity, they inevitably sustained the loss of highly experienced men, who could not easily be replaced. The idea at Brunswick was to ascertain the ability of main force crews to locate and bomb an urban target entirely on the strength of their own H2s, without the presence of Pathfinders. Launched on the night of the 12/13th the operation by 380 Lancasters and Halifaxes was inconclusive and not overly encouraging, some bombs finding the town centre, while others hit communities up to twenty miles distant. It was also an expensive raid costing twenty-seven aircraft, among which were three from 83 Squadron. Together with losses from the night's other operations, which included attacks on Rüsselsheim by almost 300 aircraft and one against troop concentrations at Falaise by around 140, failures to return reached forty-nine aircraft from over 1,100 sorties.

The morning of the 13th brought a return to Brest for 617 squadron, whose element of thirteen Lancasters was joined by fourteen others from 9 Squadron in the first of what would become a series of joint Tallboy operations. Some crews were briefed to attack the U-Boot pens, and others the derelict French cruiser *Gueydon*. This was one of a number of ships, which, it was thought, the enemy might use to block the harbour entrance ahead of advancing American forces, and it was decided to sink them in safe positions. The *Gueydon* was straddled by a number of sticks, but there were no confirmed hits, and she was still afloat as the force withdrew. Undaunted, the two squadrons returned on the following morning for another tilt at the *Gueydon*, when the payload for each aircraft on this occasion was six 2,000 lb armour-piercing bombs. A number of hits were scored, but the vessels remained afloat.

The afternoon of the 14th saw 800 aircraft engaged in support of Canadian forces in the Falaise area. It was on this occasion that friendly bombs inflicted casualties on troops positioned in a quarry. Their identification smoke was the same colour as that from the marker bombs, but it is also clear, that some crews ignored instructions given at briefings, and a number of squadron commanders were apparently disciplined afterwards as a result. That evening, 5 Group sent 150 Lancasters to Brest to sink the French battleship *Clemenceau* and the cruiser *Gueydon* in the harbour. With the ground forces firmly established and pressing eastwards, Harris could now think again about a gradual return to industrial Germany. In preparation for his new night offensive, he launched a thousand aircraft by daylight on the 15th to attack nine airfields in Holland and Belgium. Losses amounted to just three aircraft, two of them from Deelen, one of the targets assigned to 5 Group. Nos 617 and 9 Squadron joined forces on the 16th for another tilt at the pens at La Pallice, but cloud made it difficult to identify the target and Tait sent the boys home. That night more than 400 Lancasters raided the city and port of Stettin, a target which never seemed to escape lightly at the hands of the Command. On this night 1,500 houses and a few dozen industrial premises were destroyed, and five ships were sunk in the harbour. A simultaneous raid on Kiel by over 300 Lancasters and Halifaxes caused serious damage to the docks area, including the shipyards, but many bombs also fell outside of the town. An additional operation on this night involved a small force of Lancasters mining the Swinemünde Canal. Leading the proceedings as Master Bomber was W/C Porter, who had guided 9 Squadron through the harrowing Battle of Berlin period. He was flying a 97 Squadron Lancaster, which was hit at low level by fire from flak ships moored along the canal, and crashed with the loss of all on board. The fact that a modest ten aircraft were lost from the two major raids involving more than 800 aircraft suggested that the days of prohibitive bomber casualties might be over. Nos 617 and 9 Squadron returned to La Pallice on the afternoon of the 18th, and scored two more confirmed direct hits with Tallboys but no penetration.

The Davey crew returned to the fray also on the 18th, for an afternoon raid by elements of 5 Group against a supply dump at L'Isle Adam near Paris. Flying in yet another different aircraft, PB424 KM-X, they experienced a relatively uneventful trip out, although later commented on the leader's tendency to wander off track. The bombs were delivered from 11,000 feet at 14.10, and an excellent raid was reported at debriefing. That night Bremen was pounded by over 250 Lancasters and Halifaxes, and more than 8,000 houses were reduced to rubble. A week of minor operations ensued, during which, on the 24th, a 617 Squadron element targeted the pens at Ijmuiden used by the enemy's light, fast surface fleet. Tait had foregone the use of a Mosquito, and had been flying a Lancaster since the operation on the 12th. Only eight aircraft were employed on this raid, and their Tallboys inflicted severe damage on the structure. The Command was back out in strength on the 25/26th to attack targets in Germany and France. The main operation was carried out by 400 Lancasters from 1, 3, 6 and 8 Groups against the Opel motor works at Rüsselsheim, while 200 aircraft of 5 Group attacked the nearby city of Darmstadt. A predominantly Halifax force of 300 aircraft took off some hours later to attend to coastal batteries around Brest. Additional minor operations brought the total number of sorties to a new record for a single night of 1,311. Some parts of the Opel factory were put out of action for several weeks, but stocks of ready made components prevented a major loss of production. Still searching for the perfect Lancaster, the Davey crew were in PB190 KM-J on this night, and bombed the target from 9,000 feet at 01.36. The operation was a rare failure for the 5 Group method, however, probably caused by the early return of the Master Bomber and the shooting down of his two deputies. Most of the bombing missed the mark, but it would prove to be only a temporary reprieve for this southern German city. 106 Squadron had a new commanding officer to preside over this operation, W/C Stevens having replaced W/C Piercy earlier in the day.

It had been a nine hour trip to Darmstadt and back, but the following night brought an even longer one as 5 Group sent a force of 174 Lancasters to the eastern Baltic port of Königsberg, where the enemy was landing supplies for its eastern front. The Davey crew were again in 'J' for this operation, which represented the halfway point in their tour. The route to the target passed over neutral Sweden, where the obligatory gesture of annoyance was betokened by a flak barrage exploding well below the bomber stream. The attack was carried out from quite low level, in the case of the Davey crew from 7,250 feet, and the resulting fires could be seen 200 miles into the return flight. The east coast was fog bound as the exhausted crews arrived back, and the Davey crew eventually put down on the 8 Group station at Wyton after ten and a half hours aloft. It turned into a bad night for 50 Squadron after four of its crews failed to return. Later on the 27th Tait led elements from 617 and 9 Squadrons to Brest to attack a number of ships to prevent their strategic sinking by the enemy. The final operations in the flying bomb campaign were carried out against twelve sites in the Pas-de-Calais on the 28th, and shortly afterwards the region fell under Allied control. Also on that day G/C Deane was posted from 83 Squadron to be replaced by W/C Ingham, who would be the unit's last wartime commanding officer.

There was probably a degree of surprise at briefings on 5 Group stations on the 29th, when the target map revealed Königsberg to be the destination again that night. The Davey crew, having obviously given PB190 the stamp of approval, were in this Lancaster again, and would be so for all but four of their remaining operations. Take-off for the 189 Lancasters began around 20.00 hours and continued for the next fifty minutes or so, and the target was reached at 01.30. W/C Woodroffe, one of 5 Group's most experienced Master Bombers, delayed the start of the attack for some twenty minutes because of cloud, but once the marker crews could see their four aiming points, the marking and bombing proceeded accurately. The delay allowed the night fighters time to catch the bombers over the target, and Lancasters began to fall in flames into the Bay. JB593 of 106 Squadron was one of those failing to return, and was lost without trace, presumably in the sea. The pilot was the Metheringham station commander, G/Captain McKechnie. This time it was 467 that had to bear the heaviest losses with three missing crews. Nevertheless, this highly successful operation, carried out at the limit of range with a worthwhile bomb load, left 41% of the town's housing and 20% of its industry in ruins for the loss of fifteen aircraft. It was another exhausting trip, one of the longest major operations ever mounted, and the Davey crew arrived safely home after eleven hours and twenty minutes in the air. Although the V-1 threat had now been largely nullified, the V-2 was just beginning its reign of terror, and its mobile launching sites would make it an elusive target. It was most vulnerable at its points of storage, and August's operations ended with attacks by 600 aircraft on nine sites on the 31st. The operations were mounted in the early evening, and the Davey crew bombed their target at Auchy-les-Hesdin shortly after 18.00 hours from 11,750 feet. In quite a contrast to the recent mammoth flights to north-eastern Germany, they were back home after being airborne for just three hours and fifty minutes.

September was to be dominated by the need to liberate the three major French ports of Le Havre, Boulogne and Calais, which were still in enemy hands. First, however, a 5 Group force of sixty-seven Lancasters paid a visit to Brest on the afternoon of the 2nd, and left two ships sitting on the bottom in the harbour. The Davey crew completed this, their eighteenth sortie, without incident in six hours forty minutes. Early on the following evening more than 600 aircraft pounded six airfields in southern Holland including Deelen, which the Davey crew bombed from 14,000 feet. This was considerably below the rest of the main force, but problems with PB190's starboard-outer engine prevented them from getting any higher. On the way home the engine had to be shut down and the weather deteriorated, forcing them to land at North Bickenham. The first of six attacks against enemy strong points around Le Havre took place in daylight on the 5th, and involved a predominantly Lancaster force of over 300 aircraft. A second operation was mounted on the 6th, a third on the 8th and a fourth on the 9th, although the last two-mentioned were hampered by cloud, the former being curtailed and the latter abandoned altogether. The Davey crew was off the order of battle during this period until the night of the 9/10th, when elements of 5 and 8 Groups joined forces to deliver the first of a number of crushing blows against the town of Mönchengladbach. Situated just inside the German border with Holland it was a short trip of four hours and ten minutes, and it was a momentous occasion for the crew's navigator,

F/L Grant. This was the twentieth and final trip of his second tour, and from now on a selection of spare bods would fill his seat. Almost one thousand aircraft continued the assault on Le Havre and its surrounds on the 10th, and the campaign ended on the following day with a sixth attack, after which, the German garrison surrendered to British forces.

It was also on the 11th that 617 and 9 Squadrons set off on the gruelling flight to Yagodnik in the Archangel region of north-western Russia. Using it as a launching pad they would traverse the 600 miles to Norway's Kaa Fjord wherein lay at anchor the mighty battleship *Tirpitz*. Remarkably, all the Lancasters reached the general area of Yagodnik, but not all found the airfield because of the absence of an expected guiding beacon. Two 617 and four 9 Squadron aircraft were written off in forced-landings, although without crew casualties. The Russians provided fuel for the other Lancasters dotted around the countryside, and all eventually made it into Yagodnik to await suitable weather conditions for the operation.

On the night of the 11/12th 5 Group returned to Darmstadt, the city in southern Germany that had escaped serious damage two weeks earlier. The 226 Lancasters adopted a complex system known as line-bombing, which required the force to approach on two different headings, and the individual aircraft to overshoot the aiming point by a given number of seconds. This created an even spread of bombs, and on this night produced a firestorm, which killed an estimated 12,000 inhabitants and bombed out 70,000 more. Twelve aircraft failed to return. A small-scale firestorm was also reported in Stuttgart on the following night, after a concentrated 1 and 5 Groups' raid destroyed much of the centre of the city and killed over 1,100 people. Having sat out the Darmstadt operation, the Davey crew was back on duty on this night, and delivered their bomb load from 16,000 feet at 23.15 after a twenty second overshoot. A simultaneous raid by over 350 Lancasters of 1, 3 and 8 Groups on Frankfurt was also highly destructive, but cost seventeen aircraft. Operation Paravane was mounted against the *Tirpitz* from Yagodnik on the 15th, and it was a momentous occasion for 9 Squadron's W4964, which notched up its one hundredth sortie. Having begun its career in April 1943 the Lancaster flew against the *Tirpitz* in the hands of F/L Doug Melrose, and returned safely, to eventually clock up 106 operations before becoming a ground instruction airframe. As the force closed in upon its quarry, some carrying Tallboys and others Johnny Walker mines, the defenders operated smoke pots, and the ship gradually disappeared from view just as the first bombs began to fall. One large explosion was observed by some crews, but it was impossible to make an accurate assessment of the attack. In fact, a near-miss had severely damaged *Tirpitz*, and she would never put to sea again, although this would not be appreciated by the British authorities, who would order further attacks. No aircraft were lost during the operation, but F/O Levy crashed into high ground in Norway during his return flight from Yagodnik on the 17th, and all nine men on board were killed. German positions around the port of Boulogne were pounded by over 700 aircraft in daylight also on the 17th, and the 3,000 tons of bombs were considered to have done their job. Ground forces followed up, and the port was taken a week later. This was the twenty-second trip for the Davey crew, whose captain had been promoted to Flight Lieutenant since the last operation, and it was the shortest completed operation of their tour, lasting just three hours and twenty minutes. It also signalled a break for them from operational activity until October.

On the night of the 18/19th, two hundred 5 Group Lancasters attacked the town and port of Bremerhaven for the first time, and protected by an RCM screen laid on by 100 Group, destroyed over 2,600 buildings for the loss of one Lancaster and one Mosquito. On the following night elements of 1 and 5 Groups were briefed for an operation against the twin towns of Mönchengladbach and Rheydt. The attack required a complex plan involving the marking of three aiming points, one at Rheydt and two at Mönchengladbach, each with a different colour of marker to which crews were assigned accordingly. The role of Master Bomber was inexplicably handed to W/C Guy Gibson VC, who was currently serving as base operations officer at 54 Base, Coningsby, the home of 83 and 97 Squadrons. Perhaps more significantly, it was where 5 Group's complement of Master Bombers was stationed, men of great experience, and, crucially, current experience, like Owen, who had controlled the recent raid on the same target, Jeudwine and Woodroffe. Even for these men, controlling such a complicated operation would have been challenging, but for Gibson, who was not trained as a Master Bomber, had little up-to-date operational experience, and had only a fleeting acquaintance with the Mosquito, it was asking a great deal. Gibson's arrogance and determination to get back into the war before it ended led him to dismiss the advice freely given, and for some reason, to reject the 627 Squadron Mosquito prepared for him at Woodhall Spa, and demanded another one. The illumination and marking of the aiming points at Mönchengladbach went according to plan, but at Rheydt, the primary target, unforeseen problems arose, which Gibson was not able to correct. This caused a delay, during which night fighters appeared on the scene, and three Lancasters were shot down in the target area. Some of the crews assigned to Rheydt joined in the bombing of the other aiming points, but the operation was generally successful. On the way home, Gibson's Mosquito crashed on the outskirts of Steenbergen in Holland, and he and his navigator, S/L Warwick, were killed. They lie side-by-side in the town's Catholic cemetery, where their graves are tended by Jan and Connie Van Dreeschen who live in Rotterdam.

The campaign to capture Calais began on the 20th, when more than 600 aircraft attacked enemy positions in good visibility. The next assault would take place on the 24th, but in the meantime, on the night before, over 500 aircraft from 1, 3, 4 and 8 Groups bombed the Ruhr town of Neuss to good effect. 5 Group was also active on this night, renewing acquaintances with a target of almost personal association. The Group had been attacking the

Dortmund-Ems Canal on and off since the summer of 1940, and it will be recalled, that 44 Squadron's fifth wartime commander, W/C Learoyd, had earned a Victoria Cross as a result. Now, four years on, the aircraft and weaponry were different, and this attack by 136 Lancasters and five Mosquitoes against the twin branch viaduct section at Ladbergen was led by 617 Squadron with Tallboys. They were probably responsible for the breaches, and the waterway was left drained over a six-mile stretch. Night fighters were active on this night, and three 61 Squadron Lancasters fell victim. The ace Heinz-Wolfgang Schnaufer was out and about, and shot down four bombers in the space of thirty-two minutes. His first victim was F/L Geoff Stout of 617 Squadron, who was on his way home over Holland with his Tallboy still on board. Most of the crew got out, but Stout and his navigator perished in the wreckage of NF923. Schnaufer would survive the war as Germany's leading night fighter ace with a total of 121 kills to his credit. While this operation was in progress a second 5 Group formation carried out a diversionary attack on the nearby airfield at Handorf near Münster, but this did not prevent the loss of fourteen aircraft from the main raid.

Low cloud interfered with operations against Calais on the following evening, and this persuaded some crews to come below the cloud base to bomb. Here they were forced to run the gauntlet of light flak, which claimed seven Lancasters and a Halifax, four of the former from 5 Group. Cloud was similarly disruptive on the 25th, and only a third of almost 900 aircraft were able to bomb through breaks. This was the day on which W/C Doubleday stood down as commanding officer of 61 Squadron, and W/C Pexton took up the baton. On the 26th the strength was divided between Calais and four coastal batteries at Cap Gris Nez, and returning crews reported accurate and concentrated bombing. That night 5 Group went to Karlsruhe, and devastated a large part of the city for the loss of just two Lancasters. The 27th brought further attacks on enemy positions around Calais, and raids on oil targets at Bottrop and Sterkrade. The night was given over to a 5 Group raid on Kaiserslautern, the first major operation by Bomber Command against this town, and an estimated 36% of its built-up area was reduced to rubble. The final operations against the Calais area took place on the 28th, and shortly thereafter, the port was surrendered to Canadian forces. Earlier in the day 619 Squadron moved from Dunholme Lodge to Strubby, where it would see out the war. On the last day of the month 44 Squadron made its final wartime change of address with a move to Spilsby at the southern end of the Lincolnshire Wolds, and within sniffing distance of Skegness. There were now so many operational bomber stations around Dunholme Lodge, that the overlapping circuits posed an insurmountable problem. The station at Spilsby had been completed earlier in the year, and boasted uncommonly long runways. 207 Squadron had been its only resident until the arrival of 44 Squadron, and the two units would see out the war together.

October was to bring a full-scale return to targets within Germany as a second Ruhr campaign began, and an unprecedented weight of bombs would soon fall upon those towns and cities, whose names had dominated target lists from the earliest days of strategic bombing. First, however, the Command's assistance was enlisted to capture the Belgian port of Antwerp. Access to it along the River Scheldt was barred by heavy gun emplacements, particularly those on the island of Walcheren in the estuary. A number of attacks against these small targets during September had failed to eliminate them, and it was decided instead to destroy the sea walls by bombing, and thereby to inundate the island and its defences. This would also create difficult terrain for the defenders when the ground attack began. The campaign began on the 3rd, when eight waves of thirty Lancasters each attacked the sea wall at Westkapelle. The fifth wave created a breach, and this was widened by those following. 617 Squadron arrived during the main force attack, and having established that the job was done, Tait sent his crews home with their bombs. The 3rd was also the day on which a new commanding officer was appointed at 97 Squadron. G/C Johnson, had previously commanded 49 Squadron between March and mid September 1943, and had been at Woodhall Spa since. He would now preside over 97 Squadron until after war's end. On the following morning over 200 Lancasters of 5 Group took off for Wilhelmshaven. Among them was the Davey crew, who, after a break, were entering the final phase of their tour. Cloud was encountered at the enemy coast, and crews were ordered to bomb blind on H2s. The Davey crew complied at 11.07 from 17,750 feet, knowing that the attack would be scattered and indiscriminate.

The new Ruhr offensive opened at Dortmund on the evening of the 6th, when 500 aircraft from 3, 6 and 8 Groups inflicted serious damage upon industry and communications. 5 Group was over northern Germany at the same time, delivering the final heavy raid of the war on Bremen. In clear visibility the low level visual marking system worked perfectly, and the line bombing method employed by the main force resulted in the destruction of or serious damage to around 5,000 buildings. The Davey crew bombed at 20.30 from 18,750 feet after a twenty-three second overshoot, and were back home after just four hours fifty-five minutes in the air. Following the failure of Operation Market Garden the Allied right flank was perceived to be vulnerable to attack by enemy forces via the frontier towns of Cleves and Emmerich. To forestall such an eventuality the towns were heavily bombed on the afternoon of the 7th, and left in a state of disarray. 5 Group sent an element to Walcheren to attack the sea walls at Flushing, while 617 Squadron carried out an operation against the Kembs barrage near the German/Swiss/French frontiers. Seven crews were assigned to the high force, and were briefed to deliver their Tallboys from 6/9,000 feet. Six other crews, led by Tait were to attack in pairs from a few hundred feet, and this exposed them to the full fury of anti-aircraft fire from the flanks and from ahead. Two Lancasters from the low-level force were brought down by the defences, F/L

Kit Howard and crew perishing in the wreckage of theirs in a nearby wood. S/L Wyness ditched his Lancaster in the Rhine, and he and three of his crew inflated the dinghy to attempt to reach the neutral Swiss bank, while three others ran along the wing and jumped onto the French side. The latter were never seen again, and were almost certainly murdered by the Germans or those loyal to them. Wyness and the others were captured and shot by the local Burgomeister, their bodies thrown unceremoniously into the Rhine. A 627 Squadron Mosquito remained over the target until the delayed fuses of the low force Tallboys detonated, and the crew was able to report a breach in the left hand sluice.

Otherwise it was a relatively inactive period for 5 Group, and a small-scale unsuccessful attempt to breach the sea walls at Veere on Walcheren was its only outing during the following week. W/C Blome-Jones concluded his tour as commanding officer of 630 Squadron at about this time, and would ultimately be awarded the DFC. His citation spoke of his skill and determination as a pilot and captain, and his coolness in the face of opposition. The new commanding officer was W/C John Grindon, who was posted in from 106 Squadron where he had been a flight commander. He would see the squadron through to the end of the strategic bombing war. W/C Brill's tour as commanding officer of 467 Squadron came to an end on the 12th, and he thus became the unit's first commanding officer to survive to be posted. He was replaced by W/C Jack Douglas, who arrived from 1 Group's 460 Squadron RAAF, where he had been in command since May.

The start of the new Ruhr campaign led inexorably to Operation Hurricane, a series of mighty attacks against the region's major centres, as a demonstration to the enemy of the overwhelming superiority of the Allied air forces ranged against it. Duisburg was selected to host the first round, which was undertaken by almost 1,000 aircraft on the morning of the 14th. More than 4,500 tons of bombs were unloaded into the already devastated city, and that night, similar numbers returned to press home the point about superiority. It was an incredible effort by the ground staff on the stations, the fitters, armourers, refuellers etc., to launch 2,018 aircraft with 9,000 tons of bombs in something like eighteen hours. Almost as remarkable, was that these figures were achieved without the assistance of 5 Group, which sat out the morning operation, but took advantage of the night-time activity over the Ruhr to nail Brunswick. After so many failures during the year to date, the historic town finally succumbed to an accurate and concentrated attack, which left enormous damage in its wake. (I have a very good friend, who was born on D-Day in the village of Geitelde, about four miles south-west of Brunswick, and one of many small communities on the outskirts of the town. Years after the war, he learned from the locals, that they believed Bomber Command had intentionally bombed the surrounding villages, to force the populations into the town before the 'big' raid took place. In view of the previous attacks, which had fallen predominantly outside of the town, it is easy to see how this belief occurred).

It is remarkable to imagine that Bomber Command was still expanding at this stage of the war, when Germany was surrounded and collapsing in on itself. A number of new heavy squadrons were added during October, including two within 5 Group, both of which took form at Bardney. 227 Squadron was formed on the 7th from A Flight of 9 Squadron and B Flight of 619 Squadron, with W/C David Balme as its commanding officer. 189 Squadron was re-formed on the 15th under the command of W/C Jack Shorthouse, an officer of long experience, whose operational career extended back to the Battle of France during May and June 1940, when he was a Fairey Battle pilot with 12 Squadron. Later in the war he served with 44 Squadron, ending his tour as the B Flight commander, before moving on to instructional duties at a training unit. Unlike 227 Squadron, which was formed with experienced crews, and was therefore able to gain operational status within days of its formation, 189 Squadron had only a sprinkling of seasoned and second tour crews, and seems to have drawn most of its manpower straight from the training system. As a result its first operation would not take place until the 1 November. It did, however, avail itself of a number of 9 Squadron Lancasters, and working up to operational status began immediately under the watchful eyes of the flight commanders, S/Ls Gordon and McCracken. 9 Squadron, meanwhile, went to the Sorpe Dam on the 15th to attack it with Tallboys. Despite a handful of direct hits with these earthquake bombs, the structure remained intact, demonstrating that the efforts made against it during the Dams raid were doomed to failure from the start. 49 Squadron changed address again with a move to Fulbeck on the 16th, where it would be joined by 189 Squadron on the 2 November. The 16th was also the day on which W/C Black was installed as 207 Squadron's new commanding officer, and he would remain in post until the end of hostilities.

The next major operation for 5 Group came on the night of the 19/20th, when Nuremberg was the objective for 263 Lancasters and seven Mosquitoes, while over 500 aircraft from the other Groups attacked Stuttgart. The Davey crew was back in harness for this occasion, their twenty-fifth operation, but they were to be frustrated by a rare technical failure afflicting PB190. The starboard-outer engine sprang a coolant leak forty-five minutes out of Spilsby, and it had to be shut down, forcing the crew to abandon the sortie. The remainder pressed on to find the target covered by cloud, and the ensuing attack fell mainly into the southern districts rather than the city centre. Nevertheless, this was where most of the industry was situated, and from that viewpoint, the operation could be seen as a partial success for the loss of just two aircraft. 227 Squadron moved to Balderton on the 21st, and would remain there almost until the end. The assault on Walcheren continued on the 23rd with an attack on a gun battery at Flushing in the late afternoon. F/L Davey's rear gunner, Sgt Morley, had missed a number of trips through illness, and as his crew was to sit this one out, he joined the crew of F/O Russell for this operation to pull one back. They were flying in LM645, which was brought down in the target area, killing all on board. This was obviously a blow to the Davey crew, as it would be to any close-knit team who risked their lives together, and they would now have a partial stranger in the rear turret for the remainder of their tour.

The Hurricane force went to Essen on the evening of the 23rd and again on the afternoon of the 25th, by which time much of its industry had been dispersed, and it had lost its status as an important centre of production. Cologne's turn came first on the afternoon of the 28th, and that night, 5 Group undertook the long trek to Bergen in Norway, where the U-Boat pens were the objective. A total of 237 Lancasters were involved, but they encountered cloud over the port, and it proved impossible to pick out the glow from the Mosquito-laid markers. The Master Bomber tried to bring the force down to 5,000 feet, but this was still above the cloud base, and the operation was abandoned after just forty-seven aircraft had bombed. It was another frustrating night for the Davey crew, who reached the target at 01.45, but were unable to identify the aiming point, and jettisoned the bomb load 'safe'. They were flying in ME694 KM-L, which developed a problem with its port-inner engine on the way home, and a landing was made at the 4 Group station at Melbourne. Even as the activity over Bergen was in progress 617 and 9 Squadrons were departing their Scottish forward bases to undertake the long flight to Tromsö, where *Tirpitz* now lay at anchor. As they approached the ship a layer of cloud slid across the aiming point, concealing it from most crews as they were about to release their Tallboys. Nevertheless, the bombs went scything down, and flashes from the vicinity of the *Tirpitz* suggested at least one hit. The crews returned home uncertain of the outcome, and photo-reconnaissance showed the vessel to be on an even keel. In fact, *Tirpitz* had been dealt a fatal blow, but as this was not apparent, a further attack would have to be scheduled. A 5 Group force of 102 Lancasters and eight Mosquitoes carried out the final raid on Walcheren at lunchtime on the 30th, and Cologne was targeted again that evening by 900 aircraft. This operation, and another by under 500 aircraft on the evening of the 31st, left the city severely damaged and almost in a state of paralysis.

With just four operations to go to complete their tour, the Davey crew were probably anticipating a posting fairly early in November. In fact, the availability of crews and aircraft generally within the Command, and a slight reduction in the frequency of operations, would keep them at 44 Squadron for a further five weeks. Operation number twenty-seven came for them on the 1st of the new month, with a trip to the Meerbeck oil plant at Homberg. It was predominantly a 5 Group show, although fourteen Oboe Mosquitoes were on hand from 8 Group to provide an initial target reference. The force of more than 200 Lancasters arrived in the target area at dusk to find hazy cloud, and they then had to orbit, while the Pathfinder element tried to overcome problems caused by the jamming of their VHF communications. Ultimately, around two-thirds of the force bombed in the face of heavy flak, the Davey crew in ME694 doing so on H2s from 17,000 feet at 16.05.

189 Squadron vacated Bardney on the 2nd and moved into Fulbeck. The following night brought a massive attack on Düsseldorf by the Hurricane force, and this proved to be the last major raid of the war on this city. Extensive destruction resulted, particularly in the northern districts, but at the relatively high cost off eleven Halifaxes and eight Lancasters. Over 700 aircraft were dispatched to the Ruhr town of Bochum on the evening of the 4th, while a 5 Group contingent returned to the Dortmund-Ems Canal at Ladbergen, which had been repaired following the September attack. There was no cloud at the latter, and visibility was excellent. Despite the ferocity of the flak protecting this vital part of the enemy's communications system, the bombing found the mark, once more breaching the twin branches of the viaduct, and rendering a large section unnavigable for the loss of three Lancasters. The Davey crew's NG195 sustained slight damage, and there was a temporary problem with the intercom, but their bombs went down at 19.34 from 10,000 feet, and a safe return was made. The somewhat elusive oil town of Gelsenkirchen was visited by over 700 aircraft on the 6th, some crews briefed for the Nordstern oil plant and the others for the town itself. The attack was accurate and highly destructive, and cost a fairly modest 5 bombers.

It seemed to be a fact, that the odds against survival fell dramatically during the final few sorties of a tour, and the Davey crew were about to experience a close call. While the above-mention Gelsenkirchen force was on the way home, 235 Lancasters set out from 5 Group stations to resume their canal-busting activities at the junction of the Mittelland and Dortmund-Ems Canals at Gravenhorst. The marker crews experienced great difficulty in locating the aiming point, and when a marker did go down, it was too accurate and fell into the water. The appearance of night fighters over the target made it very uncomfortable, and the operation was ultimately abandoned after only a few dozen aircraft had bombed. The Davey crew were again in ME694 for this their twenty-ninth and penultimate operation, and the Lancaster was hit during the return journey, creating a catalogue of damage to be contended with. Trim cables were severed, an elevator control rod was damaged, hydraulic fluid was leaking onto the fuselage floor, the turrets were out of action and the ammunition feeds were shattered. F/L Davey headed for the emergency landing strip at Woodbridge, where a safe landing was made with only partial flap and on an undercarriage pumped down using the emergency air supply. The cold light of day revealed large holes in the fuselage and the need for extensive repair work before 'L' could fly again. F/O Daggett turned up at lunchtime to ferry the crew back to Spilsby, where they would have to wait for a whole month before undertaking the final operation of their tour. 463 Squadron lost three Lancasters on this operation, and a fourth crashed while approaching to land, although without crew casualties.

On the 9th W/C Newmarch became 44 Squadron's penultimate wartime commanding officer, having previously served as a flight commander, and he presided over his first operation two nights later, when the Group attacked the Rhenania-Ossag oil refinery at Harburg. Much of the bombing fell into residential areas and caused extensive damage, while the fate of the refinery was uncertain. In the early hours of the 12th 617 and 9 Squadrons returned to Tromsö, and as they flew back home they knew *Tirpitz* was finished, having observed her lying keel uppermost at her moorings after a number of direct hits. As American ground forces approached the Rhine, they asked for the small towns of Düren, Jülich and Heinsberg to be bombed in order to cut communications behind enemy lines. Situated in an arc respectively north to east of Aachen, each town was assigned to a proportion of the 1,188 participating bombers. The morning of the 16th was devoted to briefings, in the case of 1 and 5 Group crews for Düren, and aircraft began taking off around half an hour after noon. American aircraft were also in action against other targets in the area, and the afternoon saw over 9,000 tons of bombs pour down onto these hapless communities, all but erasing them from the map.

5 Group was not called into action again until the night of the 21st/22nd, when its canal-busting credentials were once more put to the test. A total of 138 Lancasters were sent to the Mittelland at Gravenhorst, while 123 others targeted the Dortmund-Ems at Ladbergen, and both operations resulted in draining of the waterways, in the case of the Mittelland over a thirty mile stretch. This outstanding result was achieved despite confusion caused by communications problems. A call to bomb beneath the 4,000 foot cloud base was heard by only a proportion of the force, who complied, while others bombed through cloud on the glow of the target indicators. Just two Lancasters were lost, both from 49 Squadron. The sole survivor was G/C 'Ginger' Weir, the station commander at Fulbeck and former 61 Squadron commanding officer. He was blown clear when his Lancaster exploded, and came to on his back in the muddy bottom of the drained canal. He remembers nothing of the event, and it is assumed that his aircraft was the victim of bombs falling from above, and that the other 49 Squadron Lancaster was caught in the detonation. G/C Weir's navigator on this night was S/L Pat Kelly, who had been Cheshire's navigator during 617 Squadron's development of the low level marking system in Mosquitoes. The Group was out in force on the 26/27th for an assault on Munich, and returning crews reported the bombing to have been accurate and destructive. Although the other Groups were kept busy at major targets such as Cologne, Neuss, Essen, Dortmund and Duisburg over the final days and nights of the month, 5 Group sat things out and waited for December to begin.

Having effectively destroyed most of the major towns and cities in the Reich, worthwhile urban targets were becoming scarce. Possibly as a result, the Command found itself attacking targets of seemingly little importance, as in the case of Freiburg, a minor railway centre close to the frontier with southern France. This was subjected to a pounding by 1 and 8 Groups on the 27/28th of November, in which 2,000 houses were destroyed, and over

2,000 people lost their lives. 5 Group's first operation in December would be against the similarly minor railway centre of Heilbronn, a little to the north of Stuttgart. The operation was mounted on the evening of the 4th by 282 Lancasters, while more than 500 other aircraft attended to the nearby city of Karlsruhe. After a few terrifying minutes of concentrated bombing, Heilbronn became engulfed in flames, probably experiencing a firestorm, and 80% of the built-up area was destroyed. In human terms it was a catastrophe, claiming the lives of over 7,000 people. In return, the defenders brought down twelve Lancasters.

The Davey crew most likely knew early on the 6th, that, barring a scrub, this day would see them conclude their tour one way or another. Over 1,300 sorties would be launched from England during the course of the late afternoon and early evening, among them 265 by 5 Group. Their targets were the railway yards and town centre of Giessen, a town to the north of Frankfurt. The Davey crew were back in their beloved PB190, and they bombed the target at 20.21 in good visibility from 12,100 feet after a thirty-eight second overshoot, and many explosions and fires were observed. To ensure that this final operation produced some additional tension, the starboard-outer engine developed problems on the way home and had to be shut down, but a safe landing was made at Spilsby after five minutes short of seven hours aloft, and the celebrations could begin. The night's other operations, each involving over 400 aircraft, were against an oil refinery at Leuna on the western approaches to Leipzig, and the town and railway yards at Osnabrück. The former inflicted serious damage on the installations, despite the presence of cloud, while the latter enjoyed only moderate success. The Davey crew departed 44 Squadron shortly afterwards, flight engineer Jack Rawcliffe ending up at Bruntingthorpe in Leicestershire as an instructor. His colleagues eventually joined 99 Squadron, which was posted to the Cocos Islands in July 1945, from where it was intended to fly Liberators against the Japanese.

5 Group's next outing was against the Urft Dam in the Eiffel region of western Germany. This target had already been attacked on the 4th by a small 8 Group contingent, and when almost 200 Lancasters of 5 Group, including nineteen from 617 Squadron, arrived overhead on the 8th, they encountered almost complete cloud cover, and the results of the raid were inconclusive. Another attack was mounted by the Group on the 11th, and although some of the crest was blown away, no breach occurred. The final heavy night raid of the war on Essen was delivered by over 500 aircraft from 1, 4 and 8 Groups on the 12/13th, and it caused massive industrial damage. 617 Squadron sent seventeen Lancasters to the E-Boot pens at Ijmuiden on the 15th. An accurate attack ensued, and two Tallboys penetrated the roof, destroying one Schnellboot and damaging six others. Two chemicals factories at Ludwigshafen and nearby Oppau, owned by the infamous I G Farben company, which was engaged in synthetic oil production and used slave workers, were seriously damaged during a raid by 1, 6 and

8 Groups on the 15/16th. Duisburg was hit again by 4, 6 and 8 Groups on the 17/18th, while the old city of Ulm was visited for the first and only time in the war, and had the greater part of its built-up area reduced to ashes by 1 and 8 Groups. 5 Group, meanwhile, attended to Munich in its customary efficient way. Long distance operations seemed to be a speciality for 5 Group, and the following night saw more than 200 of its Lancasters undertaking the slog to Gdynia on the Baltic coast, where shipping, port installations and housing fell victim. An oil refinery at Pölitz took another 200 aircraft from the Group in the same general direction on the 21st/22nd, and at least a part of the plant was hit. 617 Squadron took part in the operation, and the crews found it a strange experience to have to deliver their Tallboys onto an approximate rather than exact aiming point. The final wartime Christmas came and went in relative peace, but the celebrations were curtailed for some on Boxing Day, as each Group provided crews for operations against enemy positions around St Vith in the Ardennes, as the German break-out known as the Battle of the Bulge began to stall. A number of small-scale operations to Oslo Fjord and an attack on a supply bottleneck at Houffalize in the Ardennes brought the month and the year to an end for 5 Group.

On the 28th W/C Tait bade farewell to 617 Squadron, as did G/C Philpott, the station commander, to Woodhall Spa, in a joint party held in their honour, at which was announced the award of a record third Bar to Tait's DSO. His replacement, the grizzled, tough and highly experienced Canadian, Group Captain Johnny Fauquier, was also introduced to the squadron during this occasion. Fauquier was a legend in 4, 6 and 8 Groups, and would end the war as Canada's most decorated airman. He was born in Ottawa in 1909 as the son of a construction tycoon who built the Ontario leg of the transcontinental railway. He excelled at all forms of sport, and academically he was particularly accomplished in mathematics. His family connections opened up a whole world of opportunity to him, and he initially became a stockbroker. This, however, was anathema to a man with a taste for fast cars, motorcycles and brawling. He learned to fly, proving to be a natural pilot, and started a bush-pilot operation during the mining boom in Quebec. He joined the RCAF at the outbreak of war, and was frustratingly put to basic instructing duties for the first eighteen months. By the time he got into the war with 405 (Vancouver) Squadron RCAF in 4 Group Bomber Command in 1942 he was already thirty-two years of age, and ten or more years older than most of his contemporaries. He eventually gained command of 405 Squadron while it was a 4 Group unit in 1942, and returned again in 1943, when it became the only RCAF squadron to become a member of the Pathfinder Force. He acted as Master Bomber or deputy on a number of major operations, and like his predecessors at 617 Squadron, he was accustomed to leading from the front. S/L Jock Calder led 617 Squadron to Rotterdam on the 29th to attack the E-Boot pens, and a number of direct hits caused extensive damage to the shelters. However, the Germans had learned to disperse the vessels, and they escaped the carnage. Fauquier got his chance to lead the squadron into battle on the following day, when shipping in Oslo Fjord was the intended target. It was difficult to land a Tallboy on a ship making for open water, and no hits were scored, although the Emden was brought to a standstill by a near miss.

The New Year approached with the scent of victory in the air, but any thoughts that the enemy defences were spent were misplaced. There would continue to be stubborn opposition for a further four months before this proud and tenacious enemy finally laid down his arms.

1945. Victory

The juggernaut lays waste

New Year's Day began with a flourish on the Continent, as the *Luftwaffe* launched its ill-conceived and ultimately ill-fated Operation Bodenplatte at first light. The intention to destroy the Allied air forces on the ground at the recently liberated airfields in France, Holland and Belgium was only modestly realized, and any such success was nowhere near in proportion to the scale of the losses sustained. Those aircraft surviving the low-level attacks into the teeth of strong airfield flak defences then had to run the gauntlet of Allied fighters, and many failed to make it home. Hundreds of front line BF109 and FW190s crashed or were written off with battle damage, and a large number of pilots were killed, wounded or taken prisoner. This was a setback from which the *Luftwaffe* day-fighter force would never recover, although the night-fighter force remained intact, if short of experienced crews and fuel supplies. No. 5 Group crews were also out of bed early on New Year's Day, preparing for a return to the Dortmund-Ems Canal near Ladbergen, which had once more been repaired. Some 102 Lancasters departed their stations either side of 08.00 hours, and some three hours later the repair work had been undone. It was during this operation that F/S George Thompson, a 9 Squadron wireless operator, displayed selfless courage in the most difficult of circumstances, which earned him a posthumous Victoria Cross. The Lancaster in which he was flying was hit by flak shortly after bombing and a fierce fire developed, which trapped both mid-upper and rear gunners. Thompson, a hardy Scotsman, disregarded his own welfare and fought through the flames even as a howling gale whipped through the gaping holes in the floor and fuselage. He dragged his injured colleagues from their turrets and beat out the flames with his bare hands. The Lancaster was eventually crash-landed in Holland, where the afflicted were taken to hospital. One of the gunners succumbed to his injuries, but the other survived, and owed his life to Thompson's gallantry and self-sacrifice. So badly burned was Thompson, however, that he too lost his fight for life three weeks later. This was the second 5 Group VC to be gained at this target. It was a testing operation altogether for 9 Squadron, which lost two aircraft to crashes soon after take-off, and another to the defences. Later, in the early evening, the Group followed up with an attack on the Mittelland Canal at Gravenhorst, and this was also successfully dealt with.

5 Group sat out heavy raids on Nuremberg and Ludwigshafen on the 2nd/3rd, which involved a total of 900 aircraft. The former was hit harder than ever before, suffering the destruction of over 4,600 houses and apartment blocks, along with 2,000 preserved medieval houses. Industry was also smashed, and more than 1,800 people lost their lives. In the early hours of the 5th, 1, 5 and 8 Groups carried out a controversial two-phase attack on the French town of Royan, in response to requests from Free French forces laying siege on their way to Bordeaux. An offer by the German garrison commander to the inhabitants of free passage from the town had already been declined, and they suffered the consequences of their decision as their community was all but erased from the map. An element from the Group returned to Houffalize on the 5/6th to deliver another accurate attack on the supply line, and the Group contributed to a raid on Munich by over 600 aircraft on the 7/8th. After a number of cancellations due to the inhospitable weather conditions, 617 and 9 Squadrons flew to Norway to attack the U-Boot pens, shipping and a floating harbour in the port of Bergen. They arrived at the target at around 13.00 hours and met up with a Mustang escort. Ground haze became a problem, and numerous runs were made across the individual aiming points before some Tallboys were released and others brought home. Photo-reconnaissance suggested three direct hits on the pens had achieved penetration, and it was later learned that much internal damage had resulted. After a five night break, during which W/C Tomes became 57 Squadron's final wartime commanding officer, the Group launched a major operation against the oil refinery at Pölitz near Stettin. Last targeted just before Christmas, it hosted a very accurate attack on this night in clear conditions. An element from the Group was present in a two-phase raid on a similar target at Leuna on the 14/15th, and then went alone to yet another at Brüx in Czechoslovakia on the 16/17th. Both operations effectively ended oil production at these sites, and although the Group lent a small number of aircraft to a modest area raid on Gelsenkirchen on the 22nd/23rd, this concluded the month's activity for the 'Independent Air Force'. On the 22nd 627 Squadron welcomed W/C 'Darky' Hallows to its bosom as successor to W/C Curry. It will be recalled that Hallows was another veteran of the Augsburg raid of April 1942. By this time AVM Constantine had become the Group's new and final wartime AOC in place of AVM Cochrane, whose new brief was to form Transport Command.

A period of bad weather over Germany at the start of February hampered some operations, and this was 5 Group's experience at Siegen on the 1st/2nd, when some damage was inflicted on the railway station, but most of the bombs missed the town altogether. Two of the three operations conducted on the following night also missed the mark, and the 5 Group raid on

Karlsruhe fell into this category. The attack failed largely through the presence of complete cloud cover, and fourteen Lancasters were lost. 189 Squadron at Fulbeck alone suffered the loss of four aircraft and crews. This operation was cause for celebration, though, after F/L Hayter of 44 Squadron brought ND578 to a safe landing at the conclusion of its one hundredth sortie. This venerable Lancaster would end its wartime career on a reputed total of 123. Fauquier led 617 Squadron to Poortershaven on the 3rd to attack the concrete shelters housing midget submarines. The Biber was an ill-conceived and desperate attempt by Germany to interfere with Allied naval supply and support operations at a time when the war was essentially lost. The one-man craft was hastily developed and put into service. It carried a torpedo on each side, was powered on the surface by a petrol engine and when submerged by batteries. Once its power was exhausted it was at the mercy of the current, and many drifted into oblivion with their pilots. Other unfortunate pilots died of carbon-monoxide poisoning as exhaust fumes infiltrated the tiny cockpit compartment. Sadly, life in Germany was cheap at this stage of the war, and few Biber pilots survived to tell their sorry tale. The operation inflicted sufficient damage on the port installations to prevent Biber operations for a month, and this allowed Allied supply convoys unmolested access to the River Scheldt. The 6th brought the first of a number of operations by 617 Squadron against the Bielefeld Viaduct, a massive and beautiful structure on the edge of the town of Schildesche. On this occasion bad weather forced the effort to be abandoned before any precious Tallboys were delivered. The night of the 7/8th brought misery and destruction to the frontier towns of Goch and Cleves, as 4, 6 and 8 Groups pounded the former, while 1 and 8 Groups attended to the latter. 5 Group, meanwhile, sent 188 Lancasters and Mosquitoes to take another swipe at the Dortmund-Ems Canal at Ladbergen. Post operation reconnaissance showed no breaches in the banks of the waterway, but the disappointment was at least not compounded by heavy losses. Just three Lancasters failed to return, one of them was 467 Squadron's NG455, containing the crew of the squadron commander, W/C Douglas. This veteran of over 100 operations died with two others on board, one man evaded capture, and the remaining four became PoWs. W/C Douglas was the third of the squadron's four commanding officers thus far to lose his life in action, and his replacement was to suffer a similar fate. W/C Langlois stepped immediately into the breach, and presided over his first operation that night. This was another attack on the distant oil refinery target at Pölitz, last targeted in mid January. This time, however, it was to be a two-phase affair in the company of 1 and 8 Groups. The first phase was carried out entirely by 5 Group employing the low level marking technique, while standard Pathfinder marking paved the way for the 1 Group element. An extremely accurate operation ensued, which caused severe damage to the synthetic oil plant, and it made no further contribution thereafter to the German war effort. Twelve Lancasters failed to return from this operation, including three from 61 Squadron. Earlier on the 8th 617

Squadron returned to Ijmuiden for another crack at the pens, and two direct hits were claimed.

The Group was involved in no major activity between the above mentioned and the start of the Churchill inspired series of raids against Germany's eastern cities under Operation Thunderclap. These began at Dresden on the 13/14th in another two-phase attack begun by 5 Group using its low-level visual marking system. A layer of cloud interfered to an extent with the accuracy of this initial blow, but 800 tons of bombs rained down onto the beautiful and historic old city. Fires took hold, and they acted as a beacon to the 1, 3, 6 and 8 Group Lancasters following three hours behind. A further 1,800 tons of bombs completed the destruction, and resulted in a firestorm of unprecedented proportions. The population had been massively swelled by an influx of refugees from the eastern front, and it is believed that 35,000 people died on this night, although some commentators have claimed a substantially higher figure. During the morning of the 14th 617 Squadron returned to the Bielefeld Viaduct, only to be thwarted by cloud, and the Tallboys were once more returned to store. 5 Group was not present when Thunderclap targeted Chemnitz on the following night, but it too was over eastern Germany, attacking the oil refinery at Rositz near Leipzig with moderate success. A similar objective at Böhlen escaped serious damage on the 19/20th, after the Master Bomber was shot down by flak over the target.

While a large contingent of the main force was attending to the southern half of Dortmund on the 20th/21st, 5 Group was forced to abandon an attempt to breach the Mittelland Canal at Gravenhorst in the face of complete cloud cover. A return was made on the following night in clear conditions, however, and this time the operation was concluded successfully, although with moderately heavy losses. The most high-profile casualty was G/C Evans-Evans, the station commander at Coningsby, who so wanted to be 'one of the boys' and fly operations. He was a fine officer, who had commanded 3 Group's 115 Squadron for six months in 1941. Now, though, at the age of 43, good living, a healthy appetite and flying a desk had increased his girth to the extent that he found it difficult to squeeze into a pilot's seat. He was in every way a big man, who rejoiced in the nickname of 'Tiny'. It is unlikely that airmen clammered to be in his crew because of his lack of recent and relevant operational experience, and it is a tragedy that seven of the eight men on board the 83 Squadron Lancaster perished, the navigator, S/L Wishart DSO, DFC & Bar, a mere 22 years of age. 463 Squadron lost three crews from this operation, among them that of W/C Forbes, the commanding officer. He was killed along with two of his crew, while the remaining five became PoWs. W/C Kemp was appointed in his place, and would remain in post until the end of hostilities. 617 Squadron went back to Schildesche on the 22nd to try again at the Bielefeld Viaduct, and despite an accurate attack which appeared to have done the job, photo-reconnaissance showed the target to be still intact. Meanwhile, 9 Squadron was turning its attention to another architecturally impressive viaduct at

Altenbeken. On the 23rd W/C Scott became the final wartime commander of 61 Squadron. An attack on the Dortmund-Ems Canal had to be abandoned because of cloud on the 24th, but as in the case of the Mittelland Canal, this too was only a temporary reprieve. On the 25th W/C Birch became 619 Squadron's final wartime commanding officer.

The much-bombed and now barely recognisable city of Cologne was attacked for the final time on the 2 March, and four days later it fell to American forces. On the night of the 3rd/4th the *Luftwaffe* launched Operation Gisella, a large-scale intruder effort designed to catch the heavy bombers at their most vulnerable, as they approached their stations at low speed with flaps and undercarriage deployed with a tired crew on board. It was a highly successful night for the enemy, which accounted for twenty Bomber Command aircraft. 5 Group had sent over 200 aircraft to the Dortmund-Ems Canal at Ladbergen and left it completely out of action for the loss of seven Lancasters, including that of the recently appointed commanding officer of 467 Squadron, W/C Langlois, who died with all but two of his crew. His replacement was W/C Ian Hay, who would see the squadron through to the end of hostilities. The night's other main fare was a successful attack by 4 Group with Pathfinder support on the synthetic oil refinery at Kamen. Two nights later a return to Böhlen by 5 Group caused damage to the synthetic oil plant, while over 700 other aircraft dealt a severe blow to Chemnitz On the night of the 6/7th almost 200 aircraft from the Group were sent to attack the little port of Sassnitz on the island of Rügen near Peenemünde in the Baltic. The northern part of the town sustained heavy damage and three ships were sunk in the port. The oil refinery at Harburg was the target for the Group on the 7/8th, and again it was an outstanding success, although at a cost of fourteen Lancasters. For the second time in just over a month 189 Squadron lost four aircraft and crews and 61 Squadron three. Cloud ruined yet another attempt by 617 Squadron to destroy the Bielefeld Viaduct, and the Tallboys came home again.

W/C Frogley was posted from 50 Squadron on the 11th to be replaced by the long-serving W/C Flint, who had risen through the ranks from Sgt pilot and completed at least one tour with 49 Squadron. An all time record was set on this day, when 1,079 aircraft took off in the late morning to raid Essen for the final time. The record was short-lived, however, and was surpassed a fraction over twenty-four hours later, when 1,108 aircraft departed their stations for Dortmund in the early afternoon of the 12th. This time the new mark would stand until the end of the war. On the 13th 617 Squadron set off once more for Schildesche, and this time G/C Fauquier and S/L Calder had 22,000 lb Grand Slams slung beneath their Lancaster B1 Specials, for what was intended to be the first employment of this Barnes Wallis designed monster weapon. Yet again the weather had the last word, and PD119 and PD112 became the first Lancasters to land with the world's heaviest bomb still attached. It was only delaying the inevitable, however, and the operation went ahead again on the following afternoon. Fine weather conditions greeted the force of fifteen Lancasters, and Calder's Grand Slam accompanied a cluster of Tallboys all falling within seconds of each other. When the smoke cleared, the local residents were relieved to see five collapsed arches covering a distance of 130 yards. After months of bombing, particularly by the Americans, the Allied bombers would have no reason to return to the area. Fauquier, much to his chagrin, missed the operation because of an engine failure at start-up, but his chance would come to drop a Grand Slam. The Group delivered a moderately successful attack on the Wintershall oil refinery at Lützkendorf on the 14/15th, losing eighteen of 244 Lancasters in the process. W/C Levis became 106 Squadron's final wartime commanding officer on the 15th. On the 16/17th 225 Lancasters from the Group went to Würzburg with Mosquito support, and a horrifyingly successful raid ensued, in which almost 90% of this minimally industrial town's built up area was destroyed. Around five thousand of its inhabitants lost their lives. The night's other major operation was carried out at Nuremberg by a 1 Group main force with Pathfinder support. Although serious damage was caused, the defenders took some consolation by bringing down twenty-four Lancasters of 1 Group. Fauquier delivered his first Grand Slam on the 19th, when the Arnsberg Viaduct was successfully destroyed. A third raid by 5 Group on the synthetic oil refinery at Böhlen took place on the 20th/21st, and afterwards the plant remained out of action for the remainder of the war. A railway bridge at Arbergen in the suburbs of Bremen was the target for 617 Squadron on the morning of the 21st, and it was duly reduced to rubble by Grand Slams and Tallboys. On the following night the Group went to Hamburg to attend to the Deutsche Erdölwerke refinery. It was effectively dealt with for a loss of four Lancasters. Two bridges were attacked by elements from the Group on the 22nd, one in the Bremen area, and another by 617 Squadron at Nienburg near Hanover. The latter was successful, while the outcome at the former is uncertain, and it may have been the same railway bridge targeted by 617 Squadron on the 23rd, which definitely resulted in destruction. The town of Wesel had been persistently and unmercifully bombed since February, simply for being located close to the ground action. The final attack was delivered by a 5 and 8 Group force on the 23rd/24th, and after the dust had settled only around 3% of the buildings were still standing. The month ended with an attack on U-Boat pens and an oil storage depot at Farge on the Weser north of Bremen on the 27th, 617 Squadron successfully targeting the former, the largest concrete structure in existence, with Grand Slams and Tallboys.

It was becoming increasingly difficult to find worthwhile targets to keep the giant bomber force gainfully employed, but the oil campaign continued into April. 44 Squadron's final wartime commanding officer, and indeed the thirteenth in all, was appointed on the 1st, in the form of W/C Flett. He presided over his first operation on the 4th, when the Group carried out an attack on what was believed to be a military barracks at Nordhausen, following up an attack by 1 Group the day before. It was, in fact, a camp for slave workers at the underground secret weapons factory constructed after Peenemünde, and many casualties were inflicted upon the unfortunate inmates. 227 Squadron moved into Strubby on the 5th, and would now stay put until the end. 617 Squadron opened its April account on the 7th, with a return to Ijmuiden to attack shipping. A benzol plant at Molbis near Leipzig provided the target for over 180 Lancasters and Mosquitoes of 5 Group on the 7/8th, and all production was halted. It was a similar story when the Group returned to Lützkendorf on the 8/9th and ended production at this oil refinery. 189 Squadron returned to Bardney on the 8th, and would now remain there. 617 Squadron attacked U-Boot pens at Hamburg on the 9th under the umbrella of a heavy fighter escort, and the operation was a complete success. W/C Hallows had left 627 Squadron on the 17th of March for a spell in hospital, and he was only now replaced by W/C Kingsford-Smith, the former 463 Squadron commander, on the 10th of April. It was the turn of the Wahren railway yards at Leipzig to face seventy-six Lancasters and nineteen Mosquitoes of 5 Group on the 10/11th. Two attempts by 617 Squadron to take out the warships *Prinz Eugen* and *Lützow* at Swinemünde on the Baltic coast were thwarted by weather on the 13th and 15th. A third operation was launched on the 16th, and a number of direct hits and near misses were reported. The *Lützow* did sink two days later, but this was scant consolation for the loss of S/L Powell and crew, the squadron's final casualties of the war. As the bombing war began to wind down, 5 Group carried out an accurate attack on railway yards at Pilsen on the 16/17th, and sent a modest force to a similar target at Cham, on the German border with Czechoslovakia, on the following night. Heligoland was left looking like a cratered moonscape by 900 aircraft on the 18th, and that night 5 Group returned to Czechoslovakia to hit the railway yards at Komotau. 617 Squadron went to Heligoland on the afternoon of the 19th to deal successfully with the heavy gun emplacements barring the approaches to Germany's north-western ports. 49 Squadron changed its wartime address for the final time on the 22nd with a move to Syerston. The Group operated for the last time on the 25th, as part of a force targeting the SS barracks at Hitler's Eaglesnest retreat at Berchtesgaden in the morning, and later that night attacked an oil refinery in the Norwegian town of Tonsberg.

On the 28th, G/C Fauquier relinquished command of 617 Squadron on a posting to the Air Ministry. He had completed three tours and almost 100 operations, and was the proud bearer of the DSO and two Bars and a DFC. He was succeeded at 617 Squadron by W/C John Grindon, who had been in command of 630 Squadron at East Kirkby since October. Grindon was a native of Newquay in Cornwall, where he was born in 1917, just a few weeks before his father was killed at Ypres. He was educated at Dulwich College and the RAF's University of the Air at Cranwell. After passing out in 1937 he joined 98 Squadron, before moving on to 150 Squadron in 1939. Equipped with the Fairey Battle 150 Squadron became part of the Advanced Air Striking Force, which moved to France as the Second World War began.

Grindon was absent from the squadron on a navigation course during May 1940, when 150 Squadron and the others equipped with Battles suffered massive casualties during the German advance across the Low Countries and France. He spent the next four years as an instructor in Canada and as a staff officer at Bomber Command, before re-entering the operational scene as a flight commander with 106 Squadron at Metheringham in July 1944. He completed sixteen sorties with 106 Squadron, beginning at Kiel on the night of the 23rd/24th of July, and ending at Bremen on the 6/7th of October. The posting of Grindon to 617 Squadron was testimony to his calibre as 630 Squadron's commanding officer, and later in the year he would be awarded the DSO in recognition of his wartime service. W/C Wild took over at 630 Squadron, but he would have no offensive operations to oversee before hostilities ceased.

5 Group believed itself to be the elite of Bomber Command. Perhaps this was an attitude engendered by 'Bomber' Harris during his time as Air-Officer-Commanding, and it is, perhaps, true to say, that he remained its patron from his lofty position for the remainder of the war. Nevertheless, 5 Group demonstrated its prowess throughout the conflict by consistently setting and maintaining the highest standards in terms of its record on early returns, delivering a high tonnage of bombs to the target, innovation and generally lower casualties.

CHAPTER TWO

Quick Reference Facts, Figures and General Information

AIR OFFICERS COMMANDING

Air Commodore	W B Callaway	17.08.37 to 11.09.39
Air Vice Marshal	A T Harris	11.09.39 to 22.11.40
Air Vice Marshal	N R Bottomley	22.11.40 to 12.05.41
Air Vice Marshal	J C Slessor	12.05.41 to 25.04.42
Air Vice Marshal	W A Coryton	25.04.42 to 28.02.43
Air Vice Marshal	R A Cochrane	28.02.43 to 16.01.45
Air Vice Marshal	H A Constantine	16.01.45 to 15.12.45

OPERATIONAL STATIONS

Balderton	Coningsby	Fiskerton
Bardney	Dunholme Lodge	Fulbeck
Bottesford	East Kirkby	Hemswell
Langar	Skellingthorpe	Swinderby
Metheringham	Scampton	Spilsby
North Luffenham	Strubby	Waddington
Waddington	Woodhall Spa	Woolfox Lodge
Lindholme	Cottesmore	

AIRCRAFT TYPES

Hampden	Manchester	Lancaster	Mosquito	Mustang

QUICK REFERENCE AIRCRAFT/SQUADRON

9 Squadron

Lancaster	First received	R5196	12.8.42
	First operation	Düsseldorf	10/11.9.42

44 Squadron

Hampden	Last disposed of		12.41
Lancaster	First received	L7530	24.12.41
	First operation	Mining	3/4.03.42

49 Squadron

Hampden	Last operation	Rostock	23/24.04.42
	Last disposed of		27.04.42
Manchester	First received		17.04.42
	First operation	Rennes/Leaflet	2/3.05.42
	Last operation	Bremen	25/26.6.42
Lancaster	First received		21.07.42
	First operation	Düsseldorf	31.7/01.08.42

(First actual sortie was by a conversion flight Lancaster R5850, Essen 1/2.6.42.)

50 Squadron

Hampden	Last disposed of		04.42
Manchester	First received		30.03.42
	First operation	Leaflet	8/9.04.42
	Last operation	Bremen	25/26.6.42
Lancaster	First received		4.05.42
First operation	Cologne		30/31.05.42

57 Squadron

| Lancaster | First received | | 5.09.42 |
| | First operation | Wismar | 12/13.10.42 |

61 Squadron

Hampden	Last disposed of		10.41
Manchester	First received	L7307	8.03.41
	First operation	Boulogne	21/22.06.41
	Last operation	Bremen	5/26.6.42
Lancaster	First received		12.04.42
	First operation	Leaflets/France	5/6.05.42

83 Squadron

Hampden	Last disposed of		01.42
Manchester	First received		12.41
	First operation	Boulogne	28/29.01.42
	Last operation	Essen	1/2.06.42
Lancaster	First received		16.04.42
	First operation	Gennevilliers	29/30.04.42

97 Squadron

Manchester	First received		27.02.41
	First operation	Kiel	8/9.04.41
	Last operation	Bremen	17/18.01.42
Lancaster	First received		14.01.42
	First operation	Mining	20/21.03.42

106 Squadron

Hampden	Last disposed of		03.42
Manchester	First received		02.42
	First operation	Mining	20/21.03.42
	Last operation	Bremen	25/26.06.42
Lancaster	First received		28.04.42
	First operation	Cologne	30/31.05.42

189 Squadron

Lancaster	First received		16.10.44
	First operation	Homberg	1.11.44

207 Squadron

Manchester	First received		6.11.40
	First operation	Brest	24/25.02.41
	Last operation	Essen	10/11.03.42
Lancaster	First received		9.03.42
	First operation	Rostock	24/25.04.42

227 Squadron

Lancaster	First received		7.10.44
	First operation	Walcheren	11.10.44

463 Squadron

Lancaster	First received		25.11.43
	First operation	Berlin	26/27.11.43

467 Squadron

Lancaster	First received		9.11.42
	First operation	Mining	2/3.01.43

617 Squadron

Lancaster	First received		26.03.43
	First operation	Dams	16/17.05.43

619 Squadron

Lancaster	First received		29.04.43
	First operation	Düsseldorf	11/12.06.43

627 Squadron

Mosquito	First received		11.43
	First operation (5 Group)	La Chapelle	11/12.06.43

630 Squadron

Lancaster	First received		15.11.43
	First operation	Berlin	18/19.11.43

GROUP STRENGTH

As of September 1939

Operational Squadrons
44, 49, 50, 61, 83, 144

Non-operational Squadrons
106, 185

GROUP STRENGTH

As of April 1945

Operational Squadrons
9, 44, 49, 50, 57, 61, 83*, 97*, 106, 189, 207, 227, 463, 467,
617, 619, 627*, 630,
* On permanent loan from 8 Group.

Quick Reference Station/Squadron

Balderton	227, 408
Bardney	9, 189, 227
Bottesford	207, 467
Coningsby	61, 83, 97, 106, 617, 619
Cottesmore	106
Dunholme Lodge	44, 619
East Kirkby	57, 630
Finningley	106
Fiskerton	49
Fulbeck	49, 189
Hemswell	61, 144
Langar	207
Lindholme	50, 408
Metheringham	106
North Luffenham	61, 144
Scampton	49, 57, 83, 467, 617
Skellingthorpe	50 61
Spilsby	44, 207
Strubby	227, 619
Swinderby	50, 455
Syerston	61, 106, 408
Waddington	9, 44, 50, 97, 207, 420, 463, 467
Wigsley	455
Woodhall Spa	97, 617, 619, 627
Woolfox Lodge	61

Quick Reference Station/Squadron Dates

Balderton	408	09.12.41 to 13.09.42
	227	21.10.44 to 05.04.45
Bardney	9	14.04.43 to 06.10.44
	9, 227	07.10.44 to 14.10.44
	9, 227, 189	15.10.44 to 21.10.44
	9, 189	22.10.44 to 02.11.44
	9	03.11.44 to 07.04.45
	9, 189	08.04.45
Bottesford	207	17.11.41 to 20.09.42
	467	22.11.42 to 12.11.43
Coningsby	106	23.02.41 to 09.03.41
	106, 97	10.03.41 to 02.03.42
	106	03.03.42 to 01.10.42
	617	30.08.43 to 09.01.44
	618	10.01.44 to 17.04.44
	83, 97	18.04.44
Cottesmore	106	01.09.39 to 06.10.39
Dunholme Lodge	44	31.05.43 to 16.04.44
	44, 619	17.04.44 to 28.09.44
	44	29.09.44 to 30.09.44
East Kirkby	57	28.08.43 to 14.11.43
	57, 630	15.11.43

Hampden crossing the coast.

Two 50 Squadron Hampdens at Waddington bearing pre-war codes.

Hampdens operating from grass. At the outbreak of war most permanent stations still had grass runways.
617 Squadron mounted its epic attack on the dams from Scampton's grass track as late as May 1943.

Hampden crews returning from an early war raid to Norway. The Hampden carried a crew of four.

Bombing up a Hampden of 49 Squadron at Scampton.

Hampden air and ground crew of 50 Squadron

Hampden and Hereford of 14 OTU Cottesmore

Hampdens of 5 Group's Canadian 408 (Goose) Squadron.

An early Manchester I of 50 Squadron showing the original ventral fin,
small rudders and short elevator span.

50 Squadron Lancaster crew.

Manchester crew of 83 Squadron at Scampton in front of their Mk IA aircraft with modified tailplane.

83 Squadron Lancaster

A standard 617 Squadron Lancaster probably at Coningsby late 1943. Its 33 foot long bomb bay made evident by the open bomb-bay doors.

*AOC No. 5 Group
Ralph Cochrane.*

106 Squadron Lancaster at Metheringham.

View from the cockpit of a parked 617 Squadron Lancaster at Yagodnik during the first Tirpitz *operation in September 1944.*

Modified Type 464 Provisioning Lancaster used for trials in preparation for Operation Chastise, showing cut-away underside of fuselage and calliper arms.

617 Squadron Lancaster at dispersal 1943.

ED932 AJ-G. W/C Gibson's 617 Squadron Lancaster carrying Barnes Wallace's so-called "bouncing" bomb, but more accurately described as a revolving depth charge.

617 Squadron Lancaster B1 Special, which operated with a 5-man crew from March 1945 against bridges and E and U-Boot pens. The full side camouflage scheme is clearly evident.

617 Squadron Lancaster B1 Special carrying the C Flight YZ code. The faired-over front turret and absent mid-upper were weight-saving expedients to facilitate the lifting of the 10 ton Grand Slam Wallis-designed earthquake bomb.

A reconnaissance photo of the breached Möhne Dam taken on the morning of 17 May 1943, just hours after the raid.

The breach seen from the lake. Before the attack the water level almost reached the parapet.

John Cockshott in his 617 Squadron Lancaster B1 Special YZ-B PD114 over the Arbergen railway bridge near Bremen as the first Grand Slams and Tallboys find the mark on 23 March 1945.

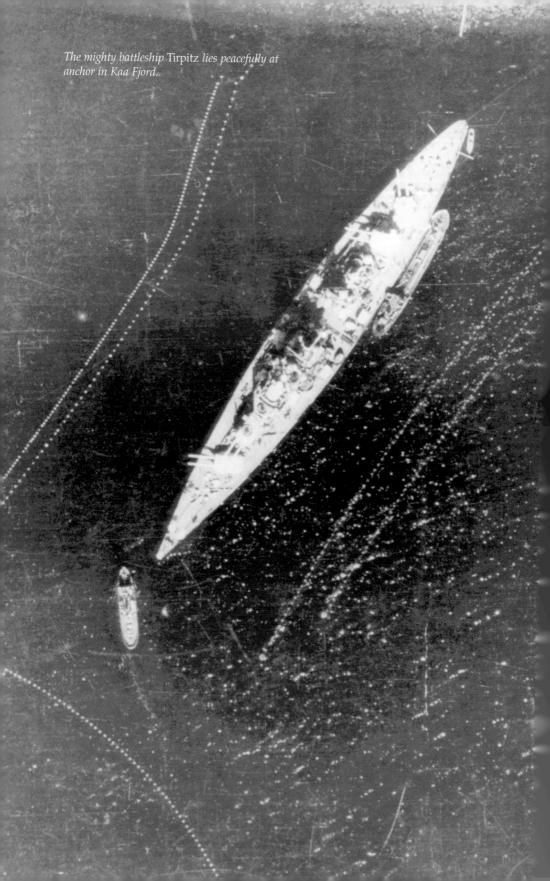

The mighty battleship Tirpitz lies peacefully at anchor in Kaa Fjord.

High altitude photo of Tirpitz *in Alten Fjord.*

Canadian aircrew looking at bomb plots after the final attack on Tirpitz.

A de Havilland Mosquito IV of 692 (Fellowship of the Bellows) Squadron of the Pathfinders Light Night Striking Force. 617 and 627 Squadrons of 5 Group operated similar versions of this aircraft, mostly in the low-level visual marking role pioneered by W/C Leonard Cheshire in early 1944 while he was the commanding officer of 617 Squadron.

Finningley	106	06.10.39 to 23.02.41
Fiskerton	49	02.01.43 to 16.10.44
Fulbeck	49	16.10.44 to 01.11.44
	49, 189	02.11.44 to 07.04.45
	49	08.04.45 to 22.04.45
Hemswell	61, 144	17.07.41
Langar	207	20.09.42 to 12.10.43
Lindholme	50	10.07.40 to 23.06.41
	50, 408	24.06.41 to 18.07.41
	408	19.07.41 to 20.07.41
Metheringham	106	11.11.43
North Luffenham	61, 144	17.07.41 to 15.10.41
	144	16.10.41 to 21.04.42
Scampton	49, 83	14.08.42
	49	15.08.42 to 03.09.42
	49, 57	04.09.42 to 06.11.42
	49, 57, 467	07.11.42 to 21.11.42
	49, 57	22.11.42 to 01.01.43
	57	02.01.43 to 20.03.43
	57, 617	21.03.43 to 27.08.43
	617	28.08.43 to 30.08.43
Skellingthorpe	50	26.11.41 to 20.06.42
	50	17.10.42 to 14.11.43
	50, 61	15.11.43 to 31.01.44
	50	01.02.44 to 14.04.44
	50, 61	15.04.44
Spilsby	207	12.10.43 to 29.09.44
	207, 44	30.09.44
Strubby	619	28.09.44 to 04.04.45
	619, 227	05.04.45
Swinderby	455	06.06.41 to 18.07.41
	455, 50	19.07.41 to 25.11.41
	455	26.11.41 to 08.02.42
Syerston	408	20.07.41 to 09.12.41
	61	05.05.42 to 30.09.42
	61, 106	01.10.42 to 10.11.43
	61	11.11.43 to 15.11.43
Waddington	44, 50	10.07.40
	44	11.07.40 to 31.10.40
	44, 207	01.11.40 to 24.02.41
	44, 207, 97	25.02.41 to 10.03.41
	44, 207	11.03.41 to 16.11.41
	44	17.11.41 to 18.12.41
	44, 420	19.12.41 to 06.08.42
	44, 9	07.08.42 to 13.04.43
	44	14.04.43 to 31.05.43
	467	12.11.43 to 24.11.43
	467, 463	25.11.43.
Wigsley	455	08.02.42 to 20.04.42
Woodhall Spa	97	02.03.42 to 17.04.43
	619	18.04.43 to 09.01.44
	617	10.01.44 to 14.04.44
	617, 627	15.04.44
Woolfox Lodge	61	16.10.41 to 05.05.42

5 Group Sorties And Losses

Aircraft	Sorties	Losses
Hampden	15,771	417 (2.6%)
Manchester	1,185	69 (5.8%)
Lancaster	52,262	1,389 (2.7%)
Mosquito	1,133	13 (1.1%)
Mustang	6	0
Total	70,357	1,888 (2.7%)

VCs

F/L R A B Learoyd	49 Squadron	Dortmund-Ems Canal	August 40
Sgt J Hannah	83 Squadron	Antwerp	September 40
S/L J D Nettleton	44 Squadron	Augsburg	April 42
F/O L T Manser	50 Squadron	Cologne	May 42
W/C G P Gibson	617 Squadron	Dams	May 43
F/L W Reid	61 Squadron	Düsseldorf	November 43
W/C G L Cheshire	617 Squadron	Career to	July 44
F/S G Thompson	9 Squadron	Dortmund-Ems Canal	January 45
Sgt N C Jackson	106 Squadron	Schweinfurt	April 44

Of 21 VCs awarded to Bomber Command and AASF airmen, 9, or 42%, went to 5 Group.

Quick Reference Records

Bomber Command

Most overall operations	50 Squadron (767)
Most bombing raids	50 Squadron (620)
Highest % losses	57 Squadron (3.3%)

5 Group

Most overall operations	50 Squadron (767)
Most bombing raids	50 Squadron (620)
Highest aircraft operational losses	44 Squadron (192)
Highest % losses	207 Squadron (3.2%)
Most sorties	50 Squadron (7135)
Bomb tonnage	50 Squadron (21,000)

CHAPTER THREE

The Squadrons

9 SQUADRON

Motto: Per Noctem Volamus (Through the night we fly)   Code WS

No. 9 Squadron has one of the longest histories in British military aviation, dating back to its original formation on the 8 December 1914, when it became the first radio equipped unit, and was employed in the role of artillery spotting. A decision to equip all artillery spotting squadrons with a radio flight resulted in the dispersal of 9 Squadron, which eventually lost its identity and was disbanded in March 1915. Resurrected in April 1915 as a radio training unit the squadron also undertook coastal defence duties until moving to France in November. The squadron operated as a bomber and reconnaissance unit until the end of 1916, when it reverted to its former role of artillery spotting, but carried out some bombing operations from June 1918. On the last day of 1919 the squadron was again disbanded, only to reappear as a night bomber unit in April 1924. In February 1939, the squadron began converting to Wellingtons, the type with which it would enter the impending conflict, and in July took up residence at Honington as one of 3 Group's six Wellington equipped front-line squadrons. No. 9 Squadron was involved in the very first raid undertaken by Wellingtons, which was to Brunsbüttel on the 4 September, the second day of hostilities. As a result it sustained the first failures to return of the type after two were brought down. The squadron continued to serve 3 Group with distinction until posted to 5 Group in August 1942. After operating successfully with Lancasters as a standard squadron of the line, it was selected to operate with the Barnes Wallis designed Tallboy bomb, previously the preserve of 617 Squadron. Beginning in September 1944, 9 and 617 squadrons undertook a series of joint operations, including the three against the German battleship *Tirpitz*. With an overall loss rate of 3% 9 Squadron suffered slightly higher than average casualties.

Posted in from 3 Group   07.08.42

STATIONS

Waddington	07.08.42 to 14.04.43
Bardney	14.04.43 to 06.07.45

COMMANDING OFFICERS

Wing Commander J M Southwell	27.06.42 to 15.03.43
Wing Commander K B F Smith DSO	15.03.43 to 12.04.43
Wing Commander P Burnett	12.04.43 to 14.11.43
Wing Commander E L Porter DFC	14.11.43 to 15.06.44
Wing Commander J M Bazin DFC	15.06.44 to 18.05.45

AIRCRAFT

Lancaster I/III   08.42 to 11.45

OPERATIONAL RECORD

Operations	Sorties	Aircraft Losses	% Losses
301	3,495	111	3.2

Category of Operations

Bombing	Mining
289	12

22 further Lancasters were destroyed in crashes.

TABLE OF STATISTICS

(Heavy squadrons)

14th highest number of overall operations in Bomber Command.
15th highest number of sorties in Bomber Command.
7th highest number of aircraft operational losses in Bomber Command.
7th highest number of bombing operations in Bomber Command.
27th highest number of mining operations in Bomber Command.

Out of 59 Lancaster Squadrons

14th highest number of overall Lancaster operations in Bomber Command.
21st highest number of Lancaster sorties in Bomber Command.
9th highest number of Lancaster operational losses in Bomber Command.

Out of 22 squadrons in 5 Group

12th highest number of overall operations in 5 Group.
10th highest number of sorties in 5 Group.
7th highest number of aircraft operational losses in 5 Group.
Highest equal (with 207 Sqn) percentage loss rate of long serving 5 Group squadrons.

Out of 17 Lancaster squadrons in 5 Group

8th highest number of Lancaster overall operations in 5 Group.
9th highest number of Lancaster sorties in 5 Group.
5th highest number of Lancaster operational losses in 5 Group.

Lancaster	From August 1942.
L7580	From 207 Sqn to 5LFS.
R5700 WS-N	From 106 Sqn via 5MU. FTR Hanover 22/23.9.43.
R5744 WS-E	From 44 Sqn. FTR Mannheim 5/6.9.43.
R5894 WS-U	From 49 Sqn to 57 Sqn.
R5904	To 15 Sqn via 1661CU.
R5907 WS-M	From 83CF. FTR Wismar 23/24.9.42.
R5915 WS-X	To 97 Sqn.
R5916 WS-R	From 49 Sqn twice. Collided in Waddington circuit with W4265 (9 Sqn) on return from Genoa 8.11.42.
R5917 WS-N	To 97 Sqn.
W4122 WS-W	To 1661CU via 9CF.
W4132	From 57 Sqn to 103 Sqn via 1661 & 1667CUs.
W4133 WS-S/Z	Crashed at Bardney during air-test 7.8.43.
W4155 WS-A/D	From 50 Sqn twice. FTR Diepholz 17/18.12.42.

W4157 WS-V/U	FTR Berlin 17/18.1.43.
W4158 WS-O/S	To 622 Sqn.
W4159 WS-Y	FTR Duisburg 8/9.1.43.
W4164	From 207 Sqn CF only to 1661CU.
W4182 WS-B	Collided in circuit with W4259 (44 Sqn) on return from Duisburg 20/21.12.42.
W4184 WS-A	FTR Munich 19/20.9.42.
W4185 WS-G	FTR Munich 21/22.12.42.
W4186 WS-S	FTR Essen 16/17.9.42.
W4197 WS-J	To 97 Sqn after 18 operations.
W4200 WS-U	To 97 Sqn after 20 operations.
W4230 WS-P	FTR Wismar 23/24.9.42.
W4235 WS-C	From 156 Sqn via NTU.
W4237 WS-W	FTR from mining sortie 29/30.9.42.
W4239 WS-T	To 97 Sqn.
W4248 WS-A	To 460 Sqn after 12 operations.
W4249 WS-M	To 97 Sqn after 15 operations.
W4253 WS-W	To 106 Sqn after 14 operations.
W4254 WS-P	To 57 Sqn after 9 operations.
W4265 WS-L	Collided in Waddington circuit with R5916 (9 Sqn) on return from Genoa 8.11.42.
W4271	9 Conversion Flight only to 1661CU.
W4358 WS-P	From 57 Sqn to 1661CU.
W4379 WS-A	FTR Berlin 17/18.1.43.
W4380 WS-S	From 12 Sqn. Became ground instruction machine.
W4761 WS-P	From 49 Sqn. FTR Berlin 17/18.1.43.
W4764 WS-K	FTR Turin 9/10.12.42.
W4765 WS-T	FTR Essen 16/17.9.42.
W4819 WS-O	To 44 Sqn.
W4821	From 103 Sqn. No operations. Returned to 103 Sqn.
W4829 WS-T	To 44 Sqn.
W4830 WS-D	To 61 Sqn.
W4831 WS-K	To 44 Sqn.
W4840 WS-B	FTR Essen 3/4.1.43.
W4843 WS-K	FTR Essen 13/14.1.43.
W4964 WS-J	Completed 106 operations. Became ground instruction machine.
W5006 WS-X	From 207 Sqn. FTR Nuremberg 30/31.3.44.
W5010 WS-L	From 49 Sqn. FTR Leipzig 19/20.2.44.
W5011 WS-Z	To 5MU.
DV161 WS-N	From 57 Sqn to 50 Sqn.
DV198 WS-U	FTR Tours 10/11.4.44.
DV284 WS-G	FTR Berlin 18/19.11.43.
DV293 WS-Y	FTR Berlin 16/17.12.43.
DV327 WS-N	Crashed in Lincolnshire on return from Berlin 23.11.43.
DV332 WS-D	FTR Berlin 2/3.12.43.
DV334 WS-C	Crashed in Nottinghamshire on return from Berlin 3.12.43.
DV340 WS-Q	From 460 Sqn to 1651CU.
DV393 WS-K	From 617 Sqn to 38MU.
DV395 WS-V	FTR Duisburg 21/22.5.44.
DV396 WS-G	To 467 Sqn.
ED307	No operations to 44 Sqn.
ED308 WS-R	To 57 Sqn.
ED347 WS-N	FTR Duisburg 20/21.12.42.

ED349 WS-S	FTR Cloppenburg 17/18.12.42.
ED395 WS-T	From 156 Sqn to 15 Sqn.
ED420	From 83 Sqn to 106 Sqn.
ED436 WS-G	FTR Berlin 17/18.1.43.
ED476 WS-M	To 12 Sqn and back. FTR Duisburg 12/13.5.43.
ED477 WS-O	FTR Hamburg 30/31.1.43.
ED479 WS-Z	FTR Essen 3/4.4.43.
ED480 WS-U	FTR Gelsenkirchen 9/10.7.43.
ED481 WS-N	Crashed near Topcliffe on return from Hamburg 30/31.1.43.
ED487 WS-D	FTR Cologne 16/17.6.43.
ED489 WS-B	Crashed on landing at Sibson while training 21.5.43.
ED490 WS-B	Crashed near Waddington on return from Berlin 1/2.3.43.
ED492 WS-W	FTR Wilhelmshaven 18/19.2.43.
ED493 WS-A	FTR Hamburg (Operation Gomorrah) 2/3.8.43.
ED494 WS-G	FTR from mining sortie 13/14.3.43.
ED495 WS-V/Y	FTR Nuremberg 25/26.2.43.
ED496	Crashed in Lincolnshire during air test 4.2.43.
ED499 WS-X	FTR Hanover 18/19.10.43.
ED501 WS-R	FTR Frankfurt 10/11.4.43.
ED502 WS-V/Y	FTR Duisburg 9/10.4.43.
ED503	Crashed in Lincolnshire during fighter affiliation 29.1.43.
ED520 WS-T	FTR Nuremberg 25/26.2.43.
ED551 WS-M/N	FTR Mönchengladbach 30/31.8.43.
ED556	From 100 Sqn. Returned to 100 Sqn.
ED558 WS-N	FTR Bochum 12/13.6.43.
ED566 WS-J/P	FTR Duisburg 9/10.4.43.
ED589 WS-O/P	FTR Pilsen 13/14.6.43.
ED648 WS-D	Crashed in sea off Mablethorpe during operation to Bochum 29/30.9.43.
ED654 WS-W	FTR Stuttgart 20/21.2.44.
ED656 WS-V	Crashed in Lincolnshire on return from Berlin 23.11.43
ED662	Crashed near Mildenhall while training 7.4.43.
ED666 WS-S/G	FTR Mannheim 5/6.9.43.
ED689 WS-K	FTR Cologne 3/4.7.43.
ED694 WS-G	FTR Essen 3/4.4.43.
ED696 WS-T	FTR Kiel 4/5.4.43.
ED699 WS-L	TR Mulheim 22/23.6.43.
ED700 WS-O	Ditched off Norfolk coast on return from Frankfurt 20.12.43.
ED721 WS-S	From 49 Sqn. Completed 10 operations to Berlin. FTR Brunswick 14/15.1.44.
ED799 WS-G	FTR from mining sortie 22/23.4.43.
ED806 WS-K	FTR Duisburg 9/10.4.43.
ED831 WS-H/Y	To 1656CU and back. FTR Gelsenkirchen 25/26.6.43.
ED834 WS-Z	FTR Dusseldorf 25/26.5.43.
ED836 WS-C/T	FTR Stuttgart 7/8.10.43.
ED838 WS-R	From 156 Sqn. FTR Essen 30.4/1.5.43.
ED871 WS-Z	From 467 Sqn. FTR Berlin 18/19.11.43.
ED975 WS-Y	Crashed in Lincolnshire on return from Munich 7.9.43.
EE122 WS-F	To 156 Sqn.
EE136 WS-R	To 189 Sqn.
EE188 WS-B	FTR Berlin 16/17.12.43.
HK540 WS-H	FTR Stuttgart 15/16.3.44.
HK788 WS-E	Caught fire in the air and crashed in Berkshire during an operation to Molbis 7/8.4.45.

HK791 WS-M	
HK803 WS-Q	To 619 Sqn.
JA679 WS-P	FTR Reggio Emilia 15/16.7.43.
JA690 WS-M	From 49 Sqn. FTR St Leu d'Esserent 7/8.7.44.
JA692 WS-D	FTR Hamburg (Operation Gomorrah) 29/30.7.43.
JA711 WS-A	From 97 Sqn. FTR Berlin 1/2.1.44.
JA852 WS-L	FTR Mannheim 23/24.9.43.
JA869 WS-H	FTR Stuttgart 7/8.10.43.
JA957 WS-D	From 576 Sqn. FTR St Leu d'Esserent 7/8.7.44.
JB116 WS-T	From 61 Sqn. FTR St Leu d'Esserent 7/8.7.44.
LL742 WS-D	To 463 Sqn via 5LFS.
LL745 WS-M	FTR Berlin 27/28.1.44.
LL785 WS-F	FTR Creil 4/5.7.44.
LL787 WS-Y	FTR Mailly-le-Camp 3/4.5.44.
LL845 WS-L	Completed 97 operations.
LL853 WS-W	FTR Prouville 24/25.6.44.
LL883 WS-C	Crashed on take-off from Bardney when bound for Brunswick 22.4.44.
LL884 WS-Q	Crash-landed in Russia during transit to Yagodnik for *Tirpitz* operation 12.9.44.
LL901 WS-V	FTR Munster 23/24.9.44.
LL914 WS-V	FTR Munster 23/24.9.44.
LL970 WS-Y	FTR Prouville 24/25.6.44.
LM217 WS-O	From 463 Sqn.
LM220 WS-Y	
LM221 WS-K	FTR Culmont-Chalindrey 12/13.7.44.
LM309	To 617 Sqn.
LM329 FTR	Oberhausen 14/15.6.43.
LM361 WS-T	FTR Juvisy 18/19.4.44.
LM422 WS-N	FTR Frankfurt 22/23.3.44.
LM430 WS-B	FTR Frankfurt 22/23.3.44.
LM432 WS-O	Crashed near Bardney while training 28/29.3.44.
LM433 WS-H	FTR Schweinfurt 24/25.2.44.
LM436	To 207 Sqn.
LM445 WS-Z	FTR Munich 24/25.4.44.
LM447 WS-K	FTR Stuttgart 20/21.2.44.
LM448 WS-M	From 467 Sqn. Force-landed in Sweden following final *Tirpitz* raid (with 617 Sqn) 12.11.44.
LM453 WS-E	FTR Rilly la Montagne 31.7.44.
LM519 WS-N	FTR Brunswick 22/23.5.44.
LM520 WS-X	FTR Lille 10/11.5.44.
LM528 WS-D	FTR Lille 10/11.5.44.
LM548 WS-C	To 463 Sqn.
LM713	To 189 Sqn.
LM715 WS-O	FTR Nuremberg 19/20.10.44.
LM736	To 189 Sqn.
LM745	To 189 Sqn.
ME555 WS-Z	From 617 Sqn.
ME579 WS-A	Crashed in Rutland on return from Argentan 7.6.44.
ME704 WS-B	FTR Scholven/Buer 21/22.6.44.
ME724 WS-O	FTR Brunswick 22/23.4.44.
ME757 WS-O	FTR Brest 13.8.44.
ME759 WS-P	To 227 Sqn via 1661CU.
ME809 WS-X	

ME833 WS-Z	FTR Revigny 18/19.7.44.
ND692	From 35 Sqn.
ND733	From 550 Sqn to 463 Sqn.
ND948 WS-H	FTR Prouville 24/25.6.44.
ND951 WS-Z	FTR Bourg Leopold 11/12.5.44.
NF929 WS-P	To 619 Sqn.
NF937 WS-E	FTR Altenbeken Viaduct 14.2.45.
NF938 WS-H	Crash-landed in Russia during transit to Yagodnik for *Tirpitz* operation 12.9.44.
NF985 WS-D	Crash-landed in Russia during transit to Yagodnik for *Tirpitz* operation 12.9.44.
NG206 WS-J	
NG220 WS-B	From 61 Sqn to 619 Sqn.
NG223 WS-D	To 106 Sqn and back. FTR Dortmund-Ems Canal at Ladbergen 1.1.45.
NG233 WS-E	FTR Altenbeken Viaduct 14.2.45.
NG235 WS-H	FTR Lützkendorf 8/9.4.45.
NG242 WS-C	
NG249 WS-S	
NG252 WS-R	Crashed on take-off at Bardney when bound for the Dortmund-Ems Canal at Ladbergen 1.1.45.
NG257 WS-N	FTR Bergen 12.1.45.
NG278 WS-N	
NG341	
NG384 WS-T	
NG419 WS-U	
NG442 WS-F	
NG486 WS-A	
NG487 WS-D	
NG495 WS-R	
NG499 WS-W	
NN722 WS-Z	FTR Leuna 14/15.1.45.
PA172 WS-G	
PB146 WS-A	To 189 Sqn.
PB211	To 630 Sqn.
PB289 WS-B	To 189 Sqn.
PB371	From 7 Sqn to 582 Sqn.
PB470	From 83 Sqn.
PB594 WS-D	To 189 Sqn.
PB596 WS-H	To 61 Sqn.
PB696 WS-V	To 619 Sqn.
PB905	From 97 Sqn.
PD198 WS-W	To 103 Sqn.
PD205 WS-H	FTR Courtrai 20/21.7.44.
PD211 WS-M	Crash-landed in Russia during transit to Yagodnik for *Tirpitz* operation 12.9.44.
PD213 WS-F	Crashed while landing at Bardney on return from Pölitz 21/22.12.44.
PD368 WS-A	From 50 Sqn. Crashed on take-off at Bardney when bound for the Dortmund-Ems Canal at Ladbergen 1.1.45.
PD377 WS-U	FTR Dortmund-Ems Canal at Ladbergen 1.1.45. F/S Thompson awarded VC.
SW277	To 61 Sqn.

44 (RHODESIA) SQUADRON

Motto: Fulmina Regis Justa (The king's thunderbolts are righteous)   Code KM

Although formed as a fighter squadron on the 24 July 1917 to defend the London area, 44 Squadron would find fame as an offensive unit during the Second World War. It was destined to fly bombers against the enemy wherever targets presented themselves, whether in its heartland, in the countries it occupied, or at sea. Following a period of disbandment between 1919 and 1937 the squadron was resurrected at Waddington as a light bomber unit, before assuming a training role, in which it converted 5 Group crews to twin engine aircraft. From February 1939 the aircraft in question was the Hampden, but from the 1 June of that year the squadron reverted to a standard 5 Group frontline unit, and it was in this form that it faced the outbreak of war. No. 44 Squadron has one of the finest wartime records of service in Bomber Command. It was one of only two squadrons to serve the Command without a break from the first day of the war to the last, and although it detached aircraft for short periods to Coastal Command, the squadron as a whole was never withdrawn from the order of battle. It was also the only squadron to serve exclusively in 5 Group from start to finish without a break. It enjoyed the distinction of introducing the Lancaster to operational service, having earlier employed Hampdens. It was the only long serving 5 Group squadron not to operate Manchesters. Two of the squadron's commanding officers wore the ribbon of the Victoria Cross. In terms of casualties, it was not a lucky squadron and suffered the heaviest Lancaster losses, both in numbers and percentage, in the Group and the Command, the heaviest overall losses in 5 Group, and equal third highest losses overall in the Command.

STATIONS

Waddington	16.06.37 to 31.05.43
Dunholme Lodge	31.05.43 to 30.09.44
Spilsby	30.09.44 to 21.07.45

COMMANDING OFFICERS

Wing Commander J N Bootham AFC	03.09.39 to 08.12.39
Wing Commander W J M Ackerman	08.12.39 to 12.03.40
Wing Commander D W Reid	12.03.40 to 20.03.41
Wing Commander S T Misselbrook DSO	20.03.41 to 13.12.41
Wing Commander R A B Learoyd VC	19.12.41 to 08.05.42
Wing Commander P W Lynch-Blosse DFC	08.05.42 to 10.05.42
Wing Commander K P Smales DSO DFC	10.05.42 to 01.02.43
Wing Commander J D Nettleton VC	01.02.43 to 13.07.43
Wing Commander E A Williamson	15.07.43 to 01.08.43
Wing Commander R L Bowes	01.08.43 to 03.02.44
Wing Commander F W Thompson DFC AFC	03.02.44 to 09.11.44
Wing Commander R A Newmarch	09.11.44 to 01.04.45
Wing Commander S E Flett	01.04.45 to 12.06.45

AIRCRAFT

Hampden	02.39 to 12.41
Lancaster I/III	12.41 to 05.47

OPERATIONAL RECORD

Operations	Sorties	Aircraft Losses	% Losses
637	6,405	192	3.0

Category of Operations

Bombing	Mining	Other
518	108	11

Hampdens

Operations	Sorties	Aircraft Losses	% Losses
338	2,043	43	2.1

Category of Operations

Bombing	Mining	Other
246	81	11

Lancasters

Operations	Sorties	Aircraft Losses	% Losses
299	4,362	149	3.4

Category of Operations

Bombing	Mining
272	27

TABLE OF STATISTICS

(Heavy squadrons)

8th highest number of overall operations in Bomber Command.
12th highest number of bombing operations in Bomber Command.
6th highest number of sorties in Bomber Command.
3rd equal (with 78 and 102 Sqns) highest number of aircraft operational losses in Bomber Command.

Out of 59 Lancaster squadrons

15th highest number of Lancaster overall operations in Bomber Command.
8th highest number of Lancaster sorties in Bomber Command.
Highest number of Lancaster operational losses in Bomber Command.

Out of 22 squadrons in 5 Group

4th highest number of overall operations in 5 Group.
3rd highest number of sorties in 5 Group.
Highest number of aircraft operational losses in 5 Group.

Out of 10 Hampden squadrons in 5 Group

3rd highest number of Hampden overall operations in 5 Group.
4th highest number of Hampden sorties in 5 Group.
5th highest number of Hampden operational losses in 5 Group.

Out of 17 Lancaster squadrons in 5 Group

9th highest number of Lancaster overall operations in 5 Group.
4th highest number of Lancaster sorties in 5 Group.
Highest number of Lancaster operational losses in 5 Group.
Highest Lancaster percentage loss rate in 5 Group.

Hampden	To December 1941.
L4042	From 16 OTU.
L4074 KM-O	From 50 Sqn to 25 OTU.
L4085 KM-A	Ditched off Aberystwyth on return from mining sortie 1.8.40.
L4086	To 49 Sqn via 14 OTU.
L4087	FTR from mining sortie 19/20.7.40.
L4088	FTR from mining sortie 21/22.4.40.
L4089	Shot down by Spitfires off Berwick on return from reconnaissance sortie to Norway 21.12.39.
L4090	Shot down by Spitfires off Berwick on return from reconnaissance sortie to Norway 21.12.39.
L4091	To 16 OTU.
L4098	Crashed on landing at Waddington during training 2.5.40.
L4099	From 50 Sqn. FTR Kristiansand Norway 12.4.40.
L4100	To 106 Sqn.
L4102	FTR from reconnaissance sortie to the Elbe Estuary 25/26.3.40.
L4115	From 61 Sqn to 16 OTU.
L4153	Force-landed near Grimsby on return from patrol 27.2.40.
L4154	Force-landed near Colchester on return from Berlin 20/21.10.40.
L4168	From 7 Sqn to 50 Sqn and back to 16 OTU.
L4171	FTR from operation against communications 23/24.5.40.
L4178	From 106 Sqn to 144 Sqn.
P1152	To 50 Sqn.
P1173	FTR Kristiansand Norway 12.4.40.
P1187	To 420 Sqn.
P1322	From 106 Sqn to 25 OTU.
P1324	Force-landed in Northamptonshire on return from mining sortie 2.10.40.
P1325	FTR from targets in the Pas de Calais area 11/12.6.40.
P1331	Crash-landed at Waddington on return from patrol 23/24.4.40.
P1338	FTR Bremerhaven 11/12.9.40.
P1339	To 1 AAS.
P1340	Crashed near Harwich on return from Emmerich 3/4.6.40.
P2077	FTR Bernburg 13/14.8.40.
P2087 KM-M	FTR Krefeld 6/7.9.40.
P2121	FTR Antwerp 17/18.9.40.
P2122	To 144 Sqn after conversion for use as torpedo bomber.
P2123	Ditched off Norfolk on return from Berlin 1.9.40.
P2137	FTR Berlin 20/21.10.40.
P2142	To 16 OTU.
P4285 KM-U	From 50 Sqn. Crashed on approach to Coningsby on return from Kassel 9.9.41.
P4286	From 50 Sqn. FTR Breda 14/15.5.40.
P4290 KM-B	Ditched off Suffolk on return from Stettin 5/6.9.40.
P4310	FTR Soest 12/13.6.41.
P4352	FTR from mining sortie 3/4.7.40.
P4353	Crashed on take-off from Waddington for air-test 25.8.40.
P4371	FTR Calais 10/11.9.40.
P4372	FTR Gelsenkirchen 29/30.8.40.
P4373	To 25 OTU.

P4374 KM-J	Crashed on landing at Radlett on ferry flight 2.9.40.
P4375	FTR Hamburg 28/29.7.40.
P4393	Crashed on landing at Waddington following ferry flight 9.7.40.
P4400	From 25 OTU to 420 Sqn.
P4406	FTR from mining sortie 27/28.7.41.
P4414	To 106 Sqn.
P4415	To 1 AAS.
P5321	From 7 AAU to 408 Sqn.
P5332	From 7 AAU to 420 Sqn.
X2898	From 83 Sqn to 16 OTU.
X2910	FTR Berlin 14/15.10.40.
X2913	FTR Bremerhaven 11/12.9.40.
X2916	To 25 OTU.
X2917 KM-R	Crashed in Norfolk when bound for Calais 6.8.41.
X2918	FTR Cologne 10/11.3.41.
X2921 KM-Z	From 106 Sqn. Crashed soon after take-off from Waddington when bound for mining sortie 7.9.41.
X2965	FTR Cologne 1/2.10.40.
X2966	Force-landed on Sutton-on-Sea beach on return from Le Havre 29.11.40.
X2982	Crash-landed in Yorkshire on return from Mannheim 13.5.41.
X2995	Crashed soon after take-off from Waddington when bound for Hamburg 14.11.40.
X2996	FTR Berlin 14/15.11.40.
X2997	Crashed on landing at Waddington on return from Merseburg 17.10.40.
X2999	FTR Berlin 17/18.4.41.
X3008	Crashed on landing at Bircham Newton on return from Hamburg 17.11.40.
X3023	Crashed in Norfolk on return from Lützkendorf 20.11.40.
X3025	Hit by AE157 of 50 Sqn on the ground at Waddington and damaged beyond repair 3.9.41.
X3026	To 1 TTU after conversion for use as torpedo bomber.
X3049	FTR from mining sortie 10/11.12.40.
X3057	To 49 Sqn.
X3061	From 83 Sqn to 420 Sqn.
X3142	To 16 OTU.
X3149	To 420 Sqn.
X3150	To 455 Sqn after conversion for use as torpedo bomber.
AD726	FTR Cologne 31.8/1.9.41.
AD727	To 61 Sqn.
AD747	Crashed in Shropshire during ferry flight 19.6.41.
AD755	Crashed in Lincolnshire following early return from Cologne 31.7.41.
AD758	From 106 Sqn to 408 Sqn.
AD829	From 83 Sqn to 455 Sqn.
AD840	FTR Hamm 8/9.7.41.
AD847	Crash-landed near West Raynham on return from Hamburg 27.4.41.
AD855	From 106 Sqn to 420 Sqn.
AD864	FTR Hamburg 2/3.5.41.
AD868	From 61 Sqn. FTR Brest 17/18.12.41.

AD869	To 420 Sqn.
AD899	FTR from mining sortie 8/9.4.41.
AD904	Crashed in Shropshire during ferry flight 19.6.41.
AD913 KM-K	Abandoned over Surrey on return from Frankfurt 3.9.41.
AD915	To 420 Sqn.
AD917 KM-P	Crashed near Waddington while in transit 28.8.41.
AD920	To 144 Sqn after conversion for use as torpedo bomber.
AD930 KM-L	Crashed on approach to Waddington on return from Hamburg 16.9.41.
AD933	Crash-landed in Worcestershire on return from Düsseldorf 28.11.41.
AD939	Collided with a Spitfire near Waddington during training 31.8.41.
AD962	FTR Brest 24.7.41.
AD966 KM-R	Crashed in Lincolnshire during training 1.8.41.
AD968	To 420 Sqn.
AD975	FTR Cologne 13/14.10.41.
AD981 KM-A	Ditched off Cromer on return from Rostock 12.9.41.
AD982	To 408 Sqn.
AD983	Crashed in Lincoln on return from mining sortie 22.7.41.
AE127	FTR Soest 12/13.6.41.
AE128	From 144 Sqn to 455 Sqn.
AE129	Crashed in Lincolnshire following early return from mining sortie 14.6.41.
AE130	To 455 Sqn after conversion for use as torpedo bomber.
AE152 KM-J/R	FTR Berlin 2/3.9.41.
AE153	FTR Hamm 8/9.7.41.
AE186	From 61 Sqn to 420 Sqn.
AE192	From 207 Sqn to 408 Sqn.
AE196	From 408 Sqn. FTR from mining sortie 13.12.41.
AE201	To 455 Sqn after conversion for use as torpedo bomber.
AE202 KM-K	From 61 Sqn to 420 Sqn.
AE218	To 50 Sqn.
AE239	FTR Düsseldorf 16/17.8.41.
AE242	To 455 Sqn.
AE254 KM-W	FTR Berlin 2/3.9.41.
AE257 KM-X	FTR Bremen 21/22.10.41.
AE258	To 420 Sqn.
AE260	To 420 Sqn.
AE290	From 61 Sqn. FTR Le Havre 23/24.10.41.
AE298	To 420 Sqn.
AE313 KM-C	FTR Frankfurt 2/3.9.41.
AE377	FTR Dunkerque 8/9.11.41.
AE379	To 420 Sqn.
AE382 KM-A	FTR Dunkerque 10/11.10.41.
AE384	To 420 Sqn.
AE385	To 420 Sqn.
AE390	To 420 Sqn.
AE393	To 420 Sqn.
AE398	Crashed near Coltishall while training 26.10.41.
AE399	To 420 Sqn.
AE428	To 50 Sqn.
AE430	To 455 Sqn.
AT128	To 420 Sqn.

AT130	To 420 Sqn.
AT132	To 420 Sqn.
AT134	To 420 Sqn.
AT135	To 420 Sqn.
AT136	To 420 Sqn.
AT144	To 420 Sqn.

Manchester December1941 to June 1942.

L7382	From 83 Sqn. Training only to 6AGS.
L7385	Training only to 207 Sqn.
L7401	From 408 Sqn. Training only to 61 Sqn.
L7415	From 408 Sqn. Training only to 61 Sqn.
L7425	From 97 Sqn. Training only to 61 Sqn.
L7430 KM-N-	From 25.OTU. Conversion Flt only to 1654CU.
L7453	From 83 Sqn. Training only to 61 Sqn.
L7477	Training only to 61 Sqn.
L7480 KM-A	From 207 Sqn to 1661CU.
L7481	From 25 OTU. Conversion Flt only to 1661CU.
R5790	From 83 Sqn. Conversion Flt only to 1661CU.

Lancaster From December 1941.

BT308	From Ringway. Familiarisation/training only to 97 Sqn.
L7530	No operations to 207 Sqn.
L7531	No operations to 97 Sqn.
L7532	To 97 Sqn.
L7533 KM-K/J	FTR Warnemünde 8/9.5.42.
L7534 KM-F	To 50 Sqn via 44CF July 42.
L7536 KM-H	FTR Augsburg. Sgt Rhodes 17.4.42.
L7537 KM-L	FTR Düsseldorf 31.7/1.8.42.
L7538 KM-B	To 97 Sqn and back. Crashed on landing at Waddington while training 20.2.42.
L7539 KM-G	To 61 Sqn.
L7540	To 83 Sqn.
L7541 KM-O/U	To 1660CU.
L7542	Crash-landed at Skellingthorpe during training 7.2.42.
L7543	To 207 Sqn.
L7544	Training only to 207 Sqn.
L7545 KM-R	To 1654CU.
L7546 KM-J	First off on squadron's first Lancaster operation flown by S/L Nettleton 3.3.42 to 207 Sqn.
L7547 KM-D	To 207 Sqn.
L7548 KM-T	FTR Augsburg. W/O Crum 17.4.42.
L7549 KM-Q	To 44CF. Crashed 22.4.42.
L7565 KM-V	FTR Augsburg. W/O Beckett 17.4.42.
L7566	To 83 Sqn.
L7567 KM-C	To 49 Sqn.
L7568 KM-W	Crashed on landing at Waddington while training 10.7.42 to 83 Sqn.
L7569 KM-U	From 97 Sqn to 106 Sqn.
L7576 KM-E-	From 97 Sqn to 44CF to 1660CF.
L7581 KM-R	Crashed on take-off from Waddington for air-test 20.5.42.
L7584 KM-S	To 44CF. Crashed in Yorkshire while training 22.8.42.
R5484 KM-K	No operations to 83 Sqn.
R5489 KM-X	Crashed on approach to Waddington while training 16.8.42.

R5491	To 61 Sqn.
R5492 KM-M	To 106 Sqn.
R5493 KM-M	FTR from mining sortie 24/25.3.42. The first operational loss of a Lancaster.
R5494 KM-O	To OADU.
R5495	To 97 Sqn.
R5496	To 97 Sqn.
R5497	To 97 Sqn.
R5506 KM-P	FTR Augsburg. F/L Sandford 17.4.42.
R5508 KM-B	S/L Nettleton's aircraft for Augsburg 17.4.42 to 97CF.
R5510 KM-A	FTR Augsburg. F/O Garwell 17.4.42.
R5514	To 156 Sqn.
R5515 KM-A	Crash-landed at Waddington while training 6.6.42.
R5516 KM-F	FTR Essen 5/6.6.42.
R5542	To 83 Sqn via 44CF.
R5547	From 207 Sqn to 1654CU.
R5554 KM-Q	FTR Munich 19/20.9.42.
R5555 KM-P	FTR Warnemünde 8/9.5.42.
R5556 KM-C	To 1661CU.
R5557 KM-G	FTR Warnemünde 8/9.5.42.
R5568 KM-T	FTR Warnemünde 8/9.5.42.
R5603 KM-D	FTR Essen 4/5.8.42.
R5624 KM-P	To 1661CU.
R5631 KM-J	To 106CF.
R5664 KM-R	To OADU and back. Crashed while landing at Waddington on return from Kassel 28.8.42.
R5665 KM-A	To 106 Sqn.
R5666 KM-F	FTR Nienburg 17/18.12.42.
R5669 KM-Z	From 83 Sqn. FTR Berlin 23/24.12.43.
R5685	From 50 Sqn. Training only. Returned to 50 Sqn.
R5697 KM-H/R	To 106 Sqn.
R5726	From 50 Sqn to 100 Sqn.
R5727	To Canada as pattern aircraft November 1942.
R5729 KM-A	FTR Brunswick 14/15.1.44.
R5732 KM-G	Crashed at Waddington after early return from Mainz 12.8.42.
R5733 KM-P	From 50 Sqn to 1654CU.
R5740 KM-O	FTR Gelsenkirchen 25/26.6.43.
R5744	Completed 21 operations to 9 Sqn.
R5842	From 61 Sqn to 49CF May 1942.
R5846 KM-X-	From 61 Sqn to 1661CU.
R5858 KM-G	Ditched during Atlantic patrol 14.6.42.
R5862 KM-V	To 1660CU.
R5863	No operations to 207 Sqn.
R5898 KM-G	From 49 Sqn. FTR Duisburg 9/10.4.43.
R5901 KM-X	From 106 Sqn. FTR Hanover 18/19.10.43.
R5903 KM-C/R	FTR Osnabrück 6/7.10.42.
R5905 KM-R	FTR Wismar 23/24.9.42.
W4105 KM-K/X	FTR Frankfurt 24/25.8.42.
W4106 KM-T	Crash-landed at Waddington while training 23.3.43.
W4110 KM-K	FTR Pilsen 13/14.5.43.
W4124 KM-D	FTR Kassel 27/28.8.42.
W4125 KM-Q	FTR Munich 21/22.12.42.
W4126 KM-B	From 44CF. FTR Nienburg 17/18.12.42.

W4135	From 50 Sqn. No operations to 97 Sqn.
W4136	To 61 Sqn via 44CF.
W4137 KM-L	From 44CF. Crashed on landing at Waddington on return from St Nazaire 1.3.43.
W4162 KM-Y	Completed 17 operations to 83 Sqn.
W4169 KM-S	FTR Bremen 13/14.9.42.
W4176 KM-X	FTR from mining sortie 8/9.1.43.
W4177 KM-W	FTR from mining sortie 18/19.9.42.
W4180 KM-D	FTR Hamburg 9/10.11.42.
W4187 KM-S	FTR Wismar 1/2.10.42.
W4188 KM-G	FTR Osnabrück 6/7.10.42.
W4199 KM-H	FTR Berlin 29/30.3.43.
W4259 KM-P	From 44CF. Collided with W4182 (9 Sqn) over Lincoln when bound for Duisburg 20.12.42.
W4266	From 50 Sqn. No operations. Returned to 50 Sqn.
W4267	From 50 Sqn. Crashed in Norfolk 27.1.43.
W4268 KM-Q	To 622 Sqn via 1654CU.
W4277 KM-S	FTR from mining sortie 8/9.1.43.
W4304 KM-C	FTR Stuttgart 22/23.11.42.
W4305 KM-J/G	FTR Pilsen 13/14.5.43.
W4778 KM-T	From 106 Sqn. FTR Hamburg 2/3.8.43.
W4819 KM-G	From 9 Sqn. FTR Cologne 2/3.2.43.
W4829 KM-V	From 9 Sqn. FTR Berlin 1/2.3.43.
W4831 KM-C	From 9 Sqn. FTR Berlin 1/2.1.44. (Aircraft's 13th Berlin sortie).
W4832 KM-U	FTR Lorient 7/8.2.43.
W4838 KM-B	FTR Wuppertal 29/30.5.43.
W4839 KM-B/F/S	FTR Berlin 27/28.3.43.
W4841 KM-W	FTR from mining sortie 10/11.3.43.
W4933 KM-Y	From 156 Sqn to 50 Sqn.
W4935 KM-M	FTR Peenemünde 17/18.8.43.
W4936 KM-W	FTR Oberhausen 14/15.6.43.
W4949 KM-H	FTR Oberhausen 14/15.6.43.
W4961 KM-S	FTR Berlin 3/4.9.43.
DV155 KM-G	From 617 Sqn. FTR Berlin 3/4.9.43.
DV166 KM-B	From 49 Sqn to 1669CU.
DV202 KM-Z	FTR Peenemünde 17/18.8.43.
DV238 KM-M	From 49 Sqn. FTR Berlin 16/17.12.43.
DV263 KM-M	FTR Magdeburg 21/22.1.44.
DV283 KM-W	To 101 Sqn.
DV286	From 207 Sqn to 300 Sqn.
DV329 KM-W	FTR Berlin 23/24.11.43.
DV331 KM-T/Z	FTR Frankfurt 20/21.12.43.
DV384 KM-A/V	To 50 Sqn.
ED305 KM-G/S	From 467 Sqn to 617 Sqn on loan. FTR from mining sortie 10/11.3.43.
ED307 KM-R	FTR Cologne 28/29.6.43.
ED309 KM-S	From 50 Sqn. FTR Lorient 7/8.2.43.
ED314 KM-M	To 61 Sqn.
ED315	No operations to 460 Sqn.
ED318 KM-X	FTR Berlin 17/18.1.43.
ED331 KM-Z	FTR Turin 12/13.7.43. W/C Nettleton VC.
ED348 KM-M	From 57 Sqn. FTR Hagen 1/2.10.43.
ED351 KM-Y	FTR Duisburg 8/9.4.43.

ED355 KM-D	FTR Nienburg 17/18.12.42.
ED433 KM-V	From 101 Sqn. FTR Kassel 3/4.10.43.
ED611 KM-J	To 463 Sqn.
ED665 KM-L	FTR Berlin 31.8/1.9.43.
ED716 KM-F	To 550 Sqn.
ED723 KM-U	FTR Dortmund 23/24.5.43.
ED735 KM-K	To 617 Sqn.
ED783 KM-F	FTR Essen 30.4/1.5.43.
ED869 KM-G	From 97 Sqn to 5LFS.
ED999 KM-X	From 49 Sqn. FTR Berlin 23/24.12.43.
EE123 KM-K	FTR Wuppertal 29/30.5.43.
EE179 KM-B	From 97 Sqn. FTR Berlin 2/3.12.43.
EE184 KM-B	Ditched in the North Sea on return from Leipzig 20/21.10.43.
EE185 KM-K/A	To 617 Sqn on loan. Returned to 44 Sqn. FTR Mailly-le-Camp 3/4.5.44. Flew 13 operations to Berlin.
HK616	From 622 Sqn.
HK623	From 622 Sqn to 38MU.
JA684 KM-Q	To 5LFS.
JA700 KM-P	FTR Berlin 2/3.12.43.
JA703 KM-W	To 617 Sqn on loan. Returned to 44 Sqn. FTR Mannheim 5/6.9.43.
JA843 KM-O	FTR Berlin 30/31.1.44.
JA895 KM-H	FTR Remscheid 30/31.7.43.
JA897 KM-F/H	FTR Peenemünde 17/18.8.43.
JA903	From 5LFS to 75 Sqn.
JB136 KM-T	FTR Munich 2/3.10.43.
LL885	From 622 Sqn.
LL920 KM-V	FTR Schweinfurt 26/27.4.44.
LL938 KM-S	FTR Wesseling 21/22.6.44.
LL965 KM-C/V	FTR Darmstadt 11/12.9.44.
LM170 KM-E	To 1668CU.
LM171 KM-R	FTR Stuttgart 28/29.7.44.
LM192 KM-K	To BCIS 12.44.
LM306 KM-L	From 49 Sqn. FTR Frankfurt 18/19.3.44. Flew 11 Berlin operations.
LM330 KM-Q	FTR Krefeld 21/22.6.43.
LM373 KM-V	FTR Berlin 23/24.11.43.
LM374 KM-S	FTR Berlin 23/24.11.43.
LM434 KM-F	FTR Wesseling 21/22.6.44.
LM592 KM-Q	FTR Wesseling 21/22.6.44.
LM625 KM-H	
LM631 KM-W	FTR St Leu d'Esserent 7/8.7.44.
LM638 KM-P	FTR Culmont-Chalindrey 12/13.7.44.
LM639	To Flight Refuelling Ltd. 7.10.44.
LM645 KM-P	FTR Walcheren 23.10.44.
LM648 KM-K	From 49 Sqn. Collided with PB428 (207 Sqn) in the circuit returning from Harburg 11/12.11.44.
LM650 KM-T	Crashed in Sussex on return from Homberg 1.11.44.
LM654 KM-L	FTR Böhlen 5/6.3.45.
LM655 KM-C	
ME299 KM-E	FTR Pölitz 8/9.2.45.
ME394 KM-X	
ME442 KM-V	Shot down by an intruder over Lincolnshire on return from the Dortmund-Ems Canal at Ladbergen 4.3.45.

ME550	
ME571 KM-P	To 463 Sqn.
ME573 KM-S	To 463 Sqn.
ME574 KM-W/P	Crashed on landing at Dunholme Lodge while training 7.1.44.
ME628 KM-V	FTR Pommerval 24/25.6.44.
ME629 KM-R	FTR Nuremberg 30/31.3.44.
ME634 KM-P	FTR St Leu d'Esserent 7/8.7.44.
ME672 KM-A	FTR Berlin 24/25.3.44.
ME694 KM-L	FTR Stuttgart 25/26.7.44.
ME699 KM-T	FTR St Leu d'Esserent 4/5.7.44.
ME730 KM-R	FTR Schweinfurt 26/27.4.44.
ME743 KM-G	FTR Marquise 27/28.6.44.
ME791 KM-K	Crashed near Nottingham on return from training flight 11.6.44.
ME794 KM-V	Destroyed in landing at Westcott on return from Maisy Palaiseau 1.6.44.
ME804 KM-O	FTR Wesseling 21/22.6.44.
ME844	From 15 Sqn.
ME859 KM-S	FTR St Leu d'Esserent 7/8.7.44.
ND496 KM-A	From 7 Sqn to 75 Sqn.
ND514 KM-C	FTR Berlin 30/31.1.44.
ND515 KM-Z/E	FTR Gennevilliers 9/10.5.44.
ND517 KM-U	FTR Colombelles 18.7.44.
ND518 KM-C/D	FTR Frankfurt 22/23.3.44.
ND519 KM-E	FTR Caen 6/7.6.44.
ND520 KM-A	FTR Augsburg 25/26.2.44.
ND525 KM-Q	FTR Schweinfurt 24/25.2.44.
ND538 KM-T	FTR Frankfurt 22/23.3.44.
ND552 KM-X	FTR Wesseling 21/22.6.44.
ND565 KM-C	FTR Berlin 24/25.3.44.
ND566 KM-O	FTR Stuttgart 1/2.3.44.
ND573 KM-S	FTR La Chapelle 20/21.4.44.
ND574 KM-G	To Flight Refuelling Ltd.
ND576 KM-M	FTR Stuttgart 15/16.3.44.
ND578 KM-Y	
ND631 KM-B	To 617 Sqn. Returned to 44 Sqn. FTR Leipzig 10/11.4.45.
ND689 KM-G/O	FTR Amiens 19/20.5.44.
ND698 KM-Q	Crashed on landing at Oakley on return from Maisy Palaiseau 1.6.44
ND741 KM-K	FTR Salbris 7/8.5.44.
ND751 KM-J	FTR Pommerval 24/25.6.44.
ND795 KM-C	FTR Nuremberg 30/31.3.44.
ND843	To Flight Refuelling Ltd.
ND869 KM-M	Ditched in the sea off Skegness when bound for Würzburg 16.3.45.
ND973 KM-A	FTR Wesseling 21/22.6.44.
ND974 KM-P	From 83 Sqn.
ND976 KM-R	FTR Duisburg 21/22.5.44.
NE138 KM-Z	FTR from mining sortie 26/27.8.44.
NF991 KM-D	
NG195 KM-C	
NG396 KM-G	From 1661CU. FTR Sassnitz 6/7.3.45.

NG397	From 1661CU.
NG415 KM-F	
NN697 KM-R	FTR Etampes 9/10.6.44.
NN765	From 1661CU to 57 Sqn.
NN768 KM-K	From 619 Sqn. FTR Harburg 7/8.3.45.
PA195 KM-V	From 1661CU. FTR Karlsruhe 2/3.2.45.
PA256 KM-C	
PA276	
PB182	To 83 Sqn.
PB189 KM-A	FTR Stuttgart 12/13.9.44.
PB190 KM-J	
PB192 KM-F	FTR Ladbergen 4/5.11.44.
PB205	To 619 Sqn.
PB206 KM-Q	FTR from mining sortie 15/16.7.44.
PB235 KM-C	FTR from mining sortie 4/5.10.44.
PB251 KM-O	FTR Hamburg 21/22.3.45.
PB266 KM-S	FTR Stuttgart 28/29.7.44.
PB283 KM-K	To 1661CU.
PB346	To 619 Sqn.
PB360	From 49 Sqn to 57 Sqn.
PB380 KM-S	To 75 Sqn.
PB417 KM-R	FTR Harburg 7/8.3.45.
PB424 KM-X	To 75 Sqn.
PB534 KM-Q	
PB535 KM-Z	FTR Darmstadt 11/12.9.44.
PB732	To 189 Sqn.
PB733	To 1661CU.
PB743	To 189 Sqn.
PB751 KM-G	From 619 Sqn. FTR Heilbronn 4/5.12.44.
PB818 KM-C	From 195 Sqn.
PB819 KM-K	From 622 Sqn.
PB869	To 1661CU.
PD222 KM-U	FTR Brest 14.8.44.
PD225	From 622 Sqn.
PD228 KM-A	From 622 Sqn.
PD366	From 622 Sqn.
PD372 KM-Z	
PD373 KM-X	FTR Heilbronn 4/5.12.44.
PD381	From 207 Sqn.
PD422 KM-T	To 75 Sqn.
RA603	
RE131 KM-E	
RE132 KM-G	
RF203	
RF206	
RF210 KM-O	
RF234	To 619 Sqn.
RF238	
RF240	
RF265	
SW251 KM-X	FTR Karlsruhe 2/3.2.45.

Heaviest single loss

21/22.06.44	Wesseling. 6 Lancasters FTR.

49 SQUADRON

Motto: Cave Canem (Beware of the dog)   Code EA

Formed on the 15th of April 1916, 49 Squadron began life as a training unit until moving to France in November 1917 for day bombing and reconnaissance duties. At the conclusion of the Great War the squadron remained in Germany as part of the force of occupation, and was disbanded there on the 18 July 1919. On the 10 February 1936 the squadron was re-formed in the light bomber role, and became the first unit to receive the Hampden in September 1938. It was with this type that the squadron faced the impending Second World War as one of 5 Group's front-line units. An operational squadron at the outset of war, 49 Squadron was in action on the first day. It remained with 5 Group throughout, other than for two brief periods of detachment to Coastal Command in 1940. It flew more Hampden sorties than any other squadron. It also operated the Manchester briefly before converting to the Lancaster. No. 49 Squadron served Bomber Command with distinction to the end of hostilities, and consistently sustained lower than average casualties.

STATIONS

Scampton	14.03.38 to 02.01.43
Kinloss (Detachment to Coastal Command).	26.01.40 to 20.03.40
Fiskerton	02.01.43 to 16.10.44
Fulbeck	16.10.44 to 22.04.45
Syerston	22.04.45 to 28.09.45

COMMANDING OFFICERS

Wing Commander J S Chick MC AFC	27.02.39 to 01.12.39
Wing Commander W C Sheen	01.12.39 to 08.04.40
Wing Commander J W Gillan DFC AFC	08.04.40 to 22.12.40
Wing Commander J N Jefferson	22.12.40 to 17.07.41
Wing Commander R D Stubbs DFC	17.07.41 to 14.05.42
Wing Commander L C Slee DSO DFC	14.05.42 to 05.04.43
Wing Commander P W Johnson DFC AFC	05.04.43 to 01.10.43
Wing Commander A A Adams	01.10.43 to 01.05.44
Wing Commander M Crocker DFC	01.05.44 to 22.06.44
Wing Commander L E Botting	23.06.44 to 12.06.45

AIRCRAFT

Hampden	09.38 to 04.42
Manchester	04.42 to 07.42
Lancaster I/Iii	07.42 to 10.49

OPERATIONAL RECORD

Operations	Sorties	Aircraft Losses	% Losses
674	6,501	163	2.5

Category of Operations		
Bombing	Mining	Leaflet
543	105	26

Hampdens

Operations	Sorties	Aircraft Losses	% Losses
342	2,636	55	2.1

Category of Operations

Bombing	Mining	Leaflet
241	82	19

Manchesters

Operations	Sorties	Aircraft Losses	% Losses
10	47	6	12.8

Category of Operations

Bombing	Mining	Leaflet
4	2	4

Lancasters

Operations	Sorties	Aircraft Losses	% Losses
323	3,818	102	2.7

Category of Operations

Bombing	Mining	Leaflet
298	21	3

TABLE OF STATISTICS

(Heavy squadrons)
7th highest number of overall operations in Bomber Command.
8th highest number of bombing operations in Bomber Command.
5th highest number of sorties in Bomber Command.
16th highest number of aircraft operational losses in Bomber Command.

Out of 59 Lancaster squadrons

8th highest number of Lancaster overall operations in Bomber Command.
16th highest number of Lancaster sorties in Bomber Command.
16th highest number of Lancaster operational losses in Bomber Command.

Out of 22 squadrons in 5 Group

3rd highest number of overall operations in 5 Group.
2nd highest number of sorties in 5 Group.
4th highest number of aircraft operational losses in 5 Group.

Out of 10 Hampden squadrons in 5 Group

2nd highest number of Hampden overall operations in 5 Group.
Highest number of Hampden sorties in 5 Group.
3rd highest number of Hampden operational losses in 5 Group.

Out of 8 Manchester squadrons in 5 Group

7th highest number of Manchester overall operations in 5 Group.
7th highest number of Manchester sorties in 5 Group.
7th highest number of Manchester operational losses in 5 Group.
Highest Manchester percentage loss rate in 5 Group.

Out of 17 Lancaster squadrons in 5 Group

6th highest number of Lancaster overall operations in 5 Group.
8th highest number of Lancaster sorties in 5 Group.
9th highest number of Lancaster operational losses in 5 Group.

Hampden	To April 1942.
L4034	From CFS. Crashed at Waddington during training 23.11.39.
L4036 EA-R	FTR Dortmund 11/12.8.40.
L4038	To 106 Sqn.
L4040	FTR from mining sortie 25/26.4.40.
L4041	To 7 Sqn.
L4042	To 44 Sqn via 7 Sqn and 16 OTU.
L4043	Crashed on a Northumberland beach on return from a mining sortie 15.4.40.
L4044 EA-R	Crashed soon after take-off from Scampton en-route to Amiens 8/9.6.40.
L4045 EA-Q	Crashed in Lincolnshire on return from Wilhelmshaven 12.1.41.
L4046	To 44 Sqn.
L4053	To 83 Sqn.
L4060 EA-H	To 5BGS.
L4066	To 83 Sqn.
L4067	To 144 Sqn.
L4068	FTR Mönchengladbach 11/12.5.40. Crew got home.
L4072	Crashed in Northumberland on return from reconnaissance sweep off Norway 21.12.39.
L4077	From 50 Sqn. Crashed in Norfolk on return from mining sortie 21.7.40.
L4086	From 44 Sqn via 14 OTU to 420 Sqn.
L4092	FTR from mining sortie 25/26.4.40.
L4125	From 144 Sqn. Crashed on take-off from Scampton when bound for a mining sortie 7.2.42.
L4129	From 144 Sqn. FTR from mining sortie 16/17.10.40
L4195 EA-H	From 185 Sqn. Crashed in Kent on return from mining sortie 17.10.40.
P1153	To 455 Sqn.
P1174	To 16 OTU.
P1175	Crashed on landing at Scampton on return from mining sortie 21/22.4.40.
P1176	To 14 OTU.
P1177	To 25 OTU.
P1206 EA-Z/K	FTR from intruder sortie to Bocholt 8/9.11.41.
P1226	Crashed in Devon during a transit flight 17.3.42.
P1310	From 14 OTU to 415 Sqn after conversion for use as torpedo bomber.
P1314	From CGS to 420 Sqn.
P1318	FTR from communications target in the Krefeld/Aachen area 25/26.5.40.
P1319	FTR from mining sortie 25/26.4.40.
P1323	From 61 Sqn to 16 OTU.
P1333 EA-F	FTR Merseburg 16/17.8.40.
P1347 EA-D	FTR Stettin 4/5.9.40.

P2063	To 144 Sqn.
P2068	Crashed soon after take-off from Scampton while training 19.6.41.
P2095	To 25 OTU.
P2111	To 25 OTU.
P2112	To 14 OTU.
P2134	Crashed in Lancashire during training 29.9.40.
P2135	Crashed soon after take-off from Scampton on a ferry flight 31.8.40.
P2143	Crashed in Hampshire on return from Bordeaux 17.10.40.
P2145	To 16 OTU.
P4299	FTR Düsseldorf 4/5.2.41.
P4304	To 489 Sqn after conversion for use as torpedo bomber.
P4305	FTR from mining sortie 26/27.6.40.
P4321	To 1 AAS.
P4322 EA-N	FTR from mining sortie 5/6.1.41.
P4350 EA-L	FTR Stettin 5/6.9.40.
P4351	Ditched off Lincolnshire coast on return from Kiel 3/4.8.40.
P4377 EA-K	From 106 Sqn. FTR from mining sortie 6/7.8.40.
P4384	Crashed in Berkshire during an operation to Bordeaux 27/28.12.40.
P4403 EA-M	Crashed on landing at St Eval on return from mining sortie 4.4.41.
P4404 EA-R	FTR from attack on airfields in France 6/7.12.40.
P4409	To 50 Sqn.
P4416 EA-L	FTR Berlin 25/26.8.40.
P5324 EA-T	From 83 Sqn. FTR from shipping strike (Channel Dash) 12.2.42.
X2900 EA-S	Crashed while landing at Abingdon after recall from a mining sortie 16/17.10.40.
X2912	From 61 Sqn to 455 Sqn after conversion for use as torpedo bomber.
X2959	To 25 OTU.
X2962	Force-landed in Cornwall on return from Berlin 20/21.10.40.
X2985 EA-W	FTR Danzig 10/11.11.40.
X3001 EA-H	FTR Hanover 10/11.2.41.
X3021	To 106 Sqn.
X3024 EA-H	FTR Lützkendorf 19/20.11.40.
X3027 EA-A	Shot down by intruder off Skegness on return from Hamburg 27/28.10.40.
X3028 EA-S	Crashed near Dunholme Lodge on return from an operation to French aerodromes 7.12.40.
X3029 EA-D	Crashed near Scampton soon after take-off when bound for Kiel 4.11.40.
X3050 EA-N	FTR from operation against aerodromes in France 6/7.12.40.
X3052 EA-C	FTR Hamburg 24/25.11.40.
X3054	Crashed in Devon on return from Lorient 21/22.3.41.
X3057	From 44 Sqn to 420 Sqn.
X3060	Crashed on landing at Scampton on return from mining sortie 26.6.41.
X3063	Crashed off Isle-of-Wight on return from Mannheim 16/17.12.40.

X3134 EA-C	FTR Düsseldorf 30.6/1.7.41.
X3135	Crashed near Scampton during training 11.11.41.
X3136 EA-K	Crash-landed in Norfolk on return from Berlin 3.9.41.
X3151 EA-T	Crash-landed near Scampton on return from Hanover 26.7.41.
AD719 EA-C	Shot down near Lincoln by intruder on return from Hanover 11.2.41.
AD729 EA-N	FTR from mining sortie 27/28.5.41.
AD733 EA-B	FTR Frankfurt 28/29.9.41.
AD739 EA-A	FTR Brest 6/7.7.41.
AD744	From 83 Sqn. Crashed in Scotland on return from mining sortie 7.9.41.
AD759	Crashed in Lincolnshire while training 25.11.41.
AD788 EA-V	FTR Kiel 25/26.6.41.
AD792	To 14 OTU.
AD799	From 106 Sqn to 144 Sqn.
AD805 EA-R	Crash-landed in Lincolnshire on return from Kassel 9.9.41.
AD824	From 50 Sqn to 144 Sqn.
AD842	To 408 Sqn.
AD845	To 14 OTU.
AD856 EA-P	Shot down by intruder off Cromer on return from Osnabrück 6.7.41.
AD865	From 83 Sqn to 455 Sqn after conversion for use as torpedo bomber.
AD896 EA-M	Crashed on approach to Scampton during training flight 6.1.42.
AD909 EA-H	FTR from mining sortie 9/10.1.42.
AD910 EA-Y	Force-landed near Pocklington on return from Bremen 13.7.41.
AD931 EA-X	FTR Dortmund 14/15.4.42.
AD960	To 420 Sqn.
AD964	From 83 Sqn to 144 Sqn.
AD967 EA-H	Collided with X3121 (83 Sqn) over Lincolnshire on return from Düsseldorf 25.8.41.
AD968	From 420 Sqn to 408 Sqn.
AD971 EA-O	FTR Duisburg 28/29.8.41.
AD973	To 144 Sqn.
AD974	From 61 Sqn to 455 Sqn.
AD976	To 455 Sqn after conversion for use as torpedo bomber.
AD979	To 144 Sqn.
AD980 EA-V	To 408 Sqn.
AE123	To 106 Sqn.
AE126 EA-N	FTR Duisburg 28/29.8.41.
AE132 EA-U	FTR from shipping strike (Channel Dash) 12.2.42.
AE145	To 455 Sqn after conversion for use as torpedo bomber.
AE194	To 455 Sqn after conversion for use as torpedo bomber.
AE203 EA-F	Crash-landed in Suffolk on return from Berlin 3.9.41.
AE224 EA-Z	FTR from Shipping strike off the Frisians 1/2.11.41.
AE227	To 408 Sqn.
AE236 EA-P	FTR Kiel 7/8.9.41.
AE237	To 83 Sqn.
AE240 EA-P	FTR from shipping strike (Channel Dash) 12.2.42.
AE241	To 5 OTU after conversion for use as torpedo bomber.

AE261	From 106 Sqn to 489 Sqn after conversion for us as torpedo bomber.
AE262	Crashed on landing at Scampton on return from Brunswick 15.8.41.
AE354 EA-S	Crashed on landing at Scampton during training 18.12.41.
AE357	Converted for use as torpedo bomber.
AE368	To 144 Sqn.
AE372	To 408 Sqn.
AE376 EA-E	Crashed in Lincolnshire soon after take-off for Frankfurt 29.9.41.
AE396 EA-W	FTR from shipping strike (Channel Dash) 12.2.42.
AE397 EA-G	Ditched off Isle of Wight on return from Mannheim 14/15.2.42.
AE419 EA-T	FTR Hüls 28/29.12.41.
AE421 EA-P	From 83 Sqn. FTR Essen 10/11.4.42.
AT111	To 489 Sqn after conversion for use as torpedo bomber.
AT112 EA-M	From 83 Sqn. Crashed near Upwood on return from Mannheim 15.2.42.
AT118	To 50 Sqn.
AT124 EA-C	FTR from mining sortie 16/17.2.42.
AT126 EA-Z	FTR Essen 6/7.4.42.
AT129 EA-O	From 83 Sqn. Crashed on take-off from Scampton when bound for Brest 25.1.42.
AT148 EA-S	FTR Emden 20/21.1.42.
AT150	To 455 Sqn after conversion for use as torpedo bomber.
AT156 EA-C	FTR Cologne 5/6.4.42.
AT174 EA-E	FTR Essen 10/11.3.42.
AT178	From 106 Sqn to 408 Sqn.
AT179	To 408 Sqn.
AT180	To 408 Sqn.
AT185	To 420 Sqn.
AT190 EA-A	From 106 Sqn. FTR Essen 10/11.4.42.
AT191	From 106 Sqn to 408 Sqn.
AT196	Abandoned over Yorkshire on return from Essen 13.4.42.
AT217 EA-S	FTR from mining sortie 19/20.4.42.
AT227	To 408 Sqn.
AT228	To 420 Sqn.
Manchester	From April 1942 to July 1942.
L7281	From 1654CU. No operations to 1661CU.
L7287 EA-G	FTR Emden 6/7.6.42.
L7290	From 97 Sqn. FTR Cologne (Operation Millennium) 30/31.5.42.
L7293	From 83 Sqn to 61 Sqn.
L7296	Conversion Flt only to 1661CU.
L7325	From 97 Sqn via 25 OTU. No operations. Became ground instruction machine.
L7386	Crash-landed at Scampton during training 5.10.42. (May have been on 57 Sqn charge)
L7387	From 83 Sqn. FTR Emden 20/21.6.42.
L7389 EA-L	From 83 Sqn to 1660CU.
L7397	From 83 Sqn. Training only to 207 Sqn.
L7398	From 106 Sqn to 1661CU.
L7420	From 25 OTU. Training only to 1660CU.

L7421	To 1660CU.
L7429	Conversion Flt only. FTR Cologne (Operation Millennium) 30/31.5.42.
L7453 EA-T	From 61 Sqn to 1661CU.
L7469	To 50 Sqn. and back. FTR Emden 6/7.6.42.
L7479	Ultimate fate unknown.
L7484	From 83 Sqn. Became ground instruction machine.
L7493 EA-F	From 25 OTU to 1661CU.
L7515	From 106 Sqn to 1656CU after 22 operations.
L7524	From 25 OTU to 1485Flt.
L7526 EA-V	From 25 OTU to 207 Sqn.
R5771	From 25 OTU to 420 Sqn.
R5772	From 25 OTU. Flew the last operation by a Manchester, to Bremen, 25/26.6.42 to 83CF.
R5775	Training only to 83 Sqn.
R5780	From 83 Sqn to 57 Sqn.
R5788	From 83 Sqn. Training only to 1660CU.
R5793	From 25 OTU. Training only to 83 Sqn.
R5794	From 25 OTU. FTR Essen 1/2.6.42.
R5835	From 83 Sqn to 50 Sqn.
R5836	From 83 Sqn to 1661CU.
Lancaster	From July 1942.
L7567	From 44 Sqn. FTR Nuremberg 28/29.8.42.
R5658	To 1654CU.
R5698	Training only to 1654CU.
R5751 EA-E	To 57 Sqn after 21 operations.
R5752 EA-D	Crash-landed at Martlesham Heath on return from Duisburg 7.9.42.
R5757	To 156 Sqn.
R5762	FTR Duisburg 20/21.12.42.
R5763	FTR Karlsruhe 2/3.9.42.
R5842	From 49CF to 1661CU.
R5850	From 83 Sqn. Conversion flight only to 1661CU.
R5855	From 83 Sqn. Conversion flight only to 1661CU.
R5889	To 97 Sqn.
R5890	FTR Essen 16/17.9.42.
R5892	To 1661CU.
R5894	To 9sqn.
R5896	To 97 Sqn.
R5897	FTR Nuremberg 28/29.8.42.
R5898	22 operations to 44 Sqn.
R5912	17 operations to 156 Sqn.
R5916	To 9 Sqn and back to 9 Sqn.
W4104	No operations to 83 Sqn.
W4107	FTR Stuttgart 22/23.11.42.
W4108	To 1654CU.
W4113	24 operations to 156 Sqn.
W4116	FTR Wismar 12/13.10.42.
W4129	No operations to 207 Sqn.
W4140	Conversion flight only to 156 Sqn.
W4181	19 operations to 15 Sqn via 1660CU.
W4183	To 1661CU.
W4196	To 156 Sqn.

W4235	To 156 Sqn.
W4245	To 156sqn.
W4258	Conversion flight only to 1661CU.
W4306	Crashed at Ford on return from Milan 24.10.42.
W4314	11 operations to 156 Sqn.
W4761	18 operations to 9 Sqn.
W4773EA-F	16 operations to 156 Sqn.
W4822	From 467 Sqn to 57 Sqn.
W4835	To 97 Sqn.
W5010	From BDU to 9 Sqn.
DV166 EA-F	To 44 Sqn.
DV178 EA-N	To 617 Sqn on loan. Returned to 49 Sqn to 50 Sqn.
DV238 EA-D/O	From 619 Sqn to 44 Sqn.
ED310	To 97 Sqn.
ED348	To 57 Sqn.
ED352	To 57 Sqn.
ED387	To 50 Sqn.
ED416 EA-J	FTR Mannheim 5/6.9.43.
ED426 EA-P	FTR Stuttgart 7/8.10.43.
ED427 EA-O	FTR Pilsen 16/17.4.43.
ED428 EA-Q	Crashed on approach to Fiskerton on return from Hamburg 31.1.43.
ED431 EA-M	FTR Essen 5/6.3.43.
ED432 EA-R/N	FTR Oberhausen 14/15.6.43.
ED434 EA-T	FTR Oberhausen 14/15.6.43.
ED435 EA-G/K	FTR Berlin 29/30.3.43.
ED438 EA-P/R	FTR Düsseldorf 3/4.11.43.
ED440 EA-L	FTR Cologne 2/3.2.43.
ED441 EA-D/E	FTR Pilsen 16/17.4.43.
ED444 EA-B/C	FTR Berlin 17/18.1.43.
ED445 EA-H	To 50 Sqn.
ED448 EA-M	Crash-landed at Dunholme Lodge after ferry flight 15.9.43.
ED450 EA-G	Hit balloon cables on return from Lorient 13/14.2.43 and crashed in sea off Plymouth.
ED452 EA-F	Crashed on landing at Fiskerton following early return from Pilsen 14.5.43.
ED453 EA-G	FTR Oberhausen 14/15.6.43.
ED467 EA-E	FTR St Nazaire 28.2/1.3.43.
ED469 EA-A	FTR Berlin 29/30.3.43.
ED497 EA-C	FTR Cologne 16/17.6.43.
ED584 EA-U	FTR Bochum 12/13.6.43.
ED590 EA-L	FTR Duisburg 8/9.4.43.
ED597 EA-B	To 619 Sqn.
ED602	From 83 Sqn to 619 Sqn.
ED620 EA-K	FTR Stettin 20/21.4.43.
ED625 EA-R	FTR Nuremberg 10/11.8.43.
ED663	FTR Cologne 8/9.7.43.
ED702 EA-D	W/C Slee's a/c. FTR Mannheim 23/24.9.43. F/S C T Anderson and crew, Dams raid survivors.
ED719 EA-K	FTR Mannheim 9/10.8.43.
ED721 EA-T	To 9 Sqn.
ED726 EA-V	FTR Turin 12/13.7.43.
ED756	To 617 Sqn.

ED785	FTR Cologne 16/17.6.43.
ED805 EA-S	FTR Peenemünde 17/18.8.43.
ED813 EA-W	FTR Dortmund 23/24.5.43.
ED999 EA-A	To 617 Sqn on loan. Returned to 49 Sqn to 44 Sqn.
EE134 EA-B/Y	To 619 Sqn.
EE186	To 106 Sqn.
JA690	To 9 Sqn.
JA691 EA-L	FTR Peenemünde 17/18.8.43.
JA851 EA-P	FTR Peenemünde 17/18.8.43.
JA892	FTR Peenemünde 17/18.8.43.
JA894 EA-C	To 617 Sqn.
JA959 EA-C	From BDU. Became ground instruction machine.
JB126	Ditched in North Sea on return from Berlin 3/4.9.43.
JB139	To 617 Sqn.
JB144	To 617 Sqn.
JB178 EA-V/U	FTR Revigny 18/19.7.44.
JB229 EA-S	Crashed on the beach at Chapel-St-Leonards on return from Berlin 24.11.43.
JB231 EA-N	FTR Berlin 2/3.1.44.
JB235 EA-B/C	Crashed on approach to Fiskerton on return from Berlin 27.11.43.
JB295 EA-R	FTR Brunswick 14/15.1.44.
JB301	FTR Mannheim 23/24.9.43.
JB305 EA-E	FTR Düsseldorf 3/4.11.43.
JB314 EA-Q	FTR Nuremberg 30/31.3.44.
JB360 EA-M	FTR Berlin 27/28.1.44.
JB362 EA-D	FTR Berlin 26/27.11.43.
JB368 EA-G	FTR Berlin 22/23.11.43.
JB371 EA-J	FTR Berlin 2/3.12.43.
JB399 EA-A/H	To 1653CU.
JB411 EA-L	Crashed on take-off from Fiskerton while training 18.10.43.
JB413	FTR Kassel 22/23.10.43.
JB416	FTR Kassel 22/23.10.43.
JB421 EA-K	FTR Salbris 7/8.5.44.
JB466 EA-A	FTR Nuremberg 30/31.3.44.
JB467 EA-T	FTR Frankfurt 20/21.12.43.
JB469 EA-B	FTR Leipzig 19/20.2.44.
JB473 EA-Q/U/W	FTR Revigny 18/19.7.44.
JB533 EA-P	Crashed on take-off from Fiskerton when bound for Modane 10.11.43.
JB545 EA-O	FTR Berlin 16/17.12.43.
JB679 EA-D	FTR Schweinfurt 26/27.4.44.
JB680 EA-P	FTR Essen 26/27.3.44.
JB701 EA-G	FTR Stuttgart 28/29.7.44.
JB710 EA-G	To 630 Sqn.
JB714 EA-J/K	FTR Etampes 9/10.6.44.
JB727 EA-S	FTR Berlin 2/3.1.44.
LL899 EA-P	FTR Aachen 11/12.4.44.
LL900 EA-T	FTR Wesseling 21/22.6.44.
LL908 EA-H	FTR Schweinfurt 26/27.4.44.
LL912	Damaged in taxiing accident at Fiskerton while training 8.5.44.
LL976 EA-A	FTR St Leu d'Esserent 7/8.7.44.

LM190 EA-R	To 1656CU.	
LM191	To 619 Sqn.	
LM207	To 619 Sqn.	
LM306 EA-F/E	To 44 Sqn.	
LM337 EA-V	FTR Milan 15/16.8.43.	
LM539 EA-D	FTR Duisburg 21/22.5.44.	
LM541 EA-N	FTR St Leu d'Esserent 7/8.7.44.	
LM572 EA-P	FTR Pommerval 24/25.6.44.	
LM648	To 44 Sqn.	
LM649 EA-T	To 630 Sqn.	
LM653	To 57 Sqn.	
ME308 EA-F	FTR Nordhausen 4.4.45.	
ME322		
ME353 EA-Q	FTR Pölitz 8/9.2.45.	
ME357 EA-U/C	From 460 Sqn. Crashed off Lincolnshire coast while training 19.4.45.	
ME454 EA-E	From 227 Sqn. FTR Würzburg 16/17.3.45.	
ME471		
ME491 EA-P		
ME675 EA-R	FTR Wesseling 21/22.6.44.	
ME787	To 619 Sqn.	
ME808 EA-D	FTR Wesseling 21/22.6.44.	
ND383 EA-E	To 1668CU.	
ND473 EA-O	To 467 Sqn.	
ND474 EA-T	FTR Stuttgart 15/16.3.44.	
ND498 EA-R	Crashed on take-off from Fiskerton when bound for Stuttgart 21.2.44.	
ND512 EA-C	To 1653CU.	
ND516 EA-N	FTR Leipzig 19/20.2.44.	
ND533 EA-M	FTR Etampes 9/10.6.44.	
ND536 EA-U/F	FTR Frankfurt 22/23.3.44.	
ND537 EA-S	FTR Munich 24/25.4.44.	
ND647 EA-N	To 1653CU.	
ND672 EA-F/U	FTR Frankfurt 22/23.3.44.	
ND676 EA-M	Crash-landed at Coltishall on return from Essen 26/27.3.44.	
ND677/G	From 460 Sqn to 115 Sqn.	
ND683 EA-K	Detached to 617 Sqn. Returned to 49 Sqn. FTR Wesseling 21/22.6.44.	
ND684 EA-V	FTR Revigny 18/19.7.44.	
ND687 EA-P	FTR Schweinfurt 26/27.4.44.	
ND695 EA-B	FTR Wesseling 21/22.6.44.	
ND713	From 460 Sqn.	
ND787 EA-F	To 1668CU.	
ND791	From 460 Sqn.	
ND792 EA-A	To 619 Sqn.	
ND957	To 619 Sqn.	
NE125 EA-K	FTR Brunswick 22/23.5.44.	
NE128 EA-J	FTR Wesseling 21/22.6.44.	
NE142	From 460 Sqn.	
NE176 EA-V	From 460 Sqn via 1LFS.	
NG327 EA-E/K	FTR Mittelland Canal at Gravenhorst 21/22.2.45.	
NG352 EA-J	FTR Würzburg 16/17.3.45.	
NX581 EA-X		

PB195 EA-P	FTR Creil (St Leu d'Esserent) 4/5.7.44.
PB207	Damaged beyond repair at St Leu d'Esserent 7/8.7.44.
PB226	From 460 Sqn.
PB231 EA-H	FTR Revigny 18/19.7.44.
PB250 EA-J	FTR Stuttgart 25/26.7.44.
PB295	To 207 Sqn.
PB299	To 467 Sqn.
PB300 EA-K	FTR Mittelland Canal at Gravenhorst 21/22.11.44.
PB306	To 467 Sqn.
PB347	To 106 Sqn.
PB348	To 227 Sqn.
PB349 EA-H	To 35 Sqn.
PB353 EA-E	FTR Bremen 6/7.10.44.
PB354 EA-G	FTR Mittelland Canal at Gravenhorst 21/22.11.44.
PB355 EA-B	Crashed on Worthing beach following early return from Munich 17.12.44.
PB359	To 106 Sqn.
PB360	To 44 Sqn.
PB361 EA-R	From 35 Sqn.
PB369 EA-A	FTR Harburg 11/12.11.44.
PB370 EA-F	FTR Dortmund-Ems Canal at Ladbergen 4/5.11.44.
PB373 EA-O	To 115 Sqn.
PB374 EA-N	FTR Lützkendorf 8/9.4.45.
PB383 EA-E	From 460 Sqn.
PB385 EA-V	FTR Düsseldorf 2/3.11.44.
PB406 EA-X/L	From 460 Sqn.
PB429 EA-S	FTR Bremen 6/7.10.44.
PB432 EA-O	Crashed in Lincolnshire soon after take-off from Fulbeck when bound for Munich 26.11.44.
PB433 EA-L	To 115 Sqn.
PB455 EA-W/V	To 115 Sqn.
PB460 EA-R	
PB463 EA-Y	From 460 Sqn. Crashed at Fulbeck during transit flight 22.4.45.
PB479	From 460 Sqn.
PB484 EA-T	
PB504 EA-U	
PB519 EA-Q	Crashed on landing at Marston Moor on return from Bergen 29.10.44.
PB522	From 460 Sqn.
PB537 EA-X	FTR Harburg 7/8.3.45.
PB559 EA-B	From 460 Sqn.
PB568 EA-Y	FTR Mittelland Canal at Gravenhorst 21/22.2.45.
PB571 EA-Z	To 115 Sqn.
PB586 EA-E/V	FTR Munich 7/8.1.45.
PB791	
PB797 EA-K	
PB799 EA-G	FTR from night flying training 11.12.44.
PB844 EA-D	To 57sqn.
PB873 EA-N	From 460 Sqn.
PB875 EA-G	From 460 Sqn.
PB907 EA-Q	To 115 Sqn.
RA531 EA-R/S	FTR Lützkendorf 8/9.4.45.
RF153 EA-K	From 50 Sqn. FTR Lützkendorf 14/15.3.45.

RF179 EA-Y
RF215
RF216 EA-J
SW256   From 1661CU to 57 Sqn.
SW265   To 106 Sqn.
SW274 EA-G

Heaviest Single Loss
21/22.06.44   Wesseling. 6 Lancasters FTR.

50 SQUADRON

Motto: From Defence to Attack   Code VN

Originally formed on the 15 May 1916, 50 Squadron's initial role was as a home defence unit patrolling the southern coastal area of England. On the 13 June 1919 it was disbanded while under the command of a certain Major A T Harris, whose future career would have great significance for Bomber Command, and remained on the shelf until its re-formation at Waddington on the 3 May 1937. At the end of 1938 the squadron received Hampdens, and it was with this type under the banner of 5 Group that it would face the impending conflict. Although 5 Group was in action from the very first day of hostilities, 50 Squadron would experience a more gentle introduction, mostly undergoing training, with short periods of detachment to Coastal Command during late 1939 and early 1940. One of the mainstays of 5 Group and Bomber Command throughout the war, 50 Squadron served continuously in the bomber role apart from three short periods of detachment to Coastal Command. It was 5 Group's most prolific squadron, operating Hampdens, Manchesters and Lancasters. It carried out more bombing raids and dispatched more sorties than any other unit in the Group, and delivered the Group's highest tonnage of bombs.

STATIONS

Waddington	03.05.37 to 10.07.40
Lindholme	10.07.40 to 19.07.41
Swinderby	19.07.41 to 26.11.41
Skellingthorpe	26.11.41 to 20.06.42
Swinderby	20.06.42 to 17.10.42
Skellingthorpe	17.10.42 to 15.06.45

COMMANDING OFFICERS

Wing Commander L Young	12.07.38 to 10.04.40
Wing Commander R T Taafe OBE	10.04.40 to 12.06.40
Wing Commander N D Crockart	12.06.40 to 27.06.40
Wing Commander G W Golledge	27.06.40 to 16.12.40
Wing Commander G A Walker DSO DFC	16.12.40 to 26.10.41
Wing Commander R J Oxley DSO DFC	26.10.41 to 20.10.42
Wing Commander W M Russell DFC	20.10.42 to 11.08.43
Wing Commander R Mcfarlane DSO DFC	11.08.43 to 06.12.43
Wing Commander F Pullen DFC	06.12.43 to 21.12.43
Wing Commander A W Heward DFC AFC	21.01.44 to 21.06.44
Wing Commander R T Frogley	21.06.44 to 11.03.45
Wing Commander J Flint DFC GM DFM	11.03.45 to 25.01.46

AIRCRAFT

Hampden	12.38 to 05.42
Manchester	04.42 to 06.42
Lancaster I/Iii	05.42 to 11.46

OPERATIONAL RECORD

Operations	Sorties	Aircraft Losses	% Losses
767	7,135	176	2.5

Category of Operations

Bombing	Mining	Leaflet
620	124	23

Hampden

Operations	Sorties	Aircraft Losses	% Losses
368	2,299	57	2.5

Category of Operations

Bombing	Mining	Leaflet
266	88	14

Manchester

Operations	Sorties	Aircraft Losses	% Losses
44	126	7	5.6

Category of Operations

Bombing	Mining	Leaflet
15	10	9

Lancaster

Operations	Sorties	Aircraft Losses	% Losses
365	4,710	112	2.4

Category of Operations

Bombing	Mining
339	26

TABLE OF STATISTICS

(Heavy squadrons)
Highest number of overall operations in Bomber Command.
Highest number of bombing operations in Bomber Command.
3rd highest number of sorties in Bomber Command.
8th highest number of aircraft operational losses in Bomber Command.

Out of 59 Lancaster squadrons

5th highest number of Lancaster overall operations in Bomber Command.
3rd highest number of Lancaster sorties in Bomber Command.
8th highest number of Lancaster operational losses in Bomber Command.

Out of 22 squadrons in 5 Group

Highest number of overall operations in 5 Group.
Highest number of sorties in 5 Group.
2nd highest number of aircraft operational losses in 5 Group.

Out of 10 Hampden squadrons in 5 Group

Highest number of Hampden overall operations in 5 Group.
2nd highest number of Hampden sorties in 5 Group.
2nd highest number of Hampden operational losses in 5 Group.

Out of 8 Manchester squadrons in 5 Group

5th highest number of Manchester overall operations in 5 Group.
6th highest number of Manchester sorties in 5 Group.
6th highest number of Manchester operational losses in 5 Group.

Out of 17 Lancaster squadrons in 5 Group

4th highest number of Lancaster overall operations in 5 Group.
Highest number of Lancaster sorties in 5 Group.
4th highest number of Lancaster operational losses in 5 Group.

Hampden	To May 1942.
L4062	Crashed while landing at Lindholme on return from Calais 26.9.40.
L4063	Crashed in Scotland on return from patrol 16/17.3.40.
L4064	FTR Kristiansand Norway 12.4.40.
L4065	FTR from mining sortie 13/14.4.40.
L4073	FTR Kristiansand Norway 12.4.40.
L4074	To 44 Sqn.
L4075	To 16 OTU.
L4076	To 14 OTU.
L4077	To 49 Sqn.
L4078	FTR Langenhagen airfield Hanover 26/27.6.40.
L4079	FTR Mönchen-Gladbach 30/31.8.40.
L4080	Damaged beyond repair in taxiing accident at Waddington 17.10.39.
L4081	FTR Kristiansand Norway 12.4.40.
L4083	FTR Kristiansand Norway 12.4.40.
L4084	To 25 OTU.
L4096	Crashed soon after take-off from Waddington while training 31.10.39.
L4097	FTR Ostend 10/11.9.40.
L4099	To 44 Sqn.
L4149	From 106 Sqn. FTR Mannheim 10/11.11.40.
L4150	From 106 Sqn to 16 OTU.
L4164	From 7 Sqn to 1 AAS.
L4168	From 44 Sqn. Returned to 44 Sqn.
P1152	From 44 Sqn. Crashed in Yorkshire following early return mining sortie 16.11.41.
P1156	To 455 Sqn.
P1166	From 144 Sqn. Returned to 144 Sqn.
P1202	Force-landed near Skellingthorpe on return from Hamburg 1.12.41.
P1223	To 1404 Flt.
P1228	To 106 Sqn.
P1239	To 420 Sqn.
P1317	Crashed on approach to Hemswell on return from Leipzig 26/27.8.40.
P1321	From 106 Sqn. Landed on a Norfolk beach on return from Castrop-Rauxel 26.7.40.

P1327	SOC on return from mining sortie 1.8.40.
P1329	FTR Hanover 26/27.6.40.
P1330	To Farnborough.
P1356	From 83 Sqn to 16 OTU.
P2070	FTR Berlin 25/26.8.40.
P2093	To 1 AAS.
P2094	From 144 Sqn to 420 Sqn.
P2124	Ditched off Yorkshire coast on return from Berlin 26.8.40.
P4285	To 44 Sqn.
P4286	To 44 Sqn.
P4287	FTR Hamburg 8/9.9.40.
P4288	Crashed near Waddington while training 9.7.40.
P4289 VN-X	Crashed on approach to Waddington while training 8.6.40.
P4382	FTR from training flight 10/11.8.40.
P4383	FTR from mining sortie 31.7/1.8.40.
P4389	Crashed soon after take-off from Lindholme on air-test 18.6.41.
P4395	To 14 OTU.
P4408	Crashed in North Sea during air-sea rescue operation 15.8.41.
P4409	From 49 Sqn. Crashed on take-off from Lindholme while training 1.4.41.
P4411	Crashed on landing at Docking on return from Berlin 1.10.40.
P4417	FTR Cologne 5/6.10.40.
P5335	From 7 AAU to 144 Sqn.
X2896	Crashed in Scotland on return from Hamburg 3.10.40.
X2897	To 83 Sqn.
X2902	FTR Stuttgart 29/30.9.40.
X2907	FTR Magdeburg 5/6.11.40.
X2908 VN-Y	Crashed at Goole on return from Hamburg 15.11.40.
X2919	Crashed near Wittering on return from Berlin 3.9.41.
X2968	To 16 OTU.
X2983	FTR from mining sortie 14/15.2.41.
X2984	Crashed in Yorkshire on return from Cologne 2.3.41.
X2991	Crashed on take-off from Swinderby en-route to Mannheim 27/28.8.41.
X2992	To 25 OTU.
X2993	FTR Berlin 14/15.10.40.
X2994	Abandoned over Norfolk on return from Essen 8.11.40.
X3000	Abandoned near Linton-on-Ouse on return from Berlin 30.10.40.
X3003	To 16 OTU.
X3004	FTR Düsseldorf 7/8.12.40.
X3022	Converted for use as torpedo bomber to Russian Navy.
X3117	FTR Mannheim 10/11.12.40.
X3125	Crashed in Lincolnshire on return from Kiel 26.11.40.
X3133	FTR Kiel 29/30.6.41.
X3141	FTR Lorient 28/29.12.40.
X3143	Crashed on landing at Lindholme on return from Bremen 2.1.41.
X3145	Converted for use as torpedo bomber to 415 Sqn.
X3146	FTR Hamburg 13/14.3.41.

AD721	FTR Berlin 12/13.3.41.
AD728	FTR from mining sortie 28/29.4.41.
AD730	Crashed in Eire on return from Berlin 17/18.4.41.
AD742	Crashed on approach to Lindholme on return from mining sortie 21.3.41.
AD753	Crashed in the sea en-route to Brest 5.4.41.
AD764	Converted for use as torpedo bomber to 5 OTU.
AD766	To 144 Sqn.
AD789	FTR Düsseldorf 10/11.4.41.
AD795	From 83 Sqn. Converted for use as torpedo bomber to 144 Sqn.
AD797	FTR Düsseldorf 2/3.6.41.
AD824	To 49 Sqn.
AD828	FTR Düsseldorf 10/11.4.41.
AD830	Crashed in Leicester while training 10.4.41.
AD834	FTR from mining sortie 28/29.4.41.
AD836	Converted for use as torpedo bomber to 455 Sqn.
AD839	FTR Frankfurt 29/30.8.41.
AD843	FTR Frankfurt 23/24.7.41.
AD844	FTR Hamburg 16/17.7.41.
AD852	Converted for use as torpedo bomber to 489 Sqn.
AD853	To 420 Sqn.
AD854	Crashed in Bedfordshire on return from Kassel 9.9.41.
AD867	Crashed near Lindholme during air-test 30.5.41.
AD897	Crashed near Lindholme during practice 19.7.41.
AD902	Crashed while landing at Swinderby following early return from mining sortie 29.7.41.
AD908	To 144 Sqn.
AD927	Converted for use as torpedo bomber to 489 Sqn.
AD928	To 144 Sqn.
AD929	From 106 Sqn to 144 Sqn.
AD977	Converted for use as torpedo bomber to 455 Sqn.
AE115	To 420 Sqn.
AE116	Converted for use as torpedo bomber to 489 Sqn.
AE124	Crashed on take-off from Swinderby for mining sortie 8/9.8.41.
AE137	FTR Karlsruhe 5/6.8.41.
AE157	Hit X3025 (44 Sqn) on the ground at Waddington on return from mining sortie 3.9.41.
AE158	To 144 Sqn.
AE159	FTR from mining sortie 28/29.7.41.
AE184 VN-Z	Crashed on landing at Ratcliffe Yorkshire while training 25.10.41.
AE185	FTR Bremen 17/18.8.41.
AE218	From 44 Sqn. Crashed on approach to Skellingthorpe on from Kiel 28.2.42.
AE226	FTR Bremen 12/13.7.41.
AE228	To 455 Sqn.
AE229	Crash-landed on Lincolnshire decoy site on return from Frankfurt 29/30.8.41.
AE230	FTR Bremen 12/13.7.41.
AE231	Converted for use as torpedo bomber to 144 Sqn.
AE234	Crashed soon after take-off from Swinderby en-route to Hanover 25/26.7.41.

AE248	To 144 Sqn.
AE250	Crashed in Cumberland on return from mining sortie 10/11.1.42.
AE251	FTR Cologne 13/14.10.41.
AE256	From 455 Sqn. FTR Kiel 23/24.10.41.
AE291	To 455 Sqn.
AE305	Crash-landed in Norfolk on return from Berlin 3.9.41.
AE306	FTR from mining sortie 7.2.42.
AE316	To 144 Sqn.
AE318	FTR Kiel 7/8.9.41.
AE320	FTR Mannheim 25/26.8.41.
AE367	FTR Hüls 12/13.10.41.
AE369	FTR Norway 27.12.41.
AE370	Converted for use as torpedo bomber to 415 Sqn.
AE373	To 408 Sqn.
AE375	To 408 Sqn.
AE380	FTR Ostend 15/16.12.41.
AE381	Crashed in Derbyshire while training 21.1.42.
AE383	FTR Bremen 20/21.10.41.
AE386	To 14 OTU.
AE387	Crashed on take-off from Skellingthorpe while training 7.3.42.
AE388	From 83 Sqn. Converted for use as torpedo bomber to 144 Sqn.
AE394	Partially abandoned and crashed in York on return from Koblenz 22.2.42.
AE400	FTR from mining sortie 7/8.3.42.
AE401	To 420 Sqn.
AE420	From 83 Sqn. FTR Hamburg 14/15.1.42.
AE422	To 420 Sqn.
AE423	Converted for use as torpedo bomber to 5 OTU.
AE427	FTR from mining sortie 6/7.11.41.
AE428	From 44 Sqn. FTR Norway 27.12.41.
AE429	FTR from mining sortie 24/25.3.42.
AE431	FTR Hamburg 14/15.1.42.
AE435	Converted for use as torpedo bomber to 455 Sqn.
AT109	Converted for use as torpedo bomber to 455 Sqn.
AT118	From 49 Sqn. Force-landed in Cornwall while on air-sea-rescue patrol 26.3.42.
AT125	Converted for use as torpedo bomber to 144 Sqn.
AT139	To 408 Sqn.
AT140	Converted for use as torpedo bomber to 144 Sqn.
AT142	Crashed on approach to Cottesmore on return from Münster 22.1.42.
AT146	To 106 Sqn.
AT147	Converted for use as torpedo bomber to 489 Sqn.
AT151	FTR Essen 25/26.3.42.
AT152	Converted for use as torpedo bomber to 415 Sqn.
AT153	Converted for use as torpedo bomber to 5 OTU.
AT158	FTR from mining sortie 25/26.3.42.
AT173	Abandoned over Norfolk on return from Essen 11.3.42.
AT177	FTR from shipping strike (Channel Dash) 12.2.42.
AT216	Crashed in Lincolnshire soon after take-off from Skellingthorpe when bound for Cologne 6.4.42.

Manchester	From April 1942 to June 1942.
L7277	Flew on the last Manchester operation, to Bremen 25/26.6.42. To 1654CU.
L7289	From 83 Sqn. FTR Bremen 25/26.6.42.
L7291	From 106 Sqn. No operations to 1654CU.
L7294	From 97 Sqn to 1654CU.
L7301 ZN-D	From 106 Sqn on loan. FTR Cologne (Operation Millennium) 30/31.5.42. Manser awarded posthumous VC.
L7401	From 61 Sqn to 1485 T.T.Flt.
L7415	From 61 Sqn to 1654CU.
L7416	To 1654CU.
L7419	From 61 Sqn to 1654CU.
L7432 VN-Z	From 207 Sqn. FTR Bremen 3/4.6.42.
L7455	From 97 Sqn to 1661CU. Completed 23 ops total.
L7456 ZN-T	From 106 Sqn on loan. FTR Cologne (Operation Millennium) 30/31.5.42.
L7460	From 97 Sqn to 1656CU.
L7464	From 61 Sqn to 460 Sqn.
L7468	From 207 Sqn. Completed 19 ops. Became ground instruction machine.
L7469	From 49 Sqn. Returned to 49 Sqn.
L7471	From 61 Sqn. FTR Emden 6/7.6.42.
L7475	From 97 Sqn. Completed 21 ops. Crashed 16.8.42.
L7476 VN-Z	From 207 Sqn to 1654CU.
L7486	From 207 Sqn. Crashed on landing at Skellingthorpe during training 25.3.42.
L7489	From 97 Sqn. FTR Warnemünde 8/9.5.42.
L7491	From 207 Sqn to 1654CU.
L7492	From 97 Sqn to 1654CU.
L7496	From 207 Sqn to 1654CU.
L7516 VN-N	From 61 Sqn. FTR from mining sortie 29/30.4.42.
L7519	From 61 Sqn. Crashed in Lincolnshire while training 13.5.42.
L7521	Crashed while landing at Waddington 5.9.42.
L7525	From 83 Sqn to 1485Flt.
R5769	From 106 Sqn to 9 Sqn.
R5778	From 207 Sqn. Damaged beyond repair during operation to Warnemünde 8/9.5.42.
R5782	From 207 Sqn. FTR Hamburg 17/18.4.42.
R5784	From 61 Sqn to 1660CU.
R5786	From 61 Sqn to 1654CU.
R5833	From 83 Sqn. FTR from mining sortie 5/6.6.42.
R5835	From 49 Sqn to 408 Sqn.
Lancaster	From May 1942.
L7532	From 61 Sqn. No operations to 207 Sqn.
L7534	From 44CF. Undercarriage collapsed when landing at Swinderby while training 13.8.42.
R5503	From 1660CU to 1664CU.
R5546 VN-T	From A&AEE. FTR Nuremberg 30/31.3.44.
R5625	From 83 Sqn. No operations. Returned to 83 Sqn.
R5626	From 83 Sqn. No operations. Returned to 83 Sqn.
R5639 VN-J	FTR Osnabrück 17/18.8.42.
R5680 VN-O	To 106 Sqn.

R5685 VN-P	To 44 Sqn on loan. Returned to 50 Sqn to 460 Sqn.
R5687 VN-N/D	FTR Hamburg 27/28.7.43. (Firestorm).
R5688 VN-G	To 12 Sqn.
R5689 VN-N	Crash-landed in Lincolnshire on return from mining sortie 18/19.9.42.
R5690 VN-H	To 1654CU via 50CF.
R5691 VN-K	FTR Milan 24.10.42.
R5702 VN-S	To 106 Sqn.
R5725 VN-F	FTR Düsseldorf 10/11.9.42.
R5726 VN-B	To 44 Sqn.
R5728 VN-L	FTR Saarbrücken 29/30.7.42. Squadron's first operational loss of a Lancaster.
R5733 VN-O	Flew 31 operations to 44 Sqn.
R5735 VN-G	FTR Düsseldorf 15/16.8.42.
R5739 VN-X	To 1654CU.
R5746 VN-Q	FTR Le Havre 11/12.8.42.
R5747 VN-G	To 83 Sqn and back to 1654CU.
R5753 VN-C	Crashed on landing at Skellingthorpe while training 17.11.43.
R5851	From 207 Sqn to 1654CU.
R5902 VN-T	FTR Wismar 12/13.10.42.
R5909	FTR Wismar 23/24.9.42.
W4112 VN-L	Destroyed in explosion at Scampton 15.3.43.
W4115	To 1651CU via A.V.Roe and A&AEE.
W4117 VN-R	Crashed on landing at Skellingthorpe during training 11.12.42.
W4119 VN-Q	From 207 Sqn via 1661CU. Abandoned over East Kirkby during training 12.2.44.
W4131	To 1660CU via 50CF.
W4135 VN-Q	Flew 21 operations to 44 Sqn.
W4154 VN-A	Flew 21 operations to 100 Sqn.
W4155 VN-M	To 9 Sqn and back. Returned to 9 Sqn.
W4161 VN-J	Became ground instruction machine.
W4163 VN-M/N	To 622 Sqn via 1667CU.
W4194 VN-F	FTR Hamburg. 9/10.11.42.
W4196	From 156 Sqn. Destroyed when W4834 (57 Sqn) blew up at Scampton 15.3.43.
W4232	From 57 Sqn via 1660CU to 5LFS.
W4250	Crashed at Woodhall Spa on return from Turin 9/10.12.42.
W4266 VN-N/S	To 44 Sqn and back. FTR Soltau 17/18.12.42.
W4267	To 44 Sqn.
W4303	No operations to 1654CU.
W4315	To NTU. Returned to 50 Sqn to 61 Sqn.
W4367	To 106 Sqn.
W4380 VN-E	From 467 Sqn to 12 Sqn.
W4381 VN-G	To 207 Sqn.
W4382	From 467 Sqn. FTR Soltau 17/18.12.42.
W4383	From 467 Sqn to 207 Sqn.
W4762	From 61 Sqn. FTR Duisburg 12/13.5.43.
W4772	Conversion Flt only to 1654CU.
W4800 VN-T	FTR Duisburg 8/9.1.43.
W4823	From 467 Sqn. Destroyed on the ground at Scampton when W4834 (57 Sqn) blew up 15.3.43.
W4824 VN-Z	From 467 Sqn. FTR Bois de Cassan 6.8.44.

W4905 VN-H	From 83 Sqn. FTR Frankfurt 4/5.10.43.
W4932	From 97 Sqn. Crashed near Dunholme Lodge during night flying training 19.6.43.
W4933	From 44 Sqn. Crashed at Skellingthorpe 30.3.44.
W5004	To 5LFS.
DV156 VN-C	From 617 Sqn. FTR Turin 12/13.7.43.
DV161	From 9 Sqn to 1653CU.
DV167 VN-M	FTR Reggio Emilia 15/16.7.43.
DV178 VN-N	From 49 Sqn. FTR Berlin 26/27.11.43.
DV197 VN-T	Crash-landed in Northamptonshire on return from Remscheid 31.7.43.
DV217 VN-C	FTR Frankfurt 20/21.12.43.
DV223	Destroyed in forced-landing in Algeria following operation to Milan 7/8.8.43.
DV227 VN-F/L	FTR St Leu d'Esserent 7/8.7.44.
DV234 VN-M	FTR Frankfurt 20/21.12.43.
DV312 VN-J	From 207 Sqn. FTR Revigny 18/19.7.44.
DV324 VN-N	FTR Hanover 8/9.10.43.
DV325 VN-B	FTR Berlin 2/3.12.43.
DV363 VN-H/O/K	Flew 13 Berlin operations. FTR St Leu d'Esserent 7/8.7.44.
DV366 VN-R	FTR Berlin 22/23.11.43.
DV368	To 5LFS. Flew on 11 Berlin operations.
DV375 VN-E	FTR Berlin 29/30.12.43.
DV376 VN-F	FTR Berlin 15/16.2.44.
DV377 VN-X	Destroyed in ground accident at Melbourne on return from Berlin 27.11.43.
DV384 VN-V	From 44 Sqn. FTR Frankfurt 22/23.3.44.
ED308 VN-J	From 57 Sqn via 1661CU. FTR Frankfurt 18/19.3.44.
ED309	From 467 Sqn to 44 Sqn.
ED358	To 106 Sqn.
ED387	From 49 Sqn. FTR Nuremberg 25/26.2.43.
ED388	FTR Berlin 17/18.1.43.
ED393 VN-K	Crashed in Yorkshire on return from Berlin 26/27.11.43.
ED394 VN-R	Crashed while landing at Crosby Cumberland during training 9.1.43.
ED409 VN-S	To 106 Sqn.
ED415 VN-N	FTR Mannheim 23/24.9.43.
ED423 VN-N	FTR Berlin 1/2.3.43.
ED429	FTR Bochum 12/13.6.43.
ED430	From 97 Sqn to 622 Sqn.
ED437	To 617 Sqn.
ED442	To 207 Sqn.
ED445 VN-L	From 49 Sqn. FTR Berlin 23/24.12.43.
ED449 VN-T	FTR Essen 12/13.3.43.
ED468 VN-A	Crashed on take-off at Skellingthorpe when bound for Hamburg 29.7.43.
ED470 VN-O	To 61 Sqn.
ED471	FTR Berlin 17/18.1.43
ED472	FTR Bochum 12/13.6.43.
ED473	To 15 Sqn via 1667CU.
ED475 VN-E	Ditched off Hastings on return from Gelsenkirchen 10.7.43.
ED478 VN-G	Lost in the North Sea on return from Frankfurt 10/11.4.43.
ED482	FTR from mining sortie 2/3.4.43.
ED483 VN-R	FTR Kassel 22/23.10.43.

ED484 VN-Q	FTR Lorient 13/14.2.43.
ED486	Crashed after take-off for Düsseldorf 27.1.43.
ED488 VN-M	FTR Cologne 2/3.2.43.
ED491 VN-H	To 115 Sqn.
ED527 VN-B	Crashed in Morocco after raid on Turin 4/5.2.43
ED585 VN-G	To 1656CU.
ED588 VN-G	From 97 Sqn. Flew 116 operations, 15 to Berlin. FTR Königsburg 29/30.8.44.
ED592 VN-B	FTR Berlin 1/2.3.43.
ED617	From 57 Sqn. FTR Gelsenkirchen 9/10.7.43.
ED690	To BDU 3.43.
ED691 VN-K	FTR Pilsen 16/17.4.43.
ED693 VN-H	FTR Pilsen 13/14.5.43.
ED712	FTR Wuppertal 24/25.6.43.
ED753 VN-M	FTR Essen 25/26.7.43.
ED755 VN-Q	FTR Berlin 3/4.9.43.
ED784 VN-N	FTR Pilsen 16/17.4.43.
ED800 VN-U	FTR Pilsen 16/17.4.43.
ED810 VN-Z	FTR Oberhausen 14/15.6.43.
ED828 VN-B/S	FTR Bochum 12/13.6.43.
ED856 VN-K/A	From 156 Sqn. FTR Darmstadt 25/26.8.44.
ED870 VN-I/J	From 97 Sqn. Completed 11 Berlin raids. FTR Mailly-le-Camp 3/4.5.44.
EE124 VN-B/Z	To 300 Sqn.
EE174 VN-A	From 97 Sqn. FTR Nuremburg 30/31.3.44.
EE189 VN-S	FTR Hanover 27/28.9.43.
JA899 VN-D	Flew 13 operations to Berlin. FTR Prouville 24/25.6.44.
JA961 VN-A	Damaged in ground accident at Melbourne on return from Berlin 27.11.43.
JB143 VN-L	FTR from mining sortie 29/30.9.43.
LL741 VN-X	FTR Mittelland Canal at Gravenhorst 21/22.2.45.
LL744 VN-B	FTR Brunswick 22/23.5.44.
LL786	To 5LFS.
LL791 VN-O	FTR Augsburg 25/26.2.44.
LL840 VN-M	FTR Gelsenkirchen 21/22.6.44.
LL841 VN-O	FTR Rennes 8/9.6.44.
LL842 VN-F	FTR Stuttgart 24/25.7.44.
LL922 VN-E/T	FTR Secqueville 7/8.8.44.
LM162	Crashed in Lincolnshire after collision on return from Stuttgart 12/13.9.44.
LM210 VN-D	FTR Stuttgart 28/29.7.44.
LM212 VN-L	FTR Dortmund-Ems Canal 23/24.9.44.
LM222 VN-Y	FTR Königsburg 29/30.8.44.
LM234 VN-K	FTR Leuna 14/15.1.45.
LM236	To 1651CU.
LM264 VN-J	FTR Calais 24.9.44.
LM296 VN-T	Completed 50 operations.
LM360	From 61 Sqn. Written off at Fiskerton 11.11.44.
LM368 VN-S	From 467 Sqn to 1653CU.
LM394 VN-R	FTR Nuremburg 30/31.3.44.
LM428 VN-O	FTR Berlin 28/29.1.44.
LM429 VN-T/C	FTR Lille 10/11.5.44.
LM435 VN-E	FTR Chatellerault 9/10.8.44.
LM437 VN-P	FTR Mailly-le-Camp 3/4.5.44.

LM480 VN-U	FTR Mailly-le-Camp 3/4.5.44.
LM591	To ECDU.
LM628 VN-M	FTR Gravenhorst 6/7.11.44.
LM629 VN-O	To 5LFS.
LM656 VN-W	From 619 Sqn. FTR Munich 17/18.12.44.
LM676 VN-W	FTR Munich 17/18.12.44.
LM680	To 630 Sqn.
ME295 VN-P	To 463 Sqn.
ME319 VN-M	
ME429	
ME441 VN-W	FTR Böhlen 20/21.3.45.
ME483 VN-A	
ME567 VN-G	To 1664CU.
ME572 VN-Z	FTR Aachen 11/12.4.44.
ME578 VN-K	FTR Frankfurt 22/23.3.44.
ME700 VN-N/V	FTR Dortmund-Ems Canal 23/24.9.44.
ME797 VN-J	FTR Duisburg 21/22.5.44.
ME798 VN-Z	FTR Prouville 24/25.6.44.
ME813	Crashed while landing at Skellingthorpe 8.8.44.
ND874 VN-R	FTR St Pierre de Mont 5/6.6.44.
ND876 VN-Z	FTR Munich 24/25.4.44.
ND953 VN-S	FTR Mailly-le-Camp 3/4.5.44.
ND989	Crashed on approach to Benson on return from Tours 19/20.5.44.
ND991	To Flight Refuelling Ltd.
NE135 VN-F	FTR Rüsselsheim 12/13.8.44.
NF918 VN-N	FTR Böhlen 5/6.3.45.
NF919 VN-D	FTR Darmstadt 11/12.9.44.
NF921 VN-Q	FTR Königsburg 29/30.8.44.
NF922 VN-G/U	
NF930	To 433 Sqn.
NF984	FTR Mittelland Canal at Gravenhorst. Crash-landed at Juvincourt 1/2.1.45.
NG127 VN-D	Crashed on take-off from Skellingthorpe when bound for Mittelland Canal at Gravenhorst 1.1.45.
NG171	Crashed on landing at Florennes when bound for Wesel 23.3.45.
NG177 VN-L	FTR Lützkendorf 14/15.3.45.
NG271	From 1651CU. Crashed near Waddington when bound for Ijmuiden 6.4.45.
NG302 VN-R	Shot down by Allied flak over Holland on return from Munich 17/18.12.44.
NG326 VN-Q	
NG342 VN-S	FTR Hamburg/Finkenwerder 9.4.45.
NG381 VN-A	FTR Karlsruhe 2/3.2.45.
NG385 VN-P	From 1669CU. FTR Pölitz 8/9.2.45.
NN694 VN-L	FTR Lille 10/11.5.44.
PA222 VN-K	
PA223 VN-D	FTR Karlsruhe 2/3.2.45.
PA968 VN-S	FTR Donges 24/25.7.44.
PA994 VN-H	FTR Königsburg 29/30.8.44.
PA996 VN-J	FTR St Leu d'Esserent 7/8.7.44.
PB755 VN-Y	
PB821 VN-E	

PD237 VN-D	FTR Bordeaux 13.8.44.
PD291	To 1656CU.
PD292 VN-H	FTR Royan 4.1.45.
PD294 VN-A	FTR Darmstadt 11/12.9.44.
PD316 VN-A	FTR Dortmund-Ems Canal at Ladbergen 7/8.2.45.
PD326	FTR Bergen 28/29.10.44.
PD339 VN-J	Crashed in Northamptonshire during transit following Exodus sortie 26.4.45.
PD340 VN-C	
PD346 VN-V	FTR Siegen 1/2.2.45.
PD362	To 467 Sqn.
PD368	To 9 Sqn.
RA565	
RA591 VN-P	
RE133 VN-D	
RE135	
RF138 VN-D	FTR Mittelland Canal at Gravenhorst 21/22.2.45.
RF153	To 49 Sqn.
RF175	To 463 Sqn.
RF180	To 467 Sqn.
RF249 VN-L	
RF267 VN-M	
SW249	
SW253	
SW261	To 83 Sqn.
SW262	To 83 Sqn.
SW264 VN-F	

Heaviest Single Loss

12.04.40	Kristiansand Norway. 4 Hampdens FTR.
03/04.05.44	Mailly-le-Camp. 4 Lancasters FTR.
29/30.08.44	Königsberg 4 Lancasters FTR.

57 SQUADRON

Motto: Corpus Non Animum Muto (I change my body not my spirit)   Code DX

The history of 57 Squadron can be traced back to its original formation as a flying training unit on the 8 June 1916. In December of that year it moved to France and became a fighter squadron, before changing roles yet again in the summer of 1917, and spending the remainder of the war as a bomber and reconnaissance unit, eventually undergoing disbandment on the last day of 1919. The squadron remained on the shelf until its re-formation as a light bomber unit in October 1931, and continued in this role, eventually taking delivery of Blenheims at the end of March 1938. It was with this type that the squadron faced the impending conflict in September 1939. No. 57 Squadron was in action from the start of hostilities flying Blenheims with the Advanced Air Striking Force in France. On return to the UK the squadron joined 2 Group, before spending a short time with Coastal Command and ultimately converting to the Wellington for a move to 3 Group. In the autumn of 1942 the squadron underwent another metamorphosis, joining 5 Group as a Lancaster unit. Its C Flight became the nucleus of 617 Squadron in March 1943, and of

630 Squadron in November. In whichever aircraft and Group 57 Squadron operated it sustained higher than average percentage casualties. That not withstanding the unit served with distinction until war's end.

Posted from 3 Group 04.09.42

STATIONS

Scampton 04.09.42 to 28.08.43
East Kirkby 28.08.43 to 25.11.45

COMMANDING OFFICERS

Wing Commander E J Laine DFC 30.07.42 To 23.09.42
Wing Commander F C Hopcroft 23.09.42 to 28.07.43
Wing Commander W R Haskell 28.07.43 to 18.08.43
Wing Commander H W H Fisher DFC 19.08.43 to 15.04.44
Wing Commander H Y Humphreys DFC 15.04.44 to 08.01.45
Wing Commander J N Tomes 08.01.45 to 12.06.45

AIRCRAFT

Lancaster I/III 09.42 to 05.46

OPERATIONAL RECORD

Lancasters

Operations	Sorties	Aircraft Losses	% Losses
348	4,037	108	2.7

Category of Operations

Bombing	Mining
313	35

TABLE OF STATISTICS

(Heavy squadrons)
15th highest number of overall operations in Bomber Command.
23rd highest number of sorties in Bomber Command.
9th highest number of aircraft operational losses in Bomber Command.
17th highest number of bombing operations in Bomber Command.
21st highest number of mining operations in Bomber Command.
Highest percentage loss rate in Bomber Command.

Out of 59 Lancaster squadrons

6th highest number of Lancaster overall operations in Bomber Command.
11th highest number of Lancaster sorties in Bomber Command.
12th highest number of Lancaster operational losses in Bomber Command.

Out of 22 squadrons in 5 Group

8th highest number of overall operations in 5 Group.
7th highest number of sorties in 5 Group.
8th highest number of aircraft operational losses in 5 Group.

Out of 17 Lancaster squadrons in 5 Group

5th highest number of Lancaster overall operations in 5 Group.
6th highest number of Lancaster sorties in 5 Group.
6th highest number of Lancaster operational losses in 5 Group.

Lancaster	From September 1942.
R5751 DX-M	From 49 Sqn to 1661CU.
R5865	From 207 Sqn to 1661CU.
R5894 DX-T	From 9 Sqn. Crashed near Scampton on return from Berlin 2.3.43.
W4130 DX-B	From 207 Sqn. FTR Cologne 15/16.10.42. (Squadron's first Lancaster loss).
W4132	To 9 Sqn.
W4165 DX-R	From 207 Sqn. FTR Hamburg 9/10.11.42.
W4189 DX-A	First off on Squadron's first Lancaster operation. FTR Hamburg 30/31.1.43.
W4190 DX-N	To 1661CU.
W4201 DX-F	Crashed at Scampton on return from mining sortie 14.3.43.
W4232 DX-G/C/B	To 50 Sqn via 1660CU.
W4234 DX-P	FTR Munich 21/22.12.42.
W4240 DX-Q	To 467 Sqn.
W4246 DX-L	Abandoned over Kent on return from mining sortie 7.11.42.
W4247 DX-S/X	FTR Hamburg 9/10.11.42.
W4250 DX-K	Crashed in Lincolnshire during operation to Turin 9/10.12.42.
W4251 DX-T	FTR Milan 24.10.42.
W4252 DX-X	FTR Kiel 4/5.4.43.
W4254 DX-S	From 9 Sqn. FTR Stettin 20/21.4.43.
W4257 DX-O	FTR St Nazaire 2/3.4.43.
W4262	Crashed near Binbrook on return from mining sortie 10.11.42.
W4267	From 44 Sqn. Crashed in Lincolnshire while training 27.1.43.
W4307 DX-O	FTR Hamburg 9/10.11.42.
W4358 DX-O/L	To 9 Sqn via 1661CU.
W4359	Crashed in Cornwall while training 17.12.42.
W4360	FTR Stuttgart 22/23.11.42.
W4375 DX-X	From 467 Sqn. FTR Wilhelmshaven 18/19.2.43.
W4376	From 467 Sqn to 103 Sqn.
W4377 DX-L	From 467 Sqn. FTR Krefeld 21/22.6.43.
W4384 DX-D	From 467 Sqn. FTR Wilhelmshaven 11/12.2.43.
W4766	To 61 Sqn.
W4772	To 50CF.
W4775 DX-J	To 1661CU.
W4797 DX-S	From 467 Sqn to 1668CU.
W4822 DX-P	From 49 Sqn. FTR Düsseldorf 3/4.11.43.
W4824 DX-H	From 467 Sqn and back via 1660CU.
W4834	From 1656CU. Destroyed at Scampton when bomb load exploded 15.3.43.
W4940	To 617 Sqn.
W4944 DX-X/X-	FTR Pilsen 13/14.5.43.

W4948 DX-J/S	Shot down by intruder over Lincolnshire on return from Hanover 23.9.43.
W5008 DX-B	To 617 Sqn on loan. Returned to 57 Sqn. FTR Nuremberg 27/28.8.43.
DV161	From 460 Sqn to 9 Sqn.
DV201 DX-M	FTR Mannheim 23/24.9.43.
DV235 DX-C	FTR Munich 2/3.10.43.
ED306	Destroyed at Scampton when W4834's bomb load blew up 15.3.43.
ED308 DX-D	From 9 Sqn to 630 Sqn.
ED319 DX-H	FTR Essen 9/10.1.43.
ED320	To 101 Sqn.
ED329	From 617 Sqn. FTR Duisburg 12/13.5.43.
ED348 DX-U	From 49 Sqn to 44 Sqn.
ED352 DX-Q	From 49 Sqn. FTR Turin 4/5.2.43.
ED371 DX-Q	From 207 Sqn. No operations.
ED385	To 106 Sqn.
ED390 DX-V	FTR Dortmund 4/5.5.43.
ED392	To 12 Sqn.
ED411	To 166 Sqn.
ED412 DX-O	To 207 Sqn.
ED413 DX-C	To 630 Sqn.
ED594	From 83 Sqn. Destroyed at Scampton when W4834 blew up 15.3.43.
ED616 DX-B	FTR Hamburg 29/30.7.43.
ED617	FTR Gelsenkirchen 9/10.7.43.
ED655 DX-X/X-	To 630 Sqn.
ED667 DX-W	FTR Pilsen 13/14.5.43.
ED668 DX-B	FTR Bochum 12/13.6.43.
ED698 DX-R	To 630 Sqn.
ED706 DX-F/A	FTR Essen 30.4/1.5.43.
ED707 DX-X/J/F	FTR Dortmund 23/24.5.43.
ED757 DX-K	Crashed while landing at Scampton following air-test 10.7.43.
ED758 DX-N	To 630 Sqn.
ED761 DX-Z	FTR Berlin 29/30.3.43.
ED762 DX-Y	Crash-landed while trying to land at Scampton during training 3.5.43.
ED766 DX-P	FTR Frankfurt 10/11.4.43.
ED770 DX-E	FTR Stettin 20/21.4.43.
ED777 DX-Q	To 630 Sqn.
ED778 DX-I	FTR Duisburg 12/13.5.43.
ED779 DX-U	To 300 Sqn.
ED781 DX-E/J	From 97 Sqn. FTR Wuppertal 24/25.6.43.
ED827 DX-Z	Crashed at Scampton on return from Nuremberg 28.8.43.
ED861 DX-D	FTR Turin 12/13.7.43.
ED920 DX-A	To 630 Sqn.
ED931 DX-C	To 617 Sqn on loan and back. FTR Hamburg 29/30.7.43.
ED941 DX-V	Crashed on approach to East Kirkby during transit flight from Waterbeach 28.9.43.
ED943 DX-T	FTR Gelsenkirchen 25/26.6.43.
ED944 DX-I	To 630 Sqn.

ED946 DX-E	Crashed soon after take-off from Swinderby while training 28.8.43.
ED947 DX-G	FTR Cologne 8/9.7.43.
ED970 DX-H	FTR Dortmund 23/24.5.43.
ED989 DX-F	From 83 Sqn. FTR Peenemünde 17/18.8.43.
ED992 DX-O	FTR Nuremberg 10/11.8.43.
ED994 DX-W	To 576 Sqn.
EE193 DX-S	To 166 Sqn.
EE197 DX-Y	To 617 Sqn on loan. Returned to 57 Sqn to 207 Sqn.
JA695	To 61 Sqn via 5MU.
JA696 DX-J	FTR Hamburg 2/3.8.43.
JA872 DX-U	To 630 Sqn.
JA875 DX-K	FTR Mannheim 23/24.9.43.
JA896 DX-D	Crashed on landing at Scampton on return from Milan 16.8.43.
JA910 DX-H	FTR Bochum 29/30.9.43.
JA914 DX-O-	FTR Berlin 3/4.9.43.
JB135	To 630 Sqn.
JB233 DX-F	FTR Berlin 23/24.12.43.
JB234 DX-E	FTR Leipzig 20/21.10.43.
JB236	To 630 Sqn.
JB237 DX-Z	FTR Kassel 22/23.10.43.
JB311 DX-B	FTR Berlin 28/29.1.44.
JB315	Crashed in Leicestershire during training 17.11.43.
JB318 DX-O/Q/L	FTR Revigny 18/19.7.44.
JB320 DX-X	FTR Kassel 22/23.10.43.
JB364 DX-M	FTR Berlin 2/3.1.44.
JB366 DX-S/N	FTR Berlin 27/28.1.44.
JB370 DX-O	To 617 Sqn on loan. Returned to 57 Sqn. FTR St Leu d'Esserent 7/8.7.44.
JB372 DX-R	FTR Berlin 2/3.12.43.
JB373 DX-N	FTR Berlin 16/17.12.43.
JB418 DX-I	FTR Berlin 18/19.11.43.
JB419 DX-E	FTR Berlin 20/21.1.44.
JB420 DX-S	FTR Berlin 15/16.2.44.
JB474 DX-F	FTR Stuttgart 15/16.3.44.
JB485 DX-L	FTR Berlin 26/27.11.43.
JB486 DX-F	FTR St Leu d'Esserent 4/5.7.44.
JB526 DX-D	FTR Wesseling 21/22.6.44.
JB529 DX-P	FTR Berlin 2/3.12.43.
JB539 DX-S/X	FTR Berlin 24/25.3.44.
JB541 DX-A	FTR Stettin 5/6.1.44.
JB546	To 630 Sqn.
JB548 DX-O/Q	FTR Berlin 1/2.1.44.
JB565 DX-I	From 61 Sqn. FTR Schweinfurt 24/25.2.44.
JB681 DX-J	FTR Berlin 2/3.1.44.
JB723 DX-L/P	FTR St Leu d'Esserent 4/5.7.44.
JB725 DX-M	FTR from mining sortie 9/10.4.44.
LL893 DX-J	FTR La Chappelle 20/21.4.44.
LL935 DX-A	To 115 Sqn.
LL939 DX-B/H	FTR Harburg 11/12.11.44.
LL940 DX-S	Damaged in accident 15.1.45.
LL967	To 1651CU.
LM114 DX-O	To 38MU.

LM115 DX-M	FTR Wesseling 21/22.6.44.
LM132	From 103 Sqn.
LM186 DX-D	
LM214 DX-U	To 1653CU.
LM231 DX-T	
LM232 DX-G/F/P	FTR Königsburg 26/27.8.44.
LM278 DX-L	FTR From mining sortie 26/27.8.44.
LM279 DX-T	Crashed in Northamptonshire when bound for Brest 2.9.44.
LM284	FTR from air test 30.7.44.
LM322 DX-X	Crashed on take-off from Scampton when bound for Hamburg 3.8.43.
LM336 DX-G	FTR Mannheim 23/24.9.43.
LM340	From 405 Sqn to 1668CU.
LM517 DX-B/C	
LM522 DX-G	FTR St Leu d'Esserent 7/8.7.44.
LM573 DX-U	FTR Wesseling 21/22.6.44.
LM579 DX-O	FTR Darmstadt 25/26.8.44.
LM580 DX-L	FTR Wesseling 21/22.6.44.
LM582 DX-B/F	
LM624 DX-A	FTR Gravenhorst 6/7.11.44.
LM626 DX-M	FTR Munich 17/18.12.44.
LM653 DX-Q	From 49 Sqn. FTR Halle 20/21.3.45.
LM673 DX-U	To 630 Sqn and back. Destroyed when PB360 blew up at East Kirkby 17.4.45.
LM678 DX-V	To 227 Sqn.
ME626 DX-J	To 1653CU.
ME679 DX-K	FTR Munich 24/25.4.44.
ME845 DX-F	From 630 Sqn.
ME864 DX-E	FTR Stuttgart 28/29.7.44.
ME868 DX-K	FTR St Leu d'Esserent 7/8.7.44.
ND405	To 550 Sqn.
ND406 DX-T	To 156 Sqn.
ND468 DX-M	FTR Mailly-le-Camp 3/4.5.44.
ND471 DX-A	Ditched in North Sea on return from Wesseling 22.6.44.
ND472 DX-G/I	To 617 Sqn on loan. Returned to 57 Sqn. Destroyed when PB360 blew up at East Kirkby 17.4.45.
ND475	Crashed in Cambridgeshire on return from Juvisy 18/19.4.44.
ND503 DX-E	FTR Leipzig 19/20.2.44.
ND506 DX-C	To 166 Sqn.
ND509 DX-C/I/P	To 61 Sqn.
ND560 DX-N/M	FTR Stuttgart 24/25.7.44.
ND572 DX-F	From 103 Sqn. Collided with ME473 (207 Sqn) over Lincolnshire during fighter affiliation exercise 2.3.45.
ND582 DX-S	Crashed on landing at Croydon on return from La Chappelle 21.4.44.
ND622 DX-E	FTR Nuremberg 30/31.3.44.
ND671 DX-I	FTR Berlin 24/25.3.44.
ND786 DX-I	FTR Munich 24/25.4.44.
ND878 DX-B	FTR Brunswick 22/23.5.44.
ND879 DX-H	FTR Brunswick 22/23.5.44.
ND954 DX-Q	FTR Joigny la Roche 31.7.44.

ND960 DX-I	FTR from mining sortie 21/22.5.44.
ND977 DX-R	
NE127 DX-J	FTR Dortmund 22/23.5.44.
NG126 DX-L	FTR Bremerhaven 18/19.9.44.
NG145 DX-J	From 630 Sqn. FTR Heilbronn 4/5.12.44.
NG199 DX/L	FTR Giessen 5/6.12.44.
NG225 DX-K	
NG395 DX-J/L	
NG398 DX-N	FTR Lützkendorf 14/15.3.45.
NG410 DX-D/G	Force-landed in Warwickshire on return from Böhlen 6.3.45.
NN696 DX-H	FTR Wesseling 21/22.6.44.
NN701 DX-K	
NN723	To 619 Sqn.
NN765 DX-X	From 44 Sqn. Destroyed when PB360 blew up at East Kirkby 17.4.45.
NN769 DX-L	
NX580 DX-V	
PA332	
PB261 DX-L	From 619 Sqn.
PB280 DX-W/P	
PB297 DX-H	From 619 Sqn.
PB348 DX-T	From 227 Sqn. Abandoned over Lincolnshire when bound for Royan 5.1.45.
PB360 DX-U/N	From 44 Sqn. Blew up at East Kirkby while being prepared for operation to Cham 17.4.45.
PB382 DX-I/N	FTR Pölitz 8/9.2.45.
PB384 DX-F	FTR from mining sortie 16/17.8.44.
PB425 DX-G	FTR Nuremberg 19/20.10.44.
PB744	To 189 Sqn.
PB784 DX-H	
PB844 DX-N	From 49 Sqn.
PB852 DX-V	From 619 Sqn. FTR Harburg 7/8.3.45.
PB894	To 630 Sqn.
PD212 DX-F	FTR Stuttgart 28/29.7.44.
PD236	From 103 Sqn.
PD263 DX-G	FTR Heimbach 11.12.44.
PD264 DX-K	FTR Giessen 6/7.12.44.
PD282 DX-E	
PD347 DX-P	Destroyed when PB360 blew up at East Kirkby 17.4.45.
PD427	
RA530 DX-Y	Crashed in Lincolnshire soon after take-off from East Kirkby when bound for Böhlen 20.3.45.
RA596	
RF124 DX-M	To 630 Sqn
RF193 DX-G	From 103 Sqn.
RF195 DX-F	From 207 Sqn. Destroyed when PB360 blew up at East Kirkby 17.4.45.
RF202 DX-G	
SW245 DX-L	FTR Munich 16/17.12.44.
SW256 DX-I/L	From 49 Sqn.

Heaviest Single Loss

21/22.6.44	Wesseling. 6 Lancasters FTR (1 ditched, crew rescued).

61 SQUADRON

Motto Per Purum Tonantes (Thundering through the clear sky)   Code QR

No. 61 Squadron first came into existence in the home defence role on the 24 July 1917. In June 1919 it was disbanded, and remained on the shelf until the 8 March 1937, when it was re-formed as a bomber squadron. After operating Blenheims for thirteen months the squadron re-equipped with Hampdens in line with the rest of 5 Group, receiving its first example of the type, L4103 on the 17 February 1939. A full complement of aircraft arrived on the squadron's station at Hemswell by the 7 March. No. 61 Squadron was operational at the start of the war, but was used sparingly. It converted from Hampdens to Manchesters in mid 1941, and in May 1942 became the seventh unit in the Command to take on the Lancaster. A third Flight was added at the end of 1942 to enable the squadron to become the first in the Command to operate the radial engine Mk II Lancaster. The first operation with the type was carried out in early January 1943, but after a few months the Mk IIs were transferred to 3 Group's 115 Squadron. Thereafter the squadron served with distinction to the end of hostilities employing standard Mk I/III.

STATIONS

Hemswell	08.03.37 to 17.07.41
North Luffenham	17.07.41 to 16.10.41
Woolfox Lodge	16.10.41 to 05.05.42
Syerston	05.05.42 to 15.11.43
St Eval (Detachment)	16.07.42 to 22.08.42
Skellingthorpe	15.11.43 to 01.02.44
Coningsby	01.02.44 to 15.04.44
Skellingthorpe	15.04.44 to 16.06.45

COMMANDING OFFICERS

Squadron Leader C H Brill	22.03.37 to 26.09.39
Wing Commander C M De Crespigny	26.09.39 to 12.02.40
Wing Commander F M Denny	12.02.40 to 19.05.40
Wing Commander G H Sheen DSO	19.05.40 to 12.11.40
Wing Commander G E Valentine DSO	12.11.40 to 03.09.41
Wing Commander C T Weir DFC	05.09.41 to 19.06.42
Wing Commander C M Coad AFC	19.06.42 to 11.02.43
Wing Commander W M Penman DFC AFC	11.02.43 to 04.10.43
Wing Commander R N Stidolph DFC	04.10.43 to 22.04.44
Wing Commander A W Doubleday DSO DFC	22.04.44 to 25.09.44
Wing Commander W D Pexton DFC AFC	25.09.44 to 23.02.45
Wing Commander C W Scott AFC	23.02.45 to 12.06.45

AIRCRAFT

Hampden	02.39 to 10.41
Manchester	07.41 to 06.42
Lancaster I/III	06.42 to 05.46
Lancaster II	10.42 to 03.43

OPERATIONAL RECORD

Operations	Sorties	Aircraft Losses	% Losses
704	6,082	156	2.6

Category of Operations

Bombing	Mining	Other
613	85	6

Hampden

Operations	Sorties	Aircraft Losses	% Losses
283	1,339	28	2.1

Category of Operations

Bombing	Mining	Other
229	49	5

Manchester

Operations	Sorties	Aircraft Losses	% Losses
44	197	12	6.1

Category of Operations

Bombing	Mining
33	11

Lancaster

Operations	Sorties	Aircraft Losses	% Losses
377	4,546	116	2.6

Category of Operations

Bombing	Mining	Other
351	25	1

TABLE OF STATISTICS

(heavy squadrons)

5th highest number of overall operations in Bomber Command.
11th highest number of sorties in Bomber Command.
19th equal (with 10 Sqn) highest number of aircraft operational losses in Bomber Command.
2nd highest number of bombing operations in Bomber Command.
3rd highest number of overall Lancaster operations in Bomber Command.
5th highest number of Lancaster sorties in Bomber Command.
5th highest number of Lancaster operational losses in Bomber Command.

Out of 22 squadrons in 5 Group

2nd highest number of overall operations in 5 Group.
4th highest number of sorties in 5 Group.
5th highest number of aircraft operational losses in 5 Group.

Out of 12 Hampden squadrons in 5 Group

5th highest number of Hampden operations in 5 Group.
6th highest number of Hampden sorties in 5 Group.
8th highest number of Hampden operational losses in 5 Group.

Out of 8 Manchester squadrons in 5 Group

2nd highest number of Manchester operations in 5 Group.
2nd highest number of Manchester sorties in 5 Group.
2nd highest number of Manchester operational losses in 5 Group.

Out of 17 Lancaster squadrons in 5 Group

2nd highest number of Lancaster overall operations in 5 Group.
2nd highest number of Lancaster sorties in 5 Group.
3rd highest number of Lancaster operational losses in 5 Group.

Hampden	To October 1941.
L4103	To 106 Sqn.
L4104	To 83 Sqn.
L4105	To 16 OTU.
L4106	To 83 Sqn.
L4108	To 144 Sqn.
L4109	To 14 OTU.
L4110	To 14 OTU.
L4111	Crashed on approach to Digby on return from patrol 8.3.40.
L4112	FTR from mining sortie 27/28.6.40.
L4113	FTR from mining sortie 14/15.4.40.
L4115	To 44 Sqn.
L4116	Crashed on landing at Hemswell while training 17.4.40.
L4117	To 14 OTU.
L4119	Crashed in Leicestershire on return from Aalborg 1.5.40
L4120	To 106 Sqn.
L4146 QR-R	From 76 Sqn. FTR from rail targets in Germany 23/24.5.40.
P1170	Crashed on landing at Doncaster while training 14.10.39.
P1171	To 83 Sqn.
P1253	From 106 Sqn. Crashed in Suffolk on return from Cologne 2.3.41.
P1323	To 49 Sqn.
P2082	FTR from mining sortie 5/6.11.40.
P2088	To 14 OTU.
P2089	Crash-landed in Dorset on return from Bordeaux 19/20.8.40.
P2090 QR-R	FTR Kiel 26/27.9.40.
P2144	Force-landed on approach to Bircham Newton on return from Düsseldorf 3.6.41.
P4298	To 25 OTU.
P4324 QR-P	FTR Merseburg 26/27.8.40.
P4335	FTR Salzbergen 12/13.8.40.
P4336	FTR from rail targets in the Ruhr 9/10.6.40.
P4337	To 5 OTU.
P4338	To 144 Sqn.
P4339 QR-H	Collided with Hampden L4138 (16 OTU) seconds after take-off from Cottesmore 13.6.40.
P4341	FTR Geestacht 29/30.6.40.
P4342	To 25 OTU.
P4343	FTR from mining sortie 20/21.7.40.
P4344	FTR from mining sortie 20/21.7.40.
P4346	FTR Schwerte 21/22.6.40.
P4349	Crash-landed in Norfolk on return from Hanover 7/8.6.40.

P4355	FTR from rail targets in Germany 20/21.6.40.
P4356	FTR Geestacht 29/30.6.40.
P4357	Ditched off Yorkshire coast during training 5.8.40.
P4358	FTR from mining sortie 20/21.7.40.
P4379	FTR Salzbergen 12/13.8.40.
P4390	FTR Dortmund-Ems Canal 7/8.7.40.
P4396	FTR Hamburg 13/14.11.40.
P4397	Damaged at Hemswell in collision with X2911 (61 Sqn) during take-off for Calais 24.9.40.
P4398	To 83 Sqn.
P4399	Crashed in Kent on return from Cologne 31.7.41.
P4400	To 25 OTU.
P4401	Converted for use as torpedo bomber.
P4405	Crashed 1n Norfolk on return from Wilhelmshaven 10.2.41.
P4418	To 14 OTU.
X2893	To A&AEE.
X2894	Crashed in Norfolk on return from Stettin 5/6.9.40.
X2906	To 25 OTU.
X2911	Collided with P4397 (61 Sqn) on take-off from Hemswell en-route to Calais 24.9.40.
X2912	To 49 Sqn.
X2920	Crashed in Yorkshire on return from mining sortie 5/6.10.40.
X2922	FTR Boulogne 13/14.9.40.
X2967	FTR Berlin 14/15.11.40.
X2971	FTR Kiel 25/26.10.40.
X2975	FTR Düsseldorf 8/9.12.40.
X2979	Crashed in Norfolk on return from Merseburg 17.10.40.
X2980	To 16 OTU.
X2981	Exploded in the air during trials of Imp Mine 20.12.40.
X2987	Crashed while landing at Hemswell on return from Duisburg 22.11.40.
X2989	To 408 Sqn.
X3005	Abandoned over Yorkshire on return from Kiel 24.3.41.
X3006	Crashed on take-off from Hemswell en-route to Hamburg 14.11.40.
X3058	To 106 Sqn.
X3064	Crashed in Lincolnshire on return from Kiel 26.11.40.
X3120	FTR Düsseldorf 2/3.6.41.
X3126	Crashed on approach to Hemswell on return from abortive operation to Bremen 3.1.41.
X3127	FTR Kiel 8/9.8.41.
X3128	FTR Mannheim 16/17.12.40.
X3138	To 5 AOS.
X3140	To 408 Sqn.
X3147	Crashed in Norfolk on return from Cologne 2.3.41.
AD723	Crashed in Lincolnshire on return from Cologne 2.3.41.
AD725	Crashed on landing at Hemswell during training 1.2.41.
AD727	From 44 Sqn. FTR from mining sortie 11/12.6.41.
AD732	FTR Cherbourg 18.4.41.
AD752	To 144 Sqn.
AD754	From 144 Sqn to 408 Sqn.
AD804	To 144 Sqn.
AD806	FTR Osnabrück 5/6.7.41.
AD825	Abandoned near Swindon on return from Brest 18.4.41.

AD826	To 455 Sqn.
AD827	FTR Kiel 8/9.4.41.
AD868	To 44 Sqn.
AD937	FTR Mönchengladbach 7/8.7.41.
AD963	To 408 Sqn.
AD974	To 49 Sqn.
AE135	To 455 Sqn.
AE186	From 207 Sqn to 44 Sqn.
AE189 QR-G	FTR Kiel 24/25.7.41.
AE200	To 144 Sqn.
AE202	To 44 Sqn.
AE219	From 207 Sqn to 408 Sqn.
AE235	To 144 Sqn.
AE247	From 207 Sqn. FTR Frankfurt 29/30.8.41.
AE256	To 455 Sqn.
AE259	Crashed in Lincolnshire on return from Kiel 9.8.41.
AE263	FTR Kiel 8/9.8.41.
AE266	Crashed on landing at Upwood on return from Cologne 31.7.41.
AE286	To 408 Sqn.
AE288	To 408 Sqn.
AE289	To 408 Sqn.
AE290	To 44 Sqn.
AE308	To 455 Sqn.
AE352	To 455 Sqn.
Manchester	From June 1941 to June 1942.
L7276	From A&AEE. No operations to 25 OTU.
L7284	From 207 Sqn. No operations to 39MU.
L7288	From 97 Sqn. No operations to 1654CU.
L7292	From 97 Sqn. No operations to TDU.
L7293	From 49 Sqn to 207 Sqn.
L7304	From 207 Sqn. FTR Kiel 26/27.6.41.
L7307	No operations to 97 Sqn.
L7315	From 97 Sqn. Crashed in Lincolnshire while training 29.6.41.
L7388	FTR Berlin 2/3.9.41.
L7395	Abandoned near Wittering following abortive sortie to Cologne 13/14.3.42.
L7396	FTR Brest 31.1/1.2.42.
L7401	From 44 Sqn to 50 Sqn.
L7415	From 44 Sqn to 50 Sqn.
L7419	From 207 Sqn to 50 Sqn.
L7422	From 207 Sqn. Ultimate fate unknown.
L7425	From 44 Sqn to 1661CU.
L7426	To 83 Sqn.
L7433	FTR from mining sortie 16/17.2.42.
L7453	From 44 Sqn to 49 Sqn.
L7454	From 207 Sqn. FTR from mining sortie 29/30.3.42
L7458 QR-A	To 1660CU.
L7464	To 50 Sqn.
L7470	FTR Essen 6/7.4.42.
L7471	To 50 Sqn.
L7472	FTR Brest 31.1/1.2.42.
L7473	From 97 Sqn to 1485 Flt.

L7475 QR-D	From 97 Sqn to 50 Sqn.
L7477 QR-N	From 44 Sqn to 1661CU.
L7486	From 207 Sqn. Returned to 207 Sqn.
L7494	FTR Boulogne 7/8.12.41.
L7495	Abandoned over Lincolnshire on return from Hamburg 16.1.42.
L7496	To 207 Sqn.
L7497	FTR Essen 25/26.3.42.
L7516 QR-F	To 50 Sqn.
L7518 QR-O	FTR Essen 25/26.3.42.
L7519	To 50 Sqn.
L7520	No operations. Crashed in Bedfordshire during training 2.11.41.
L7521	To 50 Sqn.
R5784	To 50 Sqn.
R5785 QR-M	FTR Le Havre 10/11.4.42.
R5786	To 50 Sqn.
R5787 QR-M	FTR Brest 31.1/1.2.42.
R5789	Crashed in Wiltshire following aborted sortie to Cherbourg 9.1.42.
R5796	To 207 Sqn.
R5832	To 1660CU.
R5834	Force-landed in Norfolk on return from Brest 10.2.42.
Lancaster	From April 1942.
L7532	From 97CF to 50 Sqn via 61CF.
L7539	From 44 Sqn. Training only to 50CF.
L7571 QR-S	From 97 Sqn to 207 Sqn.
R5488 QR-F	From 97 Sqn. FTR from mining sortie 3/4.7.42.
R5491	From 44 Sqn to 1656CU via 61CF.
R5505	From 207 Sqn. Training only to ECFS.
R5511	Completed 21 operations to 1654CU.
R5517	FTR Emden 22/23.6.42.
R5540	To 1661CU via 44CF.
R5541	From 207 Sqn to 97 Sqn.
R5543	FTR from Atlantic Patrol 20.8.42.
R5544	FTR Essen 1/2.6.42.
R5545	No operations. Crashed while landing at North Luffenham during training 1.5.42.
R5560	To 1654CU.
R5561	FTR Cologne 30/31.5.42. (Operation Millennium).
R5562	FTR Essen 2/3.6.42.
R5563	FTR from attack on SS *Corunna* off the Spanish coast 19.8.42.
R5565 QR-S	From 83 Sqn via NTU. FTR Magdeburg 21/22.1.44.
R5605	FTR from attack on SS *Corunna* off the Spanish coast 19.8.42.
R5613 QR-B	FTR Essen 2/3.6.42.
R5615 QR-H	FTR Bremen 27/28.6.42.
R5618 QR-H	To 1654CU.
R5627	FTR Bremen 3/4.6.42.
R5660	From A&AEE to 1654CU via 50CF.
R5661	FTR from attack on SS *Corunna* off the Spanish coast 19.8.42.

R5662 QR-A	FTR Frankfurt 24/25.8.42.
R5663 QR-B	FTR from mining sortie 3/4.7.42.
R5679 QR-O	FTR from mining sortie 24/25.9.42.
R5682 QR-R	FTR Bremen 4/5.9.42.
R5699 QR-H	Completed 34 operations. Crashed while landing at Syerston following early return from Munich 21.12.42.
R5703 QR-D	Crashed soon after take-off from Syerston through dinghy inflating when bound for Wismar 1.10.42.
R5724 QR-F	Crash-landed at Wittering on return from mining sortie 25.9.42.
R5734 QR-V	From 1654CU. FTR Nuremberg 30/31.3.44.
R5737	FTR Saarbrücken 29/30.7.42.
R5742	From 106 Sqn. FTR Nuremberg 28/29.8.42.
R5757	From 156 Sqn to 1661CU.
R5759	FTR Wismar 1/2.10.42.
R5842	From A.V.Roe to 44 Sqn 3.42.
R5843	To 1654CU via 50CF.
R5844	To 106 Sqn via 50CF.
R5845	To 1660CU via 97CF.
R5846	To 44 Sqn.
R5853	From 97 Sqn to 576 Sqn via 1660CU.
R5856 QR-Q/U	From 83 Sqn via 1660CU. FTR St Leu d'Esserent 7/8.7.44.
R5859 QR-G	To 61CF. Crash-landed on approach to Bodney on return from Mannheim 7.12.42.
R5864 QR-X	From 106 Sqn and back. Returned to 61 Sqn. Destroyed at Syerston when bomb load detonated 8.12.42.
R5866	To 1654CU.
R5888	FTR Düsseldorf 10/11.9.42.
R5910	From 106 Sqn. Returned to 106 Sqn.
W4111	FTR Düsseldorf 10/11.9.42.
W4136	From 44CF. FTR Karlsruhe 2/3.9.42.
W4166	FTR Munich 19/20.9.42.
W4168	Completed 21 operations. Crashed on landing at Swinderby on return from Turin 10.12.42.
W4173	FTR Essen 16/17.9.42.
W4192 QR-E	FTR Essen 12/13.1.43.
W4198 QR-L/H	FTR Berlin 26/27.11.43.
W4233	Crashed in Yorkshire on return from Kiel 14.10.42.
W4236 QR-K	FTR Mannheim 9/10.8.43.
W4244 QR-F	Crashed on approach to Exeter on return from mining sortie 10/11.11.42.
W4257	FTR St Nazaire 2/3.4.43.
W4269 QR-G	FTR Duisburg 12/13.5.43.
W4270	Crashed in Bottesford circuit while training 18.2.43.
W4272	Conversion Flt only to 15 Sqn via 1654CU.
W4279 QR-S/Z	FTR Kassel 3/4.10.43.
W4301	To 460 Sqn.
W4315 QR-Q	From 50 Sqn. Ditched on return from Berlin 27/28.1.44.
W4317 QR-R	FTR Pilsen 16/17.4.43.
W4357 QR-A	FTR Kassel 22/23.10.43.
W4381	From 106 Sqn to 1661CU.
W4762	To 50 Sqn.
W4763	To 106 Sqn.
W4766 QR-J	From 57 Sqn. FTR Peenemünde 17/18.8.43.

W4767 QR-J	FTR Berlin 17/18.1.43.
W4769 QR-V	Completed 18 operations. FTR Essen 3/4.1.43.
W4774	FTR Montchanin 17.10.42.
W4789	From 12 Sqn. FTR Cologne 16/17.6.43.
W4795	From 207 Sqn. FTR Stettin 20/21.4.43.
W4798	From 207 Sqn. Ultimate fate unclear in records.
W4830 QR-E	Abandoned over Lincolnshire on return from Gelsenkirchen 26.6.43.
W4884	From 5LFS.
W4898	FTR from mining sortie 28/29.4.43.
W4899	To 1668CU.
W4900 QR-Q	To 1669CU.
W4903 QR-P	FTR Nuremberg 8/9.3.43.
W4920 QR-O	FTR Berlin 1/2.3.43.
W4929	To 617 Sqn.
W4934 QR-S	FTR Peenemünde 17/18.8.43.
W4950 QR-L	From 156 Sqn to 6LFS.
W4957	From 83 Sqn via NTU to 46MU.
W5000 QR-B	FTR Hamburg 2/3.8.43.
W5002 QR-L	FTR Milan 15/16.8.43.
DS603	No operations to 115 Sqn.
DS604 QR-W	No operations to 115 Sqn.
DS605 QR-X	No operations to 115 Sqn.
DS607 QR-N	To 115 Sqn.
DS608 QR-O	To 115 Sqn.
DS609 QR-R	To 115 Sqn.
DS610 QR-S	To 115 Sqn.
DS612	To 115 Sqn.
DS613	To 115 Sqn.
DS621	To 115 Sqn.
DV186	FTR Milan 15/16.8.43.
DV228	FTR Leverkusen 22/23.8.43.
DV232 QR-K	Crashed near Nottingham on return from Mannheim 6.9.43.
DV239 QR-V	FTR Hanover 8/9.10.43.
DV294 QR-K	FTR Augsburg 25/26.2.44.
DV297 QR-O	From 106 Sqn. FTR Berlin 26/27.11.43.
DV304 QR-V	From 101 Sqn. FTR Revigny 18/19.7.44.
DV311 QR-P	FTR Nuremberg 30/31.3.44.
DV312 QR-Z	To 207 Sqn.
DV339 QR-W	From 106 Sqn. FTR Berlin 26/27.11.43.
DV344 QR-Z/V	From 106 Sqn. FTR Berlin 1/2.1.44.
DV397 QR-N/W	FTR Berlin 24/25.3.44.
DV399 QR-R	FTR Berlin 29/30.12.43.
DV400 QR-Y	FTR Berlin 27/28.1.44.
DV401 QR-Z	FTR Berlin 2/3.1.44.
ED314 QR-Y	From 44 Sqn. FTR Hanover 27/28.9.43.
ED332 QR-D	FTR Berlin 16/17.1.43.
ED359 QR-F	FTR Lorient 7/8.2.43.
ED470 QR-W	From 50 Sqn. FTR Münster 24.9.44.
ED613	FTR Essen 25/26.7.43.
ED630 QR-C-	FTR Kassel 22/23.10.43.
ED661	From Vickers Armstrong. FTR Peenemünde 17/18.8.43.
ED703	FTR Munich 9/10.3.43.
ED717 QR-S	Ditched off Isles of Scilly on return from La Spezia 14.4.43.

ED718 QR-P	FTR Munich 2/3.10.43.
ED722 QR-B	FTR Milan 15/16.8.43.
ED782	FTR Hamburg 29/30.7.43.
ED826	From 1654CU to 15 Sqn via 1654CU.
ED860 QR-N	From 156 Sqn. Crashed on take-off from Skellingthorpe when bound for Cologne 28.10.44.
EE176 QR-M	From 97 Sqn to 1653CU. Completed 122 operations
EE186 QR-D	From 106 Sqn. FTR St Leu d'Esserent 4/5.7.44.
EE190 QR-M	Crash-landed in North Africa following a raid on Italy 16.7.43.
HK538 QR-F	FTR Leipzig 19/20.2.44.
JA695 QR-W	From 57 Sqn via 5MU. FTR Aachen 11/12.4.44.
JA872 QR-K	From 630 Sqn to 46MU.
JA873	FTR Hamburg 2/3.8.43.
JA874 QR-E	To 617 Sqn.
JA900	FTR Peenemünde 17/18.8.43.
JB116 QR-R	To 9 Sqn.
JB129 QR-G	FTR Berlin 24/25.3.44.
JB132	Crashed in Nottinghamshire after collision with Lancaster R5698 (1654CU) on return from Berlin 1.9.43.
JB137	To 5LFS.
JB138 QR-J	Completed 113 operations to 5LFS.
JB351	From 83 Sqn. Damaged beyond repair during operation to Scholven 22.6.44.
JB532 QR-A	To 630 Sqn.
JB534	To 106 Sqn.
JB546	To 57 Sqn.
JB561	To 630 Sqn.
JB565	To 57 Sqn.
JB597	To 630 Sqn.
LL775 QR-O	FTR Augsburg 25/26.2.44.
LL777 QR-S	Crash-landed in Belgium on return from Giessen 6/7.12.44.
LL843	From 467 Sqn to 1659CU.
LL911 QR-X	FTR Pölitz (99th operation) 8/9.2.45.
LL918	From 460 Sqn.
LM274 QR-F	Completed 69 operations.
LM310 QR-E	From 106 Sqn. FTR Schweinfurt 24/25.2.44.
LM339	FTR Milan 7/8.8.43.
LM359 QR-B	FTR Munich 24/25.4.44.
LM360 QR-O	Aircraft in which Bill Reid won a VC during an operation to Düsseldorf 3/4.11.43 to 50 Sqn.
LM377 QR-F	From 106 Sqn. FTR Berlin 1/2.1.44.
LM452 QR-T	FTR Stuttgart 28/29.7.44.
LM454 QR-Z	FTR Bourg Leopold 11/12.5.44.
LM476 QR-E	FTR Brunswick 22/23.4.44.
LM478	Crashed on landing at Skellingthorpe on return from Bourg-Leopold 12.5.44.
LM481	To 1653CU.
LM483 QR-Y	SOC 17.3.45.
LM518 QR-C	FTR Prouville 24/25.6.44.
LM590	To 1669CU 12.44.
LM718 QR-K	FTR Dortmund Ems Canal at Ladbergen 23/24.9.44.
LM720	Crashed in Norfolk on return from Leuna 14/15.1.45.
LM729 QR-V	FTR Munich 17/18.12.44.

ME373	
ME385 QR-O	FTR Lützkendorf 8/9.4.45.
ME430	
ME439	
ME443 QR-N	
ME474 QR-V	FTR Harburg 7/8.3.45.
ME481	
ME493	
ME591 QR-C	FTR Leipzig 19/20.2.44.
ME595 QR-R/Y	FTR Brunswick 14/15.10.44.
ME596 QR-H	FTR Rüsselsheim 12/13.8.44.
ME719	To 1661CU.
ME725 QR-G	FTR Giessen 6/7.12.44.
ME732 QR-P	FTR Dortmund Ems Canal at Ladbergen 23/24.9.44.
ME783 QR-E	FTR Chatellerault 15/16.6.44.
ND509	From 57 Sqn.
ND727 QR-C	FTR Frankfurt 18/19.3.44.
ND865	From 83 Sqn to 5LFS.
ND867 QR-V	FTR St Leu d'Esserent 7/8.7.44.
ND896	To 5LFS.
ND902 QR-R	Damaged beyond repair during operation to Bergen 28/29.10.44.
ND987 QR-B	FTR Prouville 24/25.6.44.
ND988 QR-E	FTR Dortmund Ems Canal at Ladbergen 23/24.9.44.
NF912	Crashed at Skellingthorpe soon after take-off for Siegen 1.2.45.
NF914 QR-T	FTR Calais 24.9.44.
NF988 QR-T	FTR Harburg 7/8.3.45.
NF997	
NG178	
NG179 QR-C	FTR Trondheim 22/23.11.44.
NG182 QR-K	FTR Harburg 7/8.3.45.
NG220	
NG231	
NG241 QR-Y	FTR Karlsruhe 2/3.2.45.
NG367	
NG380	
NG386 QR-P	From 1669CU. FTR Böhlen 20/21.3.45.
NG490	
PA162 QR-L	FTR Trossy-St-Maximin 3.8.44.
PA165 QR-V	FTR Houffalize 5/6.1.45.
PA329 QR-R	
PA998 QR-O	FTR Darmstadt 27/28.8.44.
PB342 QR-B	To 617 Sqn.
PB434 QR-R	Crashed on landing at Skellingthorpe on return from the Mittelland Canal at Gravenhorst 6/7.11.44.
PB436 QR-D	FTR Königsburg 29/30.8.44.
PB596	From 9 Sqn.
PB649	To 227 Sqn.
PB666	To 227 Sqn.
PB725 QR-E	FTR Mittelland Canal at Gravenhorst 6/7.11.44.
PB727	
PB737 QR-E	FTR Pölitz 8/9.2.45.
PB759 QR-N	FTR Pölitz 8/9.2.45.

PD199 QR-C	FTR Düsseldorf 2/3.11.44.
PD266	
RA560 QR-K	FTR Böhlen. 20/21.3.45.
RA561	
RA593	
RF121 QR-J	FTR Hamburg 9.4.45.
RF123	
RF137 QR-E	Blew up on the ground at Skellingthorpe 24.2.45.
RF160	
RF176 QR-T	FTR Würzburg 16/17.3.45.
RF201 QR-C	
SW277	From 9 Sqn. Destroyed when RF137 blew up at Skellingthorpe 24.2.45.

Heaviest Single Loss

17/18.08.43   Peenemünde. 4 Lancasters FTR.

83 SQUADRON

Motto: Strike To Defend   Code OL

First formed on the 7 January 1917, 83 Squadron eventually moved to France in March 1918 to assume a night bombing and reconnaissance role. Disbandment followed on the last day of 1919, and it was not until the 4 August 1936 that the squadron was re-formed as a day bomber unit. In March 1938 the squadron took up residence at Scampton to become part of 5 Group, and re-equipping with Hampdens began on the 31 October. By the 9 January a full complement of the type was on charge, and this aircraft would be the one to carry the squadron into the Second World War, during which it would distinguish itself as one of Bomber Command's finest units. An operational squadron at the outset, 83 Squadron went to war on the very first night. The squadron operated Hampdens until converting to the Manchester in December 1941. The squadron became the fourth to receive the Lancaster in April 1942, and retained the type until the end of hostilities. A founder member of the Pathfinder Force in August 1942, the squadron returned to 5 Group on permanent loan in April 1944 as one of its heavy marker squadrons, and continued to serve in that role until war's end.

Posted to Pathfinder Force   15.08.42

Permanently attached to 5 Group   18.04.44

STATIONS

Scampton	14.03.38 to 15.08.42
Lossiemouth (Detachment)	21.02.40 to 20.03.40
Coningsby	18.04.44 to 05.11.46

COMMANDING OFFICERS

Wing Commander R B Jordan	21.08.39 to 01.10.39
Wing Commander L S Snaith AFC	01.10.39 to 09.06.40
Wing Commander J C Sisson	09.06.40 to 03.12.40
Wing Commander D A Boyle AFC	03.12.40 to 16.02.41
Wing Commander W W Stainthorpe	16.02.41 to 28.02.41

Wing Commander R A B Learoyd VC	28.02.41 to 20.06.41
Wing Commander H V Satterly	20.06.41 to 06.09.41
Wing Commander S O Tudor DFC	06.09.41 to 14.04.42
Wing Commander M D Crighton-Biggie	14.04.42 to 10.02.43
Group Captain L C Deane DSO DFC	03.01.44 to 28.08.44
Group Captain J A Ingham DSO DFC	28.08.44 to 10.06.45

AIRCRAFT

Hampden	11.38 to 01.42
Manchester	12.41 to 06.42
Lancaster I/Iii	05.42 to 07.46

OPERATIONAL RECORD

Operations	Sorties	Aircraft Losses	% Losses
456	2,881	87	3.0

Category of Operations

Bombing	Mining	Others
357	90	9

Hampdens

Operations	Sorties	Aircraft Losses	% Losses
283	1,987	43	2.2

Category of Operations

Bombing	Mining	Others
205	72	6

Manchesters

Operations	Sorties	Aircraft Losses	% Losses
33	152	9	5.9

Category of Operations

Bombing	Mining	Others
21	10	2

Lancasters

Operations	Sorties	Aircraft Losses	% Losses
140	1,642	35	2.1

Category of Operations

Bombing	Mining	Others
131	8	1

TABLE OF STATISTICS

(Heavy squadrons)

9th highest number of overall operations in Bomber Command.
18th highest number of sorties in Bomber Command.
23rd highest number of aircraft operational losses in Bomber Command.
11th highest number of bombing operations in Bomber Command.
9th highest number of mining operations in Bomber Command.

Out of 59 Lancaster squadrons

12th equal (with 460 Sqn) highest number of overall Lancaster operations in Bomber Command.
23rd highest number of Lancaster sorties in Bomber Command.
19th highest number of Lancaster operational losses in Bomber Command.

Out of 22 squadrons in 5 Group

7th highest number of overall operations in 5 Group.
9th highest number of sorties in 5 Group.
10th highest number of aircraft operational losses in 5 Group.

Out of 10 Hampden squadrons in 5 Group

5th equal (with 61 Sqn) highest number of Hampden overall operations in 5 Group.
5th highest number of Hampden sorties in 5 Group.
5th equal (with 44 Sqn) highest number of Hampden operational losses in 5 Group.

Out of 8 Manchester squadrons in 5 Group

6th highest number of Manchester overall operations in 5 Group.
3rd highest number of Manchester sorties in 5 Group.
3rd equal (with 106 Sqn) highest number of Manchester operational losses in 5 Group.

Out of 17 Lancaster squadrons in 5 Group

14th highest number of Lancaster overall operations in 5 Group.
14th highest number of Lancaster sorties in 5 Group.
14th highest number of Lancaster operational losses in 5 Group.

Hampden	To January 1942.
L4048	To 14 OTU.
L4049 OL-L	FTR Berlin 23/24.9.40.
L4050 OL-L	To 16 OTU.
L4051 OL-M	FTR Berlin 14/15.11.40.
L4053 OL-N	From 49 Sqn. FTR Ludwigshaven 8/9.8.40.
L4054	Abandoned over Yorkshire on return from patrol 6/7.4.40.
L4055	Crashed in Yorkshire on return from operations against communications targets 23.5.40.
L4057 OL-F	FTR Berlin 14/15.11.40.
L4058	To 16 OTU.
L4059	Crashed while landing at Newton while training 18.5.40.
L4066	From 49 Sqn. Crashed in Essex on return from Frankfurt 7/8.7.40.
L4069 OL-O	Crashed in Lincolnshire on return from the Ruhr 15.5.40.
L4070 OL-C	To 14 OTU.
L4071	Crashed on take-off from Scampton during training 30.10.39.
L4093 OL-J	FTR Kiel 3/4.11.40.
L4094 OL-R	FTR Dortmund-Ems Canal 25/26.7.40.
L4095 OL-R	FTR Danzig 10/11.11.40.
L4104	From 61 Sqn. Abandoned over Yorkshire on return from Hamburg 18/19.10.40.
L4106	From 61 Sqn. Crashed on approach to Scampton during training 18.8.40.
L4124	From 144 Sqn to 25 OTU.

L4133	From 144 Sqn to 14 OTU.
L4152 OL-S	From 76 Sqn. FTR from mining sortie 14/15.4.40.
P1171 OL-P	From 61 Sqn. FTR Kiel 1/2.7.40.
P1178 OL-H	FTR Emmerich 3/4.6.40.
P1183 OL-K	From R.A.E. FTR Le Havre 18/19.9.40.
P1334	Crashed on landing at Scampton following early return from Gelsenkirchen 29.8.40.
P1348	FTR Hamburg 5/6.6.40.
P1354 OL-Y	From 144 Sqn. Ditched in the Wash on return from Berlin 25/26.8.40.
P1355 OL-W	To 5BGS.
P1356	To 50 Sqn.
P2096	Crashed on approach to Scampton while training 27.9.40.
P2097 OL-S	Crashed near Abingdon on return from Lorient 28.12.40.
P2125 OL-L	Crashed on take-off from Scampton when bound for Cologne 27.11.40.
P2126	Converted for use as torpedo bomber to 455 Sqn.
P2138	To 16 OTU.
P4340	FTR Dortmund-Ems Canal 12/13.8.40.
P4376 OL-E	Crashed near Scampton after early return from Hanover 2.8.40.
P4380 OL-Z	Ditched off Grimsby on return from Berlin 25/26.8.40.
P4381	Crashed in Lincolnshire during training flight 3.11.40.
P4392 OL-P	Abandoned over Lincolnshire on return from Lorient 27/28.9.40.
P4398	From 61 Sqn to 106 Sqn.
P4402 OL-D	Abandoned over Lincolnshire on return from Munich 9.11.40.
P4410 OL-H	FTR Dortmund-Ems Canal 12/13.8.40.
P4412	To 25 OTU.
P5322	From 7 AAU to 14 OTU.
P5324	From 7 AAU to 49 Sqn.
P5393 OL-T	From 7 AAU. Destroyed at Scampton when bomb load exploded following taxiing collision with Hampden AE374 (83 Sqn) when bound for a mining sortie to Brest 14/15.12.41.
X2895	Crashed in Co Durham on return from Berlin 26.8.40.
X2897	From 44 Sqn. Ditched off Lincolnshire coast on return from Berlin 29.8.40.
X2898	To 44 Sqn.
X2899 OL-D	FTR from mining sortie 6/7.4.41.
X2901 OL-B	Force-landed on Southwold beach on return from Magdeburg 15/16.10.40.
X2904	Converted for use as torpedo bomber to 455 Sqn.
X2905	Converted for use as torpedo bomber to 489 Sqn.
X2964 OL-X	Crashed on take-off from Scampton when bound for Lorient 10.11.40.
X2969	To 144 Sqn.
X2972	To 14 OTU.
X2974	To 16 OTU.
X2977	Crashed on approach to Hemswell after early return from Gelsenkirchen 5.10.40.
X2978 OL-K	Crashed in Lincolnshire during air-test 3.11.40.
X2990 OL-Z	FTR from mining sortie 26/27.10.40.
X3053	Converted for use as torpedo bomber to 144 Sqn.

X3059 OL-A	Crashed near Scampton while training 3.7.41.
X3061	To 44 Sqn.
X3062 OL-Z	Shot down off Lincolnshire coast by intruder during operation to Hamburg 8/9.5.41.
X3116	To 25 OTU.
X3118 OL-J	FTR Essen 7/8.8.41.
X3119 OL-R	FTR Cologne 20/21.4.41.
X3121 OL-F	Collided with Hampden AD967 (49 Sqn) near Scampton during an operation to Düsseldorf 25.8.41.
X3122	To 420 Sqn.
X3123	To 5 AOS.
X3124 OL-H	Crashed in Staffordshire on return from Cologne 27.2.41.
X3131	To 106 Sqn.
X3132 OL-L	FTR from mining sortie 20/21.3.41.
X3139 OL-V	FTR Hamm 8/9.7.41.
X3144 OL-N	FTR from mining sortie 2/3.9.41.
AD722 OL-X	Crashed on approach to Finningley on return from Bremen 11/12.2.41.
AD731 OL-M	FTR Wilhelmshaven 16/17.1.41.
AD734 OL-K	Abandoned over Birmingham on return from Bremen 12.2.41.
AD740	To 25 OTU.
AD744	To 49 Sqn.
AD748 OL-M	Crashed in Devon on return from mining sortie 4.4.41.
AD794	To 144 Sqn.
AD795	To 50 Sqn.
AD796 OL-D	FTR Hamburg 26/27.4.41.
AD800 OL-X	FTR from mining sortie 29/30.3.41.
AD829	From 185 Sqn to 44 Sqn.
AD835 OL-G	FTR Hanover 25/26.7.41.
AD837 OL-E	Ditched off Northumberland coast on return from Bremen 18.8.41.
AD850 OL-L	From 16 OTU. FTR from mining sortie 5/6.11.41.
AD859 OL-O	From 6BAT Flt. FTR Cologne 31.8/1.9.41.
AD865	To 49 Sqn.
AD870	To 408 Sqn.
AD898 OL-K	Crashed soon after take-off from Scampton for a transit flight 21.5.41.
AD907 OL-K	FTR Kiel 19/20.8.41.
AD911 OL-M	FTR Essen 10/11.10.41.
AD912 OL-Y	FTR Cologne 31.8/1.9.41.
AD916 OL-Z	FTR Düsseldorf 30.6/1.7.41.
AD934 OL-T	Crashed on landing at Swanton Morley on return from Mannheim 23.10.41.
AD935 OL-U	Crashed in Worcestershire while training 14.8.41.
AD964	To 49 Sqn.
AD969 OL-X	FTR Bremen 22/23.6.41.
AD978 OL-C	Crashed in Norfolk on return from Berlin 3.9.41.
AE131 OL-W	FTR Brunswick 14/15.8.41.
AE133 OL-X	FTR Wilhelmshaven 10/11.1.42.
AE154 OL-H	Ditched in the North Sea on return from Kiel 2/3.8.41.
AE155	To 455 Sqn.
AE156	Converted for use as torpedo bomber to 489 Sqn.
AE187 OL-L	FTR Cologne 31.8/1.9.41.

AE188 OL-D	Crash-landed near Boscombe Down on return from Kassel 9.9.41.
AE191 OL-Z	FTR Aachen 7/8.12.41.
AE223 OL-V	Exploded on the ground at Scampton on return from Wesel 25.8.41.
AE237	From 49 Sqn to 408 Sqn.
AE312	To 455 Sqn.
AE314	To 420 Sqn.
AE315 OL-X	FTR from mining sortie 2/3.9.41.
AE319 OL-J	FTR from mining sortie 6/7.9.41.
AE356	Converted for use as torpedo bomber to 144 Sqn.
AE358 OL-U	FTR Kiel 1/2.11.41.
AE359	To 144 Sqn.
AE362 OL-S	Crashed while landing at Scampton on return from Hamburg 15/16.9.41.
AE363	Converted for use as torpedo bomber to 144 Sqn.
AE364	Converted for use as torpedo bomber to 144 Sqn.
AE365 OL-N	Crashed while landing at Scampton on return from Le Havre 15/16.9.41.
AE366	To 420 Sqn.
AE371	Converted for use as torpedo bomber to 144 Sqn.
AE374 OL-R	Collided with P5393 while taxiing at Scampton when bound for Brest and destroyed in the ensuing explosion 14/15.12.41.
AE388	To 50 Sqn.
AE389	To 420 Sqn.
AE420	To 50 Sqn.
AE421	To 49 Sqn.
AT110	To 144 Sqn.
AT112	To 49 Sqn.
AT127 OL-L	Crash-landed in Lincolnshire on return from Brest 9.1.42.
AT129	To 49 Sqn.
Manchester	From December 1941 to June 1942.
L7285	From 207 Sqn. No operations to R.A.E.
L7286	From 207 Sqn via 61CF. No operations to 1660CU.
L7289	To 50 Sqn.
L7293	From Rolls Royce to 49 Sqn.
L7297	From Rolls Royce to 1661CU.
L7382	From 207 Sqn. Training only to 44 Sqn.
L7385 OL-C	To 44 Sqn.
L7387 OL-A	To 49 Sqn.
L7389	To 49 Sqn.
L7394	To 106 Sqn.
L7397	To 49 Sqn.
L7423 OL-S	From 97 Sqn. FTR Cologne 13/14.3.42.
L7426 OL-D	From 61 Sqn. FTR Essen 8/9.3.42.
L7427 OL-Q	From 97 Sqn. FTR Hamburg 8/9.4.42.
L7453 OL-K	From 97 Sqn to 44 Sqn.
L7457	From 97 Sqn to 106 Sqn.
L7465 OL-H	From A.V.Roe. FTR Essen 25/26.3.42.
L7484	From 207 Sqn to 49 Sqn.
L7522 OL-N	From 97 Sqn. FTR Stavanger 21/22.2.42.
L7525 OL-O	From 97 Sqn to 50 Sqn.

R5768	From A.V.Roe to 1656CU.
R5772	From 49 Sqn. Conversion Flt only.
R5775	From 49 Sqn to 1654CU.
R5779 OL-G	FTR Essen 8/9.3.42.
R5780 OL-D/X	To 106 Sqn and back to 49 Sqn.
R5781 OL-R	FTR Lübeck 28/29.3.42.
R5783	From 97 Sqn. SOC 8.42.
R5788	From 207 Sqn to 49 Sqn.
R5790 OL-F	From 207 Sqn to 44CF.
R5793	From 49 Sqn. Training only to 1656CU.
R5830 OL-L	From A&AEE to 1656CU.
R5831 OL-I	FTR Essen 25/26.3.42.
R5833 OL-N	From 207 Sqn to 50 Sqn.
R5835	From 207 Sqn to 49 Sqn.
R5836 OL-T	To 49 Sqn.
R5837 OL-R	FTR from leafleting sortie to the Paris area 8/9.4.42.
R5838 OL-S	Ultimate fate unrecorded.
Lancaster	From May 1942.
L7540 OL-U	From 44 Sqn to 207 Sqn.
L7566	From 44 Sqn. Training only to 207 Sqn.
L7568	From 44 Sqn. Returned to 44 Sqn.
R5484 OL-V	From 44 Sqn. FTR Pilsen 16/17.4.42.
R5542 OL-E	From 44CF to 1667CU.
R5564 OL-P	FTR Essen 1/2.6.42.
R5565 OL-K	To 61 Sqn via NTU.
R5566 OL-B	From 83CF. FTR Genoa 6/7.11.42.
R5567 OL-D	From 83CF. Destroyed by fire at Wyton 25.9.42.
R5569 OL-E	From 97 Sqn. Returned to 97 Sqn.
R5570	To 207 Sqn.
R5610 OL-G	FTR Frankfurt 24/25.8.42.
R5619 OL-S	FTR Duisburg 25/26.7.42.
R5620 OL-H	FTR Bremen 25/26.6.42.
R5621 OL-R	FTR from mining sortie 11/12.6.42.
R5622 OL-C	FTR Pilsen 16/17.4.43.
R5623 OL-C	FTR Frankfurt 24/25.8.42.
R5625 OL-O	To 50 Sqn and back to 622 Sqn.
R5626 OL-M	To 50 Sqn and back. FTR Essen 3/4.4.43.
R5629 OL-J	FTR Dortmund 4/5.3.43.
R5630 OL-T	FTR Berlin 17/18.1.43.
R5636 OL-K	FTR from mining sortie 11/12.6.42.
R5640 OL-D	FTR Essen 8/9.6.42.
R5659 OL-B	FTR Essen 8/9.6.42.
R5667	To 1656CU.
R5669 OL-E	To 44 Sqn.
R5670 OL-R	Crashed while trying to land at Mildenhall on return from Genoa 7.11.42.
R5671 OL-F/K	To NTU.
R5672 OL-L	From 97 Sqn to 1656CU.
R5673 OL-L	FTR Genoa 6/7.11.42.
R5686 OL-G	From 207 Sqn. FTR Münster 11/12.6.43.
R5743 OL-H	FTR Wilhelmshaven 19/20.2.43.
R5747 OL-H	From 50 Sqn. Returned to 50 Sqn.
R5754 OL-K	FTR Berlin 29/30.3.43.

R5850	No operations to 49CF.
R5852 OL-Y	From 207 Sqn to 1654CU via 83CF.
R5855	To 49CF.
R5856	To 106 Sqn.
R5857 OL-F	Crashed soon after take-off from Mildenhall in transit following return from Genoa 7.11.42.
R5868 OL-Q	To 467 Sqn.
R5907	Conversion Flt only to 9 Sqn.
R5911 OL-C	FTR Kiel 13/14.10.42.
R5913 OL-G	FTR St Nazaire 28.2/1.3.43.
W4103 OL-S	To 1668CU.
W4104 OL-A	From 49 Sqn. FTR Düsseldorf 10/11.9.42.
W4123 OL-P/A	To 576 Sqn via NTU.
W4138	Conversion Flt only to 1654CU.
W4162 OL-H/E	From 44 Sqn to 460 Sqn via NTU.
W4191 OL-Z	No operations to 207 Sqn.
W4193 OL-A	To 1662CU.
W4231 OL-P/U	To 101 Sqn via 1662CU and 1667CU.
W4260	Conversion Flt only to 1654CU.
W4799 OL-S	FTR Düsseldorf 31.12/1.1.43.
W4846 OL-S	FTR Cologne 26/27.2.43.
W4847 OL-V	FTR Essen 5/6.3.43.
W4904 OL-C	To 1667CU.
W4905 OL-M/S	To 50 Sqn.
W4928 OL-S	FTR Essen 12/13.3.43.
W4953 OL-W	To 1656CU.
W4955 OL-R	FTR Duisburg 12/13.5.43.
W4957 OL-B	To 61 Sqn via NTU.
W4959 OL-X	To 207 Sqn.
W4981 OL-A	FTR Pilsen 13/14.5.43.
W4982 OL-O	FTR Mülheim 22/23.6.43.
ED311 OL-X/K	FTR Stuttgart 22/23.11.42.
ED312 OL-F	FTR Stettin 20/21.4.43.
ED313 OL-B	FTR Stuttgart 11/12.3.43.
ED334 OL-R	FTR Essen 3/4.4.43.
ED353 OL-N	FTR Duisburg 20/21.12.42.
ED368 OL-L	To NTU.
ED372 OL-O	To 101 Sqn.
ED420 OL-A	To 9 Sqn.
ED439 OL-N	Crashed near Sleaford while training 18.6.43.
ED594	To 57 Sqn.
ED599	From SIU to 156 Sqn.
ED601 OL-T	To 207 Sqn.
ED602 OL-F	From 467 Sqn to 49 Sqn.
ED603 OL-L	From SIU. FTR Bochum 12/13.6.43.
ED861	To 57 Sqn.
ED876 OL-V	From SIU. FTR Nuremberg 27/28.8.43.
ED907 OL-H	From SIU. FTR Cologne 16/17.6.43.
ED908 OL-J	From SIU to 15 Sqn via NTU.
ED974 OL-Y	From SIU. FTR Berlin 20/21.1.44.
ED984 OL-A	From SIU. FTR Berlin 23/24.8.43.
ED989	To 57 Sqn.
ED997 OL-R	From SIU. FTR Krefeld 21/22.6.43.
EE119	To 7 Sqn.

EE120 OL-L/T	To 97 Sqn.
EE121 OL-K	FTR Krefeld 21/22.6.43.
EE129	To 7 Sqn.
EE175 OL-C	From 7 Sqn to 207 Sqn.
EE201 OL-N/D	To NTU.
JA677 OL-H/U	To 7 Sqn.
JA678	To 7 Sqn.
JA682	To 7 Sqn.
JA686 OL-K	Blew up at dispersal at Wyton 26.11.43.
JA693	To 7 Sqn.
JA701 OL-E	FTR Leipzig 20/21.10.43.
JA705 OL-M	To 617 Sqn.
JA712 OL-B	From 7 Sqn to 166 Sqn.
JA913 OL-G	FTR Berlin 26/27.11.43.
JA920	To 405 Sqn.
JA924	To 405 Sqn.
JA927 OL-O	FTR Berlin 23/24.8.43.
JA928 OL-W	From 101 Sqn. FTR Schweinfurt 26/27.4.44. after completing 11 operations to Berlin.
JA940 OL-T/E	Crash-landed in Huntingdonshire on return from Berlin 29.1.44.
JA967 OL-S	FTR Berlin 28/29.1.44.
JA972 OL-D	FTR Kassel 3/4.10.43.
JB114 OL-Q	FTR Berlin 2/3.1.44.
JB118 OL-R	FTR Mannheim 5/6.9.43.
JB154 OL-A	FTR Leipzig 20/21.10.43.
JB180 OL-H/T	From 405 Sqn. FTR Wesseling 21/22.6.44.
JB187 OL-R	Abandoned over Norfolk following early return from Bochum 29.9.43.
JB232	To 97 Sqn.
JB284 OL-C	FTR Berlin 23/24.11.43.
JB302 OL-V	From 156 Sqn. Returned to 156 Sqn.
JB304	To 156 Sqn.
JB309 OL-N	From 156 Sqn to 207 Sqn.
JB344 OL-O	Crashed at Wyton on return from Berlin 17.12.43.
JB345	To 7 Sqn.
JB351 OL-D	To 61 Sqn.
JB352 OL-J/C	From SIU. FTR Berlin 30/31.1.44.
JB355 OL-J	From SIU. FTR Berlin 2/3.1.44.
JB365 OL-A/Z/G	From A.V.Roe. FTR Magdeburg 21/22.1.44.
JB402 OL-R	From SIU. FTR Mailly-le-Camp 3/4.5.44.
JB412 OL-X/B	From SIU. FTR Berlin 28/29.1.44.
JB414	From SIU to 7 Sqn.
JB424 OL-B	FTR Berlin 22/23.11.43.
JB453 OL-F/F	FTR Berlin 2/3.1.44.
JB455 OL-H	To 7 Sqn.
JB459 OL-T	From 97 Sqn. FTR Berlin 26/27.11.43.
JB461 OL-N/L	From SIU. FTR Berlin 20/21.1.44.
JB472	To 156 Sqn.
JB476	To 156 Sqn.
JB488 OL-X	From 7 Sqn. FTR Magdeburg 21/22.1.44.
JB538	To 7 Sqn.
JB553	To 156 Sqn.
JB706 OL-M/F/H	To 97 Sqn.

JB708	To 97 Sqn.
JB711	To 156 Sqn.
JB719	To 7 Sqn.
JB724 OL-V	From SIU 1.44. FTR Berlin 27/28.1.44.
LM302 OL-H	FTR Essen 3/4.4.43.
ME311 OL-B/C	
ME354/G OL-K	From 514 Sqn.
ME358/G OL-M	From 514 Sqn.
ME363 OL-P	From 514 Sqn.
ME364/G OL-S	From 514 Sqn.
ME417 OL-Q	
ME423 OL-C	FTR Leipzig 10/11.4.45.
ME525	
ME527 OL-Y	
ME528 OL-T	
ME620	From SIU to 35 Sqn.
ME621	From SIU to 35 Sqn.
ND330 OL-E/O	FTR Berlin 2/3.1.44. (405 Sqn crew).
ND333 OL-F	From 97 Sqn to 106 Sqn 9.44.
ND354 OL-A	From 7 Sqn. FTR Berlin 1/2.1.44.
ND387 OL-H	To 7 Sqn.
ND389 OL-A	FTR Aachen 11/12.4.44.
ND390 OL-U	To 97 Sqn.
ND395 OL-A/E	From 7 Sqn. FTR Aachen 11/12.4.44.
ND400 OL-Q	FTR Schweinfurt 26/27.4.44.
ND414 OL-K	FTR Berlin 20/21.1.44.
ND418	From Rolls Royce. No operations. To 7 Sqn.
ND442 OL-O	To 1666CU.
ND448 OL-K/S	From 97 Sqn. FTR Leipzig 19/20.2.44.
ND455 OL-U	From 635 Sqn. FTR Darmstadt 25/26.8.44.
ND464 OL-S	From 405 Sqn. Crashed near Coningsby while training 16.7.44.
ND465 OL-L	From SIU. Crashed on landing at Coningsby on return from Givors 11/12.8.44.
ND467 OL-L/B	FTR Caen 6/7.6.44.
ND469 OL-C	FTR Munich 24/25.4.44.
ND494 OL-G	FTR Gennevilliers 9/10.5.44.
ND499 OL-J	From SIU. FTR Schweinfurt 26/27.4.44.
ND505 OL-T	FTR Leipzig 19/20.2.44.
ND507	From SIU to 405 Sqn.
ND523	From SIU to 7 Sqn.
ND524	From SIU to 405 Sqn.
ND529 OL-D	From 405 Sqn.
ND551 OL-V	From SIU. FTR Wesseling 21/22.6.44.
ND591 OL-A	To 156 Sqn. Returned to 83 Sqn.
ND646	To 35 Sqn.
ND696 OL-H/O	From 35 Sqn. FTR Pölitz 8/9.2.45.
ND740 OL-H	From 97 Sqn. FTR Darmstadt 11/12.9.44.
ND818 OL-T	From 35 Sqn. FTR Lanveoc 8/9.5.44.
ND824 OL-B/G	
ND840 OL-A	To 97 Sqn.
ND854 OL-G/F	From 156 Sqn. FTR Brest 14.8.44.
ND856 OL-E	FTR Givors 26/27.7.44.
ND858 OL-A	To 5LFS.

ND865 OL-L	To 61 Sqn.
ND907	From 106 Sqn.
ND922 OL-J	FTR Stuttgart 24/25.7.44.
ND930 OL-Q	FTR Bois de Cassan 6.8.44.
ND963 OL-H	FTR Brunswick 22/23.5.44.
ND966 OL-C	FTR St Leu d'Esserent 7/8.7.44.
ND974 OL-T	From 405 Sqn to 44 Sqn.
ND979 OL-G/K/Q	
NE165 OL-Y	To Rolls Royce. Returned to 83 Sqn. FTR Mittelland Canal at Gravenhorst 21/22.2.45.
NG453 OL-M	Destroyed at Coningsby when bomb detonated after falling from its trolley 9.2.45.
NG454 OL-E	
PB134 OL-R/N	From 35 Sqn. FTR Horten 23/24.2.45.
PB135	From 582 Sqn.
PB138 OL-D	From 156 Sqn. FTR Brunswick 12/13.8.44.
PB140 OL-H	From 635 Sqn. Crash-landed at Ford on return from attacks on flying bomb sites 6.8.44.
PB157	From 97 Sqn.
PB181 OL-C	From 97 Sqn. FTR Dortmund-Ems Canal at Ladbergen 7/8.2.45.
PB182	From 44 Sqn to 582 Sqn.
PB188 OL-A	From 405 Sqn. FTR Harburg 11/12.11.44.
PB230 OL-V	From 582 Sqn. FTR Brunswick 12/13.8.44.
PB240 OL-J	From 156 Sqn. FTR Brunswick 12/13.8.44.
PB249 OL-C	From 635 Sqn. FTR Königsburg 29/30.8.44.
PB292 OL-S	From 405 Sqn. FTR Königsburg 26/27.8.44.
PB341 OL-J	
PB345 OL-Q	FTR Darmstadt 25/26.8.44.
PB362 OL-W	From 35 Sqn. FTR L'Isle Adam 18.8.44.
PB367	From 35 Sqn.
PB368 OL-S	From 35 Sqn.
PB376 OL-F	From 97 Sqn.
PB438	From 97 Sqn.
PB452 OL-W	From 405 Sqn.
PB458	
PB470 OL-F	To 9 Sqn.
PB478 OL-E	From 635 Sqn. Destroyed at Coningsby when NG453 blew up 9.2.45.
PB533 OL-Q	Crashed while landing at Metheringham on return from Pölitz 21/22.12.44.
PB616 OL-A	From 156 Sqn.
PB694 OL-T	
PB697	From 635 Sqn to 149 Sqn.
PB702 OL-G	Crashed in the sea off Skegness while training 14.11.44.
SW261OL-N	From 50 Sqn.
SW262OL-R	From 50 Sqn.

Heaviest Single Loss

31.08/01.09.41	Cologne. 3 Hampdens FTR.
02/03.01.44	Berlin. 3 Lancasters FTR.
20/21.01.44	Berlin. 3 Lancasters FTR.
26/27.04.44	Schweinfurt. 3 Lancasters FTR.
12/13 08.44	Brunswick. 3 Lancasters FTR.

97 (STRAITS SETTLEMENTS) SQUADRON

Motto: Achieve your aim   Code OF

First formed on the 1 December 1917, 97 Squadron began life as a training unit, until acquiring operational status as a bomber squadron in March 1918. Following a move to France in August, strategic bombing operations were conducted against Germany until the end of hostilities. After returning to the UK in March 1919, 97 Squadron was posted to India in July, and was eventually renumbered. The 97 Squadron number remained on the shelf until its resurrection as a night bomber unit on the 16 September 1935, but then undertook training duties from June 1938. It was in this form that the squadron faced the outbreak of the Second World War, equipped with Whitleys, but it again lost its identity when being retitled 10 OTU on the 6 April 1940. A short-lived re-formation took place on the 1 May, but it was a false dawn, and disbandment followed on the 20th, before any aircraft were taken on charge. On the 25 February 1941, 97 Squadron was again re-formed, this time at Waddington under the banner of 5 Group, where it would become the second unit in the Command to receive the Manchester. The Lancaster followed in early 1942, and the squadron gave magnificent service to 5 Group until a posting in April 1943 took it to the Pathfinders. One year to the day later 97 Squadron returned to 5 Group on permanent loan to act as a heavy marker unit, a role it retained for the remainder of the war.

Posted to 8 Group   18.04.43

Permanently attached to 5 Group   from 18.04.44

STATIONS

Waddington	25.02.41 to 10.03.41
Coningsby	10.03.41 to 02.03.42
Woodhall Spa	02.03.42 to 18.04.43
Coningsby	18.04.44 to 11.46

COMMANDING OFFICERS

Wing Commander D F Balsdon	25.02.41 to 18.12.41
Wing Commander J H Kynoch DFC	23.12.41 to 31.03.42
Wing Commander J D D Collier DFC*	31.03.42 to 26.10.42
Wing Commander G D Jones DFC*	26.10.42 to 01.07.43
Wing Commander E J Carter DFC	01.01.44 to 06.06.44
Wing Commander A W Heward DFC AFC	25.06.44 to 03.10.44
Group Captain P W Johnson DFC AFC	03.10.44 to 05.06.45

AIRCRAFT

Manchester	02.41 to 02.42
Hampden	07.41 to 08.41
Lancaster I/III	01.42 to 07.46

OPERATIONAL RECORD

Operations	Sorties	Aircraft Losses	% Losses
328	2,469	51	2.1

Category of Operations

Bombing	Mining
279	49

Manchesters

Operations	Sorties	Aircraft Losses	% Losses
36	151	8	5.3

Category of Operations

Bombing	Mining
33	3

Lancasters

Operations	Sorties	Aircraft Losses	% Losses
292	2,318	43	1.9

Category of Operations

Bombing	Mining
246	46

The above figures do not include those relating to Hampden operations, which were few, and conducted mostly in 106 Squadron aircraft.

TABLE OF STATISTICS

(Heavy squadrons)

28th highest number of overall operations in Bomber Command.
33rd highest number of sorties in Bomber Command.
34th highest number of aircraft operational losses in Bomber Command.

Out of 59 Lancaster squadrons

Highest number of overall Lancaster operations in Bomber Command.
17th highest number of Lancaster sorties in Bomber Command.
17th highest number of Lancaster operational losses in Bomber Command.

Out of 22 squadrons in 5 Group

9th highest number of overall operations in 5 Group.
13th highest number of sorties in 5 Group.
15th highest number of aircraft operational losses in 5 Group.

Out of 8 Manchester squadrons

3rd highest number of overall Manchester operations.
4th highest number of Manchester sorties.
5th highest number of Manchester operational losses.

Out of 17 Lancaster squadrons in 5 Group

10th highest number of Lancaster overall operations in 5 Group.
13th highest number of Lancaster sorties in 5 Group.
13th highest number of Lancaster operational losses in 5 Group.

Hampden	From July 1941 to August 1941.
AD735 ZN-R	From 106 Sqn on loan. FTR Mönchengladbach 7/8.7.41.
AD861	From 106 Sqn on loan. Crashed off Plymouth on return from Brest 7.7.41.
AE293	To 106 Sqn.

AE300	To 106 Sqn.
AE301	To 106 Sqn.
AE302	To 106 Sqn.
AE303	FTR Essen 7/8.8.41.
Manchester	From March 1941 to February 1942.
L7282	From 207 Sqn. No operations. Became ground instruction machine.
L7283	From 207 Sqn via 25 OTU. No operations to1660CU.
L7288	From 207 Sqn to 61 Sqn.
L7290	To 49 Sqn.
L7291	To 106 Sqn.
L7292	From 207 Sqn to 61 Sqn.
L7294	To 50 Sqn.
L7298	From 207 Sqn to 1654CU.
L7299	From 207 Sqn. No operations to 39MU.
L7306	Crashed on take-off from Coningsby during training 13.9.41.
L7307	From 61 Sqn. No operations to 1654CU.
L7308	Crashed on take-off from Coningsby 28.10.41.
L7315	To 61 Sqn.
L7323 OF-A	FTR Berlin 10/11.5.41.
L7324	FTR Berlin 15/16.5.41.
L7325	To 49 Sqn via 25 OTU.
L7374	FTR Kiel 26/27.6.41.
L7375 OF-B	Crashed in Lincolnshire during air-test 28.9.41.
L7382 OF-D	To 207 Sqn.
L7383 OF-F	Crashed in Norfolk during training 14.9.41.
L7384	FTR Düsseldorf 16/17.8.41.
L7423 OF-S	To 83 Sqn.
L7424 OF-Z	FTR Berlin 12/13.8.41.
L7425 OF-G	To 44 Sqn.
L7427	To 83 Sqn.
L7453 OF-X	To 83 Sqn.
L7455 OF-X	From 207 Sqn to 50 Sqn.
L7457 OF-Y	To 83 Sqn.
L7459 OF-N/V	Crashed on take-off from Coningsby for night flying training 8.1.42.
L7460 OF-J	To 50 Sqn.
L7461 OF-R	To 106 Sqn.
L7462 OF-Z	FTR Bremen 20/21.10.41.
L7463 OF-P	To 106 Sqn.
L7464 OF-N	To 61 Sqn.
L7466 OF-N	FTR from air-sea-rescue operation 8.11.41.
L7467	From 25 OTU. Conversion Flt only. To 106 Sqn.
L7473 OF-H	To 61 Sqn.
L7474 OF-Z	To 106 Sqn.
L7475 OF-B	To 50 Sqn.
L7476 OF-K	To 207 Sqn.
L7482	From 25 OTU. Conversion Flt only. To 1660CU.
L7488 OF-F	To 207 Sqn.
L7489 OF-T/K	To 50 Sqn.
L7490 OF-A/U	Crashed on approach to Coningsby on return from Brest 18.12.41.
L7491 OF-C	To 207 Sqn.

L7492 OF-A	To 50 Sqn.
L7522 OF-V	To 83 Sqn.
L7525 OF-D/O	To 83 Sqn.
R5783 OF-V	Force-landed in Lincolnshire on return from Bremen 21.10.41. To 83 Sqn.
R5792	Crashed near Kings Lynn after collision with a Hurricane during training 24.11.41.
R5795 OF-W	FTR Brest 18.12.41.
R5797	To A.V.Roe.
Lancaster	From January 1942.
BT308	From 44 Sqn. Training only to 207 Sqn.
L7531	From 44 Sqn. Crashed on take-off from Coningsby during training 24.3.42.
L7532	From 44 Sqn to 61 Sqn via 97CF.
L7538	From 44 Sqn. Returned to 44 Sqn.
L7569 OF-A	To 44 Sqn.
L7570 OF-B	Crashed in Lincolnshire during a mining sortie 20.3.42.
L7571 OF-X	To 61 Sqn.
L7572 OF-L	FTR Trondheim (*Tirpitz*) 27/28.4.42.
L7573 OF-K	FTR Augsburg S/L Sherwood 17.4.42.
L7574 OF-N	Completed 27 operations to 467 Sqn.
L7575 OF-Y	F/O Deverill's aircraft for Augsburg raid 17.4.42 to 1654CU.
L7576	Conversion Flt only. To 44 Sqn.
L7577 OF-T	To 106 Sqn on loan for one operation to 106CF.
L7578	To 207CF.
R5482 OF-C	To 101 Sqn.
R5483 OF-C/D	To 1654CU.
R5486 OF-P	Crashed while landing at Finningley during training 23.3.42.
R5487 OF-V	FTR Hamburg 26/27.7.42.
R5488 OF-F	F/O Rodley's aircraft for Augsburg raid 17.4.42. To 61 Sqn.
R5490 OF-B/M/H	To 1654CU.
R5495 OF-U/N	From 44 Sqn. FTR Essen 8/9.6.42.
R5496 OF-U	From 44 Sqn. F/L Penman's aircraft for Augsburg raid 17.4.42. FTR Bremen 4/5.9.42.
R5497 OF-W/Z	From 44 Sqn. FTR Neustadt 17/18.12.42 while on 39th operation.
R5502 OF-M	Temporary detachment to 207CF. FTR Nuremberg 28/29.8.42.
R5512 OF-C	Completed 23 operations. FTR Duisburg 20/21.12.42.
R5513 OF-P	FTR Augsburg W/O Mycock 17.4.42.
R5537 OF-B	F/L Hallows aircraft for Augsburg raid 17.4.42. FTR Frankfurt 24/25.8.42.
R5538 OF-H	Completed 41 operations. To 1660CU.
R5541	From 61 Sqn. Crash-landed in Lincolnshire while training 30.4.42.
R5548 OF-A	Completed 32 operations. Burned out on the ground at Woodhall Spa 28.12.42.
R5551	To 106 Sqn.
R5552 OF-P	To 166 Sqn.
R5553 OF-S	Crash-landed at Woodhall Spa on return from Stuttgart 5.5.42.
R5558 OF-J/T	Crashed off Norfolk coast on return from Duisburg 14.7.42.
R5559 OF-W	Completed over 30 operations. To 1662CU.

R5569 OF-X/D/B	To 83 Sqn and back. Crashed in Scampton circuit while training 13/14.11.42.
R5571 OF-A	FTR Essen 1/2.6.42.
R5572 OF-F	To 106 Sqn.
R5575 OF-T/L	To 106CF and back. FTR Berlin 17/18.1.43.
R5607 OF-X	FTR Essen 12/13.3.43.
R5609 OF-S	To 106 Sqn.
R5612 OF-R	To ETPS.
R5614 OF-G	To 106 Sqn.
R5634 OF-L	To 1664CU after 17 operations.
R5672 OF-D	To 83 Sqn.
R5675 OF-H	FTR Bremen 27/28.6.42.
R5696 OF-H	FTR Danzig 11.7.42.
R5701 OF-Y	FTR Aachen 5/6.10.42.
R5738 OF-D	FTR Essen 9/10.1.43.
R5741 OF-K	FTR Saarbrücken 1/2.9.42.
R5845 OF-T	From 61 Sqn. Conversion Flt only to 1660CU.
R5853	Conversion Flt only to 61CF.
R5854	From 106 Sqn to 1660CU.
R5889 OF-T/V	From 49 Sqn to 1661CU.
R5895	Conversion Flt only to 207 Sqn via 1660CU.
R5896 OF-Y	From 49 Sqn to 15 Sqn via 1660CU.
R5915 OF-Q	From 9 Sqn to 622 Sqn via 1660CU.
R5917 OF-K	From 9 Sqn to 1660CU.
W4127	Conversion Flt only to 619 Sqn via 1660CU.
W4135 OF-A	From 44 Sqn. FTR Düsseldorf 27/28.1.43.
W4139 OF-V	FTR Kassel 27/28.8.42.
W4170 OF-K	FTR Cologne 15/16.10.42.
W4175 OF-U	Crashed at Swinderby on return from Berlin 29/30.3.43.
W4197	From 9 Sqn to 1667CU.
W4200 OF-W	From 9 Sqn to 1656CU.
W4239	From 9 Sqn. Crashed in Woodhall Spa circuit while training 31.10.42.
W4249 OF-L	From 9 Sqn to 1661CU.
W4255 OF-V	To 1654CU.
W4278 OF-T	Crash-landed at North Luffenham on return from Genoa 23.10.42.
W4355 OF-T	To 15 Sqn via 1661CU.
W4356	Crashed in Cumberland while training 6.12.42.
W4825 OF-H	FTR Berlin 1/2.3.43.
W4835 OF-H	From 49 Sqn. FTR Hamburg 30/31.1.43.
W4887 OF-N	To 1660CU.
W4926 OF-Z	To 617 Sqn.
W4932 OF-N	To 50 Sqn.
ED310	From 49 Sqn to 15 Sqn via 1654CU.
ED323 OF-O	To 15 Sqn via 1661CU.
ED333 OF-B	FTR Neustadt 17/18.12.43.
ED425 OF-E	To 622 Sqn via 1660CU & 1654CU.
ED430 OF-C	To 50 Sqn.
ED588	To 50 Sqn.
ED591 OF-M	To 1654CU.
ED754 OF-A	FTR St Nazaire 28/29.3.43.
ED781 OF-Z	To 57 Sqn.
ED814 OF-D	To 100 Sqn.

ED816 OF-U	FTR Bochum 12/13.6.43.
ED839 OF-C	To 619 Sqn.
ED862 OF-P	FTR Hamburg 29/30.7.43.
ED866 OF-G	To 619 Sqn.
ED867 OF-F/Q	To 467 Sqn.
ED868 OF-A	From A&AEE. FTR Mannheim 23/24.9.43.
ED869 OF-S/P	To 44 Sqn.
ED870 OF-T	To 50 Sqn.
ED871 OF-K	To 467 Sqn.
ED873 OF-O	To 106 Sqn.
ED874 OF-L	To 106 Sqn.
ED875 OF-R	To 166 Sqn.
ED880 OF-D/N	Collided with Stirling BF393 near Waterbeach on return from Dortmund 5.5.43.
ED882 OF-H	To 103 Sqn.
ED911 OF-E	To 405 Sqn.
ED917 OF-Q/U	FTR Cologne 3/4.7.43.
ED923 OF-V	FTR Cologne 8/9.7.43.
ED928 OF-B	FTR Mülheim 22/23.6.43.
ED938 OF-J	To 100 Sqn.
ED939 OF-M	FTR Nuremberg 10/11.8.43.
ED940 OF-N	To 625 Sqn.
ED948 OF-W	Damaged beyond repair at Wyton 9.8.43.
ED950 OF-X	FTR Berlin 23/24.8.43.
ED953 OF-H/W/X/Y	To 467 Sqn.
EE105 OF-L/Q	Shot down by intruder at Marham on return from Berlin 23/24.8.43.
EE107 OF-F/L	To 100 Sqn.
EE120	From 83 Sqn to 1655CU.
EE168 OF-B	To 619 Sqn.
EE172 OF-O	FTR Hamburg 29/30.7.43.
EE174 OF-W	To 50 Sqn.
EE176 OF-N/O	From 7 Sqn to 61 Sqn.
EE179 OF-U/T	From 7 Sqn to 44 Sqn.
JA707 OF-W/T	FTR Nuremberg 27/28.8.43.
JA708 OF-Z/P	FTR Mannheim 23/24.9.43.
JA711 OF-Y	To 9 Sqn.
JA715 OF-H/X	To 576 Sqn.
JA716 OF-V	FTR Nuremberg 10/11.8.43.
JA846 OF-E/M/N/O	From 7 Sqn to 5LFS.
JA857 OF-G	To 35 Sqn.
JA908 OF-N/W	To 1668CU.
JA916 OF-L	FTR Berlin 31.8/1.9.43.
JA923 OF-A/H	FTR Frankfurt 4/5.10.43.
JA939 OF-M	FTR Nuremberg 10/11.8.43.
JA958 OF-K	FTR Nuremberg 27/28.8.43.
JA960 OF-E	FTR Berlin 1/2.1.44.
JA963 OF-Q	FTR Berlin 16/17.12.43.
JA966 OF-S	Damaged beyond repair during operation to Berlin 3/4.9.43.
JA970	To 7 Sqn.
JA974	To 405 Sqn.
JA976	To 405 Sqn.
JB117 OF-C	Crashed on landing at Bourn on return from Berlin 16/17.12.43.

JB119 OF-F	Crashed on landing at Bourn on return from Berlin 16/17.12.43.
JB174 OF-S	FTR Hanover 8/9.10.43.
JB176 OF-K	Crashed on landing at Bourn on return from Berlin 16/17.12.43.
JB183	To 405 Sqn.
JB189 OF-G	Destroyed on the ground at Bourn 9.10.43.
JB190 OF-V	FTR Berlin 2/3.12.43.
JB191 OF-B/A	FTR Stettin 5/6.1.44.
JB218 OF-Y	FTR Berlin 23/24.11.43.
JB219 OF-R	Crashed near Gransden on return from Berlin 16/17.12.43.
JB220 OF-O	FTR Hanover 18/19.10.43.
JB221 OF-W	FTR Frankfurt 25/26.11.43.
JB224	To 7 Sqn.
JB227 OF-J	FTR Berlin 22/23.11.43.
JB232 OF-U	From 83 Sqn. FTR Leipzig 3/4.12.43.
JB238 OF-A	FTR Berlin 22/23.11.43.
JB239	To 156 Sqn via NTU.
JB243 OF-P	Crashed at Graveley on return from Berlin 16/17.12.43.
JB275 OF-H	FTR Leipzig 20/21.10.43.
JB299 OF-D/W	FTR Magdeburg 21/22.1.44.
JB300 OF-D/B	FTR Frankfurt 18/19.3.44.
JB312 OF-Z/L/B/A	Crashed on approach to Bourn on return from Stuttgart 21.2.44.
JB348	To 405 Sqn.
JB353 OF-F/L	From 156 Sqn. FTR Berlin 28/29.1.44.
JB356 OF-X	From NTU. Completed 10 ops to Berlin. To 635 Sqn
JB361 OF-B	FTR Stuttgart 15/16.3.44.
JB367 OF-S	FTR Berlin 18/19.11.43.
JB410	To 405 Sqn.
JB422 OF-H/N	To 635 Sqn.
JB459	To 83 Sqn.
JB470 OF-T/M	To 635 Sqn.
JB482 OF-S	From 405 Sqn. Abandoned on return from Berlin 16/17.12.43.
JB531 OF-Y	Abandoned on return from Berlin 16/17.12.43.
JB535 OF-Q	FTR Berlin 30/31.1.44.
JB653	To 7 Sqn.
JB659 OF-T/J	FTR Berlin 30/31.1.44.
JB671 OF-V/A	From 7 Sqn. FTR Berlin 24/25.3.44.
JB683/G OF-C	To 12 Sqn.
JB706 OF-F/H	From 83 Sqn. To 635 Sqn.
JB708 OF-J	From 83 Sqn. FTR Lille 10/11.5.44.
JB712 OF-U	FTR Berlin 28/29.1.44.
JB720 OF-S	From 156 Sqn. FTR Stettin 5/6.1.44.
JB726 OF-Y	From 156 Sqn. FTR Brunswick 14/15.1.44.
JB728 OF-P/S	From 405 Sqn to 635 Sqn.
JB731 OF-A/F	From 7 Sqn. Abandoned over sea on return from Frankfurt 22/23.3.44.
LM314 OF-R	From 156 Sqn to 103 Sqn.
LM323 OF-U	FTR Cologne 28/29.6.43.
LM327 OF-B	FTR Wuppertal 24/25.6.43.
LM346 OF-N/O/U	From NTU. To 35 Sqn.

ME382	To 50 Sqn.
ME533 OF-O/Q	
ME623 OF-G	From 582 Sqn.
ME625 OF-O/T	From 32MU. Collided with ND981 over Lincolnshire while training 23.6.44.
ME630	To 106 Sqn.
ND333	To 83 Sqn.
ND340	To 156 Sqn.
ND343	To 405 Sqn.
ND346 OF-N/O/T/V	To 467 Sqn.
ND351 OF-P	FTR Frankfurt 22/23.3.44.
ND355 OF-T	To 635 Sqn.
ND359 OF-M	To 635 Sqn.
ND367 OF-K	FTR Berlin 20/21.1.44.
ND390 OF-S	From 83 Sqn. FTR Nuremberg 30/31.3.44. F/L R A D Trevor-Roper, rear gunner in Gibson's Dams crew, killed.
ND415 OF-Z/B	Collided with LL967 (57 Sqn) over Lincolnshire on return from Brunswick 22/23.5.44.
ND421 OF-S	FTR Brunswick 14/15.1.44.
ND440 OF-K/H	FTR Berlin 24/25.3.44.
ND448	To 83 Sqn.
ND450 OF-Y	To 635 Sqn.
ND451 OF-W/R/L	FTR Gelsenkirchen 21/22.6.44.
ND452 OF-E/S	To 625 Sqn.
ND455 OF-G	To 635 Sqn.
ND478 OF-Q	FTR Berlin 15/16.2.44.
ND495 OF-Q/M/N	
ND497 OF-Q	FTR Schweinfurt 24/25.2.44.
ND500 OF-L/P/G	FTR Munich 24/25.4.44.
ND501 OF-U/M/Q	To 106 Sqn.
ND508 OF-J	To 635 Sqn.
ND589 OF-D	From SIU. Converted for Coastal Command duties.
ND617	To 405 Sqn.
ND640 OF-F/R	FTR Nuremberg 30/31.3.44.
ND706 OF-H/A	FTR Mailly-le-Camp 3/4.5.44.
ND739 OF-E/Z	FTR Pierre-du-Mont 5/6.6.44.
ND740/G OF-F	From 35 Sqn. To 83 Sqn.
ND746 OF-N/W	From 35 Sqn.
ND748 OF-O/M	FTR La Chappelle 20/21.4.44.
ND764 OF-E/B	FTR Etampes 9/10.6.44.
ND807 OF-P	FTR Königsburg 26/27.8.44.
ND813 OF-Q	From 582 Sqn. FTR Lille 10/11.5.44.
ND815 OF-M/G	From 156 Sqn. FTR St Pierre-du-Mont 5/6.6.44.
ND840 OF-J	From 83 Sqn. FTR Bois de Cassan 6.8.44.
ND961 OF-U	FTR Dortmund-Ems Canal at Ladbergen 7/8.2.45.
ND981 OF-H	Collided with ME625 (97 Sqn) over Lincolnshire while training 23.6.44.
NE121 OF-E	FTR Cahagnes 30.7.44.
NE124 OF-J	FTR Prouville 24/25.6.44.
NE167 OF-Y	FTR from mining sortie 16/17.8.44.
PA973 OF-A/C	FTR Böhlen 20/21.3.45.
PA974 OF-B	FTR Münster 23/24.9.44.
PA979 OF-R	To 582 Sqn and back. FTR Courtrai 20/21.7.44.
PB133	From 7 Sqn.

PB156 OF-R/O	From 7 Sqn.
PB157 OF-B	From 582 Sqn. To 83 Sqn.
PB181 To 83 Sqn.	
PB200 OF-G	From 35 Sqn. Crashed in France during night exercise 10/11.11.44.
PB358 OF-J	Ditched on return from Deelen 15.8.44.
PB372	From 35 Sqn.
PB376 OF-S	To 83 Sqn.
PB398 OF-N	FTR Darmstadt 25/26.8.44.
PB408	
PB409 OF-F	FTR Dortmund Ems Canal at Ladbergen 23/24.9.44.
PB410 OF-J	From 7 Sqn.
PB422	
PB438 OF-U	From 156 Sqn. To 83 Sqn.
PB450 OF-G/D	FTR from night exercise over France10/11.11.44.
PB461 OF-E/M	FTR Pölitz 21/22.12.44.
PB473 OF-F	From 7 Sqn.
PB510 OF-Q	FTR Darmstadt 11/12.9.44.
PB521 OF-Q	From 405 Sqn. FTR Hamburg 21/22.3.45.
PB588 OF-E	From 635 Sqn. FTR Horten 23/24.2.45.
PB624	
PB691	To 189 Sqn.
PB700 OF-H	
PB706	
PB881	
PB895 OF-M	
PB900	
PB905 OF-K	To 9 Sqn.
PD200	From 625 Sqn.
PD400	From 218 Sqn.
RE115 OF-C/G	
RE119 OF-G	
RE129	

Heaviest Single Loss

16/17.12.43	Berlin. Eight Lancasters. One FTR. Seven crashed or abandoned on return.

106 SQUADRON

Motto: Pro Libertate (For freedom)   Code ZN

First formed on the 30 September 1917, 106 Squadron fulfilled a corps reconnaissance role, moving to Ireland in May 1918, and eventual disbanding in October 1919. It remained on the shelf until being resurrected at Abingdon on the 1 June 1938, and swapped its Battles for Hampdens in May 1939. The outbreak of war found 106 Squadron at Cottesmore in Rutland, to where it had moved on the 1 September 1939. It would spend the first year of war as the Group's training squadron, before becoming a standard bomber unit late in 1940. A succession of outstanding commanding officers raised the squadron's profile and reputation, and under W/C Guy Gibson it even managed a high rate of serviceability on the ill-fated Manchester. No. 106 Squadron remained at the forefront of 5 Group operations operating Lancasters until war's end, maintaining throughout its status as one of the Command's finest.

STATIONS

Cottesmore	01.09.39 to 06.10.39
Finningley	06.10.39 to 23.02.41
Coningsby	23.02.41 to 01.10.42
Syerston	01.10.42 to 11.11.43
Metheringham	11.11.43 to 18.02.46

COMMANDING OFFICERS

Squadron Leader W C Sheen	09.38 to 10.39
Wing Commander G R Montgomerie	10.39 to 06.40
Squadron Leader R D Stubbs DFC	06.40 to 11.40
Wing Commander W J H Lindlay	11.40 to 04.41
Wing Commander P J Polglase	04.41 to 05.04.41
Wing Commander R S Allen DFC	06.04.41 to 20.03.42
Wing Commander G P Gibson DSO DFC	20.03.42 to 14.03.43
Wing Commander J H Searby DFC	14.03.43 to 09.05.43
Wing Commander R E Baxter DFC	09.05.43 to 13.03.44
Wing Commander E K Piercy DFC	13.03.44 to 25.08.44
Wing Commander M M J Stevens DFC	25.08.44 to 15.03.45
Wing Commander L G Levis	15.03.45 to 18.02.46

AIRCRAFT

Hampden	05.39 to 03.42
Manchester	02.42 to 06.42
Lancaster I/III	05.42 to 02.46

OPERATIONAL RECORD

Operations	Sorties	Aircraft Losses	% Losses
557	5,745	169	2.9

Category of Operations

Bombing	Mining	Other
471	82	4

Hampden

Operations	Sorties	Aircraft Losses	% Losses
150	1,230	55	4.5

Category of Operations

Bombing	Mining
106	44

Manchester

Operations	Sorties	Aircraft Losses	% Losses
36	151	9	6.0

Category of Operations

Bombing	Mining	Other
19	14	3

Lancaster

Operations	Sorties	Aircraft Losses	% Losses
371	4,364	105	2.4

Category of Operations

Bombing	Mining	Other
346	24	1

TABLE OF STATISTICS

(Heavy squadrons)

16th highest number of overall operations in Bomber Command.
17th highest number of sorties in Bomber Command.
12th equal (with 460 Sqn) highest number of aircraft operational losses in Bomber Command.
19th highest number of bombing operations in Bomber Command.
13th highest number of mining operations in Bomber Command.

Out of 59 Lancaster squadrons

4th highest number of overall Lancaster operations in Bomber Command.
7th highest number of Lancaster sorties in Bomber Command.
13th highest number of Lancaster operational losses in Bomber Command.

Out of 22 squadrons in 5 Group

5th highest number of overall operations in 5 Group.
5th highest number of sorties in 5 Group.
3rd highest number of aircraft operational losses in 5 Group.

Out of 12 Hampden squadrons in 5 Group

8th highest number of Hampden overall operations in 5 Group.
8th highest number of Hampden sorties in 5 Group.
3rd equal (with 49 Sqn) highest number of Hampden operational losses in 5 Group.

Out of 8 Manchester squadrons in 5 Group

3rd equal (with 97 Sqn) highest number of Manchester overall operations in 5 Group.
4th equal (with 97 Sqn) highest number of Manchester sorties in 5 Group.
3rd equal (with 83 Sqn) highest number of Manchester operational losses in 5 Group.

Out of 17 Lancaster squadrons in 5 Group

3rd highest number of Lancaster overall operations in 5 Group.
3rd highest number of Lancaster sorties in 5 Group.
7th highest number of Lancaster operational losses in 5 Group.

Hampden	To March 1942.
L4038	From 49 Sqn. To 25 OTU.
L4042	From 44 Sqn. To 408 Sqn.
L4100	From 44 Sqn to 14 OTU.
L4103	From 61 Sqn. Crashed in circuit at Finningley during night training 7.12.40.
L4120	From 61 Sqn. Crashed at Finningley while training 16.12.40.
L4139	From 76 Sqn. To 7 Sqn.
L4149	From 76 Sqn. To 50 Sqn.
L4150	To 50 Sqn.

L4174	Crashed near Finningley while training 31.5.40.
L4175 ZN-B	Crashed on landing at Finningley 24.10.39.
L4176	To 7 Sqn.
L4178	To 44 Sqn.
L4180	FTR from mining sortie 29/30.10.40.
L4181	Crashed on landing at Finningley while training 6.7.40.
L4182	To 1 AAS.
L4183 ZN-P	Crashed on take-off at Finningley while training 29.11.40.
L4184 ZN-Q	Crashed on take-off at Finningley while training 13.10.40.
L4185 ZN-S	Crashed in the Thames Estuary on return from Dortmund 4/5.7.41.
L4186 ZN-T	Crashed in Lincolnshire while training 11.11.39.
L4187	Crashed in Lincolnshire while training 7/8.8.40.
L4188 ZN-V	Blew up over Buckinghamshire while training 1.9.40.
L4189	Crashed in Derbyshire while training 30.9.40.
L4194	From 195 Sqn. FTR from mining sortie 22/23.11.40
P1198	To 144 Sqn.
P1228 ZN-L	From 50 Sqn. FTR Hamburg 30.11/1.12.41.
P1253	To 61 Sqn.
P1254	To 14 OTU.
P1255	To BTU.
P1256	Crashed near Finningley during training 27.9.40.
P1258	To 25 OTU.
P1259	FTR from mining sortie 18/19.9.40.
P1290	FTR from mining sortie 7/8.11.41.
P1303	To 5Gp TF.
P1304 ZN-Y	Crashed in Yorkshire while training 21.12.40.
P1311	To 32 OTU.
P1320 ZN-B	Crashed in Lincolnshire during training 25.11.40.
P1321	To 50 Sqn.
P1322	To 44 Sqn.
P1336	Crashed at Coventry during training 24.5.40.
P1337	To 5Gp TF.
P1341	From 16 OTU. FTR Hamburg 15/16.1.42.
P2071	Abandoned over Shropshire while training 23.12.40.
P2073	To 408 Sqn.
P2083	To 5Gp TF and back. Force-landed at Wellesbourne on return from mining sortie 27.5.41.
P2098	FTR from mining sortie 27/28.12.40.
P2099 ZN-K	Force-landed in Rutland during training 17.5.41.
P2129	To 16 OTU.
P4302	To 25 OTU.
P4314	From 14 OTU. Crashed near Finningley while training 3.1.41.
P4318	To 25 OTU.
P4323	From 16 OTU. FTR from mining sortie 23/24.2.42.
P4377	To 49 Sqn.
P4398	From 83 Sqn. FTR Münster 28/29.1.42.
P4413 ZN-J	Crashed while landing at Pocklington on return from Hamburg 16.9.41.
P4414	From 44 Sqn. FTR from an intruder operation to the Cologne area 21/22.2.42.
P5323	From 7 AAU. Converted for use as torpedo bomber to 455 Sqn.

P5330	From 7 AAU to 420 Sqn.
X2914	Abandoned over Somerset on return from mining sortie 27.9.40.
X2921	To 44 Sqn.
X2960	Force-landed near Finningley while training 18.9.40.
X2970	To 25 OTU.
X2986 ZN-F	FTR Cologne 20/21.4.41.
X3002	FTR Cologne 3/4.3.41.
X3021	From 49 Sqn. FTR Schiphol 29/30.10.41.
X3058	From 61 Sqn. FTR Münster 28/29.1.42.
X3131	From 83 Sqn. Converted for use as torpedo bomber to 455 Sqn.
X3148 ZN-E	FTR Düsseldorf 10/11.4.41.
X3152	To 5BGS.
X3153	FTR Düsseldorf 10/11.4.41.
X3154 ZN-A	Crashed in Derbyshire during navigation exercise 21.12.40.
AD735 ZN-R	FTR Mönchengladbach (97 Sqn crew) 7/8.7.41.
AD736	To 16 OTU.
AD738	FTR Brest 4/5.4.41.
AD743	To 25 OTU.
AD746	Crashed on approach to Coningsby on return from Bremen 21.10.41.
AD749	To 14 OTU.
AD750	FTR from mining sortie 4/5.2.41.
AD756	FTR Düsseldorf 16/17.8.41.
AD758	To 44 Sqn.
AD760	FTR from mining sortie 7/8.11.41.
AD763	Crashed on landing at Coningsby during a ferry flight 1.3.41.
AD765	To 144 Sqn.
AD768	Abandoned over Ireland on return from Karlsruhe 1/2.10.41.
AD785	Blew up over Yorkshire on return from Hamburg 27.10.41.
AD790	Crashed on take-off at Coningsby while training 25.2.41.
AD799	To 49 Sqn.
AD802	To 14 OTU.
AD803	To 455 Sqn and back to 408 Sqn.
AD848	From 16 OTU. To 14 OTU.
AD855	To 44 Sqn.
AD857	To 408 Sqn.
AD861	Crashed off Plymouth on return from Brest (97 Sqn crew) 7.7.41.
AD862	FTR Duisburg 2/3.7.41.
AD863	FTR Cologne 15/16.6.41.
AD873	FTR Duisburg 2/3.7.41.
AD895	FTR Bremen 29/30.6.41.
AD914	FTR Dortmund 4/5.7.41.
AD919	Force-landed soon after take-off from Coningsby when bound for Cologne 18.8.41.
AD925	To A&AEE.
AD929	To 50 Sqn.
AD932	FTR from mining sortie 7/8.11.41.

AD970	Crashed off Skegness during air test 30.7.41.
AD984	FTR Bremen 20/21.10.41.
AD986	FTR Dortmund 4/5.7.41.
AD988	To 14 OTU.
AE120	FTR Mannheim 5/6.8.41.
AE123 ZN-D	From 49 Sqn. FTR Bremen 21/22.1.42.
AE134	FTR Düsseldorf 16/17.8.41.
AE136	FTR Hamburg 26/27.10.41.
AE144	FTR Essen 10/11.10.41.
AE151	FTR from intruder sortie over Germany 21.12.41.
AE186	From 420 Sqn to 408 Sqn.
AE193 ZN-A	FTR Duisburg 28/29.8.41.
AE220	FTR Mannheim 22/23.8.41.
AE232	FTR Hamburg 15/16.9.41.
AE246	To 420 Sqn.
AE255	To 5 OTU.
AE261	To 49 Sqn.
AE292	Crashed in Lincolnshire during training 14.1.42.
AE293	From 97 Sqn to 408 Sqn.
AE299	From 207 Sqn. FTR Berlin 7/8.9.41.
AE300	From 97 Sqn. FTR Rostock 11/12.9.41.
AE301	From 97 Sqn. FTR from mining sortie 26/27.8.41.
AE302	From 97 Sqn. FTR Cologne 26/27.8.41.
AE307	Converted for use as torpedo bomber to 455 Sqn.
AE317	FTR Emden 26/27.11.41.
AE378	To 420 Sqn.
AE391	FTR Gelsenkirchen 12.12.41.
AE425	Crashed on take-off from Coningsby en-route to Mannheim 11.2.42.
AE426	To 408 Sqn.
AT115	FTR Hamburg 30.11/1.12.41.
AT121	FTR Münster 28/29.1.42.
AT122	FTR Münster 28/29.1.42.
AT123	FTR from mining sortie 3/4.1.42.
AT131	To 455 Sqn.
AT141	To 408 Sqn.
AT146	From 50 Sqn. FTR from mining sortie 22/23.1.42.
AT178	To 49 Sqn.
AT190	To 49 Sqn.
AT191	To 49 Sqn.
AT219	To 420 Sqn.
Manchester	From February 1942 to June 1942.
L7291	From 97 Sqn. No operations to 50 Sqn.
L7301 ZN-D	FTR Cologne 30/31.5.42. 50 Sqn crew Manser VC.
L7305	From 25 OTU. Became ground instruction machine.
L7315	From 61 Sqn. No operations.
L7317	From 207 Sqn. Force-landed near Lee-on-Solent on return from Dortmund 15.4.42. 21 operations total.
L7319	From 207 Sqn. Completed at least 25 operations. Ultimate fate not recorded.
L7376	From 25 OTU. To 1654CU.
L7378	From 207 Sqn. Completed 32 operations to 1654CU
L7390	FTR Essen 25/26.3.42.

L7391	From 207 Sqn to 1485Flt.
L7394	From 83 Sqn. FTR from mining sortie 29/30.3.42.
L7398	To 49 Sqn.
L7399 ZN-X	FTR from mining sortie 2/3.5.42.
L7417 ZN-V	From 207 Sqn. Crashed on cross-country exercise 19.5.42.
L7418	FTR from training flight, presumed lost in the Irish Sea 19.5.42.
L7434	To 1656CU.
L7456 ZN-T	FTR Cologne 30/31.5.42. 50 Sqn crew.
L7457	From 83 Sqn. To 1654CU.
L7461	From 97 Sqn. To 1660CU.
L7463	From 97 Sqn. FTR Rostock 23/24.4.42.
L7467	From 97CF. To 1661CU.
L7474	From 97 Sqn. Abandoned over Lincolnshire while training 12.3.42.
L7485	From 207 Sqn. FTR from mining sortie 16/17.4.42.
L7488	From 207 Sqn. Became ground instruction machine.
L7515	From 207 Sqn to 49 Sqn.
R5769	To 50 Sqn.
R5770	From 25 OTU to 1660CU.
R5780	From 83 Sqn. Returned to 83 Sqn.
R5796	From 207 Sqn. 18 operations total to 1654CU.
R5839	To 1661CU.
R5840	FTR from mining sortie 2/3.5.42.
R5841	To 1660CU.
Lancaster	From May 1942.
L7569	From 44 Sqn. Became ground instruction machine.
L7577	From 97 Sqn on loan for one operation. Returned to 97 Sqn to 1660CU via 106CF.
L7579	From A.V.Roe. First off on Squadron's first Lancaster operation. To 1654CU via 106CF.
L7582	From 207 Sqn. To 100 Sqn.
R5492 ZN-S/Y	From 44 Sqn. To 1661CU.
R5551 ZN-V	From 97 Sqn. FTR Oberhausen 14/15.6.43.
R5572 ZN-M	From 97 Sqn. FTR Gelsenkirchen 25/26.6.43.
R5573 ZN-B	FTR Cologne 8/9.7.43.
R5574	FTR Munich 21/22.12.42.
R5576	To 106CF. Crashed on take-off from Coningsby while training 21.7.42.
R5604	FTR Düsseldorf 31.7/1.8.42. Was carrying first 8000 lb bomb.
R5608	FTR from mining sortie 25/26.7.42.
R5609	From 97 Sqn. To 1LFS.
R5611 ZN-W	From R.A.E. FTR Pilsen 13/14.5.43.
R5614	From 97 Sqn. Crashed at Syerston while training 1.8.43.
R5637 ZN-D	FTR Düsseldorf 27/28.1.43.
R5638	FTR Düsseldorf 10/11.9.42.
R5665 ZN-D	From 44 Sqn. FTR Remscheid 30/31.7.43.
R5668	To 207 Sqn.
R5676 ZN-E	To 1660CU via 106CF.
R5677 ZN-A/B	FTR Wuppertal 29/30.5.43.
R5678	FTR Düsseldorf 15/16.8.42.
R5680 ZN-T	FTR Essen 13/14.1.43.

R5681	Flown by W/C Gibson on his first Lancaster operation. FTR Essen 16/17.9.42.
R5683	Exploded over The Wash en-route to Duisburg 26.7.42.
R5684	FTR Frankfurt 24/25.8.42.
R5697 ZN-J	From 44 Sqn. FTR Duisburg 20/21.12.42.
R5700 ZN-G	Completed 34 operations. To 9 Sqn via 5MU.
R5702	From 50 Sqn. To 460 Sqn.
R5731 ZN-M	FTR Hamburg 3/4.3.43.
R5742	To 61 Sqn.
R5748 ZN-R	FTR Hamburg 26/27.7.42.
R5749 ZN-G	FTR Essen 12/13.3.43.
R5750	FTR Wilhelmshaven 18/19.2.43.
R5844	From 50CF. FTR Essen 1/2.6.42.
R5848	To 1660CU via 106CF.
R5854	To 97 Sqn.
R5856	To 61 Sqn via 1660CU.
R5861	FTR Wilhelmshaven 8/9.7.42.
R5864	To 61 Sqn and back. Returned to 61 Sqn.
R5899	FTR from mining sortie 18/19.9.42.
R5900 ZN-X	Crashed while landing at Syerston on return from Berlin 18.1.43.
R5901	To 44 Sqn.
R5906	Conversion Flt only. To 15 Sqn.
R5910	To 61 Sqn and back to 1654CU.
R5914	FTR Munich 21/22.12.42.
W4102	Crashed on approach to Langar after early return from Aachen 5.10.42.
W4109	FTR Mainz 11/12.8.42.
W4118 ZN-Y	FTR Turin 4/5.2.43.
W4156	FTR Duisburg 8/9.4.43.
W4178	FTR Essen 16/17.9.42.
W4179	FTR Essen 16/17.9.42.
W4195 ZN-W	FTR Cologne 15/16.10.42.
W4238 ZN-C	Crashed at Newton following early return from Krefeld 2.10.42.
W4242 ZN-A	FTR Hanover 8/9.10.43.
W4253	To 1661CU.
W4256 ZN-V	FTR Gelsenkirchen 25/26.6.43.
W4261 ZN-C	FTR Essen 13/14.1.43.
W4302	FTR Cologne 15/16.10.42.
W4367	From 50 Sqn. FTR Gelsenkirchen 25/26.6.43.
W4381	From 467 Sqn. To 61 Sqn.
W4763	From 61 Sqn. FTR Gelsenkirchen 9/10.7.43.
W4768	FTR Krefeld 2/3.10.42.
W4770 ZN-O	FTR Hamburg 3/4.2.43.
W4771	FTR Cologne 15/16.10.42.
W4776	To 1656CU.
W4778	To 44 Sqn via 106CF.
W4826 ZN-D	From 467 Sqn. FTR Hamburg 30/31.1.43.
W4842 ZN-H	FTR Essen 27/28.5.43.
W4886	FTR Nuremberg 25/26.2.43.
W4897	From 156 Sqn. To 463 Sqn.
W4918 ZN-D	FTR Essen 5/6.3.43.
W4921 ZN-Z	To 617 Sqn.

W4922	From 156 Sqn. FTR Mannheim 5/6.9.43.
DV181	FTR Turin 12/13.7.43.
DV182	FTR Mannheim 5/6.9.43.
DV195	FTR Nuremberg 10/11.8.43.
DV196 ZN-K	FTR Milan 7/8.8.43.
DV229	To 463 Sqn.
DV271	FTR Mannheim 23/24.9.43.
DV272 ZN-F	FTR Hanover 8/9.10.43.
DV273	To BDU.
DV274	To 463 Sqn.
DV297	To 61 Sqn.
DV339	To 61 Sqn.
DV344	To 61 Sqn.
ED303	From 467 Sqn. FTR Hamburg 27/28.7.43.
ED358 ZN-T	From 50 Sqn. FTR Leipzig 20/21.10.43.
ED360	From 467 Sqn. Crashed near Wisbech on return from Cologne 9.7.43.
ED385	From 57 Sqn. FTR Berlin 3/4.9.43.
ED409 ZN-B	From 50 Sqn. FTR Berlin 31.8/1.9.43.
ED417	Collided with a Halifax JN966 (428 Sqn) near Middleton-St-George on return from Berlin 26/27.11.43.
ED420	From 9 Sqn. To 463 Sqn.
ED451 ZN-O	FTR Essen 30.4/1.5.43.
ED542	FTR Essen 3/4.4.43.
ED593 ZN-T/Y	To 5LFS after many operations.
ED596 ZN-H	FTR Berlin 29/30.3.43.
ED649 ZN-X	FTR Oberhausen 14/15.6.43.
ED708	FTR Hamburg 27/28.7.43.
ED720 ZN-R	FTR Cologne 8/9.7.43.
ED752 ZN-H/P	FTR Stuttgart 14/15.4.43.
ED801	To 207 Sqn via 1661CU.
ED819	FTR Munich 6/7.9.43.
ED873	From 97 Sqn. Crashed while landing at Metheringham on return from aborted Berlin sortie 26.11.43.
ED874	From 97 Sqn. FTR Berlin 2/3.12.43.
EE125	FTR Gelsenkirchen 25/26.6.43.
EE186	From 49 Sqn. To 61 Sqn.
EE191 ZN-R	To 463 Sqn.
EE196	From 166 Sqn. FTR Kassel 22/23.10.43.
JA845	From SIU. No operations to BDU.
JA871	FTR Leverkusen 22/23.8.43.
JA876	To 622 Sqn.
JA893 ZN-C	Ditched in North Sea on return from Berlin 3/4.9.43.
JA973 ZN-F	To 463 Sqn.
JB146	Crash-landed at Romney Marsh on return from Berlin 1.9.43.
JB292 ZN-R	From 1660CU. FTR Salbris 7/8.5.44.
JB534	From 61 Sqn. Crashed in Lincolnshire on return from Berlin 16.2.44.
JB562 ZN-M	Completed 11 operations to Berlin. FTR Schweinfurt 26/27.4.44.
JB566 ZN-C	Completed 10 operations to Berlin. FTR Nuremberg 30/31.3.44.
JB567 ZN-E	Completed 10 operations to Berlin. FTR Brunswick 22/23.4.44.

JB592 ZN-W	FTR Berlin 26/27.11.43.
JB593 ZN-T	Completed 13 operations to Berlin. FTR Königsburg 29/30.8.44.
JB601 ZN-V	Completed 11 operations to Berlin. FTR Schweinfurt 26/27.4.44.
JB612 ZN-U	FTR Salbris 7/8.5.44.
JB638 ZN-G	FTR Berlin 16/17.12.43.
JB641 ZN-X	Completed 11 operations to Berlin. FTR St Leu d'Esserent 7/8.7.44.
JB642 ZN-J	FTR Berlin 1/2.1.44.
JB645 ZN-F	FTR Berlin 1/2.1.44.
JB648 ZN-B	FTR Frankfurt 22/23.3.44.
JB663	Completed 111 operations to 24MU.
JB664 ZN-N	FTR Vitry-le-Francois 27/28.6.44.
JB738	From 460 Sqn. Returned to 460 Sqn.
LL891 ZN-S/B	FTR Salbris 7/8.5.44.
LL948 ZN-V	FTR Lützkendorf 14/15.3.45.
LL953 ZN-C/O	FTR Gravenhorst 6/7.11.44.
LL955 ZN-E	FTR Gelsenkirchen 21/22.6.44.
LL974 ZN-F	FTR Vitry-le-Francois 27/28.6.44.
LL975 ZN-H	FTR Pommerval 24/25.6.44.
LM211	
LM215 ZN-F	Crash-landed at Juvincourt on return from Siegen 1.2.45.
LM303 ZN-M	FTR Wilhelmshaven 11/12.2.43.
LM310	From 467 Sqn. To 61 Sqn.
LM375	From 460 Sqn. To 463 Sqn.
LM377	To 61 Sqn.
LM549	Crash-landed at Carnaby on return from Nantes 28.5.44.
LM570 ZN-Z	FTR Scholven-Buer 21/22.6.44.
LM641 ZN-D	FTR Secqueville 7/8.8.44.
LM690 ZN-P	
ME313	From 582 Sqn via NTU.
ME324 ZN-R	To 1661CU.
ME355 ZN-P/S	From 514 Sqn. To 50 Sqn.
ME336	From 514 Sqn.
ME630 ZN-P	From 97 Sqn. FTR Leipzig 19/20.2.44.
ME668 ZN-L	FTR St Leu d'Esserent 7/8.7.44.
ME669 ZN-O	FTR Schweinfurt 26/27.4.44.
ME778 ZN-O	FTR Stuttgart 28/29.7.44.
ME789 ZN-B	FTR St Leu d'Esserent 7/8.7.44.
ME790 ZN-U	FTR Brunswick 22/23.5.44.
ME831 ZN-R	FTR St Leu d'Esserent 7/8.7.44.
ME832 ZN-J	FTR St Leu d'Esserent 4/5.7.44.
ND331 ZN-G/C	FTR Königsburg 29/30.8.44.
ND332	Crash-landed at Manston on return from Nuremberg 30/31.3.44.
ND333 ZN-R/S	From 83 Sqn.
ND336 ZN-Q	FTR Berlin 30/31.1.44.
ND339 ZN-U	Detached to 617 Sqn. Returned to 106 Sqn. FTR St Leu d'Esserent 4/5.7.44.
ND501 ZN-O/K	From 97 Sqn. Crashed while landing at Metheringham while training 3.4.45.
ND511 ZN-N/E	FTR Gennevilliers 9/10.5.44.
ND535 ZN-Q	FTR Nuremberg 30/31.3.44.

ND585 ZN-J	FTR Nuremberg 30/31.3.44.
ND680 ZN-P	FTR Coutances (Caen) 6/7.6.44.
ND682 ZN-X/K	FTR from mining sortie 15/16.12.44.
ND690	From 35 Sqn via NTU.
ND850 ZN-C	FTR Schweinfurt 26/27.4.44.
ND851 ZN-H	FTR Gennevilliers 9/10.5.44.
ND853 ZN-J	FTR Schweinfurt 26/27.4.44.
ND868 ZN-Q	FTR Dortmund Ems Canal 23/24.9.44.
ND870 ZN-S	FTR Salbris 7/8.5.44.
ND907	From 35 Sqn via NTU to 83 Sqn.
ND933	From 35 Sqn via NTU to 97 Sqn.
NE150 ZN-H	FTR Coutances (Caen) 6/7.6.44.
NG222 ZN-T	To 1654CU.
NG223	From 9 Sqn. Returned to 9 Sqn.
NG414 ZN-K	From 1661CU. Crashed on take-off from Metheringham when bound for Pilsen 16.4.45.
NN719 ZN-Q	
NN725	
NN726 ZN-D	FTR Gdynia 18/19.12.44.
PA194	From 1661CU.
PA232	
PA267 ZN-N	
PA310	
PA331	
PB122 ZN-Y	FTR Leuna 14/15.1.45.
PB144 ZN-P	FTR St Leu D'Esserent 7/8.7.44.
PB145 ZN-L/M	
PB191 ZN-H	
PB203 ZN-M	FTR Darmstadt 11/12.9.44.
PB232 ZN-N	
PB248 ZN-E	To 5LFS.
PB281 ZN-J	FTR Heilbronn 3/4.12.44.
PB284	
PB296 ZN-X	
PB298 ZN-B	Force-landed near Fulbeck on return from Bremerhaven 19.9.44.
PB303 ZN-R	FTR Homburg 1.11.44.
PB304 ZN-Z/S	Crashed in Lancashire on return from operation to the Normandy battle area 30.7.44.
PB347 ZN-G	From 49 Sqn. FTR Rheydt 19/20.9.44.
PB359 ZN-T	From 49sqn. FTR Rheydt 19/20.9.44.
PB617 ZN-B	FTR Royan 5.1.45.
PB618	
PB645	To 227 Sqn.
PB676	From 35 Sqn. To 189 Sqn.
PB682	From 405 Sqn.
PB724 ZN-L/N	FTR Munich 7/8.1.45.
PB732 ZN-K	From 189 Sqn.
PB734	
PD214 ZN-D	FTR Bremen 6/7.10.44.
PD429	To 186 Sqn.
RA508 ZN-B	FTR Dortmund 12.3.45.
RA567	
RE130	

RF130
RF151 ZN-E   From 189 Sqn.
RF235
RF236
SW248 ZN-R   From 1661CU.
SW265 ZN-O   From 49 Sqn.

Heaviest Single Loss

Schweinfurt 26/27.04.44	5 Lancasters FTR.
St-Leu-d'Esserent 07/08.07.44	5 Lancasters FTR.

144 SQUADRON

Motto: Who Shall Stop Us   Code PL

Formed initially as a corps reconnaissance unit at Port Said in March 1918 for army co-operation duties in Palestine and Egypt, 144 Squadron was moved to the Aegean in October for operations against the Turks. Shortly after the end of hostilities the squadron was reduced to a cadre, before returning to the UK in December, where disbandment followed on the 4 February 1919. The number remained on the shelf until the 11 January 1937, when it was resurrected at Bicester as a day bomber squadron, equipped initially with Overstrands and Ansons. In February the squadron moved to Hemswell, and in August, began to take delivery of Blenheims and transferred to 5 Group. Conversion to Hampdens began in March 1939, and it was with this type that the squadron entered the Second World War as one of 5 Group's front-line units. No. 144 Squadron played an important role within 5 Group for almost half of the war, before moving on to other duties with Coastal Command in early 1942.

Posted to Coastal Command   21.04.42

STATIONS

Hemswell	07.05.38 to 06.09.39
Speke	06.09.39 to 09.09.39
Hemswell	09.09.39 to 17.07.41
North Luffenham	17.07.41 to 21.04.42

COMMANDING OFFICERS

Wing Commander J C Cunningham	09.39 to 29.09.39
Wing Commander R B Jordan	29.09.39 to 05.40
Wing Commander A N Luxmoore	05.40 to 12.05.40
Wing Commander J J Watts DSO	12.05.40 to 13.06.40
Wing Commander J E C G F Gyll-Murray DSO	13.06.40 to 01.41
Wing Commander W S Gardner DFC	01.41 to 11.41
Wing Commander D D Christie	11.41 to 01.42
Wing Commander G F Simond	01.42 to 12.02.42
Squadron Leader J Bennett DFC	12.02.42 to 07.42

AIRCRAFT

Hampden	03.39 to 01.43

OPERATIONAL RECORD

Operations	Sorties	Aircraft Losses	% Losses
324	2,045	62	3.0

Category of Operations

Bombing	Mining	Leaflet
276	42	6

TABLE OF STATISTICS

Out of 22 Squadrons in 5 Group

10th highest number of overall operations in 5 Group.
15th highest number of sorties in 5 Group.
13th highest number of aircraft operational losses in 5 Group.

Out of 10 Hampden squadrons in 5 Group

4th highest number of overall Hampden operations in 5 Group.
Highest number of Hampden bombing operations in 5 Group.
3rd highest number of Hampden sorties in 5 Group.
Highest number of Hampden operational losses in 5 Group.

Hampden	To April 1942.
L4037	From R.A.E to 489 Sqn.
L4067	From 49 Sqn. Abandoned over East Anglia on return from Krefeld 21/22.5.40.
L4108	From 61 Sqn. To 14 OTU.
L4121	FTR Wilhelmshaven area 29.9.39.
L4124	To 83 Sqn.
L4125	To 49 Sqn.
L4126	FTR Wilhelmshaven area 29.9.39.
L4127	FTR Wilhelmshaven area 29.9.39.
L4129	To 49 Sqn.
L4131 PL-A	To 14 OTU.
L4132	FTR Wilhelmshaven area 29.9.39.
L4133	To 83 Sqn.
L4134	FTR Wilhelmshaven area 29.9.39.
L4135	Damaged beyond repair in taxiing accident at Hemswell while training 27.5.40.
L4137	From 76 Sqn. Crashed in Lincolnshire during navigation exercise 20.3.40.
L4141	From 76 Sqn to 1 AAS.
L4143	From 76 Sqn. Crashed in Lincolnshire during an air-test 22.4.40.
L4163	From 7 Sqn. Crashed on take-off from Hemswell when bound for a mining sortie 17.4.40.
L4165	From 7 Sqn. To 25 OTU.
L4166	From 7 Sqn. Damaged beyond repair in heavy landing at Hemswell while training 19.11.39.
L4167	From 7 Sqn. Crashed on landing at Doncaster while training 30.10.39.

L4172 PL-L	FTR from attack on communications targets 25/26.5.40.
L4173	To 14 OTU.
L4178	From 44 Sqn. Crashed in Yorkshire on return from Kiel 26/27.2.42.
N9086	SOC 14.1.42.
P1151	To 14 OTU.
P1164	Converted for use as torpedo bomber.
P1166	To 50 Sqn and back to 408 Sqn.
P1172	FTR Hamburg 5/6.9.40.
P1198	From 106 Sqn. Converted for use as torpedo bomber.
P1273	From 14 OTU. Crashed in Russia during transit 4/5.9.42.
P1295 PL-L	FTR Hüls 28/29.12.41.
P1326	FTR Mönchengladbach 11/12.5.40.
P1328	Crashed in Lincolnshire during training 1.2.41.
P1354	To 83 Sqn.
P2063	From 49 Sqn. FTR Norway 22/23.11.42.
P2079	Crashed on approach to Hemswell on return from Munich 8/9.11.40.
P2080	To 16 OTU.
P2081	To 25 OTU.
P2094	To 50 Sqn.
P2117 PL-N	Crashed while landing at Boscombe Down on return from Brest 23/24.8.40.
P4291 PL-E	FTR Merseburg (Leuna) 16/17.8.40.
P4338	From 61 Sqn to A&AEE.
P4345	Crashed at Felixstowe on return from target in France 12/13.6.40.
P4347	Converted for use as torpedo bomber to 489 Sqn.
P4348	To 16 OTU.
P4359 PL-S	Abandoned over Norfolk on return from Mannheim 8/9.2.41.
P4360 PL-L	FTR Dortmund-Ems Canal 21/22.8.40.
P4361	FTR Kiel 4/5.7.40.
P4362 PL-A	FTR from mining sortie 5/6.10.40.
P4363 PL-E	FTR from mining sortie 23/24.6.40.
P4364	Crashed soon after take-off from Scampton for a transit flight 18/19.6.40.
P4365 PL-K	Crashed on landing at Hemswell on return from Merseburg (Leuna) 16/17.8.40.
P4366	FTR Wanne-Eickel 11/12.7.40.
P4367	FTR from Wilhelmshaven 20/21.7.40.
P4368	FTR Homberg 10/11.8.40.
P4369	To 25 OTU.
P4370 PL-B or L	FTR Ludwigshafen 2/3.9.40.
P4378	Crashed while trying to land at Hemswell on return from Hamburg 5/6.9.40.
P4391	To 14 OTU.
P4394	Crashed at Wainfleet when bound for Hanover 1/2.3.41.
P4407	Abandoned over Northamptonshire on return from Le Havre 29/30.11.40.
P4415	From 44 Sqn via 1 AAS to Russian Navy.
P5331	From 7 AAU. Converted for use as torpedo bomber to 5 OTU.

P5335	From 50 Sqn. Converted for use as torpedo bomber. To 489 Sqn.
X2903	Converted for use as torpedo bomber.
X2915	FTR Berlin 1/2.11.40.
X2961	To CGS.
X2963	Crashed on landing at Hemswell on return from mining sortie 5/6.10.40.
X2969	From 83 Sqn. FTR from mining sortie 24/25.2.42.
X2973	FTR Merseburg (Leuna) 16/17.10.40.
X2976	To 16 OTU.
X2988	Abandoned over Norfolk on return from Merseburg (Leuna) 16/17.10.40.
X2998	Crashed near Hemswell on return from Kiel 25/26.10.40.
X3007	Abandoned over Lincolnshire on return from Hanover 11/12.2.41.
X3030	Crashed on approach to North Luffenham on return from Frankfurt 20/21.9.41.
X3047	FTR Berlin 1/2.11.40.
X3048	Crashed on landing at Hemswell on return from Homburg 15/16.2.41.
X3051	To 408 Sqn.
X3055 PL-O	Converted for use as torpedo bomber.
X3056	Abandoned over Lincolnshire on return from Lützkendorf 19/20.11.40.
X3065	Abandoned over Oxfordshire during fighter patrol 6/7.12.40.
X3066	FTR Düsseldorf 10/11.4.41.
X3129	FTR Brest 1.4.41.
X3130	Converted for use as torpedo bomber to 3FPP.
AD720	Crashed soon after take-off from Hemswell when bound for Cologne 10/11.3.41.
AD724	Converted for use as torpedo bomber to CCDU.
AD737	Crashed while landing at Hemswell on return from Hanover 1/2.3.41.
AD745	Abandoned over Northamptonshire on return from mining sortie 20/21.3.41.
AD752	From 61 Sqn. Crashed in Northamptonshire while training 9.1.42.
AD754	From 408 Sqn. To 61 Sqn.
AD761	Shot down by intruder soon after take-off from Hemswell when bound for a mining sortie 16/17.4.41.
AD762	Converted for use as torpedo bomber. To 415 Sqn.
AD765	From 106 Sqn. Crashed on take-off from North Luffenham while training 26.1.42.
AD766	From 50 Sqn. To 14 OTU.
AD767	Converted for use as torpedo bomber. To 415 Sqn.
AD783	To 455 Sqn.
AD784	FTR Cologne 30/31.7.41.
AD791	FTR Aachen 7/8.12.41.
AD793	Converted for use as torpedo bomber. To 5 OTU.
AD794	From 83 Sqn. Converted for use as torpedo bomber. To 415 Sqn.
AD799	From 49 Sqn. Converted for use as torpedo bomber. To 455 Sqn.

AD801 PL-C	Converted for use as torpedo bomber. To 489 Sqn.
AD804 PL-D	From 61 Sqn. FTR Hüls 28/29.12.41.
AD824	From 49 Sqn. FTR from mining sortie 7.2.42.
AD832	Crashed in Northamptonshire while training 17.2.42.
AD838	To 16 OTU.
AD841 PL-Q	FTR Hanover 15/16.5.41.
AD846	FTR from shipping strike 5/6.11.41.
AD866	FTR Bremen 3/4.7.41.
AD871	FTR Brest 6/7.7.41.
AD872	Crashed near Coningsby on return from Frankfurt 20/21.9.41.
AD900	FTR Bremen 11/12.5.41.
AD901 PL-M	Force-landed in Norfolk on return from Hamburg 8/9.5.41.
AD903 PL-A	FTR Calais 6/7.8.41.
AD905	FTR Cologne 1/2.9.41.
AD908	From 50 Sqn. Converted for use as torpedo bomber. To 455 Sqn.
AD918	FTR Mannheim 25/26.8.41.
AD921	FTR from mining sortie to Brest 13.12.41.
AD922	Abandoned over Norfolk on return from Frankfurt 20/21.9.41.
AD923	Crash-landed in Yorkshire on return from Frankfurt 20/21.9.41.
AD924	FTR Aachen 9/10.7.41.
AD926	Crashed on landing at Hemswell on return from Cologne 17/18.6.41.
AD928	From 50 Sqn. Converted for use as torpedo bomber. To 489 Sqn.
AD929	From 50 Sqn. Converted for use as torpedo bomber. To 489 Sqn.
AD936	FTR Berlin 7/8.9.41.
AD959	From 16 OTU. FTR from operations over north-west Germany 1/2.4.42.
AD964	From 49 Sqn. Converted for use as torpedo bomber. To 5 OTU.
AD965	FTR Hüls 12/13.10.41.
AD973	From 49 Sqn. Crashed while training 12.6.42.
AD979	From 49 Sqn. Converted for use as torpedo bomber. To 455 Sqn.
AE177	To 455 Sqn.
AE118	Crashed in Leicestershire on return from Rostock 11/12.9.41.
AE119	Crashed in Yorkshire on return from Wilhelmshaven 11/12.7.41.
AE121	Crash-landed in Rutland on return from Rostock 11/12.9.41.
AE122	Converted for use as torpedo bomber. To 455 Sqn.
AE125	Converted for use as torpedo bomber. To 455 Sqn.
AE128	To 44 Sqn.
AE140	FTR Karlsruhe 6/7.8.41.
AE141 PL-J	Crashed on landing at Norwich on return from Channel Dash 12.2.42.
AE142	To 5 OTU.

AE143	Crash-landed on approach to Driffield on return from Hamburg 29/30.9.41.
AE158	From 50 Sqn to Russian Navy 12.10.42.
AE195	To 16 OTU.
AE200	From 61 Sqn. FTR from mining sortie 26/27.3.42.
AE225	FTR Brest 24.7.41.
AE235	From 61 Sqn. Converted for use as torpedo bomber.
AE238	Crash-landed in Staffordshire on return from Cologne 7/8.11.41.
AE248	From 50 Sqn to 420 Sqn.
AE252	FTR Cologne 30/31.7.41.
AE253	FTR from shipping strike 5/6.11.41.
AE265	FTR Mannheim 25/26.8.41.
AE304	Crashed soon after take-off from North Luffenham when bound for Berlin 7/8.9.41.
AE309	Converted for use as torpedo bomber. To 5 OTU.
AE310	Converted for use as torpedo bomber.
AE311	Crashed on landing at North Luffenham on return from Hamburg 9/10.11.41.
AE316	From 50 Sqn. FTR Frankfurt 24/25.10.41.
AE353	FTR Brest 11.12.41.
AE359	From 83 Sqn. FTR Brest 31.1/1.2.42.
AE368	From 49 Sqn. Converted for use as torpedo bomber. To 415 Sqn.
AE392	FTR from mining sortie 7.2.42.
AE395	Converted for use as torpedo bomber. To 415 Sqn.
AE424	FTR from shipping strike 5/6.11.41.
AE440	Crashed in the Cotswolds on return from Düsseldorf 27/28.11.41.
AE441	Crashed in Norfolk on return from Hamburg 14/15.1.42.
AT110	From 83 Sqn. Crashed in Sussex when bound for Dortmund 14/15.4.42.
AT116 PL-F	Damaged in taxiing accident at Exeter on return from mining sortie 22/23.3.42.
AT117	Converted for use as torpedo bomber. To 5 OTU.
AT143	To 408 Sqn.
AT145	Converted for use as torpedo bomber.
AT149	FTR Brest 31.1/1.2.42.
AT155	Crashed in Rutland during air test 12.4.42.
AT157	FTR Dortmund 14/15.4.42.
AT172	Converted for use as torpedo bomber. To 415 Sqn.
AT175	FTR from Channel Dash 12.2.42.
AT182	From 455 Sqn. Returned to 455 Sqn.
AT187	Crashed at Sutton Bridge on return from Essen 10/11.4.42.
AT188	FTR Norway 4/5.5.42.
AT194	FTR from mining sortie 24/25.2.42.
AT218	FTR Essen 10/11.4.42.
AT222	To 16 OTU.
AT226	Force-landed in Buckinghamshire on return from Cologne 5/6.4.42.

Heaviest Single Loss

29.09.39	Heligoland Bight. 5 Hampdens.

189 SQUADRON

No Motto: Code CA

First formed on the 20 December 1917 as a night flying training unit, 189 Squadron enjoyed only a brief existence before being consigned to the shelf through disbandment on the 1 March 1919. It was not until the Second World War was grinding towards its inevitable conclusion, that the squadron was resurrected as part of Bomber Command's final expansion programme. Between the 1 October and the 1 November 1944, seven new Lancaster squadrons were formed in 1, 3 and 5 Groups, the last mentioned receiving 227 Squadron on the 7 October, and 189 Squadron on the 15th. Both squadrons were formed at Bardney, the home of 9 Squadron, but neither was to remain there for long. No. 189 Squadron participated in the massively heavy bombing campaigns that characterised the final seven months of the war, and on two occasions suffered unusually high losses for the period.

STATIONS

Bardney	15.10.44 to 02.11.44
Fulbeck	02.11.44 to 08.04.45
Bardney	08.04.45 to 15.10.45

COMMANDING OFFICER

Wing Commander J S Shorthouse   15.10.45 to 06.45

AIRCRAFT

Lancaster I/III   15.10.45 to 11.45

OPERATIONAL RECORD

Operations	Sorties	Aircraft Losses	% Losses
48	652	16	2.5

Category of Operations
All Bombing

TABLE OF STATISTICS

Out of 59 Lancaster squadrons

52nd highest number of Lancaster overall operations in Bomber Command.
51st highest number of Lancaster sorties in Bomber Command.
44th highest number of Lancaster operational losses in Bomber Command.

Out of 22 squadrons in 5 Group

Lowest number of overall operations in 5 Group.
20th highest number of sorties in 5 Group.
19th equal (with 227 Sqn) highest number of aircraft operational losses in 5 Group.

Out of 17 Lancaster squadrons in 5 Group

Lowest number of Lancaster overall operations in 5 Group.
Lowest number of Lancaster sorties in 5 Group.
16th highest number of Lancaster operational losses in 5 Group.

Lancaster	From October 1944.
DV310 CA-B	From 166 Sqn via 5LFS to 1659CU.
EE136 CA-R	From 9 Sqn. Became ground instruction machine.
LM216	From 186 Sqn.
LM713 CA-G	From 9 Sqn.
LM736	From 9 Sqn.
LM745	From 9 Sqn.
ME300 CA-P	Collided with ND473 (467 Sqn) and FTR Royan 4.1.45.
ME374	
ME444 CA-A/F	
ME452 CA-Q	FTR Harburg 7/8.3.45.
ME547	
NG226 CA-J	
NG307 CA-F	FTR Karlsruhe 2/3.2.45.
NG308 CA-G	FTR Harburg 7/8.3.45.
NG321 CA-V	FTR Mittelland Canal at Gravenhorst 21/22.2.45.
NG325 CA-H	Shot down by intruder over Norfolk on return from the Dortmund-Ems Canal at Ladbergen 4.3.45.
NG416 CA-M	From 1661CU. FTR Harburg 7/8.3.45.
NG417 CA-P	From 1661CU. FTR Harburg 7/8.3.45.
NG461	
NX567 CA-R	FTR Lützkendorf 14/15.3.45.
NX578 CA-N	
PA182 CA-W	
PA196	To 207 Sqn.
PA197 CA-B	FTR Dortmund-Ems Canal at Ladbergen 3/4.3.45.
PA284	
PA315	
PA316	
PB146 CA-A	From 9 Sqn.
PB289 CA-B	FTR Pölitz 21/22.12.44.
PB594 CA-D	From 9 Sqn.
PB622	From 7 Sqn.
PB676	From 106 Sqn.
PB691 CA-O	From 97 Sqn. FTR Pölitz 21/22.12.44.
PB732	From 44 Sqn. To 106 Sqn.
PB742 CA-T	From 630 Sqn. FTR Heilbronn 4/5.12.44.
PB743 CA-E	From 44 Sqn. FTR Karlsruhe 2/3.2.45.
PB744 CA-U	From 57 Sqn.
PB745 CA-Q	Crashed on take-off for Munich 26/27.11.44.
PB793 CA-X	
PB840 CA-K	FTR Karlsruhe 2/3.2.45.
PB848 CA-Q	FTR Karlsruhe 2/3.2.45.
PB879	
RA517 CA-B	FTR Rositz 14/15.2.45.
RA568 CA-C	
RF132 CA-K	FTR Böhlen 20/21.3.45.
RF151 CA-E	To 106 Sqn.
RF204	
SW270 CA-O	

Heaviest Single Loss

02/03.02.45	Karlsruhe. 4 Lancasters FTR.
07/08.03.45	Harburg. 4 Lancasters FTR.

207 SQUADRON

Motto: Semper Paratus (Always prepared)   Code EM

The history of 207 Squadron stretches back to the day on which the Royal Air Force was born, the 1 April 1918, when it was formed as a night bomber squadron, thus setting a trend which would be repeated during the next world conflict. At the conclusion of the Great War, the squadron remained in Germany until withdrawal to England in August 1919, and eventual disbandment in January 1920. Two weeks later, it was re-formed as a day bomber unit, and spent two periods of duty overseas during the inter-war years. In April 1938 Fairey Battles were taken on charge, and the squadron assumed a training role, which continued after the outbreak of war until it was absorbed into 12 OTU in April 1940. The squadron was re-formed at the beginning of November to introduce the new Avro Manchester into operational service. Beset with problems throughout its relatively brief and disappointing career, the Manchester was often grounded while modifications were carried out. Some of the Group's outstanding pilots found their way to 207 Squadron in early 1941, a few then moving on again to take their experience to 97 Squadron. The survivors of this era would permeate the Group and Command to become outstanding commanding officers. No. 207 Squadron was an early recipient of the Lancaster, and employed it to good effect for the remainder of the war. Sadly, 207 Squadron would end the war with higher than average casualties.

STATIONS

Waddington	01.11.40 to 17.11.41
Bottesford	17.11.41 to 20.09.42
Syerston (Detachment)	23.08.42 to 20.09.42
Langar	20.09.42 to 12.10.43
Spilsby	12.10.43 to 30.10.45

COMMANDING OFFICERS

Wing Commander N C Hyde	01.11.40 to 09.04.41
Squadron Leader C J D Kydd (Temp)	09.04.41 to 30.04.41
Wing Commander J N D Anderson OBE	30.04.41 to 21.05.41
Wing Commander K P Lewis	21.05.41 to 10.10.41
Wing Commander C Fothergill	10.10.41 to 28.05.42
Wing Commander F R Jeffs AFC	28.05.42 to 07.12.42
Wing Commander F G L Bain	07.12.42 to 09.12.42
Wing Commander T A B Parselle	10.12.42 to 26.05.43
Wing Commander P N Jennings	29.05.43 to 26.02.44
Wing Commander V J Wheeler DFC*	26.02.44 to 23.03.44
Wing Commander J F Grey DSO DFC	24.03.44 to 16.10.44
Wing Commander H R Black AFC	16.10.44 to 18.04.46

AIRCRAFT

Manchester	11.40 to 03.42
Hampden	07.41 to 08.41
Lancaster I/III	03.42 to 08.49

OPERATIONAL RECORD

Operations	Sorties	Aircraft Losses	% Losses
481	4,563	148	3.2

Category of Operations

Bombing	Mining	Other
426	50	5

Manchester

Operations	Sorties	Aircraft Losses	% Losses
95	360	17	4.7

Category of Operations

Bombing	Mining	Other
76	15	4

Lancaster

Operations	Sorties	Aircraft Losses	% Losses
386	4,203	131	3.1

Category of Operations

Bombing	Mining	Other
350	35	1

TABLE OF STATISTICS

(Heavy squadrons)
24th highest number of overall operations in Bomber Command.
29th highest number of sorties in Bomber Command.
22nd highest number of aircraft operational losses in Bomber Command.
4th highest percentage loss rate in Bomber Command.
25th highest number of bombing operations in Bomber Command.

Out of 58 Lancaster squadrons in Bomber Command

2nd highest number of Lancaster operations in Bomber Command.
10th highest number of Lancaster sorties in Bomber Command.
4th highest number of Lancaster operational losses in Bomber Command.

Out of 22 squadrons in 5 Group

6th highest number of overall operations in 5 Group.
6th highest number of sorties in 5 Group.
6th highest number of aircraft operational losses in 5 Group.
2nd equal (with 9 Sqn) highest percentage loss rate in 5 Group.

Out of 8 Manchester squadrons in 5 Group

Highest number of Manchester overall operations in 5 Group and Bomber Command.
Highest number of Manchester sorties in 5 Group and Bomber Command.
Highest number of Manchester operational losses in 5 Group and Bomber Command.

Out of 17 Lancaster squadrons in 5 Group

Highest number of Lancaster overall operations in 5 Group.
5th highest number of Lancaster sorties in 5 Group.
2nd highest number of Lancaster operational losses in 5 Group.

Hampden	From July 1941 to August 1941.
AE186	To 61 Sqn.
AE192	To 44 Sqn.
AE219	To 61 Sqn.
AE247	To 61 Sqn.
AE249	To 455 Sqn.
AE264	To 455 Sqn.
AE295	To 5 Group TF.
AE296	To 455 Sqn.
AE297	To 408 Sqn.
AE299	To 106 Sqn.

Manchester	From November 1940 to March 1942.
L7278 EM-B/A	Crashed in Leicestershire soon after take-off from Waddington when bound for Lorient 21.3.41.
L7279 EM-B/A	From 6MU to RAE.
L7280	To 44 Sqn.
L7282 EM-J	No operations. To 97 Sqn.
L7283	To 97 Sqn via 25 OTU.
L7284 EM-D	To 61 Sqn.
L7285	No operations. To 83 Sqn.
L7286	To 83 Sqn via 61CF.
L7288 EM-H	To 97 Sqn.
L7292	To 97 Sqn.
L7293	From 61 Sqn. To 1660CU.
L7294	To 97 Sqn.
L7298	No operations. To 97 Sqn.
L7299	No operations. To 97 Sqn.
L7300 EM-S/F	Completed 18 operations. Crashed on approach to Waddington while in transit 23.11.41.
L7302 EM-R	FTR Kiel 8.4.41.
L7303 EM-P	FTR Düsseldorf 26/27.3.41.
L7304	No operations. To 61 Sqn.
L7307 EM-P	From 97 Sqn. FTR Düsseldorf 27/28.3.41.
L7309 EM-J/O	FTR Hamburg 14/15.1.42.
L7310 EM-H	Crashed soon after take-off from Waddington for air-test 21.6.41.
L7311 EM-F	FTR Düsseldorf 16/17.8.41.
L7312 EM-L	FTR Hüls 12/13.10.41.
L7313 EM-C	Shot down by intruder on take-off from Waddington when bound for Hamburg 13.3.41.
L7314 EM-T/Y	Shot down over Northamptonshire by a 25 Sqn Beaufighter when bound for Boulogne 22.6.41.
L7316 EM-U	FTR Cologne 31.8/1.9.41.
L7317 EM-C	To 106 Sqn after 16 operations.
L7318 EM-K	Crashed on approach to Waddington while in transit 15.9.41.
L7319 EM-X	To 106 Sqn after 21 operations.
L7321 EM-D	FTR Cologne 13/14.10.41.
L7322 EM-B/Q	FTR Brest 9.1.42.
L7373 EM-T	FTR Cologne 13/14.10.41.
L7377 EM-G	FTR Berlin 12/13.8.41.
L7378 EM-A	To 106 Sqn after 24 operations.
L7379 EM-T	FTR Hamburg 2/3.5.41.
L7380 EM-W	FTR Berlin 7/8.9.41.

L7381 EM-K/R	FTR Berlin 12/13.8.41.
L7382	From 97 Sqn. Training only to 83 Sqn.
L7385 EM-U/U-	From 44 Sqn. Crashed on landing at Bottesford while training 6.8.42.
L7391	To 106 Sqn.
L7393 EM-V	Crash-landed at Perranporth during air-test 18.5.41. Became ground instruction machine.
L7397	From 49 Sqn. Training only to 1660CU.
L7417 EM-Y	To 106 Sqn.
L7419 EM-Y	To 61 Sqn.
L7422 EM-V	Crashed in Lincolnshire while training to 61 Sqn after repair.
L7432 EM-S/Z/O/J	To 50 Sqn after 16 operations.
L7454 EM-M	To 61 Sqn.
L7455 EM-G	To 97Squadron after 14 operations.
L7468 EM-Z	To 50 Sqn after 15 operations.
L7476 EM-K	From 97 Sqn. To 50 Sqn.
L7480 EM-L	To 44 Sqn.
L7483 EM-H/O	To 10 AGS.
L7484 EM-F/P	To 83 Sqn.
L7485 EM-O	To 106 Sqn.
L7486 EM-B/P	To 61 Sqn and back to 50 Sqn.
L7487 EM-N	FTR Bremen 20/21.10.41.
L7488 EM-Q	From 97 Sqn. To 106 Sqn.
L7491 EM-O	From 97 Sqn. To 50 Sqn.
L7496 EM-S	From 61 Sqn. To 50 Sqn.
L7515 EM-S	To 106 Sqn.
L7523 EM-M	Crashed in Yorkshire following early return from Hamburg 14.1.42.
L7526	From 49 Sqn. To 1656CU.
R5778	To 50 Sqn.
R5782 EM-R	To 50 Sqn.
R5788	To 83 Sqn.
R5790	To 83 Sqn.
R5791 EM-V	To 1485Flt.
R5796 EM-W	From 61 Sqn. To 106 Sqn.
R5833	Training only. To 83 Sqn.
R5835	To 83 Sqn.
Lancaster	From January 1942.
BT308	From 97 Sqn. Familiarization only to Rolls Royce.
L7530	From 44 Sqn. Training only to 467 Sqn.
L7532	From 50 Sqn. No operations to 3LFS.
L7540	From 83 Sqn. To 1654CU via 207CF.
L7543 EM-Z	From 44 Sqn. FTR Danzig 11.7.42.
L7544	From 44 Sqn. Conversion training only to 1667CU.
L7546 EM-G	From 44 Sqn. FTR Genoa 7/8.11.42.
L7547 EM-M	From 44 Sqn. FTR Lorient 13/14.2.43.
L7566 EM-A	From 83 Sqn. To 1660CU.
L7571 EM-S	From 61 Sqn. FTR Essen 16/17.9.42.
L7580 EM-C/O	To 9 Sqn.
L7582 EM-D	To 106 Sqn.
L7583 EM-A	To 1661CU.
R5498 EM-Z	No operations. Crashed near Bottesford during training 8.4.42.

R5499 EM-O	FTR from mining sortie 10/11.8.42.
R5500 EM-B	To 460 Sqn.
R5501 EM-W/G	No operations. Crashed in Lincoln after mid-air collision with a Miles Master during training 28.3.42.
R5503 EM-S	To 1660CU via 207CF.
R5504 EM-P/N	To 1660CU.
R5505 EM-X/S	To 61 Sqn.
R5507 EM-W/Z-	To 1660CU via 97CF.
R5509 EM-G	FTR from mining sortie 16/17.8.42.
R5541 EM-Y	To 61 Sqn.
R5547 EM-Y	To 44 Sqn.
R5549 EM H/P	To 12 Sqn via 1661CU.
R5550 EM-B	Destroyed at Bottesford by crash-landing Manchester L7385 while training 6.8.42.
R5570 EM-F/R	From 83 Sqn. FTR Turin 8/9.12.42.
R5616 EM-D/J	FTR from mining sortie 16/17.8.42.
R5617 EM-T	No operations. Crashed in Devon during training 24.5.42.
R5628 EM-Q	FTR from mining sortie 9/10.9.42.
R5632 EM-N	FTR Duisburg 23/24.7.42.
R5633 EM-R	FTR Mainz 12/13.8.42.
R5635 EM-N/L	To 1661CU.
R5668	From 106 Sqn to BDU.
R5674 EM-B/F/S	To 103 Sqn.
R5686 EM-T	To 83 Sqn.
R5693 EM-Q/T	To 5MU.
R5694 EM-F	From OADU. Crashed in Lincolnshire following early return from Bad Zwischenahn 25.11.42.
R5695 EM-C	FTR Haselunne 25.11.42.
R5736	From 1654CU to 1660CU.
R5745 EM-T	To 460 Sqn.
R5755 EM-N	FTR Bremen 4/5.9.42.
R5756 EM-D	To 1667CU.
R5758 EM-Z	To 1660CU via 97CF.
R5760 EM-Y	FTR Mainz 12/13.8.42.
R5761 EM-T	FTR Essen 5/6.8.42.
R5847 EM-Y	FTR Bremen 3/4.6.42.
R5851	To 50 Sqn.
R5852 EM-R	To 83 Sqn.
R5860 EM-Y	Ditched in North Sea on return from Emden 20/21.6.42.
R5863 EM-K	From 44 Sqn. Crashed in Nottinghamshire while training 19.8.42.
R5865 EM-W	To 57 Sqn.
R5867 EM-T	FTR Duisburg 23/24.7.42.
R5895 EM-B	From 1660CU. FTR Magdeburg 21/22.1.44.
R5908 EM-B	FTR Milan 24.10.42.
W4119 EM-K	To 50 Sqn via 1661CU.
W4120 EM-L	FTR Mönchen-Gladbach 30/31.8.43.
W4121 EM-B	FTR Milan 24.10.42.
W4129 EM-R	From 49 Sqn. FTR Kassel 27/28.8.42.
W4130	No operations to 57 Sqn.
W4134 EM-U	FTR Essen 3/4.1.43.
W4164 EM-G	To 9CF.
W4165 EM-L	To 57 Sqn.
W4167 EM-Q	Crashed at Langar on return from Lorient 14.2.43.

W4171 EM-T/J	FTR Duisburg 26/27.4.43.
W4172 EM-X	FTR Munich 9/10.3.43.
W4174 EM-V	To 15 Sqn via 1660CU.
W4191 EM-Q	From 83 Sqn. FTR Munich 21/22.12.42.
W4276 EM-Z-	From 101 Sqn. FTR Hanover 18/19.10.43.
W4365 EM-B	FTR Essen 21/22.1.43.
W4381 EM-B	From 50 Sqn. To 467 Sqn.
W4383 EM-S	From 50 Sqn. To 1654CU.
W4795 EM-B	From 467 Sqn. To 61 Sqn.
W4798	From 467 Sqn. No operations to 61 Sqn.
W4815 EM-C	Crashed on landing at Spilsby on return from Augsburg 26.2.44.
W4892 EM-T	From 1662CU. FTR Berlin 1/2.1.44.
W4931 EM-U	FTR Berlin 29/30.3.43.
W4938 EM-A	FTR Duisburg 12/13.5.43
W4945 EM-Z	FTR from mining sortie 28/29.4.43.
W4952 EM-T	Crashed on landing at Langar while training 12.8.43.
W4959 EM-E/S	From 83 Sqn. FTR Berlin 23/24.11.43.
W4962 EM-B-	FTR Hamburg 27/28.7.43.
W5001 EM-J	FTR Düsseldorf 25/26.5.43.
W5006 EM-G	To 9 Sqn.
DV183 EM-O/W	FTR Cislago 16/17.7.43.
DV184 EM-N/O	Crashed on take-off from Langar when bound for Munich 2.10.43.
DV188 EM-J	FTR Berlin 23/24.12.43.
DV191 EM-O/Q	Flew 10 operations to Berlin. FTR Brunswick 14/15.1.44.
DV233	From 467 Sqn. No operations. Returned to 467 Sqn.
DV243 EM-D	Ditched off Great Yarmouth on return from Frankfurt 22/23.10.43.
DV286 EM-W	To 44 Sqn.
DV312	From 61 Sqn. To 50 Sqn.
DV360 EM-U	Flew 12 Berlin operations. FTR Wesseling 21/22.6.44.
DV361 EM-V	Abandoned over Northamptonshire while training 22.12.43.
DV369 EM-D	FTR Brunswick 14/15.1.44.
DV370 EM-L	FTR Berlin 1/2.1.44.
DV371 EM-M	FTR Berlin 30/31.1.44 on 12th Berlin operation.
DV383 EM-G/O/R	Flew 14 Berlin operations to 46MU.
ED329 EM-T	To 617 Sqn.
ED330 EM-F	FTR Wilhelmshaven 18/19.2.43.
ED356 EM-W	FTR Nuremberg 25/26.2.43.
ED361 EM-R	From 467 Sqn. Collided with JA844 (619 Sqn) and abandoned over Surrey on return from Milan 13.8.43.
ED364 EM-H	From 467 Sqn to 622 Sqn via 1654CU.
ED365 EM-U	FTR Hamburg 3/4.3.43.
ED371/G	From RAE. No operations to 57 Sqn.
ED412 EM-Q	From 57 Sqn. FTR Turin 12/13.7.43.
ED413 EM-P	From 630 Sqn. To 1651CU.
ED418 EM-G	FTR Duisburg 12/13.5.43.
ED442 EM-W	From 50 Sqn. FTR Hanover 22/23.9.43.
ED498 EM-O	FTR Milan 15/16.8.43.
ED533 EM-N	FTR from mining sortie 2/3.3.43.
ED537 EM-O	FTR Düsseldorf 11/12.6.43.
ED550 EM-K	FTR Berlin 23/24.8.43.
ED554 EM-Q	FTR Duisburg 9/10.4.43.

ED569 EM-B	FTR Cologne 28/29.6.43.
ED586 EM-F	FTR Stettin 5/6.1.44.
ED600 EM-P	FTR Düsseldorf 25/26.5.43.
ED601 EM-N	From 83 Sqn. FTR Berlin 2/3.12.43.
ED604 EM-A	FTR Essen 12/13.3.43.
ED623 EM-N	To 626 Sqn.
ED627 EM-N	FTR Nuremberg 27/28.8.43.
ED692 EM-W	FTR Mülheim 22/23.6.43.
ED698	From 630 Sqn. Crashed on take-off from Spilsby when bound for Berlin 20.1.44.
ED758 EM-V	From 630 Sqn. FTR Berlin 30/31.1.44.
ED801	From 106 Sqn via 1661CU to 1653CU.
ED802 EM-M	To 5LFS.
ED832 EM-X	FTR Berlin 3/4.9.43.
EE126 EM-A	Flew 12 Berlin operations. FTR Leipzig 19/20.2.44.
EE141 EM-P	FTR Berlin 16/17.12.43.
EE173 EM-K	From 156 Sqn. FTR Berlin 30/31.1.44.
EE175 EM-S	From 83 Sqn. FTR Kassel 22/23.10.43.
EE197 EM-N	From 57 Sqn. Damaged beyond repair during operation to Brunswick 14/15.1.44.
JB309	From 83 Sqn. To 1668CU.
LL776 EM-S	FTR Dortmund 22/23.5.44.
LL902 EM-A	Crashed on approach to Little Rissington on return from Lützkendorf 14/15.3.45.
LL968 EM-K	FTR Heilbronn 4/5.12.44.
LL973 EM-M	FTR Wesseling 21/22.6.44.
LM123	Damaged in accidents during 1945 and eventually SOC.
LM125 EM-G	FTR St Leu d'Esserent 4/5.7.44.
LM129 EM-Y	FTR St Leu d'Esserent 7/8.7.44.
LM208 EM-M	FTR from mining sortie 16.10.44.
LM218 EM-N	FTR St Leu d'Esserent 7/8.7.44.
LM261 EM-L	FTR Darmstadt 11/12.9.44.
LM263 EM-N	FTR Deelen Airfield 15.8.44.
LM271 EM-L	FTR Bergen 28/29.10.44.
LM326 EM-Z	FTR Hanover 18/19.10.43.
LM334 EM-V	FTR Nuremberg 27/28.8.43.
LM366 EM-H	FTR Berlin 28/29.1.44.
LM383 EM-R	FTR Brunswick 14/15.1.44.
LM436 EM-G	From 9 Sqn. FTR Nuremberg 30/31.3.44.
LM526 EM-R	FTR Schweinfurt 26/27.4.44.
LM535	
LM540 EM-Q	FTR Brunswick 22/23.5.44.
LM543	To 195 Sqn.
LM578 EM-L	FTR Wesseling 21/22.6.44.
LM671 EM-S	FTR Gdynia 18/19.12.44.
ME386 EM-G	Crashed in Lincolnshire on return from Böhlen 5/6.3.45.
ME389	
ME472 EM-O	From 619 Sqn. FTR Leipzig 10/11.4.45.
ME473 EM-N	Collided with ND572 (57 Sqn) over Lincolnshire during night fighter affiliation exercise 2.3.45.
ME522 EM-X	FTR Hamburg 21/22.3.45.
ME532	From 630 Sqn.
ME631 EM-K	FTR Schweinfurt 26/27.4.44.
ME633 EM-Y	FTR Leipzig 19/20.2.44.

ME666 EM-A	FTR Frankfurt 22/23.3.44.
ME667 EM-X	FTR Bremen 6/7.10.44.
ME678 EM-N	FTR Etampes 9/10.6.44.
ME680 EM-R	FTR Berlin 24/25.3.44.
ME681 EM-T	FTR Revigny 18/19.7.44.
ME683 EM-W	FTR Wesseling 21/22.6.44.
ME685 EM-C	FTR Toulouse 5/6.4.44.
ME688 EM-E	FTR from mining sortie 9/10.4.44.
ME805 EM-J	FTR St Leu d'Esserent 7/8.7.44.
ME807 EM-S	FTR Nevers 15/16.7.44.
ME814 EM-E	FTR Revigny 18/19.7.44.
ME827 EM-I	FTR Wesseling 21/22.6.44.
ND510 EM-T/E	FTR Berlin 15/16.2.44.
ND513 EM-R	FTR Clermont Ferrand 10/11.3.44.
ND521	To 460 Sqn.
ND522 EM-O/J	FTR from mining sortie 21/22.5.44.
ND530	To 630 Sqn.
ND555 EM-D	FTR Mittelland Canal at Gravenhorst 6/7.11.44.
ND556 EM-F	FTR Mailly-le-Camp 3/4.5.44.
ND564 EM-H	FTR La Chapelle 20/21.4.44.
ND567 EM-V	FTR St Leu d'Esserent 7/8.7.44.
ND568 EM-L	FTR Nuremberg 30/31.3.44.
ND570 EM-Z	FTR St Leu d'Esserent 4/5.7.44.
ND575 EM-M	FTR Mailly-le-Camp 3/4.5.44.
ND862	From 582 Sqn. To 1661CU.
ND866 EM-B	FTR St Leu d'Esserent 7/8.7.44.
ND871 EM-G	FTR Brunswick 22/23.5.44.
ND872 EM-L	FTR Stuttgart 28/29.7.44.
NE168 EM-F	FTR Houffalize 5/6.1.45.
NF979 EM-B	FTR Düren 16.11.44.
NG143	FTR from mining sortie 16.10.44.
NG144 EM-G	FTR Gdynia 18/19.12.44.
NG204 EM-M	FTR Dortmund-Ems Canal at Ladbergen 3/4.3.45.
NG230 EM-F	FTR Böhlen 5/6.3.45.
NG245 EM-R	
NG286	To 619 Sqn.
NG399 EM-O	FTR Lützkendorf 14/15.3.45.
NN724 EM-X	FTR Dortmund-Ems Canal at Ladbergen 7/8.2.45.
PA183	
PA196 EM-D	From 189 Sqn. FTR Böhlen 20/21.3.45.
PA275	
PB286	
PB293 EM-W	
PB294 EM-G 24/25.7.44.	Crashed off Lincolnshire coast on return from Donges
PB295 EM-I	From 49 Sqn. FTR Mittelland Canal at Gravenhorst 21/22.2.45.
PB428 EM-T	Collided with LM648 (44 Sqn) in Spilsby circuit on return from Harburg 11.11.44.
PB699	To 619 Sqn.
PB764 EM-L	
PB765 EM-B	FTR Heilbronn 4/5.12.44.
PB814 EM-T	FTR Mittelland Canal at Gravenhorst 21/22.2.45.
PB874	

PB878	To 460 Sqn.
PD207 EM-G	From 49 Sqn. FTR Stuttgart 12/13.9.44.
PD209	To 429 Sqn.
PD210 EM-C	FTR Revigny 18/19.7.44.
PD216 EM-J	FTR Darmstadt 25/26.8.44.
PD217 EM-Z	To 1659CU.
PD220	
PD267	FTR Stuttgart 12/13.9.44.
PD280 EM-V	
PD290 EM-N	Destroyed in take-off accident at Spilsby when bound for Homburg 1.11.44.
PD318 EM-J	FTR Handorf Airfield at Münster 23/24.12.44.
PD322 EM-C	FTR Giessen 6/7.12.44.
PD381	To 44 Sqn.
RE128	
RF144	
RF194	To 630 Sqn.
RF195	To 57 Sqn.
RF208	
RF209	

Heaviest Single Loss

7/8.7.44	St Leu d'Esserent 6 Lancasters FTR.

227 SQUADRON

No Motto:

No. 227 Squadron was formed on the 18 April 1918 at Taranto from a number of RNAS flights. Absorbed into the newly created RAF the squadron was earmarked as a day bomber unit, but failed to see operational service before the armistice, and was disbanded on the 9 December 1918. The 227 number was applied to a number of detachments and flights in the Middle East between June and August 1942, before being given to a detachment of Beaufighters on Malta. In March 1943 the squadron moved to Egypt and Libya to carry out shipping sweeps in the eastern Mediterranean, and moved to Italy in August 1944, where it became part of the South African Air Force. The squadron re-formed at Bardney on the 7 October 1944 by taking 9 Squadron's A Flight and 619 Squadron's B Flight. It began operations shortly afterwards and remained a front line unit until war's end.

STATIONS

Bardney	07.10.44 to 21.10.44
Balderton	21.10.44 to 05.04.45
Strubby	05.04.45 to 08.06.45

COMMANDING OFFICERS

Wing Commander D M Balme DSO DFC	07.10.44 to 18.06.45

AIRCRAFT

Lancaster I/III	07.10.44 to 05.09.45

OPERATIONAL RECORD

Operations	Sorties	Aircraft Losses	% Losses
61	815	15	1.8

Category of Operations
All Bombing

TABLE OF STATISTICS

Out of 59 Lancaster squadrons

49th highest number of Lancaster overall operations in Bomber Command.
49th highest number of Lancaster sorties in Bomber Command.
44th equal (with 189 & 218 Sqns) highest number of Lancaster operational losses in Bomber Command.

Out of 22 squadrons in 5 Group

21st highest number of overall operations in 5 Group.
19th highest number of sorties in 5 Group.
19th equal (with 189 Sqn) highest number of aircraft operational losses in 5 Group.

Out of 17 Lancaster squadrons in 5 Group

16th highest number of Lancaster overall operations in 5 Group.
16th highest number of Lancaster sorties in 5 Group.
17th highest number of Lancaster operational losses in 5 Group.

Lancaster	From October 1944.
LM259 9J-U	From 630 Sqn. FTR Heilbronn 4/5.12.44.
LM678 9J-O	From 57 Sqn.
LM756	To 619 Sqn.
ME309 9J-Y	To 1654CU.
ME372 9J-U	FTR Hamburg 21/22.3.45.
ME454	To 49 Sqn.
ME759 9J-D	From 9 Sqn via 1661CU. FTR Karlsruhe 2/3.2.45.
NG170 9J-S	FTR Ladbergen 3/4.3.45.
NG296 9J-D	FTR Giessen 6/7.12.44.
NN778 9J-H	
NN802 9J-K	
NX566 9J-S	
PA171 9J-D	FTR Düsseldorf 2/3.11.44.
PA214 9J-P	FTR Lützkendorf 14/15.3.45.
PA258	
PA259 9J-Z	FTR Bohlen 20/21.3.45.
PA279	
PA280 9J-P	
PA283 9J-J	
PA287 9J-N	
PB348 9J-B	From 49 Sqn. To 57 Sqn.
PB404 9J-X	From 619 Sqn.
PB596 9J-L/O	From 61 Sqn. To 1668CU.
PB610 9J-O	Crashed on landing at Balderton on return from Sassnitz 7.3.45.

PB643 9J-S	FTR Harburg 11/12.11.44.
PB644 9J-R	FTR Bohlen 5/6.3.45.
PB645 9J-A	From 106 Sqn.
PB646 9J-P	FTR Giessen 6/7.12.44.
PB647 9J-Q	To 115 Sqn.
PB649 9J-K	From 61 Sqn.
PB651 9J-H	To 1654CU.
PB666 9J-J	From 61 Sqn. FTR Gravenhorst 21/22.2.45.
PB672 9J-C	FTR Heilbronn 4/5.12.44.
PB690 9J-V	FTR Gravenhorst 21/22.2.45.
PB723 9J-W	FTR Gdynia 18/19.12.44.
PB729	
PB731 9J-L	To 5MU.
PB805 9J-M	
PB847	
PD340 9J-E	From 50 Sqn.
PD342 9J-B	From 463 Sqn.
PD345 9J-F	From 463 Sqn. To 115 Sqn.
PD348	
PD349 9J-G	
RA518 9J-C	
RA546 9J-J	FTR Lützkendorf 14/15.3.45.
RF131 9J-B	
RF178	
SW247 9J-W	From 1661CU.

408 (GOOSE) SQUADRON

Motto: For Freedom   Code EQ

No. 408 Squadron was born out of Article XV of the BCATP agreement of January 1941, which called for twenty-five Canadian squadrons to be formed in the RAF by May 1942. All such squadrons were to be numbered in the 400 to 450 series to avoid confusion with RAF and other Dominion units. It was the second Canadian bomber unit to form after 405 (Vancouver) Squadron, and officially came into existence on the 24 June 1941 at Lindholme, as part of 5 Group. Operations began with the Hampden, which was approaching the end of its operation life with Bomber Command, and a few Manchesters were taken on charge shortly before the squadron transferred to 4 Group to re-equip with the Halifax. 408 would carry out no operations with 4 Group before becoming a founder member of the Canadian 6 Group on New Year's Day 1943. Later 408 Squadron operated the radial-engined Mk II Lancaster, before reverting to the new and successful marks of the Halifax.

Posted to 4 Group   17.09.42

STATIONS

Lindholme	24.06.41 to 20.07.41
Syerston	20.07.41 to 09.12.41
Balderton	09.12.41 to 17.09.42
North Luffenham (Detachment)	25.01.42 to 17.03.42

COMMANDING OFFICERS

Wing Commander N W Timmerman DSO DFC   24.06.41 to 26.03.42
Wing Commander A C P Clayton DFC*   26.03.42 to 14.04.42
Wing Commander J D Twigg   18.05.42 to 28.08.42
Wing Commander W D S Ferris DFC   01.09.42 to 26.10.43

AIRCRAFT

Hampden   06.41 to 09.42
Manchester   04.42 to 06.42

OPERATIONAL RECORD

Operations	Sorties	Aircraft Losses	% Losses
191	1,234	35	2.8

Category of Operations

Bombing	Mining	Leaflet	Reconnaissance
118	56	15	2

Hampdens

Operations	Sorties	Aircraft Losses	% Losses
190	1,233	35	2.8

Category of Operations

Bombing	Mining	Leaflet	Reconnaissance
117	56	15	2

Manchesters

Operations	Sorties	Aircraft Losses	% Losses
2	2	0	0.0

Category of Operations
Bombing
2

TABLE OF STATISTICS

(Heavy squadrons)
26th highest number of overall operations in Bomber Command.
30th highest number of sorties in Bomber Command.
29th highest number of aircraft operational losses in Bomber Command.
28th highest number of bombing operations in Bomber Command.

Out of 22 squadrons in 5 Group

15th highest number of overall operations in 5 Group.
17th highest number of sorties in 5 Group.
15th highest number of aircraft operational losses in 5 Group.

Out of 10 Hampden squadrons in 5 Group

7th highest Hampden overall operations in 5 Group.
7th highest number of Hampden sorties in 5 Group.
7th highest number of Hampden operational losses in 5 Group.

Out of 8 Manchester squadrons in 5 Group

Lowest overall Manchester operations, sorties and operational losses in 5 Group.

Hampden	To October 1942.
L4042	From 106 Sqn. To 1401Flt.
L4086	From 420 Sqn. Converted for use as torpedo bomber.
L4140 EQ-B-	From 16 OTU. FTR from mining sortie 27/28.3.42.
L4204	From 185 Sqn. To 14 OTU.
P1165 EQ-B	FTR Hüls 28/29.12.41.
P1166	From 144 Sqn. Converted for use as torpedo bomber.
P1212 EQ-T	Crashed on approach to Coningsby on return from Bremen 20/21.10.41.
P1218 EQ-Q	FTR Mannheim 22/23.10.41.
P1244 EQ-Y	From 455 Sqn. FTR Kassel 27/28.8.42.
P1314	From 420 Sqn. Converted for use as torpedo bomber. To 1402Flt.
P2064	From 14 OTU. Converted for use as torpedo bomber. To 415 Sqn.
P2073	From 106 Sqn. Converted for use as torpedo bomber. To 5 OTU.
P5321	From 44 Sqn. To 14 OTU.
P5334	From 7 AAU. To 1406Flt.
P5392 EQ-W	From 7 AAU. Crashed in Hampshire on return from Cherbourg 15.12.41.
X2989	From 61 Sqn. To 14 OTU.
X3051 EQ-U	From 144 Sqn. FTR Bremen 21/22.1.42.
X3140	From 61 Sqn. Converted for use as torpedo bomber. To 455 Sqn.
AD754	To 144 Sqn. Back to 408 Sqn via 61 Sqn. Converted for use as torpedo bomber. To 32 OTU.
AD758	From 44 Sqn. To 14 OTU.
AD782 EQ-A	From 14 OTU. Crashed soon after take-off from Balderton for Brest 25.1.42.
AD803 EQ-L	From 106 Sqn. FTR from mining sortie 15/16.5.42.
AD829 EQ-E	From 455 Sqn. FTR Saarbrücken 28/29.8.42.
AD842	From 49 Sqn. Crashed on take-off from North Luffenham for mining sortie 9.3.42.
AD853	From 420 Sqn. To 1 AAS.
AD857	From 106 Sqn. To 7FPP.
AD870 EQ-X	From 83 Sqn. Converted for use as torpedo bomber
AD960	From 420 Sqn. To 1402Flt.
AD963	From 61 Sqn. Converted for use as torpedo bomber. To 489 Sqn.
AD968	From 49 Sqn. SOC 3.2.44.
AD972	To 5Gp TF.
AD980 EQ-Y	Crashed near Balderton during air test 6.6.42.
AD982	From 44 Sqn. Converted for use as torpedo bomber. To A&AEE.
AD987	From 25 OTU. Converted for use as torpedo bomber. To 144 Sqn.
AE139	From 25 OTU. Crashed in Berkshire during transit 26.3.42.
AE148 EQ-B-	From 16 OTU. FTR from mining sortie 11/12.12.41.
AE150 EQ-M	From 25 OTU. FTR Mainz 12/13.8.42.
AE186	From 106 Sqn. To 14 OTU.
AE190	From 25 OTU. To 14 OTU.
AE192	From 44 Sqn. To 14 OTU.
AE196	To 44 Sqn.

AE197	FTR Saarbrücken 28/29.8.42.
AE219 EQ-R	From 61 Sqn. FTR from mining sortie 27/28.3.42.
AE227 EQ-D	From 49 Sqn. FTR Saarbrücken 28/29.8.42.
AE237 EQ-X	From 83 Sqn. FTR from mining sortie 22/23.4.42.
AE244 EQ-P	FTR Düsseldorf 31.7/1.8.42.
AE245	Converted for use as torpedo bomber. To 5 OTU.
AE258	From 420 Sqn. Converted for use as torpedo bomber. To 1 AAS.
AE264	From 455 Sqn. To 1404Flt.
AE267	To 420 Sqn.
AE286 EQ-T	From 61 Sqn. FTR Wilhelmshaven 10/11.1.42.
AE287	Converted for use as torpedo bomber. To 455 Sqn.
AE288 EQ-H	From 61 Sqn. FTR Warnemünde 8/9.5.42.
AE293	From 106 Sqn. Converted for use as torpedo bomber. To 455 Sqn.
AE295	From 5Gp TF. To 14 OTU.
AE297 EQ-F	From 207 Sqn. FTR Warnemünde 8/9.5.42.
AE360	Converted for use as torpedo bomber. To 415 Sqn.
AE361	Converted for use as torpedo bomber. To TDU.
AE366 EQ-U	From 420 Sqn. Crash-landed at Lakenheath on return from Duisburg 7.8.42. To 5 OTU.
AE372	From 49 Sqn. Converted for use as torpedo bomber. To 415 Sqn.
AE373	From 50 Sqn. Converted for use as torpedo bomber. To NAFDU.
AE375	From 50 Sqn. Converted for use as torpedo bomber. To 415 Sqn.
AE378	From 420 Sqn. Converted for use as torpedo bomber. To 455 Sqn.
AE385	From 420 Sqn. Crashed at Balderton during training 12.9.42.
AE393 EQ-G	From 420 Sqn. Crashed in Yorkshire on return from Hamburg 16.1.42.
AE418	Converted for use as torpedo bomber. To 415 Sqn.
AE426	From 106 Sqn. FTR Kiel 28/29.4.42.
AE432 EQ-S	FTR Düsseldorf 15/16.8.42.
AE433 EQ-D	FTR Essen 8/9.11.41.
AE437 EQ-U	FTR Düsseldorf 27/28.11.41.
AE438 EQ-N	FTR Ostend 9/10.11.41.
AE439	To A&AEE.
AT113 EQ-A	From 455 Sqn. Crashed near Balderton during air-test 29.7.42.
AT120	FTR Essen 12/13.4.42.
AT133 EQ-X	FTR Cherbourg 14/15.12.41.
AT138	Converted for use as torpedo bomber. To 144 Sqn.
AT139 EQ-A-	From 50 Sqn. FTR Duisburg 21/22.7.42.
AT141	From 106 Sqn. FTR Dortmund 14/15.4.42.
AT143	From 144 Sqn. Crashed on landing at Booker on return from Saarbrücken 28/29.8.42.
AT154 EQ-B	FTR Essen 2/3.6.42.
AT176 EQ-A	FTR from mining sortie 27/28.3.42.
AT178	From 49 Sqn. To 1404Flt.
AT179	From 49 Sqn. Converted for use as torpedo bomber. To 455 Sqn.

AT180 EQ-B	From 49 Sqn. To 1404Flt.
AT182	From 455 Sqn. To 1404Flt
AT186	Crashed in Nottinghamshire while training 11.4.42.
AT189 EQ-G	From 455 Sqn. FTR from mining sortie 18/19.6.42.
AT191 EQ-A	From 49 Sqn. FTR Essen 1/2.6.42.
AT220 EQ-G	Destroyed by fire at Balderton 3.6.42.
AT224 EQ-A	FTR from mining sortie 15/16.5.42.
AT225	From 420 Sqn. To 1404Flt.
AT227 EQ-L	From 49 Sqn. FTR from Anti-shipping operation 19.7.42.
AT228 EQ-U	From 420 Sqn. FTR Saarbrücken 28/29.8.42.
Manchester	May 1942.
L7401 EQ-N	To 44 Sqn.
L7415	Training only. To 44 Sqn.
R5776	From 1654CU. Training only. To 1654CU.
R5835	From 50 Sqn. Training only. To 1654CU.

Heaviest Single Loss

28/29.08.42	Saarbrücken. 4 Hampdens FTR.

420 (SNOWY OWL) SQUADRON.

Motto: Pugnamus Finitum (We fight to the finish) Code PT

No. 420 Squadron Royal Canadian Air Force was born out of Article XV of the British Commonwealth Air Training Plan (BCATP) Agreement, which was signed on the 7 January 1941, and called for the formation of twenty-five Canadian squadrons by May 1942. All such units were to be numbered in the 400–450 series, and 420 Squadron was the fourth to be formed in Bomber Command after 405, 408 and 419 Squadrons. 420 Squadron was formed in 5 Group at Waddington on the 19 December 1941, and although many of the Group's squadrons had converted to the ill-fated Avro Manchester by this time, 420 Squadron was to begin its operational career on the trusty, if obsolete Hampden. After taking part in ninety operations with 5 Group, 420 Squadron transferred to 4 Group in August 1942 and converted to the Wellington. Operations were undertaken with this Group before 420 Squadron became a founder member of the Canadian 6 Group on the 1 January 1943. It was not until January 1944 that the Snowy Owls went to war with four engines, having taken delivery of Hercules-powered Halifaxes.

Posted to 4 Group 06.08.42

STATIONS

Waddington	19.12.41 to 06.08.42

COMMANDING OFFICERS

Wing Commander D A R Bradshaw	19.12.41 to 11.04.43

AIRCRAFT

Hampden	12.41 to 08.42

OPERATIONAL RECORD

Hampden

Operations	Sorties	Aircraft Losses	% Losses
90	535	19	3.6

Category of Operations

Bombing	Mining	Other
44	37	9

TABLE OF STATISTICS

Out of 22 squadrons in 5 Group

20th highest number of overall operations in 5 Group.
21st highest number of sorties in 5 Group.
18th highest number of aircraft operational losses in 5 Group.

Out of 10 Hampden squadrons in 5 Group and Bomber Command

Lowest number of overall Hampden operations in Bomber Command and 5 Group.
9th highest number of Hampden sorties in Bomber Command and 5 Group.
9th highest number of Hampden operational losses in Bomber Command and 5 Group.

Hampden	From December 1941 to August 1942.
L4086	From 49 Sqn to 408 Sqn.
P1187 PT-X	From 44 Sqn. Crash-landed in Essex on return from Stuttgart 4/5.5.42.
P1239 PT-Y	From 50 Sqn. FTR Essen 12/13.4.42.
P1257	From 455 Sqn. Converted for use as torpedo bomber. To 489 Sqn.
P1314	From 49 Sqn. To 408 Sqn.
P2094 PT-Q	From 50 Sqn. Hit by 44 Sqn Lancaster L7581 at Waddington 20.5.42.
P4306	From 14 OTU. Converted for use as torpedo bomber. To 415 Sqn.
P4400 PT-J	From 44 Sqn. FTR from shipping strike (Operation Fuller) 12.2.42.
P5330 PT-J	From 106 Sqn. FTR Rostock 24/25.4.42.
P5332 PT-T	From 44 Sqn. FTR Bremen 2/3.7.42.
X3057	From 49 Sqn. SOC 21.12.43.
X3061	From 44 Sqn. To 14 OTU.
X3122	From 83 Sqn. To 519 Sqn.
X3149 PT-B	From 44 Sqn. Converted for use as torpedo bomber. To 32 OTU.
AD786 PT-L	From 455 Sqn. Crashed 20 minutes after take-off from Waddington when bound for mining sortie 23/24.6.42.
AD853	From 50 Sqn. To 408 Sqn.
AD855	From 44 Sqn. Converted for use as torpedo bomber. To 489 Sqn.
AD869 PT-L	From 44 Sqn. Crashed soon after take-off from Waddington during night navigation exercise 20.4.42.
AD915 PT-F	From 44 Sqn. FTR from mining sortie 18/19.2.42.
AD960	From 49 Sqn. To 408 Sqn.
AD968	From 44 Sqn. To 49 Sqn.

AE115	From 50 Sqn. Converted for use as torpedo bomber. To 455 Sqn.
AE155	From 455 Sqn. To 14 OTU.
AE186	From 44 Sqn. To 106 Sqn.
AE202 PT-X	From 44 Sqn. FTR Hamburg 26/27.7.42.
AE246 PT-V	From 106 Sqn. FTR Lübeck 28/29.3.42.
AE248 PT-A	From 144 Sqn. FTR Bremen 2/3.7.42.
AE258	From 44 Sqn. To 408 Sqn.
AE260 PT-O	From 44 Sqn. FTR from mining sortie 2/3.6.42.
AE267 PT-V	From 408 Sqn. FTR Hamburg 26/27.7.42.
AE298 PT-D	From 44 Sqn. FTR from mining sortie 26/27.3.42.
AE314	From 83 Sqn. Converted for use as torpedo bomber. To 455 Sqn.
AE355 PT-A	FTR Düsseldorf 31.7/1.8.42.
AE366	From 83 Sqn. To 408 Sqn.
AE378	From 106 Sqn. To 408 Sqn.
AE379	From 44 Sqn. To 455 Sqn.
AE384	From 44 Sqn. Converted for use as torpedo bomber. To 455 Sqn.
AE385	From 44 Sqn. To 408 Sqn.
AE386	From 14 OTU. Converted for use as torpedo bomber. To 455 Sqn.
AE389 PT-D	From 83 Sqn. FTR from mining sortie 7/8.5.42.
AE390 PT-Z	From 44 Sqn. FTR from mining sortie 12/13.7.42.
AE393	From 44 Sqn. To 408 Sqn.
AE399 PT-P	From 44 Sqn. Collided with 44 Con Flt Lancaster on landing at Waddington on return from Cologne 30/31.5.42.
AE401	From 50 Sqn. Converted for use as torpedo bomber. To 415 Sqn.
AE422	From 50 Sqn. Converted for use as torpedo bomber. To 415 Sqn.
AT128 PT-G	From 44 Sqn. FTR Dortmund 14/15.4.42.
AT130 PT-S	From 44 Sqn. FTR Emden 21/22.1.42.
AT132	From 44 Sqn. To 455 Sqn.
AT134 PT-K	From 44 Sqn. FTR from shipping strike (Operation Fuller) 12.2.42.
AT135	From 44 Sqn. Converted for use as torpedo bomber. To 455 Sqn.
AT136 PT-N	From 44 Sqn. FTR Essen 8/9.6.42.
AT144 PT-A	From 44 Sqn. FTR Warnemünde 8/9.5.42.
AT185 PT-A	From 49 Sqn. FTR Emden 20/21.6.42.
AT219 PT-C	From 106 Sqn. Crashed soon after take-off from Waddington when bound for Dortmund 14/15.4.42.
AT225	To 408 Sqn.
AT228	From 49 Sqn. To 408 Sqn.

455 SQUADRON RAAF

Motto: Strike And Strike Again   Code UB

No. 455 Squadron RAAF officially formed on the 6 June 1941 under the Empire Air Training Scheme, but personnel had begun gathering at Williamstown, New South Wales during the previous month. Designated a medium bomber squadron it joined

5 Group, and took up residence at Swinderby in Lincolnshire, where it received Hampdens. Operations began in October, and continued until the squadron was posted to Coastal Command in April 1942.

Posted to Coastal Command 20.04.42

STATIONS

Swinderby	06.06.41 to 08.02.42
Wigsley	08.02.42 to 20.04.42

COMMANDING OFFICERS

Flight Lieutenant J H W Lawson	05.41 to 07.41
Wing Commander J E C G F Gyll-Murray	07.41 to 15.12.41
Wing Commander G M Lindeman	15.12.41 to 06.02.43

AIRCRAFT

Hampden	06.41 to 10.42

OPERATIONAL RECORD

Hampden

Operations	Sorties	Aircraft Losses	% Losses
92	424	14	3.3

Category of Operations

Bombing	Mining	Other
56	29	7

TABLE OF STATISTICS

Out of 22 squadrons in 5 Group

19th highest number of overall operations in 5 Group.
Lowest number of sorties in 5 Group.
Lowest number of aircraft operational losses in 5 Group.

Out of 10 Hampden squadrons in 5 Group and Bomber Command

9th highest number of overall Hampden operations in Bomber Command and 5 Group.
Lowest number of Hampden sorties in Bomber Command and 5 Group.
Lowest number of Hampden operational losses in Bomber Command and 5 Group.

Hampden	From August 1941 to April 1942.
L6018	From 5 AOS. SOC 4.6.44.
P1153	From 49 Sqn. Converted for use as torpedo bomber. To 415 Sqn.
P1156 UB-F	From 50 Sqn. FTR from shipping strike (ChannelDash) 12.2.42.
P1201 UB-P	FTR Rover Patrol in Cologne area 7/8.11.41.
P1203 UB-T	FTR Essen 6/7.4.42.
P1243	From 5 OTU. Returned to 5 OTU.
P1244	From 16 OTU. To 408 Sqn.
P1257	From 16 OTU. To 420 Sqn.

P1272 UB-R	From 14 OTU. FTR Hamburg 30.11/1.12.41.
P2065	From 16 OTU. Converted for use as torpedo bomber. To 415 Sqn.
P2075	From 14 OTU. Converted for use as torpedo bomber. To 5 OTU.
P2085 UB-U	From 16 OTU. Crashed on landing at Wigsley on return from Essen 11.3.42.
P2095	From 49 Sqn.via 25 OTU. Converted for use as torpedo bomber.
P2100	From 16 OTU. To 5 OTU.
P5320	From 14 OTU. SOC 10.3.44.
P5325 UB-B	From 7 AAU. FTR from mining sortie 2/3.4.42.
P5326 UB-V	From 7 AAU. Crashed soon after take-off from Wigsley for air-test 12.3.42.
P5327	From 7 AAU. Converted for use as torpedo bomber.
P5328 UB-Q	From 7 AAU. Crashed in Buckinghamshire on return from mining sortie to La Rochelle 3.1.42.
P5329 UB-J	From 7 AAU. Crashed in Somerset during transit flight 25.3.42.
AD783 UB-U	From 144 Sqn. Crashed in Lincolnshire after early return from mining sortie 13.2.42.
AD786	From 14 OTU. To 420 Sqn.
AD803	From 106 Sqn. Returned to 106 Sqn.
AD826	From 61 Sqn. To 16 OTU.
AD829	From 44 Sqn. To 408 Sqn.
AD974	From 49 Sqn. To 5 OTU.
AE117	From 144 Sqn. SOC 19.3.44.
AE128	From 44 Sqn. To 5 OTU.
AE135	From 61 Sqn. Converted for use as torpedo bomber. To 5 OTU.
AE155	From 83 Sqn. To 420 Sqn.
AE198	Converted for use as torpedo bomber.
AE228	From 50 Sqn. Crashed in Scotland while training 11.7.43.
AE242	From 44 Sqn. Converted for use as torpedo bomber. To 415 Sqn.
AE243 UB-B	FTR Rover Patrol to Cologne area 7/8.11.41.
AE249	From 207 Sqn. FTR Hamburg 15/16.9.41.
AE256	From 61 Sqn. To 50 Sqn.
AE264	From 207 Sqn. To 408 Sqn.
AE291 UB-K	From 50 Sqn. FTR Essen 10/11.4.42.
AE296	From 207 Sqn. Converted for use as torpedo bomber. To 5 OTU.
AE308	From 61 Sqn. FTR from mining sortie 6.2.42.
AE312	From 83 Sqn. To 14 OTU.
AE352 UB-R	From 61 Sqn. FTR Emden 21/22.1.42.
AE379	From 420 Sqn. To 5 OTU.
AE430 UB-M	From 44 Sqn. FTR Hamburg 30.11/1.12.41.
AE434 UB-G	Crashed in Lincolnshire while in transit 5.11.41.
AE442	To 14 OTU.
AT113	To 408 Sqn.
AT114	Converted for use as torpedo bomber. To 415 Sqn.
AT119 UB-Y	FTR Emden 21/22.1.42.
AT131	From 106 Sqn. Converted for use as torpedo bomber. To 489 Sqn.

AT132	From 420 Sqn. Collided with a Beaufighter off Scotland while training 24.5.43.
AT137	Destroyed by fire at Leuchars 8.6.42.
AT181 UB-V	FTR from intruder sortie 21/22.2.42.
AT182	To 144 Sqn and back to 408 Sqn.
AT189	To 408 Sqn.
AT192 UB-R	FTR Essen 10/11.3.42.
AT221 UB-D	FTR Essen 10/11.4.42.

463 SQUADRON RAAF

Motto: Press On Regardless   Codes PO JO

No. 463 Squadron RAAF was formed at Waddington on the 25 November 1943. It was created by hiving off 467 Squadron's C Flight. The provision of a core of experienced air and ground crews enabled the squadron to become operational immediately, and it went to war for the first time on the following night. It was unfortunate for new crews to begin their tours during the Berlin campaign, and 463 Squadron would be among the Group's more severely afflicted.

STATIONS

Waddington   25.11.43 to 07.45

COMMANDING OFFICERS

Wing Commander R Kingsford-Smith	25.11.43 to 18.06.44
Wing Commander D R Donaldson	18.06.44 to 25.06.44
Wing Commander W A Forbes	25.06.44 to 22.02.45
Wing Commander K M Kemp	22.02.45 to 30.07.45

AIRCRAFT

Lancaster I/III   25.11.45 to 25.09.45

OPERATIONAL RECORD

Operations	Sorties	Aircraft Losses	% Losses
180	2,525	69	2.7

All bombing

TABLE OF STATISTICS

(Heavy squadrons)

Out of 59 Lancaster squadrons

35th highest number of Lancaster overall operations in Bomber Command.
32nd highest number of Lancaster sorties in Bomber Command.
22nd highest number of Lancaster operational losses in Bomber Command.

Out of 22 squadrons in 5 Group

16th highest number of overall operations in 5 Group.
12th highest number of sorties in 5 Group.
12th highest number of aircraft operational losses in 5 Group.

Out of 17 Lancaster squadrons in 5 Group

13th highest number of Lancaster overall operations in 5 Group.
11th highest number of Lancaster sorties in 5 Group.
11th highest number of Lancaster operational losses in 5 Group.

Lancaster	From November 1943.
L7539	From 1654CU. Training only to 1660CU.
W4897 JO-Q	From 106 Sqn. FTR Berlin 1/2.1.44.
DV171 JO-O/Y	From 626 Sqn. FTR Calais 24.9.44.
DV229 JO-C/P	From 106 Sqn. FTR Orleans 10/11.6.44.
DV274 JO-R	From 106 Sqn. FTR Augsburg 25/26.2.44.
DV275	From 101 Sqn. Returned to 101 Sqn.
DV280 JO-S	FTR Gelsenkirchen 21/22.6.44.
DV337 JO-N	From 467 Sqn. FTR Berlin 26/27.11.43.
DV338 JO-C	From 467 Sqn. Completed a total of 11 Berlin operations. FTR Leipzig 19/20.2.44.
DV374 JO-B	From 467 Sqn. FTR Revigny 18/19.7.44.
ED420 JO-L	From 106 Sqn. FTR Berlin 23/24.12.43.
ED545 JO-J	From 467 Sqn. FTR Berlin 30/31.1.44.
ED606 JO-E	Collided with ND637 (625 Sqn) over Lincolnshire on return from Stuttgart 15/16.3.44.
ED611 JO-T	From 44 Sqn. Flew 10 Berlin operations to BTU.
ED772 JO-G	From 467 Sqn. FTR Berlin 30/31.1.44.
ED949 JO-A	From 467 Sqn. FTR Berlin 30/31.1.44.
EE191 JO-F	From 106 Sqn. Flew 10 Berlin operations. FTR Frankfurt 18/19.3.44.
HK535 JO-N	FTR Lille 10/11.5.44.
HK536 JO-H	FTR St Leu d'Esserent 4/5.7.44.
HK537 JO-O/S	FTR Berlin 28/29.1.44.
HK803	From 619 Sqn. No operations.
JA902 JO-D	From 467 Sqn. FTR Berlin 2/3.1.44.
JA965	From 101 Sqn. Crashed at Wigsley on return from Hanover 27/28.9.43.
JA973 JO-O	From 106 Sqn. FTR Berlin 30/31.1.44.
LL740 JO-M	FTR Schweinfurt 24/25.2.44.
LL742	From 9 Sqn via 5LFS to 1660CU.
LL790 JO-O	FTR Königsburg 29/30.8.44.
LL795 JO-A	To 1660CU.
LL844 JO-R	
LL847 JO-D	FTR Munich 17/18.12.44.
LL848 JO-X	FTR Munich 24/25.4.44.
LL881 JO-E	FTR Lille 10/11.5.44.
LL882 JO-J	FTR Lille 10/11.5.44.
LL892 JO-L	FTR Brunswick 22/23.4.44.
LM130 JO-M/N	Collided with a Hurricane during fighter affiliation and crashed in Lincolnshire 11.3.45.
LM217	To 9 Sqn.
LM223 JO-P	From 467 Sqn. FTR Dortmund-Ems Canal 23/24.9.44.
LM242 JO-F	FTR Darmstadt 11/12.9.44.
LM309 JO-V	From 619 Sqn via 1661 & 1660CUs. FTR Dortmund-Ems Canal 23/24.9.44.
LM375 JO-B	From 106 Sqn. FTR Bremen 6/7.10.44.
LM444 JO-H/D	FTR Schweinfurt 24/25.2.44.

LM458 JO-G	FTR Mailly-Le-Camp 3/4.5.44.
LM548 JO-P	FTR Gravenhorst 21/22.2.45.
LM551 JO-G	FTR Revigny 18/19.7.44.
LM571 JO-E	FTR Prouville 24/25.6.44.
LM574 JO-J	FTR Prouville 24/25.6.44.
LM587 JO-L	FTR Cap Gris Nez 26.9.44.
LM589 JO-Y	FTR St Cyr 25.7.44.
LM597 JO-C/W	FTR Prouville 24/25.6.44.
LM675 JO-T	Crash-landed in France during operation to Boulogne 17.9.44.
LM683	Crash-landed at Bracebridge Heath on return from Bremerhaven 19.9.44.
LM695	To 617 Sqn.
ME295 JO-F	From 50 Sqn.
ME298 JO-B	FTR Karlsruhe 2/3.2.45.
ME325	To 1651CU.
ME327	To 1660CU.
ME329 JO-A	
ME395 JO-S	
ME427	
ME478 JO-M	FTR Lützkendorf 8/9.4.45.
ME489 JO-P	
ME563 JO-N/L	FTR Berlin 27/28.1.44.
ME571 JO-W	From 44 Sqn. FTR Duisburg 21/22.5.44.
ME573 JO-J	From 44 Sqn. FTR Stuttgart 15/16.3.44.
ME580 JO-Q	FTR Duisburg 21/22.5.44.
ME614 JO-K	FTR St Leu d'Esserent 4/5.7.44.
ME615 JO-Z/V	FTR Stuttgart 28/29.7.44.
ME701 JO-F	Damaged beyond repair during operation to Beauvoir 28/29.6.44.
ND326	From 100 Sqn.
ND733 JO-L	From 9 Sqn. FTR Pilsen 16/17.4.45.
NE133 JO-X	FTR Dortmund-Ems Canal 4/5.11.44.
NF977 JO-G	FTR Vlissingen 23.10.44.
NF990 JO-Q	FTR Gravenhorst 6/7.11.44.
NG191 JO-A	FTR Gravenhorst 6/7.11.44.
NG193 JO-D	FTR Leuna/Merseburg 14/15.1.45.
NG194	
NG234 JO-E	From 467 Sqn. FTR Dresden 13/14.2.45.
NG256	Crashed on approach to Seething on return from Gravenhorst 6/7.11.44.
NG275 JO-K	From 1651CU. FTR Siegen 1/2.2.45.
NG329 JO-Z	FTR Gravenhorst 21/22.2.45.
NG401 JO-G	Crashed on landing at Juvincourt in France on return from Bohlen 5/6.3.45.
NG439	Force-landed in Lincolnshire during an air-test 25.3.45.
NG469 JO-D	FTR Ladbergen 3/4.3.45.
NN721 JO-T	FTR Rositz 14/15.2.45.
NN804	
NX584 JO-V	FTR Lützkendorf 9.4.45.
PA187	To 467 Sqn.
PA314	
PA330	
PB246	To 582 Sqn.

PB260	From 626 Sqn.
PB263	FTR Kaiserslautern 27/28.9.44.
PB264	
PB290 JO-K	FTR Giessen 6/7.12.44.
PB620	FTR Vlissingen 23.10.44.
PB688 JO-M	Crashed near Waddington on return from Pölitz 21/22.12.44.
PB695 JO-R	FTR Royan 4/5.1.45.
PB792 JO-Q	FTR Heilbronn 4/5.12.44.
PB804 JO-A	FTR Gravenhorst 21/22.2.45.
PB845 JO-C	FTR Bohlen 20/21.3.45.
PD203	
PD258 JO-S	FTR Königsburg 29/30.8.44.
PD259 JO-P	FTR Vlissingen 23.10.44.
PD311 JO-O	FTR Gravenhorst 6/7.11.44.
PD329 JO-Y	Flew as camera aircraft on final *Tirpitz* raid 12.11.44.
PD330	
PD337	
PD338 JO-C	FTR Düsseldorf 2/3.11.44.
PD342	To 227 Sqn.
PD345	To 227 Sqn.
RA542 JO-Z	Force-landed in Sweden during operation to Tonsberg 25/26.4.45.
RA573	
RA576	
RF141	
RF152	
RF175 JO-D	From 50 Sqn.
RF177	
RF270	
SW268	

467 SQUADRON

No Motto: Code PO

No. 467 Squadron RAAF was formed at Scampton on the 7 November 1942. Its formation coming in response to the Australian government's wishes to group together, where possible, Australian flying personnel. Initially, though, like all squadrons, it was a polyglot of nationalities, predominantly from Britain, Canada and New Zealand. Ground crews were also mainly RAF, although this would change in time. Equipped with the Lancaster 467 remained in the front line of operations until war's end.

STATIONS

Scampton	07.11.42 to 22.11.42
Bottesford	22.11.42 to 12.11.43
Waddington	12.11.43 to 15.06.45

COMMANDING OFFICERS

Wing Commander C L Gomm	07.11.42 to 16.08.43
Squadron Leader A S Raphael	16.08.43 to 18.08.43
Wing Commander J R Balmer	18.08.43 to 11.05.44

Wing Commander W L Brill	12.05.44 to 12.10.44
Wing Commander J K Douglas	12.10.44 to 08.02.45
Wing Commander E Le P Langlois	08.02.45 to 04.03.45
Wing Commander I H A Hay	04.03.45 to 30.09.45

AIRCRAFT

Lancaster I/III   11.42 to 09.45

OPERATIONAL RECORD

Operations	Sorties	Aircraft Losses	% Losses
314	3,833	104	2.7

Category of Operations

Bombing	Mining
299	15

14 Lancasters destroyed in crashes

TABLE OF STATISTICS

(Heavy squadrons)

Out of 59 Lancaster squadrons

9th highest number of Lancaster overall operations in Bomber Command.
15th highest number of Lancaster sorties in Bomber Command.
14th equal (with 156 Sqn) highest number of Lancaster operational losses in Bomber Command.

Out of 22 squadrons in 5 Group

11th highest number of overall operations in 5 Group.
8th highest number of sorties in Bomber Command.
9th highest number of aircraft operational losses in 5 Group.

Out of 17 Lancaster squadrons in 5 Group

7th highest number of Lancaster overall operations in 5 Group.
7th highest number of Lancaster sorties in 5 Group.
8th highest number of Lancaster operational losses in 5 Group.

Lancaster	From November 1942.
L7530	From 207 Sqn. Training only. To 1661CU.
L7574	From 97 Sqn. Crashed on take-off from Waddington when bound for Berlin 22.11.43.
R5485 PO-S/F	From 1657CU. FTR Revigny 18/19.7.44.
R5868 PO-S	From 83 Sqn. Flew a total of 137 operations. Preserved in RAF Museum Hendon.
W4240 PO-A	From 57 Sqn. FTR Hanover 18/19.10.43.
W4375	No operations to 57 Sqn.
W4376	To 57 Sqn.
W4377	To 57 Sqn.
W4378 PO-N	FTR Berlin 17/18.1.43.
W4380	To 50 Sqn.
W4381	From 207 Sqn. To 106 Sqn.
W4382	To 50 Sqn.

W4383	To 50 Sqn.
W4384 PO-B	To 57 Sqn.
W4795	First off on Squadron's first operation to 207 Sqn.
W4797	No operation. To 57 Sqn.
W4798	To 207 Sqn.
W4822	To 49 Sqn.
W4823	To 50 Sqn.
W4824	No operations. To 57 Sqn and back via 1660CU to 50 Sqn.
W4825	To 97 Sqn.
W4826	To 106 Sqn.
W4946 PO-C/U-	FTR Hamburg 27/28.7.43.
W4983 PO-B/Z	FTR Düsseldorf 11/12.6.43.
W5003 PO-H	FTR Hamburg 27/28.7.43.
DV226	FTR Kassel 22/23.10.43.
DV233	From 427 Sqn to 207 Sqn and back. FTR Mannheim 23/24.9.43.
DV237	FTR Berlin 3/4.9.43.
DV240 PO-D	FTR Nuremberg 30/31.3.44.
DV277 PO-L	To 5LFS.
DV337 PO-N	To 463 Sqn.
DV338	To 463 Sqn.
DV372 PO-F	To 1651CU.
DV373	To 463 Sqn.
DV374	To 463 Sqn.
DV378 PO-C	FTR Berlin 30/31.1.44.
DV396 PO-B	From 9 Sqn. FTR Düsseldorf 1/2.11.44.
ED303	To 106 Sqn.
ED304 PO-B/C/D	FTR Düsseldorf 11/12.6.43.
ED305	No operations to 44 Sqn.
ED309	To 50 Sqn.
ED360 PO-D	To 106 Sqn.
ED361	To 207 Sqn.
ED363 PO-E	FTR Cologne 28/29.6.43.
ED364	To 207 Sqn.
ED367 PO-H	FTR Duisburg 8/9.1.43. Squadron's first loss.
ED500 PO-S	Crash-landed in Cheshire while training 3.8.43.
ED504 PO-K	FTR Essen 27/28.5.43.
ED523 PO-Q	FTR Stuttgart 11/12.3.43.
ED524 PO-T	FTR Essen 3/4.4.43.
ED525	FTR Wilhelmshaven 19/20.2.43.
ED526 PO-J	FTR Nuremberg 25/26.2.43.
ED529	FTR Wilhelmshaven 19/20.2.43.
ED530 PO-O	Ditched in Channel on return from Munich 2/3.10.43.
ED531 PO-T	FTR Turin 12/13.7.43.
ED532 PO-H	FTR Scholven Buer 21/22.6.44.
ED534 PO-R	FTR Hamburg 29/30.7.43.
ED535	To 460 Sqn.
ED538 PO-O	Crashed on landing in North Africa following operation to Cislago 16/17.7.43.
ED539 PO-V/P	FTR Berlin 27/28.1.44.
ED541 PO-A	FTR Berlin 3/4.9.43.
ED543 PO-H	FTR Pilsen 13/14.5.43.
ED545 PO-F/G	To 463 Sqn.
ED546	Crashed while landing at Wittering during training 15.10.43.

ED547 PO-M/U	FTR Berlin 29/30.12.43.
ED561	To 100 Sqn.
ED602	To 83 Sqn.
ED606 PO-X	To 463 Sqn.
ED621 PO-P/V	FTR Munich 2/3.10.43.
ED651 PO-Y	FTR Pilsen 16/17.4.43.
ED657 PO-T	FTR Duisburg 21/22.5.44.
ED695 PO-J	FTR Düsseldorf 25/26.5.43.
ED737 PO-F/G/P	FTR Cologne 16/17.6.43.
ED763	To 617 Sqn.
ED764 PO-N	FTR Peenemünde 17/18.8.43.
ED768 PO-N	FTR Düsseldorf 25/26.5.43.
ED771 PO-E	FTR Essen 30.4/1.5.43.
ED772	To 463 Sqn.
ED780	FTR Pilsen 16/17.4.43.
ED803 PO-B	FTR Magdeburg 21/22.1.44.
ED867 PO-T/L	From 97 Sqn. FTR Berlin 28/29.1.44.
ED871	From 97 Sqn. To 9 Sqn.
ED949 PO-U	To 463 Sqn.
ED953	From 97 Sqn. Damaged at Waddington 2.6.44.
ED994 PO-A	From 576 Sqn. FTR Stettin 5/6.1.44.
ED998 PO-Y	FTR Milan 15/16.8.43.
EE135 PO-Y	FTR Mannheim 23/24.9.43.
EE143 PO-J	FTR Lille 10/11.5.44.
EE194 PO-E	FTR Nuremberg 27/28.8.43.
JA675 PO-F	From 427 Sqn. FTR Milan 15/16.8.43.
JA676 PO-B	FTR Turin 12/13.7.43.
JA901 PO-N	FTR Mailly-Le-Camp 3/4.5.44.
JA902	To 463 Sqn.
JA906 PO-K	To 427 Sqn and back. FTR Kassel 3/4.10.43.
JA909	From 405 Sqn. To 1661CU.
JB121 PO-U	FTR Düsseldorf 3/4.11.43.
JB124	FTR Berlin 23/24.8.43.
JB130	To 1668CU.
JB140	Crashed on take off from Waddington when bound for Leipzig 4.12.43.
JB286 PO-L	From 405 Sqn. Crashed in Cambridgeshire on return from Munich 8.1.45.
LL746 PO-M	FTR Augsburg 25/26.2.44.
LL788 PO-H/G	FTR Lille 10/11.5.44.
LL789 PO-P	FTR Stuttgart 12/13.9.44.
LL792 PO-E	FTR Bourg Leopold 11/12.5.44.
LL843	To 61 Sqn.
LL846 PO-V	FTR Stuttgart 28/29.7.44.
LL971 PO-N	FTR Scholven-Buer 21/22.6.44.
LM100 PO-D	FTR Karlsruhe 2/3.2.45.
LM101 PO-J	FTR Courtrai 20/21.7.44.
LM119 PO-E	FTR Courtrai 20/21.7.44.
LM205 PO-B	FTR Beauvoir 29.6.44.
LM219 PO-G	FTR St Leu d'Esserent 7/8.7.44.
LM223	To 463 Sqn.
LM226 PO-H	FTR Stuttgart 12/13.9.44.
LM233 PO-M	To 635 Sqn.
LM237 PO-N	FTR Königsburg 29/30.8.44.

LM239	FTR Karlsruhe 26/27.9.44.
LM267 PO-J	FTR Königsburg 29/30.8.44.
LM310	To 106 Sqn.
LM311 PO-L	Crashed on approach to Bottesford on return from Turin 13.7.43.
LM338 PO-U	FTR St Leu d'Esserent 7/8.7.44.
LM340	To 405 Sqn.
LM342	FTR Peenemünde 17/18.8.43.
LM368	From 101 Sqn. To 50 Sqn.
LM372 PO-K	FTR Berlin 1/2.1.44.
LM376 PO-O	FTR Nuremberg 30/31.3.44.
LM431 PO-M	FTR Stettin 5/6.1.44.
LM440	Crashed in Yorkshire on return from Rennes 8/9.6.44.
LM450 PO-K	FTR Prouville 24/25.6.44.
LM475 PO-B	FTR Lille 10/11.5.44.
LM552 PO-D	FTR from Training exercise 12.6.44.
LM583 PO-O	FTR Königsburg 29/30.8.44.
LM636 PO-U	FTR Calais 24.9.44.
LM642	
LM646 PO-A	To 156 Sqn.
LM677 PO-V	FTR Dortmund-Ems Canal at Ladbergen 3/4.3.45.
LM686 PO-X	To 156 Sqn.
LM746	Written off after collision with NN714 (467 Sqn) over Lincolnshire when bound for Cologne 28.10.44.
LM748	To 1654CU.
ME304	From 405 Sqn.
ME432	
ME453 PO-L	FTR Dortmund-Ems Canal at Ladbergen 3/4.3.45.
ME484	
ME488	
ME575 PO-C/G	FTR Berlin 27/28.1.44.
ME851 PO-B	FTR Nevers 15/16.7.44.
ME853 PO-Q	FTR Bois de Cassan 2.8.44.
ME856 PO-T	FTR Stuttgart 28/29.7.44.
ND346 PO-E	FTR Bois de Cassan 2.8.44.
ND473 PO-N	From 49 Sqn. Collided with ME300 (189 Sqn) over France on return from Royan 4.1.45.
ND729 PO-L	FTR Prouville 24/25.6.44.
ND732 PO-Y	FTR La Chapelle 20/21.4.44.
NF908 PO-C	Crashed in Staffordshire during fighter affiliation exercise 3.1.45.
NF910 PO-Q	
NF917 PO-Q	FTR Harburg 11/12.11.44.
NF989 PO-P	FTR Walcheren 23.10.44.
NG196	
NG197 PO-G	FTR Siegen 1/2.2.45.
NG234	To 463 Sqn.
NG366	
NG455 PO-H	FTR Dortmund-Ems Canal at Ladbergen 7/8.2.45.
NG485	
NN714 PO-W	FTR Harburg 11/12.11.44.
NN805	
PA169 PO-S	FTR Dortmund-Ems Canal at Ladbergen 1.1.45.
PA187 PO-F	From 463 Sqn.

PB234 PO-C	FTR Revigny 18/19.7.44.
PB299 PO-O	From 49 Sqn. FTR Rheydt 19/20.9.44.
PB306 PO-J	From 49 Sqn. FTR Karlsruhe 2/3.2.45.
PB513	From 405 Sqn.
PB653	From 405 Sqn.
PB726 PO-P	To 635 Sqn.
PB740 PO-O	FTR Heilbronn 4/5.12.44.
PB754 PO-U	To 35 Sqn.
PB762	To 35 Sqn.
PB806 PO-W	FTR Dortmund-Ems Canal at Ladbergen 3/4.3.45.
PD215	FTR Munich following collision with PD346 (50 Sqn) 17/18.12.44.
PD218	
PD230 PO-X	FTR Rüsselsheim 12/13.8.44.
PD231 PO-T	FTR Würzburg 16/17.3.45.
PD362	From 50 Sqn.
PD398	Force-landed in France on return from Munich 26/27.11.44.
PD418 PO-P	From 617 Sqn.
RE134	
RE136 PO-V	
RF139	
RF140	
RF180	From 50 Sqn.
SW259	From 156 Sqn.
SW263	

Heaviest Single Loss

12/13.07.43	Turin. 2 Lancasters FTR 1 crashed on return.
10/11.05.44	Lille. 3 Lancasters FTR.
29/30.08.44	Königsburg. 3 Lancasters FTR.
03/04.03.45	Ladbergen. 3 Lancasters FTR.

617 SQUADRON

Motto: Apres Moi Le Deluge (After me the flood).   Codes. AJ KC YZ

Formed from C Flight of fellow Scampton residents 57 Squadron on the 21 March 1943, 617 Squadron was to become the most famous squadron in RAF history. Under the command of W/C Guy Gibson the squadron's first brief was to attack the major dams serving Germany's Ruhr region, and after a period of intensive training the operation was successfully concluded, although at a very high cost in aircraft and crews. It remains the most celebrated feat of arms in aviation history. Following another expensive and this time unsuccessful low-level operation against the Dortmund-Ems Canal four months later the squadron again rebuilt, and under the leadership of Leonard Cheshire became a byword for high level precision bombing. Its association with the brilliant scientist, Dr Barnes Wallis, begun with the 'bouncing bomb' used to destroy the dams, continued with his ballistically perfect Tallboy and Grand Slam earthquake bombs in 1944 and 45. The former was employed against the battleship *Tirpitz* and V-weapon storage sites, and both proved highly effective against communications targets and U-boat bunkers. The very best in leadership, crews and equipment enabled the squadron to operate at peak efficiency at all times, and it was unquestionably one of the most effective small forces employed by the Allies in any theatre of operations.

STATIONS

Scampton	21.03.43 to 30.08.43
Coningsby	30.08.43 to 10.01.44
Woodhall Spa	10.01.44 to 17.06.45

COMMANDING OFFICERS

Wing Commander G P Gibson	21.03.43 to 03.08.43
Wing Commander G W Holden	03.08.43 to 16.09.43
Squadron Leader H B Martin (Temp)	16.09.43 to 10.11.43
Wing Commander G L Cheshire	10.11.43 to 12.07.44
Wing Commander J B Tait	12.07.44 to 29.12.44
Group Captain J E Fauquier	29.12.44 to 28.04.45
Wing Commander J E Grindon	28.04.45 to 09.08.45

AIRCRAFT

Lancaster	1/111 03.43 to 06.45
Mosquito	03.44 to 05.45
Mustang	06.44 to 05.45

OPERATIONAL RECORD

Operations	Sorties	Aircraft Losses	% Losses
101	1,599	32	2.1

Category of Operations

Bombing	Leaflet	Other
99 (D-Day spoof)	1	1

Lancaster

Operations	Sorties	Aircraft Losses	% Losses
101	1,478	32	2.2

Mosquito

Operations	Sorties	Aircraft Losses	% Losses
36 (included in above)	75	0	0.0

Mustang

Operations	Sorties	Aircraft Losses	% Losses
6 (included in above)	6	0	0.0

TABLE OF STATISTICS

Out of 59 Lancaster squadrons

42nd highest number of Lancaster overall operations in Bomber Command.
41st highest number of Lancaster sorties in Bomber Command.
36th highest number of Lancaster operational losses in Bomber Command.

Out of 19 Mosquito squadrons

Lowest number of Mosquito overall operations, sorties and operational losses in Bomber Command.

The only squadron to operate a Mustang in Bomber Command.

Out of 22 Squadrons in 5 Group

18th highest number of overall operations in 5 Group.
16th highest number of sorties in 5 Group.
17th highest number of aircraft operational losses in 5 Group.

Out of 17 Lancaster squadrons in 5 Group

3rd lowest number of Lancaster overall operations in 5 Group.
3rd lowest number of Lancaster sorties in 5 Group.
3rd lowest number of Lancaster operational losses in 5 Group.

Out of 2 Mosquito squadrons in 5 Group

Lowest number of Mosquito overall operations, sorties and aircraft operational losses in 5 Group.

Lancaster	From March 1943.
W4358 DX-L	From 57 Sqn on loan. Returned to 57 Sqn.
W4822 DX-P	From 57 Sqn on loan. Returned to 57 Sqn.
W4921 AJ-C	From 106 Sqn. No operations to 619 Sqn.
W4926 AJ-Z	From 97 Sqn. No operations to 1654CU.
W4929 AJ-J	From 61 Sqn. No operations to 619 Sqn.
W4940 AJ-B	From 57 Sqn. No operations to 1660CU.
W5008 DX-B	From 57 Sqn on loan. Returned to 57 Sqn.
DV155	To 44 Sqn.
DV156	To 50 Sqn.
DV178 EA-N	From 49 Sqn on loan. Returned to 49 Sqn.
DV246 KC-U	To 1661CU.
DV380 KC-N/X/P	To EAAS.
DV382 KC-J	Crashed in the South Downs while in transit to Woodhall Spa after the Antheor Viaduct raid 13.2.44. S/L Suggitt.
DV385 KC-A/V/T	Flew on 2 *Tirpitz* operations to 46MU.
DV391 KC-W/O/Y	Flew on all 3 *Tirpitz* operations to 46MU.
DV393 KC-T/R/E	To 9 Sqn.
DV394 KC-M	FTR Munich 24/25.4.44. F/L Cooper.
DV398 KC-Z	FTR Liege 20/21.12.43. F/L Rice.
DV402 KC-P/X	Landed in Sardinia following operation to the Antheor Viaduct 12.2.44. F/L Martin.
DV403 KC-L/G/X	FTR Wizernes 24.6.44. F/L Edward.
DV405 KC-J	Flew on all 3 *Tirpitz* operations to 44MU.
ED305 KM-S	From 44 Sqn on loan. Returned to 44 Sqn.
ED329 AJ-T	From 207 Sqn. Training only to 57 Sqn.
ED437 AJ-N/V	From 50 Sqn. Training only to 622 Sqn via 1661CU.
ED631 KC-E-	From 622 Sqn. To 115 Sqn.
ED735 AJ-R	From 44 Sqn. Lost without trace in the Bay of Biscay area during transit from Rabat 17/18.11.43. F/L Youseman.
ED756 AJ-H	From 49 Sqn. Training only to 619 Sqn.
ED763 AJ-D/KC-Z	From 467 Sqn. Flew all 3 *Tirpitz* operations.
ED765/G AJ-M	Type 464 1st prototype. Crashed on Ashley Walk Range while training 5.8.43. F/L Kellaway.
ED817/G AJ-C/X-	Type 464 2nd prototype to 46MU.
ED825/G AJ-T/E	Type 464 3rd prototype. McCarthy, Operation Chastise. FTR from SOE sortie for 138 Sqn, F/O Weeden 9/10.12.43.
ED864/G AJ-B	Type 464. Astell. FTR Operation Chastise 16/17.5.43.
ED865/G AJ-S	Type 464. Burpee. FTR Operation Chastise 16/17.5.43.

ED886/G AJ-O	Type 464 townsend, Operation Chastise. FTR from SOE sortie for 138 Sqn, W/O Bull 10.12.43.
ED887/G AJ-A	Type 464. Young. FTR Operation Chastise 16/17.5.43.
ED906/G AJ-J	Type 464. Maltby, Operation Chastise.
ED909/G AJ-P/P-	Type 464. Martin, Operation Chastise.
ED910/G AJ-C	Type 464. Ottley. FTR Operation Chastise 16/17.5.43.
ED912/G AJ-N/S	Type 464. Knight, Operation Chastise to 46MU.
ED915/G AJ-Q	Type 464 to 46MU.
ED918/G AJ-F	Type 464. Brown, Operation Chastise. Crashed on Snettisham beach during training 20.1.44. F/L O'Shaughnessy.
ED921/G AJ-W	Type 464. Munro, Operation Chastise to 46MU.
ED924/G AJ-Y	Type 464. Anderson, Operation Chastise to 44MU.
ED925/G AJ-M	Type 464. Hopgood. FTR Operation Chastise 16/17.5.43.
ED927/G AJ-E	Type 464. Barlow. FTR Operation Chastise 16/17.5.43.
ED929/G AJ-L	Type 464. Shannon, Operation Chastise to 46MU
ED931 DX-C	From 57 Sqn on loan. Returned to 57 Sqn.
ED932/G AJ-G/V	Type 464. Gibson, Operation Chastise to 61 Sqn.
ED933/G KC-X/N/N-	Type 464 to 46MU 2.45.
ED934/G AJ-K	Type 464. Byers. FTR Operation Chastise 16/17.5.43.
ED936/G AJ-H	Type 464. Rice, Operation Chastise. SOC 28.7.44.
ED937/G AJ-Z	Type 464. Maudslay. FTR Operation Chastise 16/17.5.43.
ED999 EA-A	From 49 Sqn on loan. Returned to 49 Sqn.
EE130 AJ-A	FTR Dortmund-Ems Canal 15/16.9.43. F/L Allsebrook.
EE131 KC-B/L	Crash-landed in Russia during the first *Tirpitz* operation 12.9.44. F/O Ross.
EE144 AJ-S	FTR Dortmund-Ems Canal 15/16.9.43. W/C Holden.
EE145 AJ-T	Crashed on landing at Scampton while training 6.6.43. F/L Munro.
EE146 AJ-K/KC-D	Flew 2 *Tirpitz* operations (W/C Tait). SOC 24.4.45.
EE147 AJ-L	To 619 Sqn.
EE148 AJ-U	To 626 Sqn.
EE149	To 619 Sqn.
EE150 AJ-Z	To 619 Sqn.
EE170	Training only to 619 Sqn.
EE185 KM-K	From 44 Sqn on loan. Returned to 44 Sqn.
EE197 DX-Y	From 57 Sqn on loan. Returned to 57 Sqn.
JA703 KM-W	From 44 Sqn on loan. Returned to 44 Sqn.
JA705 OL-M	From 83 Sqn. Training only.
JA874 KC-E	From 61 Sqn. FTR Dortmund-Ems Canal 15/16.9.43. P/O Divall.
JA894 KC-T	From 49 Sqn. To A&AEE.
JA898 KC-X	From 619 Sqn. FTR Dortmund-Ems Canal 15/16.9.43. F/L Wilson.
JA981 KC-J	Crashed in North Sea after recall from the Dortmund-Ems Canal operation of 14/15.9.43. S/L Maltby.
JB139 KC-X/V	From 49 Sqn. FTR Brest 5.8.44. F/O Cheney.
JB144 KC-N	FTR Dortmund-Ems Canal 15/16.9.43. F/L Knight.
JB370 DX-U-	From 57 Sqn. Returned to 57 Sqn.
LM309 AJ-X	From 9 Sqn. Training only to 619 Sqn.
LM482 KC-W/Q	FTR Kembs Barrage 7.10.44. F/L Howard.
LM485 KC-N/U/H	Flew on first and last *Tirpitz* operations.
LM489 KC-L/A/N	Flew on all 3 *Tirpitz* operations.
LM492 KC-Q/W	Flew on all 3 *Tirpitz* operations.
LM695 KC-N	From 463 Sqn.

ME554 KC-F	Flew on all 3 *Tirpitz* operations.
ME555 KC-C	To 9 Sqn.
ME557 KC-O/S	FTR Rilly-La-Montagne 31.7.44. F/L Reid.
ME559 KC-Q/Y	Crash-landed on arrival in Russia for the first *Tirpitz* operation 11/12.9.44. S/L Wyness.
ME560 KC-H	Crashed while landing at Woodhall Spa after a ferry flight 14.7.44. F/O Hamilton.
ME561 KC-R/T	Flew on all 3 *Tirpitz* operations. Crashed in Lincolnshire on return from Pölitz 22.12.44. F/O Joplin.
ME562 KC-Z/K	Flew on all 3 *Tirpitz* operations.
ND339 ZN-Z-	On detachment from 106 Sqn. Returned to 106 Sqn.
ND472 DX-O-	On detachment from 57 Sqn. Returned to 57 Sqn.
ND554 LE-N-	On detachment from 630 Sqn. Returned to 630 Sqn.
ND631 KM-B-/Z-	On detachment from 44 Sqn. Returned to 44 Sqn.
ND683 EA-P-	On detachment from 49 Sqn. Returned to 49 Sqn.
NF920 KC-E	FTR *Tirpitz* (force-landed in Sweden) 29.10.44. F/O Carey.
NF923 KC-M	FTR Dortmund-Ems Canal 23/24.9.44. F/O Stout.
NF992 KC-B	FTR Bergen 12.1.45. F/O Ross.
NG180 KC-S	FTR Kembs Barrage 7.10.44. S/L Wyness.
NG181 KC-M	To 195 Sqn and back. Flew 2 *Tirpitz* operations.
NG228 KC-V	FTR Swinemünde 16.4.45. S/L Powell.
NG339 KC-G	
NG340 KC-L/U	
NG445 KC-E	
NG489 KC-M	
NG494 KC-B	
NN702	From 630 Sqn.
PB342	From 61 Sqn to 1653CU.
PB415 KC-S/O	Flew on all 3 *Tirpitz* operations. SOC 4.45.
PB416 KC-V	Missing on return from Russia (First *Tirpitz* operation) 17.9.44. F/O Levy
PB996 YZ-C	B1 Special.
PB997 YZ-E	B1 Special.
PB998 YZ-D	B1 Special.
PD112 YZ-S	B1 Special.
PD113 YZ-T	B1 Special.
PD114 YZ-B	B1 Special.
PD115 YZ-K	B1 Special.
PD116 YZ-A	B1 Special.
PD117 YZ-L	B1 Special. FTR Arbergen Railway Bridge 21.3.45. F/L Gumbley.
PD118 YZ-M	B1 Special.
PD119 YZ-J	B1 Special.
PD121 YZ-S	B1 Special.
PD127 YZ-F	B1 Special.
PD128 YZ-R	B1 Special.
PD129 YZ-O	B1 Special.
PD130 YZ-D/W/U	B1 Special.
PD131 YZ-V	B1 Special.
PD132 YZ-X	B1 Special.
PD133 YZ-P	B1 Special.
PD134 YZ-Y	B1 Special.
PD135 YZ-W	B1 Special.
PD136 YZ-N	B1 Special.

PD139 YZ-W/L	B1 Special.
PD233 KC-G	FTR Bergen 12.1.45. F/L Pryor.
PD238 KC-B/H	
PD371 KC-S/W	
PD418	To 467 Sqn.

Mosquito	From March 1944.
DZ415 AZ-Q/A	From 627 Sqn on loan as required.
DZ418 AZ-L	From 627 Sqn on loan as required.
DZ421 AZ-C	From 627 Sqn on loan as required.
DZ484 AZ-G	From 627 Sqn on loan as required.
DZ521 AZ-M	From 627 Sqn on loan as required.
DZ525 AZ-S	From 627 Sqn on loan as required.
DZ534 AZ-H	From 627 Sqn on loan as required
DZ547 AZ-E	From 627 Sqn on loan as required.
DZ637 AZ-O	From 627 Sqn on loan as required.
KB215 AZ-H	From 627 Sqn on loan as required.
ML975 HS-M	From 109 Sqn on loan as required.
ML976 HS-N/L	From 109 Sqn on loan as required.
NS992 AJ-N/S	To 515 Sqn.
NS993 AJ-N/L	To 515 Sqn.
NT202 AJ-N	To 417 Sqn and back. Crashed at Wainfleet Sands while training 7.8.44. F/O Duffy.
NT205 AJ-L	

Mustang	From 22.6.44 to 2.10.44.
HB837 AJ-N	To 541 Sqn via 38MU.

Heaviest Single Loss

16/17.05.43	Operation Chastise. 8 Lancasters FTR.

619 SQUADRON

No Motto: Code PG

Formed on the 18 April 1943 in the middle of the Ruhr campaign, 619 Squadron had no previous history or tradition, and in fact, has never been awarded a badge or motto to commemorate its existence. Based at Woodhall Spa in 5 Group its nucleus was provided by three crews from 97 Squadron, who were left behind when it vacated the station on that day to join the Pathfinders, and took up residence at Bourn. The first of an intended sixteen brand new Lancasters, ED977, arrived on the 29th. Among other Lancasters taken on charge early on were some older ones, including seven from 617 Squadron. The squadron remained at the forefront of operations until war's end.

STATIONS

Woodhall Spa	18.04.43 to 09.01.44
Coningsby	09.01.44 to 17.04.44
Dunholme Lodge	17.04.44 to 28.09.44
Strubby	28.09.44 to 30.06.45

COMMANDING OFFICERS

Wing Commander I J Mcghie DFC	18.04.43 to 18.08.43
Wing Commander W Abercromby DFC	18.08.43 to 04.12.43
Wing Commander J R Jeudwine OBE	04.12.43 to 23.05.44
Wing Commander J R Maling AFC	23.05.44 to 26.07.44
Wing Commander R A Milward DFC	28.07.44 to 25.02.45
Wing Commander S G Birch	25.02.45 to 14.06.45

AIRCRAFT

Lancaster I/III   04.43 to 07.45

OPERATIONAL RECORD

Operations	Sorties	Aircraft Losses	% Losses
240	3,011	77	2.6

Category of Operations

Bombing	Mining
223	17

TABLE OF STATISTICS

Out of 59 Lancaster squadrons

20th highest number of Lancaster overall operations in Bomber Command.
25th highest number of Lancaster sorties in Bomber Command.
20th highest number of Lancaster operational losses in Bomber Command.

Out of 22 squadrons in 5 Group

13th highest number of overall operations in 5 Group.
11th highest number of sorties in 5 Group.
11th highest number of aircraft operational losses in 5 Group.

Out of 17 Lancaster squadrons in 5 Group

11th highest number of Lancaster overall operations in 5 Group.
10th highest number of Lancaster sorties in 5 Group.
10th highest number of Lancaster operational losses in 5 Group.

Lancaster	From April 1943.
W4127 PG-D	From 1660CU. FTR La Chapelle 20/21.4.44.
W4921	From 617 Sqn. To 1654CU.
W4929	From 617 Sqn. To 1661CU.
DV238	To 49 Sqn.
DV326 PG-P	Completed 10 Berlin operations to 5LFS.
DV328 PG-L	FTR Berlin (11th Berlin operation.) 24/25.3.44.
DV330 PG-O	FTR Berlin 15/16.2.44.
DV335 PG-H	To 46MU.
DV336 PG-U	Crashed near Elvington on return from Berlin 27.11.43.
DV381 PG-B	FTR Berlin 26/27.11.43.
ED597	From 49 Sqn. Crashed on take-off from Coningsby while training, and damaged beyond repair 17.3.44.
ED602 PG-X	From 49 Sqn. FTR Karlsruhe 26/27.9.44.

ED756	From 617 Sqn to 1654CU.
ED839 PG-C	From 97 Sqn. Crashed on take-off from Woodhall Spa when bound for Hanover 8.10.43.
ED859 PG-G/V	From 156 Sqn. FTR Wesseling 21/22.6.44.
ED866 PG-E	From 97 Sqn. To 5LFS.
ED977 PG-A	FTR Stettin 5/6.1.44.
ED978 PG-B	FTR Düsseldorf 11/12.6.43.
ED979	FTR Cologne 28/29.6.43.
ED980	FTR Oberhausen 14/15.6.43.
ED981 PG-V	FTR Berlin 23/24.8.43.
ED982 PG-D	FTR Peenemünde 17/18.8.43.
ED983 PG-W	Crashed in Lincolnshire on return from Bochum 30.9.43.
EE106 PG-C/E	FTR Antheor Viaduct 16/17.9.43.
EE109 PG-F	FTR Hanover 18/19.10.43.
EE110 PG-U	Crashed in Bristol Channel on return from Hagen 1/2.10.43.
EE111 PG-S	Abandoned over Yorkshire coast on return from Berlin 27.11.43.
EE112 PG-T	FTR Nuremberg 10/11.8.43.
EE113	FTR from air-test 9.6.43.
EE114 PG-B	FTR Leipzig 20/21.10.43.
EE115 PG-G	FTR Berlin 31.8/1.9.43.
EE116 PG-Q	FTR Aachen 11/12.4.44.
EE117 PG-L	FTR Peenemünde 17/18.8.43.
EE118	To 156 Sqn.
EE134 PG-X/Y	From 49 Sqn. To 5LFS.
EE147 PG-P	From 617 Sqn. FTR Peenemünde 17/18.8.43.
EE149 PG-U	From 617 Sqn. Written off on return from Gelsenkirchen 25/26.6.43.
EE150 PG-F	From 617 Sqn.. Crash-landed on approach to Woodhall Spa on return from Berlin 17.12.43.
EE168 PG-R	From 97 Sqn. Crashed in Yorkshire on return from Berlin 27.11.43.
EE170 PG-N	From 617 Sqn. FTR Berlin 2/3.12.43.
EE198 PG-H	FTR Krefeld 21/22.6.43.
HK803	From 9 Sqn. To 463 Sqn.
JA844 PG-J	Collided over Sussex with ED361 (207 Sqn) on return from Milan 13.8.43.
JA847 PG-C	FTR Berlin 2/3.12.43.
JA848 PG-R	FTR Berlin 31.8/1.9.43.
JA867 PG-X	FTR Berlin 16/17.12.43.
JA898	To 617 Sqn.
JB123 PG-D	FTR Berlin 2/3.1.44. on 10th Berlin operation.
JB125	To 5LFS.
JB131 PG-T	To 5LFS after 10 Berlin operations.
JB133	FTR Mannheim 5/6.9.43.
JB134 PG-Y/G	FTR Mailly-Le-Camp 3/4.5.44. after 12 Berlin operations.
JB186 PG-G/O	From 156 Sqn. FTR Revigny 18/19.7.44.
LL778 PG-A	To 5LFS.
LL783 PG-G/C	FTR Caen 6/7.6.44.
LL784 PG-M/W	FTR Aachen 11/12.4.44.
LL808 PG-D	FTR Wesseling 21/22.6.44.
LL904 PG-S	FTR Schweinfurt 26/27.4.44.
LL919 PG-W	FTR Schweinfurt 26/27.4.44.
LL969 PG-G	FTR Revigny 18/19.7.44.

LL977 PG-H	FTR Wesseling 21/22.6.44.
LM191PG-O	From 49 Sqn. FTR Darmstadt 11/12.9.44.
LM207	From 49 Sqn. Crashed while landing at Brussels-Evere on return from Essen 11.3.45.
LM209 PG-H	FTR Darmstadt 11/12.9.44.
LM309	From 617 Sqn. To 463 Sqn via 1661 & 1660CU.
LM378 PG-J	FTR Revigny 18/19.7.44.
LM418 PG-R/S	Crash-landed at Woodbridge on return from Nuremberg 30/31.3.44.
LM419 PG-N	FTR Schweinfurt 24/25.2.44.
LM420 PG-R	To 5LFS.
LM423 PG-H	FTR Berlin 2/3.1.44.
LM446 PG-H	FTR Gennevilliers 9/10.5.44.
LM484 PG-M/H	FTR Givors 26/27.7.44.
LM536 PG-Q	FTR Stuttgart 28/29.7.44.
LM630 PG-D	
LM640 PG-L	FTR Revigny 18/19.7.44.
LM643 PG-E	FTR Donges 24/25.7.44.
LM656 PG-M	FTR Königsburg 29/30.8.44.
LM657 PG-R/Q	
LM737 PG-A	
LM742 PG-S	FTR Mitteland Canal 7.11.44.
LM751 PG-X	FTR Heilbronn 4/5.12.44.
LM756 PG-F	From 227 Sqn. FTR Berchtesgaden 25.4.45.
ME314 PG-W	FTR Pölitz 9.2.45.
ME472 PG-J	To 207 Sqn.
ME568 PG-F	FTR Trossy-St-Maximin 3.8.44.
ME569 PG-X	To 1668CU.
ME723 PG-X	FTR Munich 24/25.4.44.
ME745 PG-L	FTR St-Leu-d'Esserent 7/8.7.44.
ME747 PG-Q	Crashed into North Sea during exercise 23.4.44.
ME787 PG-J	From 49 Sqn.
ME846 PG-E/G/C	FTR Wesseling 21/22.6.44.
ME855 PG-X	FTR Brunswick 12/13.8.44.
ME866 PG-W	FTR Chatellerault 9/10.8.44.
ND728 PG-N	FTR Royan 4/5.1.45.
ND730 PG-O	FTR Salbris 7/8.5.44.
ND792	From 49 Sqn. Crashed while landing at Strubby during training 4.2.45.
ND932 PG-U	FTR Heilbronn 4/5.12.44.
ND935 PG-Z/K	FTR Stuttgart 25/26.7.44.
ND957 PG-M	From 49 Sqn. Broke up in the air on return from Munich 7/8.1.45.
ND986 PG-S	FTR Wesseling 21/22.6.44.
NE151 PG-W	FTR Wesseling 21/22.6.44.
NF929	From 9 Sqn.
NG198	
NG286 PG-Y	From 207 Sqn. FTR Harburg 7/8.3.45.
NG483	
NG503 PG-W	FTR Würzburg 16/17.3.45.
NN695 PG-X	Shot down over Norfolk by intruder on return from Duisburg 21/22.5.44.
NN723 PG-G/H/J	From 57 Sqn. FTR Mitteland Canal 5/6.11.44.
NN751 PG-H	

NN768	To 44 Sqn.
NX574 PG-E	
PA180 PG-G	
PA198	
PA255 PG-V	
PA277	
PB205	From 44 Sqn to 1661CU.
PB208 PG-S	FTR Kiel 23/24.7.44.
PB210 PG-U/V	FTR Karlsruhe 2/3.2.45.
PB245 PG-L/Z	FTR Revigny 18/19.7.44.
PB261 PG-L	From SIU. To 57 Sqn.
PB297	From SIU. To 57sqn.
PB346 PG-J	From 44 Sqn. FTR Givors 26/27.7.44.
PB356 PG-G	FTR Harburg 11/12.11.44.
PB404 PG-F	To 227 Sqn.
PB405 PG-S	FTR Mönchen-Gladbach 19/20.9.44.
PB481	From 7 Sqn to 5LFS.
PB540 PG-Z	Crash-landed at Woodbridge on return from Homburg 1.11.44.
PB590 PG-Z/V	
PB696	From 9 Sqn.
PB699 PG-Z	From 207 Sqn. FTR Harburg 7/8.3.45.
PB751	To 44 Sqn.
PB758 PG-S	To 1661CU.
PB782	
PB842 PG-Y	FTR Pölitz 13/14.1.45.
PB852	To 57 Sqn.
PB862	To 1660CU.
PD425 PG-T	From 1661CU. FTR Böhlen 20/21.3.45.
PD441 PG-B	From 1661CU.
RA519 PG-U	
RA521 PG-D	
RA527 PG-M	
RA588 PG-W	
RA590 PG-Y	
RF234 PG-T	From 44 Sqn.
RF239 PG-K	
SW254 PG-S	From 1661CU. FTR Leipzig 10/11.4.45.

Heaviest Single Loss

21/22.06.44	Wesseling 6 Lancasters FTR.

627 SQUADRON

Motto: At First Sight   Code AZ

Formed at Oakington on the 12 November 1943, 627 Squadron was born out of the planned expansion of 8 Group's Mosquito capability, which, with the addition of further squadrons in 1944, would become the Light Night-Striking Force. Faced with an option to maintain 139 Squadron as a three flight unit, or to form a new squadron, AVM Bennett opted for the latter, and C Flight was duly transferred. Over the succeeding twelve days, eleven pilots, some with navigators, were involved in the postings, along with their Mk IV Mosquitoes to form the nucleus of the new squadron. After 617 Squadron demonstrated the effectiveness of the Mosquito in a low-level marking role, which became known as the '5 Group method', 627 Squadron was transferred on permanent loan to perform that function. It also carried out daring precision low-level attacks against individual buildings.

Permanently attached to 5 Group from 8 Group   15.04.44

STATION

Woodhall Spa   15.04.44 to 30.09.45

COMMANDING OFFICERS

Wing Commander R P Elliott DSO DFC*	13.11.43 to 03.06.44
Wing Commander G W Curry DSO DFC*	03.06.44 to 22.01.45
Wing Commander B R Hallows DFC	22.01.45 to 17.03.45
Wing Commander R Kingsford-Smith DSO DFC	10.04.45 to 01.06.45

FLIGHT COMMANDERS

A Flight

Squadron Leader W G Lockhart DSO DFC	23.11.43 to 01.01.44
Squadron Leader E R Nelles DFC	19.01.44 to 15.07.44
Squadron Leader R Churcher DFC*	15.07.44 to 14.12.44
Squadron Leader P F Mallender	14.12.44 to 25.03.45
Squadron Leader W Topper DFC	25.03.45 to 30.09.45

B Flight

Squadron Leader E I J Bell DFC	13.11.43 to 08.01.44
Squadron Leader N W Mckenzie DFC	16.01.44 to 21.09.44
Squadron Leader R W G Oakley	21.09.44 to 01.05.45
Squadron Leader J H Penney DFC	01.05.45 to 30.09.45

Trials And Development Flight

Squadron Leader B J Hooper	01.03.45 to 30.09.45

AIRCRAFT

Mosquito IV	11.43 to 09.45
Mosquito XVI	03.45 to 09.45
Mosquito XX	07.44 to 09.45
Mosquito XXV	10.44 to 09.45

OPERATIONAL RECORD

Operations	Sorties	Aircraft Losses	% Losses
166	1,058	15	1.4

Category of Operations

Marking/Recce	Mining	Window	Met/Photo
121	6	4	35

TABLE OF STATISTICS

Out of 19 Mosquito squadrons in Bomber Command

10th highest number of overall Mosquito operations in Bomber Command.
7th highest number of Mosquito sorties in Bomber Command.
4th highest number of Mosquito operational losses in Bomber Command.

Out of 22 squadrons in 5 Group

17th highest number of overall operations in 5 Group.
18th highest number of sorties in 5 Group.
21st highest number of operational losses in 5 Group.
The only squadron in 5 Group completely equipped with Mosquitoes.

Mosquito	From November 1943.
W4072 AZ-Q	From 105 Sqn via 1655MTU. Crashed in the sea off Essex coast on return from Berlin 9.1.44.
DK293 AZ-L	From 109 Sqn. FTR Frankfurt 8/9.1.44.
DK313 AZ-A/N	From 139 Sqn. To 1655MTU.
DZ344 AZ-E	From 1655MTU. To 692 Sqn and back to 2Gp CS.
DZ353 AZ-T/B	From 139 Sqn. FTR Rennes airfield 9/10.6.44.
DZ370	From 139 Sqn. Returned to 139 Sqn.
DZ414 AZ-O	From 139 Sqn. To Marshalls.
DZ415 AZ-Q/A	From 105 Sqn.
DZ418 AZ-F/B	From 139 Sqn.
DZ421 AZ-C	From 139 Sqn. To 1655MTU.
DZ422 AZ-D	From 139 Sqn. Crashed onto Woodhall Spa airfield on return from training 7.5.44.
DZ426 AZ-C/A	From 139 Sqn. To NTU.
DZ441	From 140Wg. To 605 Sqn.
DZ442 AZ-A/D	From 139 Sqn. To 1655MTU.
DZ461 AZ-U	From 1655MTU. To 109 Sqn.
DZ462 AZ-N	From 105 Sqn.
DZ468 AZ-D	From 692 Sqn. FTR Nantes 27/28.5.44.
DZ477 AZ-K	From 139 Sqn. To 1655MTU.
DZ478 AZ-R	From 139 Sqn. Crashed on approach to Woodhall Spa while training 7.5.44.
DZ479 AZ-B/F	From 139 Sqn. FTR Berlin 2/3.12.43.
DZ482 AZ-P	From 139 Sqn. FTR Beauvoir 29.6.44.
DZ484 AZ-G	From 109 Sqn. To 1655MTU.
DZ516 AZ-O	From 139 Sqn. FTR Beauvoir 29.6.44.
DZ518 AZ-F/A/P	From 139 Sqn.
DZ521 AZ-M	From 139 Sqn. Crashed in Norfolk on return from Karlsruhe 27.9.44.
DZ525 AZ-S/B	From 692 Sqn.
DZ530 AZ-N/D	From 618 Sqn.
DZ534 AZ-H	From 618 Sqn. To 692 Sqn and back. Ditched near Cherbourg on return from Givors 26/27.7.44.
DZ547 AZ-O/E/D	From 618 Sqn. To 692 Sqn and back.
DZ551 AZ-E	From 109 Sqn. FTR Berlin 1/2.2.44.
DZ559	From 618 Sqn. Returned to 618 Sqn.
DZ594 AZ-X	From A&AEE.
DZ599 AZ-A/F	From 692 Sqn. FTR from mining sortie to the River Elbe 27/28.3.45.

DZ601 AZ-A	From 139 Sqn.
DZ606 AZ-M/H	From 692 Sqn. To 1655MTU and back to 109 Sqn.
DZ611 AZ-G	From 692 Sqn.To 109 Sqn.
DZ615 AZ-M/H/Y	From 139 Sqn. To 16 OTU.
DZ616 AZ-Z/G	From 139 Sqn. Crashed soon after take-off from Oakington when bound for Berlin 5.1.44.
DZ631 AZ-L/W	From 692 Sqn. Damaged on the ground 12.4.45.
DZ632 AZ-C	From 692 Sqn. To 139 Sqn.
DZ633 AZ-D	From 693 Sqn.
DZ634 AZ-P/Z/E	From 692 Sqn. To 109 Sqn.
DZ635 AZ-H/N	From 1655MTU. FTR Bremerhaven 18/19.9.44.
DZ636 AZ-N	From 692 Sqn. FTR Givors 26/27.7.44.
DZ637 AZ-O/X	To 692 Sqn and back. FTR Siegen 1/2.2.45.
DZ640 AZ-N/K/U	From 692 Sqn. FTR Walcheren 30.10.44.
DZ641 AZ-U/C	From 692 Sqn. To 109 Sqn.
DZ642 AZ-N/J/H	From 692 Sqn. Crashed near Sumburgh on return from Trondheim 22.11.44.
DZ643 AZ-P/O	From 692 Sqn. To 109 Sqn.
DZ644 AZ-R	To 139 Sqn.
DZ645 AZ-F	From 139 Sqn. To 109 Sqn.
DZ646 AZ-A	From 692 Sqn. To 139 Sqn.
DZ647	To 692 Sqn.
DZ650 AZ-Q	From 692 Sqn. Crashed on take-off from Woodhall Spa 29.12.44.
KB122 AZ-T	From 139 Sqn. To 109 Sqn.
KB153	Damaged beyond repair 28.11.44.
KB195 AZ-B	From 139 Sqn. FTR Vlissingen 7.10.44.
KB197	To 608 Sqn.
KB213 AZ-R	
KB215 AZ-H	From 139 Sqn via 1655MTU. Broke up over Wainfleet range while training 19.10.44.
KB223	To 16 OTU.
KB240	To 1655MTU.
KB242	To 608 Sqn.
KB265	From 608 Sqn. To 109 Sqn.
KB267 AZ-E	From 139 Sqn. FTR Mönchengladbach/Rheydt 19/20.9.44. W/C Guy Gibson VC killed.
KB329	To 139 Sqn.
KB345 AZ-J	From 608 Sqn. To 109 Sqn.
KB349	To 139 Sqn.
KB362 AZ-K	From 1655MTU to 5 Group Film Unit.
KB366 AZ-O	From 608 Sqn. FTR Kaiserslautern 27/28.9.44.
KB401 AZ-E	From 608 Sqn. FTR Böhlen 19/20.2.45.
KB409 AZ-Y	From 608 Sqn. To 109 Sqn.
KB413 AZ-P	To 142 Sqn.
KB416 AZ-F	From 608 Sqn.
KB419 AZ-K	To 109 Sqn.
KB433 AZ-Z	From 142 Sqn. To 5 Group Film Unit.
KB446 AZ-P	From 142 Sqn. Force-landed in Belgium on return from Sterkrade 18/19.1.45.
KB462	From 142 Sqn. To 109 Sqn.
KB486	From 142 Sqn. To 109 Sqn.
KB490 AZ-U/Q	To 109 Sqn.
KB521 AZ-M	To 13MU

KB533 AZ-N	To 109 Sqn.
KB561 AZ-V	To 109 Sqn.
KB625 AZ-L	Crashed on take-off from Woodhall Spa while 5.5.45.
LR497	From 105 Sqn. To 109 Sqn.
LR510	From 109 Sqn. To TRE.
LR511	From 109 Sqn. To 1317Flt and back to Little Snoring.
ML906 AZ-C-	From 1409Met Flt. Crashed on landing at Woodhall Spa after navigation exercise 17.3.45.
ML914	From 105 Sqn. To 1317Flt and back to 109 Sqn.
ML934	From 1409Met Flt to 1317Flt and back to 109 Sqn.
ML935 AZ-A-	From 1409Met Flt to 1317Flt and back to 109 Sqn.
MM128	To 692 Sqn.
MM133	To 692 Sqn.
MM138	To 692 Sqn.
MM140	To 692 Sqn.
MM144	To 692 Sqn.
MM204	To 128 Sqn.
MM205	To 109 Sqn.
MM219	To 139 Sqn.
MM223	To 571 Sqn.
MM229 AZ-D-	From 1409Met Flt to 1317Flt and back.
NS536 AZ-B-	Crashed on landing at Boscombe Down following navigation exercise 13.3.45.
NT205 AZ-L-	
PF382	To 105 Sqn.
PF415	To 128 Sqn.
PF428	To 128 Sqn.
PF444 AZ-N-	To 109 Sqn.
PF498	From TFU.
PF499	From TFU.
PF503	From TFU.
RV324	

630 SQUADRON

Motto: Nocturna Mors (Death by night)   Code LE

Formed in 5 Group on the 15 November 1943 at East Kirkby, 630 Squadron was an entirely new unit with no past history or tradition. It was one of many squadrons created during the second half of the year as part of the Command's expansion programme, and as was generally the case, it was sporned by an existing operational unit. Its parent was 57 Squadron, whose B Flight, under the command of an American, Squadron Leader Crocker DFC, transferred en-masse across the tarmac to form the nucleus. The squadron remained at the forefront of operations until war's end.

STATION

East Kirkby   15.11.43 to 18.07.45

COMMANDING OFFICERS

Wing Commander M Crocker DFC	15.11.43 to 12.12.43
Wing Commander J D Rollinson DFC	12.12.43 to 28.01.44
Wing Commander W Deas DFC	01.02.44 to 07.07.44

Wing Commander L M Blome-Jones DFC   12.07.44 to 09.44
Wing Commander J E Grindon DFC   09.44 to 28.04.45
Wing Commander F W L Wild DFC   28.04.45 to 18.07.45

AIRCRAFT

Lancaster I/III   15.11.43 to 18.07.45

OPERATIONAL RECORD

Operations	Sorties	Aircraft Losses	% Losses
202	2,453	59	2.4

Category of Operations

Bombing	Mining
180	22

11 further Lancasters were destroyed in crashes

TABLE OF STATISTICS

Out of 58 Lancaster squadrons

28th equal (with 35 Sqn) highest number of Lancaster overall operations in Bomber Command.
33rd highest number of Lancaster sorties in Bomber Command.
26th equal (with 550 Sqn) highest number of Lancaster operational losses in Bomber Command.

Out of 22 squadrons in 5 Group

14th highest number of overall operations in 5 Group.
14th highest number of sorties in 5 Group.
14th highest number of aircraft operational losses in 5 Group.

Out of 17 Lancaster squadrons in 5 Group

12th highest number of Lancaster overall operations in 5 Group.
12th highest number of Lancaster sorties in 5 Group.
12th highest number of Lancaster operational losses in 5 Group.

Lancaster	From November 1943.
ED308	From 57 Sqn. To 1661CU.
ED413 LE-T	From 57 Sqn. To 207 Sqn.
ED655 LE-J	From 57 Sqn. Crashed in Lincolnshire during operation to Berlin (619 Sqn crew) 15/16.2.44.
ED698	From 57 Sqn. To 207 Sqn.
ED758	From 57 Sqn. To 207 Sqn.
ED777 LE-Q	From 57 Sqn. FTR Berlin 2/3.12.43.
ED920 LE-D	From 57 Sqn. FTR Leipzig 3/4.12.43.
ED944 LE-Z	From 57 Sqn. To 5LFS.
JA872 LE-N	From 57 Sqn. To 61 Sqn.
JB135 LE-L	From 57 Sqn. FTR Berlin 23/24.11.43.
JB236 LE-O-	From 57 Sqn. FTR Berlin 23/24.11.43.
JB288 LE-H	From 1660CU. FTR Nuremberg 30/31.3.44.
JB290 LE-C/D	From 1660CU.
JB294	From 1660CU. FTR Berlin 21/22.1.44.
JB532 LE-X	From 61 Sqn. FTR Berlin 1/2.1.44.

JB546 LE-A	From 57 Sqn. FTR Brunswick 22/23.5.44.
JB556 LE-Y	Crashed on take-off from East Kirkby when bound for Munich 24.4.44.
JB561	From 61 Sqn. To 12 Sqn.
JB597	From 61 Sqn. Crashed while landing at Holme-on-Spalding-Moor on return from Berlin 27.11.43.
JB654 LE-C	FTR Berlin 28/29.1.44.
JB665 LE-B	FTR Berlin 15/16.2.44.
JB666	FTR Berlin 28/29.1.44.
JB672 LE-U/F	FTR Duisburg 21/22.5.44.
JB710 LE-W	From 49 Sqn. FTR Leipzig 19/20.2.44.
LL886 LE-I	FTR Berlin 24/25.3.44.
LL949 LE-E	Crashed in the Humber Estuary on return from Trondheim 22/23.11.44.
LL950 LE-Y	FTR from mining sortie 21/22.5.44.
LL966 LE-P	FTR Rositz 14/15.2.45.
LL972 LE-T	FTR Stettin 16/17.8.44.
LM117 LE-J	FTR Revigny 18/19.7.44.
LM118 LE-V	FTR Wesseling 21/22.6.44.
LM216 LE-K	To 186 Sqn.
LM259 LE-F	To 227 Sqn.
LM260 LE-S	FTR Würzburg 16/17.3.45.
LM262 LE-G	FTR Secqueville 7/8.8.44.
LM269 LE-I	FTR Bordeaux 18.8.44.
LM287 LE-O	To 1651CU.
LM537 LE-X	FTR Revigny 18/19.7.44.
LM637 LE-V	FTR Urft Dam 8.12.44.
LM649	From 49 Sqn.
LM673	From 57 Sqn. Returned to 57 Sqn.
LM680 LE-Z	From 50 Sqn.
ME312 LE-A	To 1661CU.
ME532	To 207 Sqn.
ME650 LE-B	FTR Königsburg 26/27.8.44.
ME664 LE-T	FTR Nuremberg 30/31.3.44.
ME717 LE-G	Crash-landed in Corsica following operation to Munich 24/25.4.44.
ME729	Crashed in Scotland while training 18.7.44.
ME737 LE-E/S	FTR Bourg Leopold 11/12.5.44.
ME739 LE-F/T	FTR Leipzig 10/11.4.44.
ME782 LE-N	FTR Wesseling 21/22.6.44.
ME795 LE-G	Abandoned over Henlow on return from Wesseling 21/22.6.44.
ME796 LE-S	FTR Revigny 18/19.7.44.
ME843 LE-U	FTR Wesseling 21/22.6.44.
ME845 LE-Q	To 57 Sqn.
ME867 LE-N	FTR St Leu d'Esserent 4/5.7.44.
ND335 LE-L	To 1668CU.
ND337 LE-S	FTR Nuremberg 30/31.3.44.
ND338 LE-T/Q	FTR Stuttgart 20/21.2.44.
ND412 LE-H	From 405 Sqn.
ND527 LE-O	FTR Givors 26/27.7.44.
ND530 LE-P	From 207 Sqn. FTR Stuttgart 15/16.3.44.
ND531 LE-K	FTR Wesseling 21/22.6.44.
ND532 LE-N	FTR Leipzig 19/20.2.44.

ND554 LE-A	From 617 Sqn. FTR Politz 8/9.2.45.
ND561 LE-R	FTR Stuttgart 1/2.3.44.
ND563	Crashed on take-off from East Kirkby when bound for Stuttgart 20.2.44.
ND580 LE-G	FTR Bourg Leopold 11/12.5.44.
ND583 LE-V	FTR Stuttgart 15/16.3.44.
ND655 LE-J	FTR Brunswick 22/23.5.44.
ND657 LE-W	FTR Berlin 24/25.3.44.
ND685 LE-Q	FTR Caen 6/7.6.44.
ND686 LE-M	FTR Frankfurt 18/19.3.44.
ND688 LE-R	FTR St Leu d'Esserent 7/8.7.44.
ND788 LE-U	FTR Berlin 24/25.3.44.
ND789 LE-I	FTR Schweinfurt 26/27.4.44.
ND793	To Flight Refuelling Ltd.
ND797 LE-W	FTR Stuttgart 28/29.7.44.
ND949 LE-Z	Crashed in Leicestershire on return from Lützkendorf 9.4.45.
ND982 LE-Y	From 405 Sqn. FTR Königsburg 29/30.8.44.
NF961 LE-L	Crashed in Yorkshire while night-flying training 18.10.44.
NG123 LE-U	
NG125 LE-F/N	
NG145	To 57 Sqn.
NG258	Crashed in Lincolnshire on return from Politz 22.12.44.
NG259 LE-N	
NG413 LE-M	From 1661CU.
NN702 LE-J	To 617 Sqn.
NN703	
NN774 LE-L	
PA322 LE-V	
PA992 LE-Y	FTR Stuttgart 24/25.7.44.
PB121 LE-F	FTR Etampes 9/10.6.44.
PB211 LE-H	From 9 Sqn. Crashed in North Sea during mining sortie 23/24.7.44.
PB236 LE-F	FTR Revigny 18/19.7.44.
PB244 LE-N	FTR L'Isle Adam 18.8.44.
PB344 LE-R	
PB742	To 189 Sqn.
PB865	To 1661CU.
PB880 LE-B	FTR Politz 13/14.1.45.
PB894	From 57 Sqn. FTR from mining sortie 31.12/1.1.45
PD253 LE-D	
PD254 LE-W	
PD283 LE-G	FTR Darmstadt 11/12.9.44.
PD317 LE-G	Crashed on landing at East Kirkby following early return from Munich 7.1.45.
PD327 LE-E/Y	To 75(NZ)Sqn.
RA520 LE-E	
RF122 LE-S	FTR Leipzig 10/11.4.45.
RF124 LE-S	From 57 Sqn.
RF194	From 207 Sqn.
RF266	

Heaviest Loss

21/22.6.44	Wesseling 4 Lancasters FTR, 1 abandoned on return.
18/19.7.44	Revigny 4 Lancasters FTR.

Key to Abbreviations

A&AEE	Aeroplane and Armaments Experimental Establishment.
AA	Anti-Aircraft fire.
AACU	Anti-Aircraft Cooperation Unit.
AAS	Air Armament School.
AASF	Advance Air Striking Force.
AAU	Aircraft Assembly Unit.
ACM	Air Chief Marshal.
ACSEA	Air Command South-East Asia.
AFDU	Air Fighting Development Unit.
AFEE	Airborne Forces Experimental Unit.
AFTDU	Airborne Forces Tactical Development Unit.
AGS	Air Gunners School.
AMDP	Air Members for Development and Production.
AOC	Air Officer Commanding.
AOS	Air Observers School.
ASRTU	Air-Sea Rescue Training Unit.
ATTDU	Air Transport Tactical Development Unit.
AVM	Air Vice-Marshal.
BAT	Beam Approach Training.
BCBS	Bomber Command Bombing School.
BCDU	Bomber Command Development Unit.
BCFU	Bomber Command Film Unit.
BCIS	Bomber Command Instructors School.
BDU	Bombing Development Unit.
BSTU	Bomber Support Training Unit.
CF	Conversion Flight.
CFS	Central Flying School.
CGS	Central Gunnery School.
C-in-C	Commander in Chief.
CNS	Central Navigation School.
CO	Commanding Officer.
CRD	Controller of Research and Development.
CU	Conversion Unit.
DGRD	Director General for Research and Development.
EAAS	Empire Air Armament School.
EANS	Empire Air Navigation School.
ECDU	Electronic Countermeasures Development Unit.
ECFS	Empire Central Flying School.
ETPS	Empire Test Pilots School.
F/L	Flight Lieutenant.
Flt	Flight.
F/O	Flying Officer.
FPP	Ferry Pilots School.

F/S	Flight Sergeant.
FTR	Failed to Return.
FTU	Ferry Training Unit.
G/C	Group Captain.
Gp	Group.
HCU	Heavy Conversion Unit.
HGCU	Heavy Glider Conversion Unit.
LFS	Lancaster Finishing School.
MAC	Mediterranean Air Command.
MTU	Mosquito Training Unit.
MU	Maintenance Unit.
NTU	Navigation Training Unit.
OADU	Overseas Aircraft Delivery Unit.
OAPU	Overseas Aircraft Preparation Unit.
OTU	Operational Training Unit.
P/O	Pilot Officer.
PTS	Parachute Training School.
RAE	Royal Aircraft Establishment.
SGR	School of General Reconnaissance.
Sgt	Sergeant.
SHAEF	Supreme Headquarters Allied Expeditionary Force.
SIU	Signals Intelligence Unit.
S/L	Squadron Leader.
SOC	Struck off Charge.
SOE	Special Operations Executive.
Sqn	Squadron.
TF	Training Flight.
TFU	Telecommunications Flying Unit.
W/C	Wing Commander.
Wg	Wing.
WIDU	Wireless Intelligence Development Unit.
W/O	Warrant Officer.

Bibliography

Air War over France. Robert Jackson. Ian Allan.
Als Deutschlands Dämme Brachen. Helmut Euler. Motor Buch Verlag.
At First Sight. Alan B Webb.
Avenging in the Shadows. Ron James. Abington Books.
Avro Lancaster. The definitive record. Harry Holmes. Airlife.
Avro Manchester. Robert Kirby. Midland Counties Publications.
Battle-Axe Blenheims. Stuart R Scott. Budding Books.
Battle Under the Moon. Jack Currie. Air Data.
Beam Bombers. Michael Cumming. Sutton Publishing.
Beware of the Dog at War. John Ward.
Black Swan. Sid Finn. Newton.
Bomber Command. Max Hastings. Pan.
Bomber Command War Diaries. Martin Middlebrook/Chris Everett. Viking.
Bomber Group at War. Chaz Bowyer. Book Club Associates.
Bomber Harris. Dudley Saward. Cassel.
Bomber Harris. Charles Messenger. Arms and Armour Press.
Bomber Intelligence. W E Jones. Midland Counties Publications.
Bomber Squadron at War. Andrew Brookes. Ian Allan.
Bomber Squadrons at War. Geoff D Copeman. Sutton Publishing.
Bombers over Berlin. Alan W Cooper. Patrick Stephens Ltd.
Bombing Colours 1937-1973. Michael J F Bowyer. Patrick Stephens Ltd.
Confounding the Reich. Martin W Bowman/Tom Cushing. Patrick Stephens Ltd.
De Havilland Mosquito Crash Log. David J Smith. Midland Counties Publications.
Despite the Elements. 115 Squadron History. Private.
Diary of RAF Pocklington. M Usherwood. Compaid Graphics.
Each Tenacious. A G Edgerley. Square One Publications.
Feuersturm über Hamburg. Hans Brunswig. Motor Buch Verlag.
Forever Strong. Norman Franks. Random Century.
From Hull, Hell and Halifax. Chris Blanchett. Midland Counties Publications.
Gordon's Tour with Shiney 10. J Gordon Shirt. Compaid Graphics.
Great Raids. Vols 1 and 2. Air Commodore John Searby DSO DFC. Nutshell Press.
Halifax at War. Brian J Rapier. Ian Allan.
Hamish. The story of a Pathfinder. Group Captain T G Mahaddie. Ian Allan.
Heavenly Days. Group Captain James Pelly-Fry DSO. Crecy Books.
In Brave Company. W R Chorley. P A Chorley.
Joe. The autobiography of a Trenchard Brat. Wing Commander J Northrop DSO
    DFC AFC. Square One Publications.
Lancaster at War. Vols 1,2,3. Mike Garbett/Brian Goulding. Ian Allan.
Lancaster. The Story of a Famous Bomber. Bruce Robertson. Harleyford Publications
    Ltd.
Lancaster to Berlin. Walter Thompson DFC*. Goodall Publications.

Low Attack. John de L Wooldridge. Crecy.

Massacre over the Marne. Oliver Clutton-Brock. Patrick Stephens Ltd.

Master Airman. Alan Bramson. Airlife.

Melbourne Ten. Brian J Rapier. Air Museum Publications (York) Ltd.

Mission Completed. Sir Basil Embry. Four Square Books.

Mosquito. C Martin Sharp & Michael J F Bowyer. Crecy.

Night Fighter. C F Rawnsley/Robert Wright. Collins.

Night Flyer. Squadron Leader Lewis Brandon DSO DFC. Goodall Publications.

Night Intruder. Jeremy Howard-Williams. Purnell Book Services.

No Moon Tonight. Don Charlwood. Goodall Publications.

On The Wings Of The Morning. RAF Bottesford 1941-45. Vincent Holyoak.

On Wings of War. A history of 166 Squadron. Jim Wright.

Only Owls And Bloody Fools Fly At Night. Group Captain Tom Sawyer DFC. Goodall Publications.

Pathfinder. AVM D C T Bennett. Goodall Publications.

Pathfinder Force. Gordon Musgrove. MacDonald and Janes.

Reap the Whirlwind. Dunmore and Carter. Crecy.

Royal Air Force Aircraft Serial Numbers. All Volumes. Air-Britain.

Royal Air Force Bomber Command Losses. Vols 1,2,3,4,5,6. W R Chorley. Midland Counties Publications.

Silksheen. Geoff D Copeman. Midland Counties Publications.

Snaith Days. K S Ford. Compaid Graphics.

Start im Morgengrauen. Werner Girbig. Motor Buch Verlag.

Stirling Wings. Jonathon Falconer. Alan Sutton Publications.

Strike Hard. A bomber airfield at war. John B Hilling. Alan Sutton Publishing.

Sweeping the Skies. David Gunby. Pentland Press.

The Avro Lancaster. Francis K Mason. Aston Publications.

The Berlin Raids. Martin Middlebrook. Viking Press.

The Dambusters Raid. John Sweetman. Arms and Armour Press.

The Halifax File. Air-Britain.

The Hampden File. Harry Moyle. Air-Britain.

The Handley Page Halifax. K A Merrick. Aston Press.

The Hornets' Nest. History of 100 Squadron RAF 1917-1994. Arthur White. Square One Publications.

The Lancaster File. J J Halley. Air-Britain.

The Other Battle. Peter Hinchliffe. Airlife.

The Pedulum and the Scythe. Ken Marshall. Air Research Publications.

The Starkey Sacrifice. Michael Cumming. Sutton Publishing Ltd.

The Stirling Bomber. Michael J F Bowyer. Faber.

The Stirling File. Bryce Gomersall. Air-Britain.

The Wellington Bomber. Chaz Bowyer. William Kimber.

The Whitley File. R N Roberts. Air-Britain.

The Squadrons of the Royal Air Force. James J Halley. Air-Britain.

They Led the Way. Michael P Wadsworth. Highgate.

To See The Dawn Breaking. W R Chorley.

Valiant Wings. Norman Franks. Crecy.

Wellington. The Geodetic Giant. Martin Bowman. Airlife.

White Rose Base. Brian J Rapier. Aero Litho Company (Lincoln) Ltd.

Wings of Night. Alexander Hamilton. Crecy.

2 Group RAF. A Complete History. Michael J F Bowyer. Crecy.

101 Squadron. Special Operations. Richard Alexander.

207 Squadron RAF Langar 1942-43. Barry Goodwin/Raymond Glynne-Owen. Quacks Books.

408 Squadron History. The Hangar Bookshelf. Canada.

Other Publications by Chris Ward

RAF Bomber Command Squadron Profile Series

Squadron Numbers
7, 9, 10, 12, XV, 35, 40, 44, 49, 50, 51, 57, 61, 75(NZ), 77, 78, 83, 90, 97, 100, 101,102, 103, 105, 106, 115, 138, 139, 144, 149, 150, 153, 156, 189, 207, 214, 218, 405, 408, 415, 419, 420, 424, 425, 426, 427, 428, 429, 431, 432, 433, 434, 460, 467, 550, 578, 617, 619, 622, 625, 626, 627, 630

Mosquito Squadrons of the Pathfinder Force

Operational Statistics of Bomber Command and its Squadrons

Dambusters